Britain and the German Question

Britain and the German Question

Perceptions of Nationalism and Political Reform, 1830–63

Frank Lorenz Müller
Stevenson Junior Research Fellow
University College
Oxford

palgrave

First published 2002 by
PALGRAVE
Houndmills, Basingstoke, Hampshire RG21 6XS and
175 Fifth Avenue, New York, N. Y. 10010
Companies and representatives throughout the world

PALGRAVE is the new global academic imprint of
St. Martin's Press LLC Scholarly and Reference Division and
Palgrave Publishers Ltd (formerly Macmillan Press Ltd).

ISBN 0–333–96615–5

This book is printed on paper suitable for recycling and made from fully managed and sustained forest sources.

A catalogue record for this book is available from the British Library.

Library of Congress Cataloging-in-Publication Data
Müller, Frank Lorenz, 1970–
    Britain and the German question: perceptions of nationalism
    and political reform, 1830–63 / Frank Lorenz Müller.
        p. cm.
    Includes bibliographical references and index.
    ISBN 0–333–96615–5 (cloth)
    1. Great Britain—Foreign relations—Germany. 2. Great Britain–
    –Foreign relations—19th century. 3. Germany—Foreign relations–
    –Great Britain. 4. Germany—Foreign relations—1789–1900. I. Title.

DA47.2.M85 2001
327.41043'09'034—dc21
                                                                2001035428

10   9   8   7   6   5   4   3   2   1
11   10   09   08   07   06   05   04   03   02

Printed and bound in Great Britain by
Antony Rowe Ltd, Chippenham, Wiltshire

für Hedi und Erhard

Contents

Acknowledgements

During the writing of this book, I was very fortunate in the generous support I received from numerous individuals and institutions. I am delighted to use this opportunity to record my gratitude and indebtedness to them.

Merton and University Colleges, Oxford, have been my academic homes since 1996. Throughout this time, I have greatly benefited from being part of such learned, generous and caring communities. For that I would like to thank the Warden and Fellows of Merton, its Middle Common Room and domestic staff, as well as the Master, Fellows and staff of 'Univ'.

Without the financial support I received from the Rhodes Trust I could not have undertaken my research. I would therefore like to express my gratitude to the Rhodes Trustees and the friendly people at Rhodes House. I would also like to thank Hugh and Catherine Stevenson whose generosity enabled me to complete this study.

In the course of my work I was greatly assisted by archivists and librarians. I am particularly grateful to the staff at the Public Record Office, but also to the staff of Southampton University Library, Balliol College Library, the Bodleian Library, the British Library and the County Record Offices in Northampton, Winchester and Hertford. For their permission to consult and quote from archival material I would like to register my gratitude to the Earl of Clarendon, the Trustees of the Broadlands Archives, the Controller of Her Majesty's Stationary Office, the British Library and the Hampshire Record Office.

My doctoral supervisor, Professor Hartmut Pogge von Strandmann, first taught me in 1993, then encouraged me to return to Oxford in 1996, and has since helped me in many kind ways. This study owes much to his keen interest, judgement and experience. I am also grateful to Professor Timothy Blanning, Professor Robert Evans, Peter Ghosh, Philip Waller and Dr Leslie Mitchell for their advice and encouragement.

My friends and colleagues Dr Dominik Geppert and Dr Benjamin Novick, my mother-in-law, Susan Chesters, and Cameron Laux of Palgrave Publishers proof-read all or parts of the manuscript. Thanks to their efforts many opaque phrases and infelicities of style have been weeded out. What blemishes remain result from my stubbornness.

Celia, my wife, helped me tremendously during the writing of this book. She took a consistently lively interest in my work and was an inspiring, constructively critical reader. Her greatest contribution, however, is the happiness she gives to the author.

I owe an even greater, deeper debt of gratitude to my parents, Hedi and Erhard Müller, for everything they have done for me. It is to them, my oldest and best friends, that this book is gratefully and affectionately dedicated.

FLM

Abbreviations

Add.Mss.	Additional Manuscripts, British Library (London)
AHR	*The American Historical Review*
AP	Aberdeen Papers, British Library (London)
BD	Despatches (part of BP)
BEM	*Blackwood's Edinburgh Magazine*
BFR	*The British and Foreign Review*
BlP	Bloomfield Papers (PRO/FO/356)
BP	Broadlands (= Palmerston) Papers, Southampton University Library
BQR	*The British Quarterly Review*
CaP	Cartwright Papers, Northamptonshire Record Office (Northampton)
CEH	*Central European History*
ClP	Clarendon Papers, Bodleian Library (Oxford)
CM	Cornhill Magazine
CoP	Cowley Papers (PRO/FO/519)
ER	*The Edinburgh Review*
FaC	Correspondence of John Fane, Bodleian Library (Oxford)
FM	*Fraser's Magazine for Town and Country*
FO	Foreign Office Files, PRO (Kew/Surrey)
FQR	*The Foreign Quarterly Review*
FR	*The Fortnightly Review*
GC	General Correspondence (as part of BP)
GWU	*Geschichte in Wissenschaft und Unterricht*
HFR	*The Home and Foreign Review*
HJ	*The Historical Journal*
HZ	*Historische Zeitschrift*
IHR	*The International History Review*
JMH	*The Journal of Modern History*
MaP	Malmesbury Papers, Hampshire Record Office (Winchester)
MGM	*Militärgeschichtliche Mitteilungen*
MM	Memoranda (part of BP)
MoP	Morier Papers, Balliol College Library (Oxford)
NBR	*The North British Review*
PeP	Peel Papers, British Library (London)
PRO	Public Record Office (Kew/Surrey)

QR   *The Quarterly Review*
QVL   *The Letters of Queen Victoria. A Selection from Her Majesty's Correspondence between the Years 1837 and 1861*, eds A. C. Benson and Viscount Esher, 3 vols (London 1908)
QVP   The Papers of Queen Victoria on Foreign Affairs [files from the Royal Archives (Windsor); microfilm edition]
RC   Royal Correspondence (part or BP)
RuP   Russell Papers (PRO/30/22)
TEM   *Taits's Edinburgh Magazine*
WeP   Westmorland Papers, British Library (London)
WR   *The Westminster Review*

Introduction

In July 1862, only weeks before he was appointed Prussian Minister-President, Otto von Bismarck visited England. During his week in London he met both Viscount Palmerston and Earl Russell. His conversations with these grand old men of British politics left Bismarck decidedly unimpressed. 'The English ministers know less about Prussia than about Japan and Mongolia,'[1] he complained to his wife. Far from indicating the barrenness of studying British attitudes to German politics during the early and mid-Victorian period, this remark points to the very heart of the subject. As Bismarck's report to the Prussian King shows, Palmerston and Russell were certainly not ignorant of the complexities of German and Prussian politics. However, the Prussia which they desired to see – a liberal, constitutional Prussia, whose governments relied on parliamentary majorities – struck the Prussian diplomat as so fanciful that he falsely dismissed the British cabinet as ignorant.

The issues raised by Bismarck were by no means new to Palmerston and Russell. By the early 1860s, they had been hearing about German constitutionalism and Prussia's German role for decades. The notion of a united Germany was on the agenda ever since 1815. It was present both in the dreams of Germany's liberal-national movement[2] and in the fears of many conservative German politicians. The tension between the challenge posed by an opposition demanding liberal, constitutional and national progress and the various governmental responses became the dominant theme in German politics from the Congress of Vienna to the foundation of the *Reich*. This study is concerned with the British attitude to this 'German Question'. It does not aim to provide a comprehensive analysis of the British picture of Germany with all its cultural, scholarly, economic, dynastic and religious facets, but focuses on the British perception of Germany as a political issue. It investigates how

1

Britain's foreign political establishment – the politicians, diplomats and writers who informed, made and executed British foreign policy – perceived, analysed and reacted to the struggle for political reform and national unity in the German Confederation between the July Revolution of 1830 and the *Fürstentag* meeting of German Princes in 1863.

Although conflicts between the liberal-national aspirations of some sections of German society and the defenders of the status quo erupted soon after 1815, the governments successfully suppressed the forces of opposition for some time. The July Revolution, however, breached the defences of the Restoration. The ensuing process of oppositional challenge and governmental response commanded the continued interest of British observers of Germany. The failure of the *Fürstentag* initiative in 1863 ended the attempts to improve Germany's political organization through essentially peaceful reforms. Neither governmental concessions to popular demands, the method employed in 1848, nor intergovernmental compromise, as attempted in 1849–51 and 1861–3, had produced any lasting results. In 1864, 1866 and 1870–1 political change was wrought by action on the battlefield, and thus a dramatic new quality of means was introduced into German politics. With the parameters of the political process so drastically altered, patterns of perception and analysis which had emerged since the *Vormärz* no longer sufficed. It therefore makes sense to treat the years between 1830 and 1863 as a distinct period in the British perception of German politics.[3]

The study of Anglo-German relations between 1815 and the First World War has been dominated by the decades after 1871. The intensifying rivalry between Britain and the German Empire has attracted a great deal of scholarly attention.[4] For the decades preceding the foundation of the *Reich*, the situation is less satisfactory. Until recently, there was no source-based account of Anglo-German relations during the years of the *Vormärz*.[5] Günther Heydemann's incisive study of Britain's Italian and German policies from 1815 to 1847 goes some way towards closing this gap.[6] Some older works on Britain's policy towards Germany in 1848–9 are no longer adequate. Hans Precht's and Alexander Scharff's books were written without consulting British archives and are marred by prejudice. Veit Valentin's study extensively summarizes Foreign Office files, but offers little analysis.[7] These books were superseded by Günther Gillessen's thorough study of Palmerston's policy towards Germany from 1848 to 1851.[8] Thanks to him and Anselm Doering-Manteuffel,[9] the Austro-Prussian struggle of 1849–51 is the period most satisfactorily studied. The years between 1858 and 1863, on the other hand, have fared much worse. No study of the British perception of the 'New Era' and the subsequent struggle for federal reform has been published since Valentin's book of 1937.[10]

The works by Heydemann, Gillessen, Doering-Manteuffel, Davis and Metzler have illuminated several aspects of the relationship between Britain and the German states during the second third of the nineteenth century. There are, however, some perspectives which have not yet been adequately explored. With the notable exception of Heydemann's book, the existing works on British attitudes to the prehistory of the German nation state have focused on international relations. The present study emphasizes the multidimensional character of British perceptions. Analyses of the international repercussions of a closer uniting of Germany will therefore be complemented by scrutinizing the perceptions of the internal parameters of this process. Particular attention will be devoted to the British assessment of the liberal-national forces of opposition and of proposed changes to the federal constitution. The study will thus attempt to give the issue of reform a more distinct profile by emancipating it from the role of a mere contributory to the overarching objective of national unity. Moreover, no study has so far traced the long-term development of British perceptions of the questions of reform and unity in Germany from the July Revolution right up to the eve of the 'Wars of German Unification'.

One objective of this study is to establish the criteria and interests by which contributors to and makers of British foreign policy assessed the aims pursued and measures employed by Germany's liberal-national opposition and the German governments, and thus to outline the characteristics of a German nation-state acceptable or even welcome to Britain. An understanding of the intellectual background to Britain's reactions to the prehistory of the *Reich*, as well as a knowledge of the analytic traditions which emerged in the Foreign Office with regard to German nationalism, will not only illuminate British policy towards the German states before 1863, but should also contribute towards a better understanding of Anglo-German relations after 1871.

Between 1830 and 1863, German politics confronted British observers with revolution and reaction, nationalism and particularism, liberalism and radicalism, free trade and protectionism, reform and stagnation. By studying British perceptions of this kaleidoscope, this book will furthermore endeavour to throw light on the British attitude to national movements in nineteenth-century Europe. There was considerable strain between Whig beliefs in the necessity and inevitability of political change in a liberal, parliamentary and constitutional direction, and

Britain's interest in the peaceful maintenance of the power-political and social status quo established in 1815. Thus fear of revolutionaries and adherence to the monarchical principle co-existed uneasily in the minds of the makers of British foreign policy with opposition to reactionary policies and suspicion of monarchs. In observing German politics, British politicians and diplomats had to confront these contradictions.

A further objective of this study is to explore the European dimension of the genesis of the German nation-state by analysing it not from a teleological perspective of eventual German unity, but through the eyes of relatively detached observers with a different agenda. An examination of British perceptions of this process should help to determine whether the German national movement was perceived to be undermining or consolidating the European order, and how its demands could be reconciled with the interests of the other European powers. The book will therefore provide further observations on the central problem of how a united German nation state – both the result of and a new starting-point for German nationalism – could be accommodated within a European states system.

For both quantitative and qualitative reasons this study of British reactions to German politics focuses on an elite group of diplomats, politicians and writers, rather than scanning the broad spectrum of public opinion. Apart from sporadic outbursts of popular feeling, the politics of foreign countries was at best a minority interest in nineteenth-century Britain. 'The very phrase "foreign affairs,"' Disraeli wryly remarked in 1872, 'makes an Englishman convinced that I am about to treat of subjects with which he has no concern.'[11] The lack of public interest in foreign politics was reflected in the House of Commons which, between 1830 and 1863, dedicated, on average, a meagre 7.7 per cent of its time to them.[12] Even the relatively few with a keen interest in foreign affairs often ignored the arcane politics of the German Confederation. Consequently, as the *Times* observed in September 1832, 'more is known in England respecting South America than of the true state of Germany.'[13] The official and private correspondence of British diplomats posted in the German Confederation, supplemented by articles in newspapers and periodicals, can therefore be said to constitute Britain's only rich and continuous stream of information and commentary on German politics. Owing to its federal structure, the German Confederation provides a uniquely plentiful harvest of diplomatic sources. There were British legations in Berlin, Hanover, Munich, Stuttgart, Frankfurt, Dresden and Vienna. In 1851, for instance, 26

British ambassadors, envoys, secretaries of legation and attachés were posted in Germany. In the same year there were only 8 British diplomats in France and 5 in Russia.[14]

The letters and despatches written and received by Britain's diplomats in the German Confederation are not merely a copious source, but also one of high quality. Far from being the 'gigantic system of out-door relief for the aristocracy of Great Britain' of John Bright's famous gibe,[15] Britain's diplomatic service was on the whole a body of conscientious, experienced and not infrequently perceptive officials. A closer study of the group of diplomats[16] who provided a large share of the source material considered here broadly vindicates Charles Middleton's description of them as men 'of mediocre but adequate ability.'[17] British diplomats in Germany were a body of experienced officials, each serving an average of just over 22 years in the German Confederation.[18] They therefore generally enjoyed good and trusting relations with the governments to which they were accredited. Their despatches contain numerous accounts of frank discussions with German foreign ministers and sovereigns. British missions in Germany also analysed the German press and supplied the Foreign Office with translations of newspaper articles. Individual diplomats differed in the intensity of their contacts with the non-governmental sphere. Cowley and Morier were personally acquainted with Germany's leading liberals; Bligh and Westmorland had little time for such groundwork. Most British diplomats in Germany, however, appear to have entertained good relations with their colleagues from other countries, and frequently reported the local 'French' or 'Russian' perspective on the issues under discussion. Being posted on average at three different German capitals, their experience of German politics was fairly wide.[19] British diplomats spent an average of 61 per cent of their service careers in Germany and can therefore be considered specialists on German affairs, though not overly focused or exclusively parochial.

In addition to drawing attention to British diplomats' experience, it is also important to emphasize that the unreformed diplomatic service of the 1830s to 1860s – at least as far as it was represented in the German Confederation – had largely become a professional body relatively free from patronage. Of the group considered here, only two diplomats – Lord John Russell's brother William and Earl Aberdeen's brother Robert Gordon – were clear party appointments who came and went with their patrons.[20] A high number of diplomats were promoted by both Whig and Tory administrations,[21] and changes of government in Britain rarely led to changes in diplomatic personnel.[22] As a result of its gradual depoliticization and professionalization in the course of the nineteenth century, the diplomatic corps included more and more capable 'career diplomats'. In addition to these trusty 'work horses', British interests in the German Confederation were represented by some outstanding diplomats such as Sir Frederick Lamb, the First Earl Cowley and Sir Robert Morier.

Given that the diplomatic service was a 'part of the parliamentary, governmental and political élite of early Victorian society,'[23] however, it is not surprising that the diplomats' coverage of German politics contained numerous exaggerations and oversights reflecting British prejudice, preferences and apprehensions. At several points during the period under discussion, British observers of Germany showed signs of being influenced by domestic politics. Their attitude to German Radicalism after 1830 echoed the conflict over parliamentary reform before the Great Reform Act. Views of the *Zollverein* were coloured by the debate over the Corn Laws. The experience of Chartism clearly left its traces on the way British diplomats and politicians reacted to Germany's opposition of the *Vormärz* period and in the course of 1848. The anti-Schwarzenberg thrust of Russell's and Palmerston's policies in 1849–51 was in line with the heady mixture of popular Austrophobia and anti-Catholic agitation of 1850–1. Britain's frenetic Russophobia, which swept the country during the Crimean War, virtually rendered impossible an unbiased appraisal of the policies pursued by Prussia and the 'Third Germany' after 1854. After 1858, the domestic background proved important again when British praise for Prussia's French policy dovetailed with the popular Francophobia caused by the Orsini Affair and the invasion scare of 1859. It is from these very distortions, though, that valuable insights into the attitude and preoccupations of Britain's foreign political establishment can be gleaned. The despatches sent and instructions received by Britain's missions in the German Confederation, together with the private papers of diplomats, prime ministers and foreign secretaries, thus provide a wealth of telling source material.

While concentrating on the perceptions by British statesmen, the Foreign Office, the diplomatic corps and a number of influential newspapers and periodicals, the present study does not aim to investigate the views of the Court. This may appear surprising given the strong interest in Germany shown by King William IV, Queen Victoria and Prince Albert. It was, however, the close dynastic link between Britain's Royal Family and the German states which compromised the Court's credibility where Germany was concerned. Rather than winning British sympathies for the German governments, William IV's Metternichean line in 1832, as well as Victoria's and Albert's pro-German disposition in the Schleswig-Holstein question, and Albert's stubborn support for the 'Union' project in 1850 as well as his pro-Austrian stance in 1859, discredited the Court in the eyes of Britain's foreign political establishment. On all of these occasions the Ministers of the Crown humbly but determinedly ignored the wishes of their royal masters, readily incurring their wrath.[24] The strongly biased views of the members of the Houses of Hanover and Saxe-Coburg thus cannot be said to have either represented or dominated British perceptions of German politics.

As a leading victorious power in the wars against Napoleonic France, Britain played a crucial role at the Congress of Vienna and therefore acted as one of the midwives of the German Confederation. Considering stability and calm on the continent a necessary condition for the global pursuit of her political and commercial interests, Britain worked hard to ensure peace in Europe. The new federal organization of the German states played a key role within the framework of this peace concept. On the one hand, the German Confederation promised to guarantee the continued existence of the small and medium-sized German states. This was especially relevant because of the personal union of Great Britain and Hanover which continued until 1837. More importantly, though, it was hoped that the German Confederation would develop into a solid defensive power strengthening the centre of Europe and thus securing peace by containing possible expansionist ambitions on the parts of France and Russia.[25] Yet a mere four years after the founding of the German Confederation in 1815, British observers of German politics experienced their first doubts about its political stability. The 14 months of tension between the assassination of the right-wing playwright Kotzebue by a radical student and the Vienna Final Act of May 1820 produced several diplomatic reports highlighting the danger of revolutionary unrest in Germany.[26] However, the relative calm of the 1820s largely alleviated such fears, and it was not until the revolution of 1830 that British concern about Germany's political situation took on a more consistent form.

In spite of the strong dynastic links, the density of Britain's diplomatic representation, an awareness of Germany's importance for European peace and an appreciation of the commercial value of Germany's markets, British interest in German politics between 1830 and 1863 remained somewhat theoretical and characterized by a lack of urgency.[27] Unlike France and Russia, the German Confederation never directly endangered vital British interests. France's ambitions in the eastern Mediterranean during the late 1830s, her mounting a credible naval threat in 1858–9, Russia's designs on the Dardanelles and her expansion towards India: these were the foreign political issues which set British pulses racing between 1830 and 1863. The German states were simply incapable of such feats, and thus interest in them was often low. In the course of the four-night Commons debate on Palmerston's policies in June 1850, for example, the various speakers discussed France, Russia, Greece, Italy and Hungary at great length. Britain's policy *vis-à-vis* the recent dramatic events in Germany, however, attracted hardly more notice than a single, ill-informed and provocative paragraph from Disraeli.[28]

While questions of political reform and national unity in the German Confederation rarely occupied the forefront of their attention, British politicians never ignored them. The letters and despatches written and received by prime ministers, foreign secretaries and diplomats reflect a continuous, informed and serious interest in these issues throughout the whole period under discussion. While some individual British observers – John Ward and Robert Morier, for instance – were Germanophiles, who sincerely cared about Germany's welfare, the majority of them kept a keen eye on the British interests involved. Although the direct bilateral impact of the German states on Britain was low, the importance of the German Confederation within the multilateral European system was well-appreciated. British observers realized again and again – in the early 1830s, in 1840, in 1848–9, in 1849–51 and in 1859–60 – that Germany was doubly important for a peaceful European order: she must be safe from revolutionary insurrection, and she had to contain French and Russian ambitions.

In September 1865, with the Danish war over and the Prusso-Austrian conflict looming, Palmerston still emphasized this point. 'With a view to the future, it is desirable that Germany, in the aggregate, should be strong, in order to control those two ambitious and aggressive powers, France and Russia,' the Prime Minister wrote, only weeks before his death. Convinced that 'a strong Prussia is essential to German strength', he advocated Prussia's annexation of Schleswig and Holstein.[29] Bismarck, who only three years earlier had sneered at Palmerston's alleged ignorance, would have been pleasantly surprised to hear the Prime Minister make such a robustly pro-Prussian statement. There was little foundation, though, for both his earlier sneer and his later surprise, as Bismarck would have discovered if he had studied the illuminating story of British perceptions of political reform and of the question of national unity in the German Confederation between 1830 and 1863.

1
British Perceptions of *Vormärz* Germany, 1830–47

German history between the July Revolution, which ended the so-called Restoration, and the March Revolution some 18 years later, is frequently referred to as the period of the *Vormärz* ('Pre-March'). This retrospective characterization of the era as anticipating the revolution which concluded it reflects the precariousness of the political and social status quo of the years between 1830 and 1848. The established order was challenged by strong oppositional forces, expressing increasing tensions between state and society. Governmental responses to growing demands for constitutional change and greater national unity ranged from blunt repression to reforming initiatives and constitutional concessions. Their perceptions and analyses of German politics during the *Vormärz* show that British diplomats, journalists and politicians not only took a keen interest in the dialectic process of oppositional challenge and governmental response, but that they also had clear preferences as to the manner and direction of political change in Germany.

Subversion and reaction in the wake of the July Revolution, 1830–3

In the summer of 1830, after three days of fighting in the streets of Paris, the Bourbon dynasty fell. It soon became clear that the July Days had set a revolutionary chain reaction in motion which was to spread all across Europe. The news quickly reached England, where Wellington reacted warily though pragmatically to the new French regime. 'It is obvious that the only feeble hope we have of maintaining the peace of the world is in the moderation of the character of the Duc d'Orléans,' the Prime Minister wrote in a memorandum on 14 August 1830; 'It appears to me, then, that good policy requires that we should recognise the Duc d'Orléans as King.' British Radicals and some Whigs, however, reacted more positively. Many of them welcomed the July Monarchy, which appeared to combine order and progress, as a clarion call for reform or more extreme change.[1] Even recent and somewhat sceptical converts to the liberal cause voiced enthusiastic opinions. Viscount Palmerston was exuberant. 'Well, this is a pretty rapid process in France. [. . .] We shall drink to the cause of Liberalism all over the world,' he wrote to his brother-in-law. 'Let Spain and Austria look to themselves; this reaction cannot end where it began, and Spain and Italy and Portugal and parts of Germany will sooner or later be affected. This event is decisive of the ascendancy of Liberal Principles throughout Europe.'[2]

Palmerston's prognosis proved correct, and sooner rather than later many parts of Germany were affected. The news from Paris provoked a series of political and social conflicts. After the relative calm of the 1820s, both moderate and radical forces of opposition renewed their attacks on the regime of the Restoration. Violent ruptures occurred in the non-constitutional states of North Germany: in Brunswick, Hanover, Electoral Hesse and Saxony open rebellion forced the swift adoption of constitutional arrangements. In the constitutional states of the south and south-west the struggle against princely authority took place in the legislative assemblies, during the so-called 'Chamber Struggles'. By using their budgetary powers, liberal deputies in Bavaria, Württemberg and Baden sought to improve their positions *vis-à-vis* their governments, and pressed for greater civil liberties. Strengthened by recent elections, they caused their governments considerable embarrassment and – most noticeably in Baden – succeeded in realizing some of their objectives.[3]

However, liberal opposition in the individual states was not the only challenge to Germany's existing order triggered by the revolutionary impulse from France. Especially the Bavarian Palatinate – though also parts of Baden and Hesse – saw an upsurge of German radicalism. Its adherents disseminated their opinions through a number of newspapers, enjoyed organized support in the form of the *Preß- und Vaterlandsverein* ('Association for the Press and the Fatherland'), and voiced clearly republican aims. The efforts of the *Vaterlandsverein* famously culminated in the *Hambacher Fest* ('Hambach Festival'), a political rally on 27 May 1832 which attracted some 25,000 participants. It sparked off a number of smaller meetings in Baden, Hesse and Franconia, but German radicalism soon succumbed to the repressive measures taken by the German Diet at the behest of Austria and Prussia. The attempt by a number of radical students to trigger a German revolution by seizing the main police station in Frankfurt in April 1833, the so-called *Wachensturm* ('Storming of the Guardhouse'), proved nothing but a tragic farce.[4]

Both the radical and the moderate wings of the liberal opposition in the early 1830s came to address the question of national unity. Disappointed with the governments of the individual states, the oppositional 'party of movement' demanded a national German parliament, a national executive and ultimately a German nation state. Naturally, the hoped for monarchical-constitutional Germany of the chamber liberals was profoundly different from the radicals' German republic, but the national idea did provide a common platform. Given the liberals' and radicals' dream of a German nation-state, there is something bitterly ironic about the fact that it was Germany's only *national* institution, the Diet of the German Confederation, which decreed the repressive measures that eventually suppressed the liberal movement of 1830–3. Beginning in October 1830 and culminating in the 'Six Articles' of June 1832, the German Diet, led by Austria and Prussia, issued a number of resolutions aimed at containing the challenge to the status quo. By November 1832 all German states, even those whose earlier liberal concessions had attracted censure from the Diet, had ratified these decrees. Within 18 months a comprehensive system of political persecution was put in place.[5]

The political changes brought about in 1830, both in Britain and on the Continent, had important consequences for Britain's foreign political agenda. Rather than oppose the new French regime, the Grey government approached the July Monarchy to form a loose western liberal entente. This *rapprochement* was at least partly caused by the desire to counterbalance the revival of the Russo-Prusso-Austrian alliance, which had resulted from recent developments in the Eastern Question, and culminated in the Münchengrätz Convention of 1833. It was against the background of Palmerston's opposing the principles embodied by this Neo-Holy Alliance, and especially Russia's advances in the East, that British cooperation with France in the Belgian crisis acquired particular importance. After protracted negotiations, which brought Britain to the brink of involvement in a continental war, a solution was reached in 1833, which – by providing for an independent Belgian state, free from French and Dutch control – fully met Palmerston's demands. Even though Britain's nascent alignment with the July Monarchy was severely tested by French ambitions during this crucial period, Palmerston – unwittingly aided by a sniping Metternich – managed to keep France and Britain together.[6]

British European policy in the aftermath of the July Revolution has frequently been portrayed as a crusade in favour of liberal and constitutional progress in Europe and against the dark forces of reaction. This is the central motif in Charles Webster's classic account of Palmerston's foreign policy in the 1830s, a decade when 'Britain first took the lead in protecting the advance of democracy on the continent of Europe.' Donald Southgate presented the Palmerston of these years as the 'Patron of Liberalism', and in the leading biography of the Foreign Secretary, Kenneth Bourne deals with the same period under the heading 'Liberalism all over the World'. Heinz Gollwitzer, in a much-quoted article on 'Ideological Block Formation', even ascribed the leadership of the 'western and liberal camp' to Palmerston. After 1830, Gollwitzer argued, he styled himself as 'Metternich's antagonist' and as 'protector of the constitutional movement in the whole of Europe; he defended its cause not only in Belgium, Portugal and Spain, but also in Switzerland, Italy and at the Federal Diet in Frankfurt.'[7]

In spite of the pressing questions of the Belgian settlement, the Eastern Question and parliamentary reform, the political developments in Germany attracted a fair deal of attention from Britain's new Whig ministry and caused a lively discussion amongst her foreign political establishment. It has been argued that it was their ideological commitment which led the makers of British foreign policy to side with the liberal German constitutional movement in the aftermath of the July Revolution. Most accounts of Palmerston's clash with Metternich and the German Diet in 1832 interpret the Foreign Secretary's involvement in German politics as yet another example of his determination to advance the liberal cause. For Herbert Bell, Palmerston's 'intermeddling' in Germany revealed why his name was to become an 'elixir for hard-pressed liberals from Warsaw to Madrid'. It was in a parliamentary speech on German affairs, Donald Southgate argued, that Palmerston 'assumed the moral leadership of the Liberal cause'.[8] In the most recent analysis of Palmerston's motives, which highlights the ambivalence of Palmerston's liberalism and stresses the importance of the anti-revolutionary end of the constitutional means applied by British foreign policy, the focus is still on a Foreign Secretary talking liberal sense to reactionary statesmen and 'pursuing a clearly reform-oriented course'.[9]

The present investigation does not deny the importance of certain basic ideological convictions and Whiggish tenets (as well as rhetoric) for the conduct of British policy towards Germany between 1830 and 1833. British observers of Germany were confronted with a kaleidoscope of political phenomena: uprisings, constitutional and liberal-national

movements, radicalism, reaction and the emergence of both oppositional and governmental policies aiming at a greater cohesion of the
German states. The presence of a single dominant interpretative theme
such as 'Liberalism all over the World' is not, therefore, conducive to
the establishment of an undistorted account of the British perception
of and reaction to the multifaceted process of political change in
Germany. Rather, an attempt will be made here to identify and charac-
terize the central players in the political process as they emerge from
British analyses. The German political development in the wake of the
July Revolution suggests a study of three such players: (i) the oppositional 'party of movement', (ii) the Metternichean party of repression
and (iii) Germany's constitutional states.

The 'deep dye of Jacobinism': Germany's movement of opposition

Britain's diplomats at the German courts were quick to realize that the
July Revolution, by encouraging the various movements of opposition,
had profoundly changed the political scene in Germany. Their early
reactions indicated little sympathy with the 'party of movement'. In
August 1830, Sir Edward Disbrowe at Stuttgart informed the Foreign
Secretary, Lord Aberdeen, about the presence of 'discontent persons
and Jacobins in this part of Germany'. Three weeks later, William Chad
reported from Frankfurt on the 'spirit of insurrection which is now
abroad in Germany', and Milbanke, his Secretary of Legation, commenting on the effect of the Belgian revolution on the German states,
found it 'useless to deny that a very strong revolutionary spirit appears
to pervade many of them.' At the end of October, Disbrowe warned 'that
the party which would excite trouble in Europe has not ceased to feed
those flames.' He could not 'feel but anxiety for the tranquillity of
Germany next Spring.'[10] This critical reaction to the oppositional forces
by the British diplomats did not change with Palmerston's arrival at
the Foreign Office in November 1830, and applied in equal measure to
the revolutionaries in the streets, and to the deputies involved in the
'Chamber Struggles' in Baden, Württemberg and Bavaria. The whole
movement was frequently dismissed as part of a secret conspiracy. Disbrowe mentioned that 'money ha[d] indubitably been distributed with
no sparing hand among the discontented.' Sir Thomas Cartwright, the
new envoy at Frankfurt, believed that the spirit of insurrection was
'kept alive by agents of the Propaganda'.[11] However, Disbrowe could at
least console himself with the observation that 'the contest [was] as yet
confined to the third class, lawyers, shopkeepers, etc. on the one side,
the Sovereign and the old noblesse on the other; as yet the great mass

of the people notwithstanding every attempt on the part of the French and German democrats remain[ed] uncorrupted.'[12]

The complexion of the newly constituted chambers, on the other hand, offered the disaffected diplomats little consolation. In February 1831, Cartwright regretted the outcome of the recent elections in Baden as they had 'gone very much against the interest of the government and many individuals ha[d] been returned of the most violent democratic principles.' In the following year, the newly elected chamber in Württemberg attracted hardly more approbation: 'The more the character of the deputies who have been elected to the Chambers of the kingdom of Wurtemberg is considered the more it displeases,' Disbrowe reported from Stuttgart. 'Pettifogging attorneys, editors of radical newspapers and smaller employés of government who [. . .] find a traffic in agitation and ultra liberal doctrines more profitable, particularly when coupled with their pay as deputies have been selected in very considerable numbers as members.' The decidedly hostile opinion which Cartwright and Disbrowe had formed of the liberal opposition in the south-west of Germany was, however, based on more than merely a penchant for conspiracy theories and a somewhat arrogant disregard for 'the class of newspaper writers and professors'. It was the aims of the 'party of movement' which really disconcerted Britain's diplomats.[13]

Two items on the agenda of the liberal opposition particularly attracted Disbrowe's and Cartwright's criticism: German unity and liberty of the press. As early as October 1830, the British envoy in Württemberg felt 'convinced that a secret party directs these manoeuvres whose object is to form one great united nation of Germany by mediatizing or by destroying the different governments of which it is composed.' By February 1832, much to Disbrowe's regret, such dangerous ideas had gained a firm foothold in the chambers of Württemberg, Baden and Hesse: 'M. Pfizer, author of a pamphlet [. . .] in which he puts forward the doctrine of a German national union, which would do away with the independent sovereignties of which it is composed, has been elected in consequence of advocating that doctrine. A doctrine which in different shapes has been more or less overtly advocated by the members of opposition in Baden, Messrs Welcker and Duttlinger, also M. Hoffman in Darmstadt. Their plan, impracticable in the present state of Germany or in any probable state to which the country could be brought except through streams of blood, would most likely if successful reduce it to an infinite number of federated republics.' In March 1832, Cartwright, in a long despatch on the German liberal party and its 'pronounced aversion to the monarchical principles on which the

Confederation is based', reached the same conclusions. 'This party, termed by some the Liberal, by others the Ultra-Liberal Party [. . .] wishes to bring about a complete change in the actual system. – It calls for the introduction of the most liberal institutions, and its more moderate adherents wish for nothing further; – but the more violent have in view the dissolution of the Confederation and, in perspective, the unity of Germany. – This party is therefore regarded as directing all its efforts to revolutionize Germany.'[14]

A less ambitious but – in the eyes of the British diplomats – similarly problematic aim of the 'ultra-liberal' party was the freedom of the press, especially in view of the reportedly violent nature of the liberal newspapers. 'That there are some very mischievous publications abroad is a matter of notoriety,' Cartwright wrote in November 1831, 'as well as that they have a very pernicious influence on the public mind.' Unfortunately, things appeared to be going from bad to worse. 'It is certain,' Cartwright reported some three months later, that 'the newspapers published in the [Bavarian] Rhine Province preach the most open sedition'; this was an 'abuse of the liberty of the press'. These papers, he complained in March 1832, 'have latterly exceeded every reasonable limit and taken a very vicious course. The two Bavarian papers have daily inserted the most scandalous inflammatory articles, exciting to revolt and insurrection.'[15] It is hardly surprising, therefore, that Welcker's motion in the Baden chamber which aimed to 'enforce a universal system of freedom and of the liberty of the press throughout the Confederation' did not meet with Disbrowe's approval. 'The project itself is wild and inconsistent (incompatible with the present state of Germany).' In a similar vein, Sir Frederick Lamb, the British ambassador in Vienna, advocated the introduction of censorship in a despatch of 27 May 1832, for 'without one how can the licence of the press be suppressed, or if unsupressed how can it fail to bring on either revolution from within, or collision from without?'[16]

Common to both the demands for national unity and for complete liberty of the press was their incompatibility with the structure of the German Confederation, which Cartwright was keen to defend. He regularly drew attention to this point. 'I find that almost all the members of the Diet think these legislative bodies have pushed matters too far. – Those of the most moderate opinions think that this state of things cannot continue,' the diplomat reported in October 1831, for 'if some limits are not set to the attributes of the chambers, they will undermine the power of the Confederation altogether.' The principles and views of the 'Ultra Liberals' seemed 'directed towards a subversion of the existing order of things', and their growing influence was dangerous, because it 'rendered it probable they would ultimately compel the governments of those states to adopt a system of legislation and administration totally at variance with the federal laws and institutions and diametrically opposed to the monarchical principles which form the key stone of the federal union.' All this made for a worrying state of affairs on the eve of the Hambach Festival. 'The accounts which are received from all parts of the South and West of Germany represent the liberal party to be becoming daily more discontented and formidable,' Cartwright wrote on 26 May 1832, 'and many members of the Diet are becoming very uneasy at the agitated and feverish state of the public mind.'[17]

In the British perception of the German liberal-national movement, the Hambach rally marked a climax. The radical speeches given at the meeting attracted the most alarmist and critical comments by Britain's diplomatic representatives thus far. Cartwright saw all his warnings vindicated. 'The revolutionary sentiments, views, and intentions declared in the most undisguised and unreserved terms by all who were present [. . .] have imprinted upon that meeting a character of dangerous political importance which must exert a most pernicious influence in Germany,' he reported on 2 June 1832. The events at Hambach, Cartwright wrote to Palmerston 12 days later, had changed the whole scene: 'It is now no struggle between a liberal and an absolute system. Matters are far beyond that. It is a struggle with a revolutionary party [. . .] and the seeds of revolution are sown forth widely and deeply.' Lamb in Vienna was even more scornful about what he considered 'a gratuitous attempt of the gentlemen of the press and literati backed by the bankrupts and turbulent spirits to take advantage of the times, and get power and through it plunder into their own hands.'[18]

The reaction in the liberal British press was similarly damning. The *Times* saw in the *Hambacher Fest* the work of 'revolutionists'. The *Morning Chronicle* referred to 'violent demagogues', while regretting that the 'whole assemblage was, in fact, under the control of the Republican French, or [. . .] the Jacobinical party', and regarding the events in the Palatinate as 'the probable prelude to a speedy outburst of revolt, supported by the volunteer aid of French republicanism.' Looking back over the year, the *Annual Register* gave a sombre account of the meeting: 'The speeches which attracted most notice, and were most loudly applauded, were of a nature to excite the fears of all regular governments. Amid their smoke and heat nothing could be distinctly traced except democracy and revolution.'[19]

Despite the strong reactions to the *Hambach* rally, it was the repressive steps taken by the Federal Diet against both the Radicals in the Palatinate and the liberals in the Chambers which soon commanded the centre of British attention. However, the overwhelmingly negative attitude of British diplomats towards the opposition in Germany – and especially to its radical wing – remained largely unchanged by their critical stand against Austria, Prussia and the Diet. Time and again the forces of opposition were described as an extremist body of revolutionaries and democrats, conspiring with French republicans and always ready for revolutionary civil war. It is also interesting to note that the official and private correspondence of the British diplomats and politicians who concerned themselves with the affairs of Germany between 1830 and 1833 yields hardly any examples of a clear distinction being drawn between the radical and moderate wings of German liberalism. Cartwright, for instance, in a letter dated 14 June 1832, referred to a 'revolutionary party with which the advocates of a wholesome liberal system ha[d] nothing in common', but left it unclear who these wholesome advocates were. In two further despatches he distinguished between 'violent liberals and revolutionists' and 'the Revolutionary Party' on the one hand, and 'the real liberal party' and 'the real constitutionalists' on the other.[20] Such differentiations were the exception, however, and generally British diplomatic commentators tarred the whole oppositional spectrum with the same 'ultra-liberal' brush. It appears that in their anti-revolutionary solidarity with the German governments, Britain's more conservative diplomats, like Disbrowe, Cartwright and Lamb, dismissed every kind of oppositional challenge. The exception to this rule was Baron Erskine at Munich, who advocated official British support for the oppositional constitutional party.[21]

Moreover, the group of 'real Liberals' and 'Constitutionalists' remained strangely nameless. The only politician to be honoured with the epithet 'moderate liberal' by a British diplomat was the Prussian Foreign Minister Count Bernstorff,[22] whereas leading liberals such as Karl Rotteck, Karl Welcker and Sylvester Jordan were rarely mentioned, and if so, branded as extremists.[23] Their aims were either considered dangerous – like national unity or liberty of the press – or simply dismissed as lacking justification. Frederick Lamb, for instance, was puzzled by the existence of a German opposition. 'I am not aware what these German malcontents want', he wrote to Palmerston in June 1832 with reference to the South German chambers. 'I have not yet heard of any grievance that they have put forward, nor do I hear a complaint of injustice or oppression against any of the governments.' The same applied, according to Palmerston's speech in the House of Commons on 2 August 1832, to the German Radicals in the Palatinate. The Foreign Secretary found it 'unquestionable that there were many appearances in Germany of a disposition to disturb the internal tranquillity of the Confederacy on grounds which would not justify that disturbance.'[24]

Cartwright at Frankfurt, who worked at the very centre of the proceedings against the liberal opposition, continued to send lurid reports on the 'revolutionary Party' and their 'extravagant doctrine of the unity of Germany under republican institutions'.[25] In September 1832 he welcomed the dismissal of Professors Welcker, Rotteck and Duttlinger on account of their 'violent and in some instances extravagant principles'. The ill-fated and amateurish *Wachensturm* coup of April 1833 emerges from a whole series of Cartwright's official despatches and private letters as a vast international conspiracy of German and French revolutionaries aiming at 'the establishment at Frankfort of a Republican Central Government for Germany'. The whole venture, he assured Palmerston, was 'planned and executed with a method and secrecy and intrepidity almost unequalled' and came 'within a hair's breadth of succeeding'.[26] Yet another disquieting occurrence took place when several hundred people attended a celebration of the first anniversary of the *Hambacher Fest* on 27 May 1833. Cartwright observed that their 'speeches, songs, and general behaviour stamped the meeting as one of revolutionary character'. This second Hambach rally attracted highly critical comments in the *Times*, whose articles on Germany were usually marked by an inveterate hostility to Metternich. 'The idea also, openly advocated by Dr. Wirth [. . .] which embraces nothing less than a German republic *une et indivisible*, [. . .] is *per ipse* mischievous. [. . .] The "*idée fixe*" of Dr. Wirth and his disciples must therefore cease to be ridiculous ere it be dangerous to the government he would overthrow, but the mischief is in the meantime doing; liberalism of every shade is confounded in the deep dye of Jacobinism.'[27]

The notion of a Franco-German conspiracy of insurgents appears to have enjoyed widespread credibility amongst British observers of Germany. As early as November 1831, Cartwright had commented on the infiltration of Germany by French revolutionary agents, for he had learned that the Saxon minister at Paris had 'lately countersigned more passports for Saxony than he ever was in the habit of doing in former years.' Palmerston gave these rumours some credence. He informed Lord Durham, who was sent on a special mission to Prussia in July 1832, 'that the party which is labouring in France to produce violent and forcible changes of institutions, has been actively at work in the West of Germany; and proceedings have taken place in those countries of a decidedly revolutionary tendency.' According to Lamb, in their struggle against the sovereigns even the German chambers relied upon 'the republican and revolutionary party in Germany and upon the republicans in France.'[28]

It was because of this French connection that the patriotism of the south-west German liberals seemed less than reliable. In August 1832, gripped by the general war scare which swept Europe in the early 1830s, Disbrowe predicted that 'in case war breaks out now – they will, as far as they can, form a French party.' The Foreign Secretary took this prognosis seriously enough to inform Durham of the 'great probability, that a French party [would] be created in the heart of Germany which [might] ultimately affect the political relations of that country.' The same concern resurfaced in Palmerston's lengthy despatch to Vienna and Berlin of 7 September 1832, where he warned that overly repressive measures might lead to revolutions; this was particularly dangerous 'in countries whose geographical position is such, that if the affections and confidence of the nation should be withdrawn from the Sovereign, the people might turn their eyes to other quarters, and might be taught to look abroad for that protection and support which they believed their natural governors had ceased to afford them. [. . .] It is obvious that in such a posture of affairs a powerful foreign influence might grow up in the bosom of the state.'[29]

In the light of these observations and evaluations, Palmerston came to regard Germany's liberal-national opposition of the early 1830s as a dangerous and highly explosive charge. It had to be treated with extreme caution. Overly repressive measures on the part of the Diet, he feared, might have calamitous consequences. Ever since 1815, the German Confederation played a central role in British notions of a stable and peaceful European order, as a defensive federal league designed to protect Europe's centre against French and Russian invasions.[30] Palmerston's alarm at the threat of a revolutionary war in Germany must be seen against this background. 'There will be an outbreak,' the Foreign Secretary predicted to the British ambassador in Paris, 'which may by its reach shake even some of the possessions of Austria but will infallibly revolutionize Prussia and Italy.' He wrote to Cartwright warning of 'consequences which might in their result shake to its foundation the general settlement of Europe.' Lord Erskine at Munich was instructed to draw the Bavarian government's attention to 'consequences in the highest degree dangerous to the peace of Europe.' Finally, in his September despatch to Vienna and Berlin, Palmerston painted the ominous picture of a 'general convulsion in Europe, from which the soundest institutions, and the most firmly established thrones might not escape unharmed.'[31] Thus, even if the Foreign Secretary may not have endorsed without qualification the rejection of the German opposition by his more conservative diplomats in Frankfurt, Stuttgart and Vienna, there can be no question of his being a protector pure and simple of the German movement of opposition. It had little appeal for him. Indeed, in October 1833, reviewing the events since the July Revolution, Palmerston expressed his attitude in a letter to the King's private secretary. 'No doubt there is in Germany, and has been for many years past, a dangerous faction, whose object is the subversion of all existing institutions.'[32]

Threatening to 'play the Devil in Germany': the party of repression

When Metternich and the conservative German governments eventually set out to contain this 'dangerous faction', they became the target of a venomous campaign in Britain's liberal press. The sequence of measures agreed by the German Diet and designed to repress the growing opposition, which culminated in the 'Six Articles' of 28 June 1832 and further resolutions on 5 July 1832,[33] sparked off a dismayed and passionate reaction. The *Times* counted the 'Six Articles' amongst 'the most frightful attempts upon human independence and social happiness, recorded in the annals of Europe.' On the same day, the *Morning Chronicle* attacked 'this extraordinary document, intended to crush the spirit of freedom in Germany.' The *Spectator* was dismayed by the 'confederated despots of Germany' attempting 'to arrest the progress of knowledge and liberality in their dominions'.[34] It was indeed the German sovereigns who attracted the most spiteful outbursts, with the *Times* encouraging 'free-born Germans' to resist 'the tyrannical mandates of their coterie of Princes' and advocating British support in a war against Germany's 'domestic despots'. The journalist William Weir, in two articles for *Tait's Edinburgh Magazine*, revelled in similar dreams of a European war against Germany's 'half-feudal, half-Turkish system'.[35] Under the title 'The German Princes against the German People', John Wilks, a former Whig MP, published 16 lengthy letters in the *Morning Chronicle* between July and September 1832. Wilks accused the German princes of measures more violent than 'the decrees of Roman Emperors or Spanish Inquisitors' and raised the cry of 'Down with the Confederation'.[36]

The debate which Henry Lytton Bulwer's motion to protest officially against the measures of the Diet triggered in a thinly attended House of Commons on 2 August 1832, was equally marked by a uniformly critical reaction to the 'Six Articles'.[37] Lytton Bulwer called them 'contrary to the liberty and independence of the German people'. The Radical Joseph Hume was shocked 'that the military despots of Russia, Prussia and Austria, should be permitted to immerse Europe once more in the darkest ignorance [. . .] by crushing altogether the spirit of liberty and independence.' For the Irish reformer Thomas Wyse the question was 'whether despotism or liberty should prevail in the civilized world'. He feared 'the triumph of despotism'. Palmerston replied cautiously to Lytton Bulwer. While confirming his support for the constitutional states of Germany, he refused to accede to the motion. This was not because the Foreign Secretary supported the German princes but because – as he explained in a way which sent a clear message to Frankfurt – he could not believe that they could 'think it practicable, by mere military force, to deprive millions of men of those constitutional privileges which have been formally conceded to them; because that would be to impute to them a want of knowledge and judgement under which it is impossible to suppose persons to labour.'[38]

Britain's diplomats at the courts of these 'despots', on the other hand, did not join in the almost unanimous public condemnation of the 'Six Articles' in Britain. 'The ravings of the Times,' Lamb complained to Palmerston, 'are louder upon the subject if possible than those of the revolutionary Press in France.'[39] The disagreement between the papers and the diplomats in Germany was, however, not merely a question of style but one of substance. Shocked by what they regarded as the excesses of a revolutionary party, convinced that repressive measures were necessary, and prepared to believe that Austria's and Prussia's motives were honourable, most British diplomats broadly welcomed the steps taken by the Diet.[40] For Cartwright, desperate times called for desperate measures, and he was therefore not surprised 'to find Austria and Prussia at length determined to act with vigor to suppress a spirit which threatens to involve Germany in very serious consequences. If Austria and Prussia are not prepared to carry matters to extremities,' he wrote to Palmerston, 'it is very doubtful whether the power of the Confederation can be maintained.' Cartwright was convinced that the 'Six Articles' had been framed 'to give the sovereigns the power to fulfill their federal duties and for no other purpose.' From Stuttgart, Disbrowe reported that the liberal party had received the resolution of the Diet 'with consternation'. They had been dealt 'a blow which they were not prepared to parry'. Lamb reminded Palmerston that in 1820 Germany had been 'withdrawn from an almost equal state of excitement by similar measures' and that the calm thus produced 'was followed by years of prosperity, and the gradual development of constitutional situations.' Looking back in March 1833 Lamb happily concluded that 'Germany was becoming the prey of a set of agitators from whom a measure which is mildness itself compared to that proposed for Ireland has rescued it.'[41]

Lamb's unqualified praise for the motivation, method and success of the steps taken by the Diet in 1832 was, however, an exception. Even Cartwright and Disbrowe, who generally welcomed repressive measures, were critical of certain aspects of the 'Six Articles'. The attitude of Palmerston and the Cabinet towards Metternich's policies, on the other hand, proved wholly negative, and it was decided to confront Austria and Prussia as well as William IV, who, as King of Hanover, fully supported Metternich's line.[42] Palmerston turned against the Austrian chancellor with a vengeance. In a series of private letters to Lamb – which he probably expected to be intercepted by the Austrian police[43] – Palmerston fired broadsides of classic Whig rhetoric against his counterpart in Vienna. Metternich was described as playing 'the devil in Germany', as the 'bitter enemy of all constitutions', as full of 'never dying hatred of free institutions' and as belonging to the same school of politicians as Charles I and James II of England, Charles X of France and Polignac.[44] It is, however, important to note that, for all his passionate personal invective against Metternich, Palmerston's consistent rejection of the 'Six Articles' was based on two rational considerations. First, he believed them to be ineffectual at quelling the revolutionary movement and feared that they would, on the contrary, trigger a convulsion. Secondly, Palmerston regarded the 'Six Articles' as irreconcilable with the federal structure of the constitution of the German Confederation, and as designed to bring about a change in the German states system inimical to British interests.

As has been shown, Palmerston was concerned about the potential of the German opposition for erupting into revolutionary civil war and jeopardizing the European order. Metternich's excessively repressive measures, the Foreign Secretary feared, would bring on such a disaster. 'He will set all the constitutional sovereigns by the ears with their subjects and then he will march in so many thousand Austrian policemen to keep order,' he predicted to Lamb in June 1832, 'but this system cannot last, and must break down under him; and whenever it does there will be a crash.' In the Commons debate on 2 August, Palmerston voiced these concerns publicly. 'I will not deny, that if the resolutions of the Diet are acted on to their full extent, steps may be taken which [. . .] will cause such serious differences among the Germanic body [ ] as may render it impossible to hope that the peace of Europe can be preserved.'[45] Reports from Disbrowe in Stuttgart, Cartwright in Frankfurt, Barnard in Dresden and Abercrombie in Berlin about the extreme unpopularity of the federal decrees confirmed these apprehensions.[46] Thus, in letters to Cartwright, Erskine, Earl Grey, Lamb and the King, Palmerston continued to warn against a policy which he considered a sure path to revolution.[47] The long despatch to Vienna and Berlin, in which Palmerston comprehensively rejected the Metternichean course, consequently culminated in a terrible prognosis. 'Should the measures of the Diet unfortunately provoke resistance [. . .], a war of political opinion would begin, of which it is more easy to foretell the calamities, than to foresee the conclusion. [. . .] It is impossible not to perceive that such a war, breaking out upon the Rhine, in consequence of what would be represented and felt, as the aggression of power upon legal rights, might produce a general convulsion in Europe.'[48]

For all his discarding of Metternich's allegedly counter-productive policies, Palmerston did not hesitate to offer his own anti-revolutionary recipe. He clearly saw the need for some action. 'No doubt there are many who want revolution,' he wrote to Lamb in June 1832, 'and they should be opposed.' In a letter to Chad in Berlin, the Foreign Secretary pointed out what course Austria and Prussia ought to follow: a 'moderate degree of prudence, temper and firmness would guard them all against revolutions.'[49] In addition to advocating prudent strength on the part of the individual states, Palmerston also suggested a rather Whiggish form of defensive modernization to resolve the current crisis in Germany. 'Divide et impera should be the maxims of governments in these times,' he lectured his sceptical ambassador in Vienna; 'separate by reasonable concessions the moderate from the exaggerated, content the former by fair concessions and get them to assist in resisting the insatiable demands of the latter. This is the only way to govern now.' This advice came very close indeed to the dictum 'reform in order to preserve', which has been described as 'a core of Whiggery', and reflected fairly accurately Palmerston's attitude to the issue of parliamentary reform in Britain.[50]

Where Palmerston's rejection of the 'Six Articles' was concerned, the question of their incompatibility with the federal structure of the German Confederation proved at least as important as their potential to provoke revolutionary civil war. In his speech in the House of Commons, as well as in his despatch to Vienna and Berlin of 7 September 1832, Palmerston clearly expressed what he regarded as the essential constitutional characteristics of the German Confederation: 'not only the internal and external safety of the States which compose it,' he declared on 2 August, 'but also the maintenance inviolate of their individual independence.' Moreover, the Foreign Secretary emphasized the importance of this point by affirming 'that the independence of constitutional states [. . .] such as the minor states of Germany, never can be a matter of indifference to the British Parliament, or, I hope, to the British public.'[51] In his despatch Palmerston even went so far as to present Metternich with a hierarchy of the aims of the Confederation. 'It is clear that this league was intended to secure the separate independence of its component members; for the maintenance of that independence was set forth as one of the objects of the union, and to it, therefore, the federal obligations and engagements must be considered as subordinate and conducive.'[52]

Palmerston's correspondence in the months after the passing of the 'Six Articles' clearly showed that he considered these decrees not merely damaging to that central 'maintenance inviolate' of the independence of the German states. He regarded them as designed to damage the constitutions of the separate states and thus to create a centralized, more despotic Germany under Austrian and Prussian tutelage. Twelve days before the 'Six Articles' were decreed, Palmerston had already reported to the King that Austria and Prussia were 'about to purpose at the Diet in Frankfort a series of resolutions, the general effect of which would be, if adopted, to encroach most materially upon the political independence of the smaller states of the Confederation and to subject the internal affairs and even the legislation of those states to the supervision and control of a committee to be named for that purpose [. . .] by Austria and Prussia.' The steps eventually taken appeared to justify Palmerston's apprehensions. 'The real truth is,' he wrote to the Prime Minister on 3 August 1832, 'that the resolutions of the Diet [. . .] are nearly as inconsistent with the German constitutions as the proceedings of Charles X or James II were with those of France and England.' In his despatch to Metternich of 7 September 1832, Palmerston put the matter more diplomatically though hardly less clearly. By fully exercising the powers with which it had been invested through the 'Six Articles', he argued, the Diet would create a situation in which 'the constitutional rights of the smaller states and their political independence, might be most seriously affected.'[53]

In Palmerston's opinion, these lamentable consequences constituted the very core of Metternich's policy, whose objective – as he wrote to Granville in Paris – was 'not to check revolutions but to establish every-where despotic power.' His distrust of the Austrian chancellor and his motives went so far that in a letter to Lamb he sarcastically wondered 'how much that Fête [at Hambach had] cost the Austrian Secret Service Fund'. The Foreign Secretary certainly believed, as he wrote in a draft despatch to Erskine in August 1832, that Austria and Prussia aimed at enabling the Diet 'to exercise an absolute authority and control over the sovereigns and the legislatures of the smaller states.'[54] Research by Robert Billinger partially vindicates these suspicions, even if Palmerston appears to have overestimated the extent of the Austrian chancellor's ambitions. Billinger shows that between 1831 and 1834 Metternich was indeed trying to reassert federal power. However, rather than seeking 'absolute authority', Billinger argues, Metternich was merely concerned with buttressing the monarchical principle.[55] Palmerston, for his part, viewed these efforts as an attempt to bring about greater centralization in Germany, to which he was passionately opposed, and decided to defend the independence of the constitutional states.[56]

Palmerston's suspicious interpretation of Austria's and Prussia's motives was not wholly endorsed by his diplomats in Germany. The majority of them took a more charitable view of the objectives behind the 'Six Articles' and their compatibility with the constitution of the German Confederation. 'I have already stated to Your Lordship in my previous despatches,' Cartwright wrote to Palmerston in August 1832, 'that I do not believe Austria and Prussia started with any fixed plan for subverting the constitutions in the states of the Confederation, and I see no reason as yet to change that opinion.' On the same day he argued that the 'Six Articles' did not violate the rights of the separate states or else they would oppose them. Minto in Berlin similarly testified to a 'disposition to refrain from pushing or trying the authority of the Diet over the constitutional states,' whereas Lamb, characteristically, denied the existence of the problem altogether. He described the notion that there was a conflict between Austria and Prussia on the one hand and the liberal governments of Germany on the other as 'a perverted view' produced by the press. 'It is a question between all the German Gov-ernments including Austria and Prussia against a party and a press which have gone beyond the liberality of the most liberal among them and that to such an extent as to have been felt to menace their existence.'[57]

None of this alleviated the Foreign Secretary's deep suspicions of the motives of the conservative powers. Palmerston expressed these apprehensions most fully in a letter to the King's private secretary in October 1833. 'A great cry has been raised by Austria, Russia and Prussia, that the revolutionary spirit requires some stronger measures,' he wrote. 'May not that cry be intended to cover the ambitious views of those who raise it?' According to Palmerston, these ambitious views included plans to reduce the smaller German states to Austrian and Prussian dependencies and 'to authorize Austria and Prussia to march their troops about Germany to be the police officers of all the minor states.'[58]

'Natural allies of this country': Germany's constitutional states

In his reply to Lytton Bulwer's motion on the 'Six Articles', Palmerston expressed high regard for the importance of Germany's constitutional states by according them the status of 'natural Allies of this country'. He furthermore declared that 'no English ministry [would] perform its duty if it [were] inattentive to the interests of such states'. Indeed, throughout his clash with Metternich Palmerston consistently presented himself as the champion of the rights of the constitutional states of Germany. Their 'spirit of national independence,' he pointedly reminded Metternich in September 1832, 'is the more entitled to be respected by the governments, because it was first called into life by an appeal from the sovereigns to their people [. . .] to free them from the greatest military power, which, in modern times, has broken down the independence of Princes.'[59]

Palmerston did not only speak up for the interests and rights of the constitutional states of Germany, he also asserted their ability to cope independently with the revolutionary challenges in the wake of 1830. In his instructions for Lord Durham, Palmerston confirmed the 'opinion of His Majesty's Government that the designs of the [revolutionary] factions might be frustrated by the steady exercise of the legitimate authority belonging to the governments of those states in which agitation exists.' The Foreign Secretary expressed this conviction again in his long despatch to Vienna and Berlin of September 1832. The British government, he wrote, was 'inclined to think that a firm but temperate exercise of the Powers possessed by the Governments of those states, would have been sufficient to uphold the authority of the law, and to preserve domestic peace.'[60]

The description of the smaller German states given in the despatches and letters from Britain's diplomatic representatives was less flattering. As early as September 1830, Milbanke had complained that the progress which the revolutionary spirit had made in some German states was 'to be mainly attributable to the absence of energetic measures on the part of most of the Governments.' Cartwright regretted in March 1832 that the 'Ultra-Liberal' Party with its anti-monarchical principles had 'great ramifications [. . .] particularly in the constitutional states where from the nature of the institutions it ha[d] more scope for action', and he attacked the Bavarian government for its unwillingness to carry out its federal duties. The revolutionary unrest in the south of Germany confronted the weak German states with a situation which they failed to master. 'These small states cannot support this,' Lamb wrote in May. 'They can neither exist with a free Press, nor have they the force to control it.' After the Hambach Festival Milbanke became even more outspoken. In a private letter to Lamb, which the ambassador swiftly forwarded to Palmerston, Milbanke poured scorn over the smaller states, some of which were 'so jealous of their *miserable* independence, that they would prefer waiting till they are destroyed by revolution to acknowledging the right of the Diet to interfere in what they call their internal affairs.'[61] Lamb himself stood Palmerston's central argument on its head by declaring the subordination of the individual constitutions to the Confederation. 'The constitutions,' he explained in August 1832, 'have been in all cases gifts from the sovereigns to their subjects, but they could not give what they did not possess: exemption from the federal obligations.' These federal duties, Lamb argued, were the price the small states had to pay for their continued existence. 'It has to be recollected that absolute independence has at no period been possessed by any German state, nor in a state of absolute independence would the smaller ones have failed to be absorbed long since into their greater neighbours.'[62]

In the light of these critical comments it is worth asking whether Palmerston's commitment to upholding the rights of the constitutional states in Germany did not in fact originate from less altruistic motives than what Granville sarcastically described as 'tender feeling for the friends of freedom in Germany, or [. . .] over-anxious care for the independence of the smaller states of the Confederation.'[63] Rather, the notion which Donald Southgate called Palmerston's 'extravagant equation liberal state = independent state = pro-British state', appears to have played a significant role. Speaking in the Commons on 2 August 1832, Palmerston justified the government's interest in the independence of Germany's constitutional states as follows: 'As long as our commerce is of importance to us – as long as continental armies are in existence – as long as it is possible that a power in one quarter may become dangerous to a power in another – [. . .] so long is it proper for this country, in the maintenance of its own independence, not to shut its eyes to anything that threatens the independence of Germany.'[64]

This statement emphasizes two interests central to British European policy in the nineteenth century: security and commerce. As his correspondence with Lamb on the preferability of constitutional states in Germany indicates, Palmerston believed that specific desirable characteristics relevant to these interests were more frequently found in constitutional forms of government. 'As to constitutional states it is not as it seems to me our piece of pedantry to think well of them,' he wrote to Lamb in August 1832, 'for surely they are less likely to go to war than despotic governments because money will not be voted lightly.' Lamb, however, was not convinced. 'Constitutional states from the foundation of Rome down to the present hour have been the most warlike and quarrelsome of any,' he replied and countered the argument of their alleged Anglophilia by referring to her 'inveterate enemy', the United States of America. Lamb equally rejected Palmerston's commercial arguments in favour of constitutional states. 'The American tariff and the French prohibitive system may serve to show that it is not only in pure monarchical states that false use of commercial policy can be found and clung to.'[65] Britain's ambassador in Vienna could therefore not share his chief's optimism that by supporting the constitutionalism of the individual German states Germany could be made peaceful, safe from revolution and free-trading.

The picture of Germany in the wake of the July Revolution which emerges from the contemporary reports, statements and discussions by British diplomats, politicians and journalists is thus largely negative. Both political agents in Germany, the oppositional 'party of movement' and the governmental party of reaction, fared extremely badly in the eyes of British diplomats, politicians and journalists. The largely undiscriminating accounts of the liberal and radical opposition groups given by the majority of Britain's diplomats in Germany and at least partially endorsed by Palmerston, portrayed them as French-inspired, 'ultra-liberal', anti-monarchical demagogues posing a lethal threat to the existence of the German Confederation. Moreover, because of its alleged connection with the revolutionary party in Europe in general and in France in particular, the Foreign Secretary and his diplomats considered the German opposition a serious threat to the peace of Europe and general settlement of 1815.

Palmerston shared the belief held by the German governments and most of the British diplomats in Germany that the revolutionary movement had to be contained. He nevertheless joined Britain's liberal press and a number of radical MPs in their passionate rejection of Metternich's methods to achieve this. Palmerston was convinced that the Austrian and Prussian policy of restricting the rights of the individual German states and repressing civil liberties might trigger a revolutionary civil war in Europe. He believed the 'Six Articles' of June 1832 to be really designed to replace German federalism with despotic centralism and to stamp out the constitutions of the smaller states. Convinced that Britain's interest in European peace and free commerce would be furthered by safeguarding a process of moderate, defensive constitutionalisation in the German states, Palmerston embarked on an attack on Metternich's policy. His confrontation with the Austrian and Prussian governments and the German Diet, however, proved ineffectual. Thus, the years 1830 to 1833 saw British observers of Germany reject two competing models of German unity: an oppositional model, which could take a number of different forms ranging from a constitutional monarchy to a German republic, and a reactionary and centralizing Prusso-Austrian condominium. Both these models were considered incompatible with the German order as instituted in 1815 and inimical to British interests.

It is noticeable that amid all the criticisms of political developments in Germany by British diplomats, politicians and journalists, there is hardly a single positive statement. German politics was perceived as a piece with villains and weaklings but no heroes. The worthy 'moderate liberals' or 'reformers' appear more as a concept than reality. They play but a tiny role, have no names and no objectives worth mentioning, let alone supporting. Even Britain's 'natural allies', the constitutional states of Germany, are governed by nameless ministers and ruled by weak princes. Palmerston's fruitless campaign of opposition to Metternich is hardly an exception to this rule. It was fought much more as a struggle *against* revolutionary and counter-revolutionary attempts to change the status quo than as a crusade *for* German constitutionalism and liberalism. Thus, barring some revolutionary hotheads in Fleet Street and reactionaries in Windsor Castle, there were no English voices clearly speaking out *in favour* of a particular positive German policy. This silence on developments worth encouraging in German politics gives eloquent testimony to Britain's deep conservatism with regard to German affairs. 'Our real interest in Germany,' Frederick Lamb wrote to Palmerston in September 1832, 'is that it should be strong, united, monarchical and federal, under these conditions, incapable of aggression itself, and repelling it from the East and from the West, it becomes the key stone of the peace of Europe.'[66] In other words, in the wake of the July Revolution Britain wanted Germany to remain as it had been set up in 1815.

Reforms and no reform movement, 1834–47

During the years between the settlement of the Belgian crisis and the outbreak of the revolutions of 1848, Britain was faced with foreign political challenges in several different theatres, in Europe and beyond. In the Far East, the clash between Britain's commercial interests and China's opposition to the opium trade led to the First Opium War. After some carefully targeted gunboat action, the Chinese agreed to far-reaching concessions which were recorded in the treaty of Nanking of 1842. Another extra-European issue causing considerable concern for British diplomacy was relations with the United States. The Webster–Ashburton Treaty of 1842, which settled the delineation of the eastern section of the US–Canadian border, considerably improved the acrimonious relationship between London and Washington. During the presidential campaign of 1844, however, a call was raised for the annexation of the Oregon territory by the United States, provoking a fierce reaction in Britain. In spite of fiery talk of war and the mobilization of the Royal Navy, a compromise was reached in 1846 settling the western section of the border along the forty-ninth parallel.[67]

Britain's relations with the European powers continued to be dominated by the complex and overlapping issues of opposition to Russia and Austria, cooperation with France, advancement of constitutionalism and the Eastern Question. In Peninsular affairs Britain and France joined forces against the reactionary pretenders in Portugal and Spain, Dom Miguel and Don Carlos. The Quadruple Alliance into which Britain, France, Spain and Portugal entered in April 1834 provided for the expulsion of the pretenders and was designed, as Palmerston wrote, to 'serve as a powerful counterpoise to the Holy Alliance of the east'.[68] It was over Britain's and France's individual degrees of influence in Spanish politics, however, that tensions were beginning to creep into Anglo-French relations. Antagonism heightened after the Thiers government came to office in 1836 and culminated during the Eastern Crisis of 1840/1, which saw France subdued by an unlikely coalition of Britain, Austria, Russia and Prussia. When the crisis had blown over, it was left to Palmerston's and Thiers's successors, Aberdeen and Guizot, to mend the entente. Again, Spanish politics proved a double-edged issue. In 1845, after careful negotiations, Britain and France agreed on marrying off Queen Isabella of Spain and her sister in a way which would satisfy both British and French interests. This *rapprochement* came to grief in 1846, when Palmerston, a fierce critic of Aberdeen's conciliatory course, returned to the Foreign Office. Guizot confronted him with a *fait accompli* and settled the Spanish matter to suit French interests. Weakened by the collapse of the Anglo-French entente, Britain could do little more than register a perfunctory protest against Metternich's annexation of Cracow in the same year. Palmerston was more successful in 1847, when Metternich and Guizot wanted to support the conservative Swiss cantons in their struggle against the liberal majority. He dragged out negotiations until the progressive cantons had won the *Sonderbund* war and then prevented a European conference on Swiss affairs. The Foreign Secretary also opposed the Austrian chancellor in Italy, where the election of Pope Pius IX had raised hopes for liberal changes to which Austria was implacably opposed. Palmerston sent Earl Minto on a special mission to preach the merits of timely reform. He reinforced the implied warning to Metternich by ordering Admiral Parker's squadron into the Tyrrhenian Sea.[69]

All these foreign political challenges did not drown out a continuous British discourse on German politics during the *Vormärz*. Rather, as France's neighbour and the scene of conflict between a liberal opposition and the defenders of the status quo, Germany was inextricably tied up with the network of issues which dominated Britain's European policy. However much some British observers may have objected to the policies which the German opposition and the Metternich party pursued in the wake of the July Revolution, by the early 1830s Germany had entered a period of profound political change. The era of the German *Vormärz*, which ended with the outbreak of the March Revolution in 1848, witnessed both the growth of a powerful liberal national movement of opposition and a number of governmental policies bearing on the questions of reform and national unity. The most important initiative in German national politics of the 1830s, the foundation of the Prussian-led German *Zollverein* ('Customs Association'), attracted intensive and lasting interest amongst Britain's diplomats, politicians and wider public. The same cannot be said of the breakthrough of modern nationalism in Germany in 1840/1, which scarcely featured in the British perception of German politics. A similar pattern continued throughout the 1840s, when an appreciation of the significance of the growing national movement was clouded by a concentration on Prussia's pseudo-reform measures. In British eyes, Germany experienced something rather desirable during the *Vormärz*: reform without a reform movement.

'Every sensible Englishman must rejoice': the *Zollverein*, 1834–47

'With the last stroke of twelve and the close of the old year, the toll gates were thrown wide. The traces tightened, and amid shouts of exultation and the cracking of many whips the trains of goods moved forward across the enfranchised land.'[70] This scene, which, in Treitschke's romanticized description, sounded like a fairy-tale, really marked something rather prosaic. On 1 January 1834, the German *Zollverein*, a customs association based on the abolition of internal tariff barriers between a number of German states, was officially launched. The immediate prehistory of its formation dated back to a tariff agreement between Prussia and Hessen-Darmstadt in 1828. Under Prussian leadership this association grew, and by 1834 it included Electoral Hesse, Bavaria, Württemberg, Saxony and the Thuringian states. In 1835, 1836 and 1841 Baden, Frankfurt and Brunswick also joined. By facilitating intra-German commerce the *Zollverein* served to form a national market, boosted infrastructure, provided a stimulus to Germany's economic development and gave Prussia a powerful institutional basis for her German policy.[71] British diplomats and journalists, who had been largely unequivocal in their rejection of the steps taken both by the opposition and the governments between 1830 and 1833, proved more ambivalent with respect to the *Zollverein*.

There was some very vocal criticism of the *Zollverein's* potential and actual protectionism, which, it was believed, might inflict serious harm on British commerce. However, it will be argued here that even where commercial considerations were concerned, though more importantly with regard to its political effects, the *Zollverein* fared relatively well in the analyses of British observers. This might explain why Britain opposed the foundation of the *Zollverein* only initially and somewhat half-heartedly and soon had, in the words of the British envoy at Frankfurt, 'no objection to the plan or policy of the Prussian Union.'[72] This ambivalence has, however, not featured prominently in the literature on Britain's attitude towards the *Zollverein* during the 1830s and 1840s. Taking their cue from Treitschke's vitriolic diatribe that 'English commercial morality which, with the Bible in the right hand and the opium pipe in the left, aspire[d] to diffuse the blessings of civilisation over the surface of the globe' expressed itself in 'unconcealed hostility' towards the *Zollverein*, older studies emphasized British opposition to the Customs Association. Britain was described as having 'observed the growth of the Prussian *Zollverein* with spiteful eyes' and as being 'hostile to the construction of the Zollverein', whose foundation, it was argued, 'significantly contributed to putting strain on the English attitude towards Germany.'[73]

The intensive public discussion of the *Zollverein* in Britain undoubtedly offered much to support such a negative interpretation. On 15 August 1833, more than four months prior to the launch of the *Zollverein*, George Henry Robinson drew the attention of the House of Commons to Prussia's attempts 'to embrace within its commercial code a large part of Germany, which [. . .] would prove very detrimental to British interests', and demanded to know 'whether the Government had taken any steps to counteract the machinations of Prussia.' By then British newspapers and periodicals had been discussing the issue for more than a year. In May 1832 the economist John McCulloch published the first of two damning articles on 'Prussian Commercial Policy', arguing that 'the sooner the progress of the evil is checked the better'. In August 1832 the *Times* printed a whole series of articles attacking Prussian commercial policy for its allegedly protectionist designs. In its commentary on the foundation of the *Zollverein*, the *Spectator* reminded its readers that the 'evident object of Prussia' was 'to gain a more extensive market for her own manufactures, by excluding those of foreign states – especially England – from the greater part of Germany.'[74] From 1835 to 1848, a broad range of British periodicals published at least 13 articles by authors as prominent as David Urquhart, John Austin and Richard Monckton Milnes, which were wholly or partially devoted to a discussion of the *Zollverein*.[75] Some of them contained scurrilous attacks on the German Customs Association. In 1835 Urquhart described the *Zollverein* as a 'deep and comprehensive plan of Russia'. Seven years later John Austin predicted the imminent formation of 'a conspiracy of nations against [Britain's] manufactures and commerce, far more formidable than the continental system of Napoleon.'[76]

Journalists and writers were not alone in decrying the potentially baneful effects of the German Customs Association on Britain's trade. Diplomats and politicians were also worried. Their warnings predated the formation of the *Zollverein* and accompanied it throughout the *Vormärz*. As early as March 1828, commenting on the recent customs agreement between Prussia and Hessen-Darmstadt, Milbanke in Frankfurt gloomily predicted 'that our commerce with the interior of Germany [. . . would] be almost entirely destroyed.' In November 1831 and December 1833 Chad in Berlin and Erskine in Munich evoked the frightful image of Napoleon's continental blockade to describe the damaging effect of the German Customs Association. Palmerston, in a despatch to all his diplomats in Germany of 18 September 1832, found it 'needless to point out how prejudicial to the commerce of Britain must be the extension throughout Germany of a system, the proposed object of which is to exclude by duties practically prohibitive almost all the products of British industry.'[77] In the course of the 1840s, the irritation of the Foreign Office and the Board of Trade heightened, when the *Zollverein* was considering raising import duties on British iron. In 1843 a full 16 pages of copies of diplomatic and consular despatches on the 'Recent Modifications in the Tariff of the German Customs Union' were printed for the use of Parliament. The overall impression this question left on the British government was anything but favourable. In November 1843, Peel, in a letter to his Foreign Secretary, Aberdeen, summarized the conduct of Prussia in respect of the iron duties as 'equally unwise and ungrateful' and advocated 'the strongest remonstrance'. Four years later, in a memorandum for the Prince Consort, Palmerston still argued that as long as the Customs Association adhered to protectionism, 'so long [would] the public of England look upon the Zollverein as a league founded in hostility to England.'[78]

While this hostility towards the *Zollverein's* protectionism undoubtedly constituted an important aspect of its perception and analysis by the British, it would be misleading to describe this as the only or even the most important element. On the level of trade policies two qualifications have to be added: from the very beginning, the majority of British diplomats in Germany and the special observers who were sent to collect information on the *Zollverein* agreed that its effects on British trade would be relatively small, and thus general calmness prevailed amongst British officials. Secondly, there were even hopes that the *Zollverein* might benefit Britain's commerce.

When, in September 1829, tariff negotiations were going on between Prussia and Hessen-Darmstadt on the one hand and Bavaria and Württemberg on the other, Aberdeen concluded that His Majesty's Government could not 'find in this treaty anything immediately requiring their direct interference'. Four years later, with the negotiations still dragging on, Francis Forbes reported from Dresden that – according to the Saxon Minister of Finance – British commerce would not suffer from Saxony's accession to the proposed Customs Association. In the same year Abercrombie, chargé d'affaires in Berlin, found it 'impossible to say whether this system [would] in practice be advantageous or prejudicial to English commercial interests', but expressed general optimism. In 1835 he stated that Frankfurt's entry into the *Zollverein* was unlikely to harm British commerce. Palmerston briefly referred to the German Customs Association in the Commons in February 1836. Wondering 'whether it might operate to the advantage or detriment of England,' he came to an unspectacular answer: 'it would have little effect in either way.'[79]

The reports which John MacGregor sent from Germany were similarly reassuring. MacGregor, a statistician and economist, toured Germany in 1836 and 1838 to gather information for the Board of Trade. In 1836 he concluded that British commerce had not suffered severely from the new tariff. After he had attended the *Zollverein* conference at Dresden two years later, he reported to Palmerston that there was not enough evidence to support 'the idea generally entertained in England as to the pernicious effects of the Germanic Union of Customs on British Trade and Manufactures.' In 1840, John Bowring, another observer sent to a *Zollverein* conference, submitted a detailed report to the Foreign Secretary and to Parliament, and concluded that the German Customs Association was not 'a union formed in hostility to the commercial interests of other states' nor was it its design to 'create a manufacturing population in rivalry with or opposition to the manufacturing aptitudes of England.' In the end, even British anger at the proposed rises in the *Zollverein's* iron duties ended in a relaxed manner. 'I believe we may congratulate ourselves on the separation of the Zollverein Congress at Carlsruhe, without having done anything of consequence, or inflicted any injury upon us,' Aberdeen wrote to Peel in October 1845. 'Prussia has behaved well in resisting the clamour of the Southern States.'[80]

Some British accounts of the effects of the *Zollverein* on British commerce reflected even more optimism than the mere expectation that little harm would be done. In April 1833, Erskine in Munich argued that the Customs Association would remove 'the delays and various impediments arising from the numerous custom houses of separate states' and predicted that thereby general commerce would be 'greatly facilitated and improved which must be favourable to British trade.' Abercrombie equally believed that 'an increased field' would be 'opened for the immense resources of the English industry.' In 1838 Lord William Russell reported from Berlin that, according to the United States envoy, Britain would profit from the creation of a larger market for her products. John Bowring echoed these hopes in his report of 1840: 'There is no reason why foreign commerce should not have benefited to the same or even wider extent than internal industry.' In 1843 Samuel Laing called the view that the *Zollverein* was inimical to British commerce as 'erroneous as it is narrow. The richer our neighbours become,' he explained, 'the better customers they are to us.'[81]

Important as all these considerations of the *Zollverein's* effects on Britain's commerce were, British diplomats, economists and writers proved also very much alive to its impact on Germany herself. They realized that both on an economic and on a political level the launching of the *Zollverein* had caused profound changes, and it is fair to say that in the majority of British accounts these changes were described as beneficial to Germany. Thus in spite of its protectionist imperfections, the *Zollverein* was perceived as a successful governmental reform initiative.

A clear appreciation of the reforming effect of the *Zollverein* on Germany's economy was already apparent in Palmerston's response to G. H. Robinson's criticism of the government's alleged inaction in the House of Commons in August 1833. The Foreign Secretary declared that Prussia had entered into negotiations with the minor states of Germany 'for the purpose of including them all in one common union of custom-houses, and thus freeing the internal communications of Germany from the various impediments to which it was now liable.' This positive view of the *Zollverein*'s salutary effect on German commerce and industry was repeated by British diplomats, economists and politicians throughout the 1830s and 1840s. In 1839 William Russell reported from Berlin that the Customs Union had been 'productive of the greatest benefit to Germany by removing the barriers which had previously impeded the freedom of commerce.' In 1840 and 1842 Bowring and MacGregor stressed the same point. Bowring concluded that the *Zollverein* was 'favourable to the prosperity and to the happiness of the German community' and predicted that, if guided by 'enlightened economy and sound commercial policy', it would work as an 'instrument of incalculable and boundless good.' For MacGregor, the intra-German free trade zone had produced 'the greatest material, moral, and civilized blessings ever enjoyed by the German people.' In September 1846 Palmerston reiterated this view in a memorandum for the Queen and Prince Albert. 'The Zollverein,' he explained, 'swept away at once all these internal obstructions; and removing all the Custom Houses to the external conference of the Union gave perfectly Free Trade within the circle; and great has been to Germany the convenience and advantage thereof.'[82] Such praise for the *Zollverein*'s role in bringing about free trade gains a particular pertinence when seen against the British background of the controversy over the repeal of the Corn Laws. This British debate certainly coloured the perception of the German Customs Association, giving it progressive and reforming connotations.[83]

Even more striking than this appreciation of the *Zollverein*'s beneficial effects on Germany's economy is the British evaluation of its political dimension which emerges from official British reports and the press coverage. Two observations are particularly noticeable: (i) from the very beginning, the *Zollverein* was understood to be a Prussian bid for political preponderance; and (ii) the political effects of the *Zollverein* were judged to be clearly positive.

In its summary of the year 1836, the 'Annual Register' made a fairly dramatic declaration. 'In the present year [. . .] the gigantic object after which Prussia had so long been labouring – to unite all German states into one body, by a commercial treaty [. . .] was brought to a successful termination.' This grandiose claim was entirely in tune with opinions expressed by many other influential organs of published opinion in Britain. In May 1832 John McCulloch, in an article for the *Foreign Quarterly Review*, described Prussia as 'actuated by political as well as commercial motives.' On the eve of the launching of the *Zollverein* the *Times* predicted that Prussia would use it for her own 'political aggrandizement'. The 'ultimate tendency' of the 'Prussian system', the *Westminster Review* concluded one year later, was to 'render Prussia the centre, round which the whole material interests of Germany will revolve.' In 1836 *Blackwood's Edinburgh Magazine* observed that 'the banner of Prussia – politically as commercially – wave[d] over two-thirds, or, excluding the Austrian portion, about eight-ninths of the German population.' In the course of the 1830s and 1840s, many similar comments can be found in Britain's leading periodicals.[84]

Britain's diplomats agreed with the notion, prevalent in British newspapers and periodicals, of Prussia's political motivation in launching the *Zollverein*. Even before its establishment, Chad and Abercrombie in Berlin, Erskine in Munich, and Bingham, his Secretary of Legation, all emphasized the political importance of Prussia's commercial policies. Chad, Erskine and Abercrombie observed that the Prussian government expected the political gain to outweigh the expected loss in customs revenue, and Bingham found it 'impossible not to foresee the immense political influence which Prussia must gain.' Cartwright rated the first year of the *Zollverein*'s operation as a great success for Prussia, which had 'at length effected a grand political object at which she ha[d] been aiming for years past.'[85] A few years on Henry Wellesley in Stuttgart and William Russell in Berlin came to the same conclusion. 'The fact is,' Wellesley wrote in 1838, 'the influence of Prussia is daily increasing in all the countries that have joined the Commercial Union, and she is rapidly gaining that addition of power, which there is no doubt she proposed to herself.' William Russell echoed this account: 'in a political sense, Prussia has in great measure succeeded,' he reported; and added, 'Your Lordship is so well acquainted with the struggle for political ascendancy in Germany that took place between Austria and Prussia, and with the advantages which the formation of the Union obtained for Prussia [. . .] that it is unnecessary for me to enter into consideration of this question.' The theme of Prussia's political agenda in forming the *Zollverein* was also present in the reports by Bowring and MacGregor, with the former reminding his readers that 'the probable political consequences of the establishment of the Zoll Verein [. . .] were certainly not lost sight of by its founders', and the latter arguing that Prussia had aimed at the creation of a 'general union of its material and consequently moral and political interests.'[86]

British observers' perceptions of the political meaning of this 'general union' were broadly favourable. From its beginning, it was imbued with a clear reforming effect. On the eve of its launch, the *Times* printed an almost euphoric leader: 'The Prussian Government has established [. . .] a commercial confederation more important to the prosperity and Union of the separate States of Germany than its existing political league – a confederation which will join the people in a closer alliance than their religion or civil institutions, – a confederation, which, if successful, will do more to promote their internal peace, and to consolidate their external security, than all their joint garrisons or military contingents.'[87] In spite of some wild accusations that it was an anti-British Russo-Prussian conspiracy, in spite of its reviled protectionism, and in spite of the protracted controversy over iron duties, this positive interpretation of the *Zollverein* can be traced right through until the eve of the revolution of 1848.

For British diplomats and politicians, one of the most attractive political features of the *Zollverein* was undoubtedly its expected anti-revolutionary effect. Worried by the explosive atmosphere of the early 1830s, a number of German governments believed that the dangerous political situation could be defused by removing the vexing tariff barriers which impeded commerce and fuelled popular discontent.[88] Palmerston was aware of this argument. In September 1832, the Foreign Secretary sent a circular to all British diplomats in the German Confederation informing them that he was 'inclined to believe that much of the discontent which for some time past [had] existed in Germany [was] owing to commercial, fully as much as to political grievances. [. . .] The impediments cripple the industry of the people [. . .] and interfere with the progress of national prosperity.' Because these disadvantages were caused not by nature but by 'conventional arrangements, it is to be expected that they should be less easily endured.' It must therefore have been welcome news indeed, when Francis Forbes reported the conviction of the Saxon government that the *Zollverein* would 'deprive the revolutionary party of one of their greatest grievances, the innumerable frontiers which exist everywhere.' The same argument can be found in John MacGregor's report. He believed that it was the spread of republicanism all over Germany, Belgium and Poland in the wake of the revolution of 1830 which served to 'justify Prussia in making fiscal sacrifices in order to unite Germany under apparently only a commercial, but in reality a political and national bond.'[89]

In addition to staving off revolution, the *Zollverein* was also seen to provide a more efficient national organization than the German Confederation. 'The political Diet of Germany may still continue at Frankfort,' the *Times* predicted in a leader in January 1834, 'but its more important commercial diet will be transferred to Berlin.' In 1840 John Bowring made similar observations about the *Zollverein*: 'it has done wonders in breaking down petty and local prejudices, and has become a foundation on which future legislation, representing the common interest of the German people, may undoubtedly be hereafter raised.' In his 1842 report MacGregor called the *Zollverein* a 'far more solid and powerful confederacy than that by which all the states of Germany are politically allied.' This view was shared by the *Times*, which, in the same year, described the combination of 'the interests and the policy of the German States in one great energetic whole' by means of the Customs Association as 'in every sense beneficial to the great political interests of Europe.'[90]

Such views of the *Zollverein* were not confined to economists and journalists but were shared by British diplomats and politicians. In April 1843 William Fox-Strangways, envoy at Frankfurt, described the 'union of Germany' as 'one of the great objects of the league.' This analysis was supported by what Lord Westmorland in Berlin reported about the views of the Prussian minister von Bodelschwingh who had stressed the advantages of the *Zollverein* 'in the establishment of the political independence and power of their country.' Westmorland agreed that 'with respect to the political importance which has accrued to Germany from the commercial union of so many of its States, there [could] be no doubt that it [had] been very considerable.' All these positive evaluations of the political role of the *Zollverein* were comprehensively echoed in two memoranda which Palmerston wrote for the Queen and Prince Albert in 1846 and 1847. 'Politically,' the Foreign Secretary argued in the earlier memorandum, 'it has tended to give to the states which compose [Germany], in a certain degree, that unity of national feeling, which the separate subdivision of the country into distinct and different states was calculated in some degree to destroy. No well wisher to Germany can feel otherwise than glad at the political effect of the Zollverein.' In 1847 Palmerston was even more positive: 'Every sensible Englishman must rejoice at the establishment of the Zollverein, and must wish to see it include the whole of Germany.'[91]

It is interesting to note that for all this endorsement of the national effect of Prussia's *Zollverein* initiative by the Foreign Secretary and his diplomats, there is one notion present in the writings of some journalists and economists which is conspicuously absent from official diplomatic correspondence: the boost the *Zollverein* received from popular German nationalism. The *Zollverein* rests, Alfred Mallalieu wrote in *Blackwood's Edinburgh Magazine* in 1836, 'on the empire of opinion – it is based on moral power, a tower of strength more durable than the ephemeral action of ball and steel; it has conciliated local antipathies – it is entwined in national prejudices – [. . .] it rallied around its standard all the generous sentiments, the ardent feelings, the patriotism of – FATHERLAND.' John Bowring observed that the *Zollverein* had brought the 'sentiment of German nationality out of the regions of hope and fancy into those of positive and material interests.'[92] Two years later, the writer Samuel Laing argued that 'according to every true German, the league is to be the grand restorer of nationality to Germany, of national character, of national mind, national greatness, national everything, to a new, regenerated German nation.' He even predicted political problems for Prussia. The spirit of commercial freedom inherent in the *Zollverein* must in the end 'overturn the autocratic principle of her government.' Writing in the *Edinburgh Review* in 1844, John Ward called the *Zollverein* an expression of 'that vehement desire for national unity which so generally pervades the German mind' and aimed 'at making the "fatherland" an undivided nation.'[93]

This grass-roots oriented interpretation which portrays the *Zollverein* as fuelled by a strong popular German nationalism did not feature in the official British accounts. Their version was on the whole sympathetic and very much top-down: despite some disaffection caused by its protectionist potential, the *Zollverein* was seen as a salutary governmental reform measure, designed to enhance commercial freedom, to prevent revolutionary unrest and to bring about closer cooperation amongst the German states without compromising their independence. Moreover, the *Zollverein* was initiated and led by Prussia which was considered the German state most likely to pursue a 'liberal' tariff policy.[94] Only once did a British diplomat observe a clear connection between the development of the Customs Association and popular nationalism.

In December 1840, Fox-Strangways reported from Frankfurt that Prussia used the *Zollverein* to 'simplify the general government, and to combine the powers of Germany', and observed that these measures seemed to be 'in unison with the patriotic ideas which the circumstances of the time have lately called forth '[95] 1840 was, however, a special year in the history of German nationalism.

The 'noble spirit shown by the Germans': the 'Rhine Crisis' of 1840/1

1840–1 was a great year, in fact probably the only great year, in the life of Nikolaus Becker. In September 1840 this completely unknown and undistinguished assistant court scribe from Geilenkirchen near Aachen published his poem 'Der deutsche Rhein' ('The German Rhine'). It took Germany by storm. On 13 October it was sung to a melody by Kreutzer at the birthday celebration for Frederick William IV in Cologne. Six weeks later a crowd of 1,000 Leipzigers attended a contest where several different melodies for the poem were judged. It is believed that up and down the country more than 200 tunes for the Rhine Song were composed. Countless poems in the same vein were concocted, the public singing of 'Der deutsche Rhein' reached epidemic proportions, and the rhymester became a national celebrity. The incredible success of Becker's verses can hardly be ascribed to their intrinsic qualities, for they offered little thought and less literary merit. Rather it was owing to the current political background that Becker's words electrified the German public and made thousands enthusiastically join in the singing of:

Sie sollen ihn nicht haben	No – *they* shall never win it,
Den freien deutschen Rhein	Our free, our German stream;
Ob sie wie gier'ge Raben	No – though like starving ravens,
Sich heiser darnach schrei'n.	They Rhine-ward, Rhine-ward scream.[96]

The historical context which explains Becker's rise to fame was the Franco-German 'Rhine Crisis' which was itself part of a greater international crisis caused by the Eastern Question. In 1839–40 France had fallen out with the other European powers over the question of how to contain Mehemet Ali, the Vice-King of Egypt. With Britain, Russia, Austria and Prussia determined to protect the Ottoman Empire against Ali's aggression and France refusing to coerce the Vice-King, whom she had been supporting for a number of years, a conflict was inevitable. In March 1840 Adolphe Thiers succeeded Soult at the head of the French ministry and aggravated the situation by resorting to belligerent rhetoric. The tension rose when, in July 1840, the other powers decided to confront Ali without French agreement. Public opinion in France, especially the papers of the left, reacted with outrage to this diplomatic setback. It was interpreted as a revival of the old anti-Napoleonic coalition and as a humiliating blow to French national honour. By way of compensation a cry was raised for a reconquest of France's 'natural borders', particularly the Rhineland. Thiers's government went along with this nationalist craze and increased the size of the army and deployed troops to France's eastern regions. For some weeks a general European war threatened, but in October France backed down, Thiers resigned and the crisis petered out.[97]

France's aggressive gestures provoked reactions in Germany. Both the public and the German governments were deeply affected. Their respective reactions differed in intensity but pointed in a similar direction. Across the mass of the German population, the 'Rhine Crisis' resulted in the breakthrough of modern nationalism. Throughout the German Confederation a process of political mass mobilization took place. A passionate and scornful rejection of French claims on the Rhineland and the emotive appeal to national solidarity soon united Germans from all walks of life, and from Cologne to Königsberg. The Rhine Song movement was only the most vocal expression of this deep-reaching process. The wave of nationalism which swept the country in 1840–1 profoundly changed the political complexion of Germany. It was in the course of the 'Rhine Crisis', it has been argued, that mass nationalism established itself as an 'independent political factor against which, in the long run, no claim of a government to represent its people could hope to prevail.'[98] Consequently, with the German governments unable to contain it as efficiently as they had done before the 'Rhine Crisis', the 1840s were to witness the growth of a liberal and truly national movement of opposition in Germany.

Amongst the German governments and on the federal level, the reactions to Thiers's policy were, predictably, somewhat more muted. The threat of a French invasion led to calls for an overhaul of the military structure of the German Confederation, but apart from the establishment of the federal fortresses at Rastatt and Ulm, the half-hearted moves in this direction produced few significant results. After lengthy negotiations, Austria and Prussia did, however, agree on joint operational planning for defence purposes. Even if the German governments, and in particular Prince Metternich, did not fully embrace the public demands for greater German unity, they nevertheless displayed benevolence towards the great surge of patriotic feeling expressed across the country. For the first time since 1813, German princes were part of a national movement.[99] Nikolaus Becker was to profit directly from this. In the spring of 1841 he received an inscribed silver tankard from the King of Bavaria together with the royal wish that he may often drink from it while singing 'No – they shall never win it.'

Ludwig I's patriotic gesture is particularly relevant with respect to the British perception of the 'Rhine Crisis'. For without this gift the name of Nikolaus Becker and his virtually omnipresent poem might not have attracted as much as a single mention in the official and private correspondence of Britain's diplomats and politicians. As it was, probably the only reference to Becker occurred when Lord Erskine in Munich reported in February 1841 that King Ludwig had 'directed a handsome cup to be executed by the celebrated artist Schwanthaler [. . .] and to be presented to Nicolaus Becker – author of the song *"Sie sollen ihn nicht haben"*.' This song, Erskine explained somewhat lamely, 'has been very universally known, as having been composed as a national German air' expressing 'a sentiment of determined antipathy to an invasion by France of the German territory.'[100]

This single reference to the protagonist of the Rhine Song craze was symptomatic of the perception by Britain's diplomats and politicians of the German reaction to the 'Rhine Crisis'. The most interesting observation is that the dog did not bark, or, in other words, the almost complete failure of Britain's diplomats to appreciate the importance of the process of mass nationalization which took place in 1840–1. Rather, the few comments on the political role of the German people were characterized by initial suspicions of French sympathies, which eventually gave way to the debatable impression that the people of Germany, while hostile to French aggression, were generally content with the political status quo. The focus of British perceptions of German politics during the 'Rhine Crisis' was, however, firmly on the various sovereigns and governments. More than the poets, singers and journalists, it was they who were praised for their united stand against France.

The patriotism of the German people, on the other hand, appeared doubtful, at least initially. In May 1840 Erskine reported from Munich that even after Thiers's coming to power 'the liberal part of the population of Germany look[ed] to the support of their views from the influence of similar opinions in France.' Four months later Lord William Russell in Berlin commented on the existence of a large French party in Germany; and even as late as November 1840, when the 'Rhine Crisis' had almost blown over, Erskine mentioned the anxiety of the German sovereigns 'to keep off the contagion of the extravagant doctrines and pretensions of the turbulent people of France.'[101] Being prone to Francophile tendencies was not an endearing feature in the eyes of the makers of British foreign policy in 1840–1, a time when Palmerston wrote to Lytton Bulwer that he had never in his life been more disgusted with anything than he was with the conduct of Thiers.[102]

It was therefore with hearty approval that Britain's diplomats registered how in the course of the 'Rhine Crisis' the public mood in Germany swung in a decidedly anti-French direction. References to this phenomenon, however, remained relatively few in number and were on the whole merely descriptive. In September 1840, Russell in Berlin believed that the French deceived themselves 'in supposing they could walk into the Prussian Rhenish Provinces. They would be kicked out in disgrace.' From Frankfurt, William Fox-Strangways reported on 'a strong anti-French demonstration on the King of Prussia's birthday at Dusseldorf' and that he had been informed that 'the feeling among all classes of Germans [. . .] was very national and very hostile to France.' Lord Beauvale, the former Frederick Lamb, relying on information from Metternich and the German diplomats in Vienna, came to similar conclusions: 'the feeling of Germany is entirely national and its object is independence and peace; but if these should be violated there is every appearance that the whole country would rise as in 1813 to vindicate them.' Only once did a British diplomat clearly evaluate the relevance for the future development of Germany of what had taken place 'in the minds of the people generally', as he called it. In February 1841, when the critical phase of the 'Rhine Crisis' was long over, Erskine mused over the consequences of the emotional reaction which the French policies of 1840 had provoked amongst the German population. 'This sentiment so widely spread in Germany will have, no doubt, a strong influence in uniting the different states of its Confederation in a firm maintenance of their independence and mutual interests.'[103]

The scant attention which Britain's diplomats paid to the political mobilization of the German population and their failure to recognize the full significance of German nationalism stood in marked contrast to the acute observations and conclusions by Baron Bourgoing, the French envoy at Munich. He noticed the role of 'powerful classes' such as 'the very liberal one of scholars, professors and of the youth of the universities' in the dissemination of German nationalism: 'in spite of its liberalism it is readier than any other to be enthused by the expressions of Teutonic patriotism.' Bourgoing also identified what Germany's patriotic writers were aiming at: to persuade everyone in Germany

'that there exists a German fatherland and that the German nationality must constitute itself and unite itself by indissoluble bonds.' His
well-informed and detailed reports are full of warnings about the
growing strength of German nationalism which, as he wrote to Guizot,
the new head of government, in December 1840 'expands, consolidates
itself every day and seems to throw Germany, once fragmented and dis-
united, into entirely new pathways. [. . .] This solidarity of interests and
this unanimity of sentiment of Germany's was a political element which
Europe has never known at any period in history.' Bourgoing was
unequivocal about the importance of what he was observing: 'the creation of the German nationality is one of the most important facts of
our century.'[104]

It is fair to say that the contrast between Bourgoing's perceptiveness
and the relative obtuseness of his British colleagues with respect to the
breakthrough of nationalism in Germany was partly due to factors specific to the situation. Bourgoing was an exceptionally able diplomat, and
the anti-French thrust of the German nationalist wave of 1840–1 made
it a far more striking phenomenon for French than for British diplomats. While concentrating on the wider issue of the Eastern Question,
the British reaction indicated little interest in the domestic affairs of the
German Confederation. This was also reflected in the absence of the
topic from public discussion in Britain. Throughout the entire 'Rhine
Crisis' the *Times* referred only once to an element of the nationalist
wave in Germany, and this was yet again the silver tankard presented
to Becker in 1841. The *Spectator* and the *Annual Register* did not mention
the German reaction at all, and the only German issue which was
debated, albeit at some length, in the House of Commons in 1840–1,
was the question of the duties collected from commercial shipping
at Stade. In the periodicals there was also only one contemporary
comment on the German political scene. In October 1841 the educa-
tionalist Harry Longueville Jones published an article in 'Blackwood's
Edinburgh Magazine' where he argued that 'the noble spirit shown by
the Germans' and their 'soul-stirring cry of "No! they shall never have
the free, the German Rhine"' entitled them to the 'warm respect and
hearty good-will of the sound portion of the British public.'[105]

A more general reason for the sparse and superficial attention by
British diplomats and politicians to popular German nationalism in
1840–1 was the extent to which they focused on sovereigns and governments rather than on the people in their analyses of the political
process. This was different in the case of French diplomacy, which had
recognized the foreign political potential of France's reputation as a lib-

erator of oppressed peoples and consequently paid careful attention to them. Bourgoing was therefore able to conclude from his observations that France 'had lost whatever ideological and popular sympathies it had ever enjoyed in Germany, and would now have to work with governments, not peoples, to defend its interests.'[106] British diplomats at the German courts, on the other hand, merely noted with approbation that in 1840–1, unlike in the early 1830s or after the revocation of the Hanoverian constitution in 1837, the popular spirit served to consolidate rather than undermine the political status quo in Germany and Europe. 'Generally speaking,' Francis Forbes was happy to report from Dresden in November 1840, 'the state of the public mind is now much more satisfactory in the North of Germany, than two or three years ago.'[107] Britain's diplomats could therefore concentrate on the unspectacular steps taken by the governments of the separate German states.

In the course of the 'Rhine Crisis' the German sovereigns and their ministers earned much praise from Palmerston and his diplomats for their policies in response to French aggression. 'It is fortunate,' Beauvale wrote in August 1840, 'that Prussia has succeeded in establishing a bond of union in Germany,' and Erskine emphasized two months later that the 'German States and Sovereigns entertain[ed] a confident reliance on the sufficiency of their united strength ultimately to repel any aggression on the part of France, and a thorough conviction that their union [would] be firm.' In November, Stephen Henry Sulivan, chargé d'affaires in Munich, testified to 'a great deal of unanimity among the different German states' and observed that 'all the points of disagreement among them, have, by a sort of tacit consent, been allowed to drop.' Palmerston was impressed by the military measures taken by the German governments to prepare for a possible French attack. On 3 November 1840 he instructed his envoy in Berlin to express to the Prussian foreign minister 'the great satisfaction of Her Majesty's Government at learning that the German Confederation is taking such active steps, and making such wise and provident arrangements.'[108]

In the judgement of British observers, the overall effect of the 'Rhine Crisis' on the German body politic was therefore positive on two different levels. First, it was believed to have indicated that the people were patriotic, content with the status quo and unlikely to be affected by insurrectionary doctrines. Palmerston, in a letter to the Queen in November 1840, described how in the 1790s France had been bent on foreign war and how the peoples of Continental Europe had suffered under oppressive regimes. 'Those abuses have now in general been removed,' the Foreign Secretary continued, and 'the people in many parts of Germany have been admitted, more or less, to a share in the management of their own affairs. A German feeling and a spirit of nationality has sprung up among all the German people, and the Germans, instead of receiving the French as liberators, as many of them did in 1792–1793, would now rise as one man to repel a hateful invasion.'[109]

Secondly, the 'Rhine Crisis' was seen to have created closer cooperation between the separate German states, to have produced that 'union of Germany within itself,' which Beauvale held to be 'the keystone of Continental Europe'. Russell in Berlin was equally satisfied with the recent developments. 'Monsieur Thiers has involuntarily rendered great service to Germany by renewing the union of the confederated states which had been on the wane since 1820,' he wrote in December 1840, and concluded: 'as far as the sovereigns and governments are concerned, it is now perfect.' Eight months later, the British envoy in Prussia felt no need to revise his earlier evaluation of the effect of Thiers's policies. 'Before he held threatening language and made warlike demonstrations, the states of Germany were divided by petty jealousies, and the military contingents neglected. The policy of Monsieur Thiers induced them to unite, and to fill up their contingents to the federal complement,' Russell reported to the Foreign Secretary; 'such is the good that Monsieur Thiers has done to Germany.'[110]

The 'Rhine Crisis' thus provided British diplomats with a predominantly positive image of the state of affairs in Germany. The Confederation appeared as a union of cooperating, benevolent sovereigns, ready to stand up to foreign challenges and backed by a patriotic population which enjoyed 'a share in the management of their own affairs.' As it turned out, this image did not prepare Britain's diplomats for the political conflicts of the 1840s and reflected British interests and preferences rather than German realities.

The 'enlightened views of the Prussian Monarch': the national movement and governmental reforms, 1840–7

During the 1840s Germany experienced the establishment of nationalism as a popular mass phenomenon. Indeed, it has been described as a characteristic of the decade that governmental measures proved ineffectual at containing societal forces of opposition and national mobilization.[111] Apart from the increase in strength of the national movement and its continued pursuit of the twin objectives of liberal constitutions and greater national unity, two further observations are important in a discussion of Germany's national movement of the

1840s. First, the German nationalism underwent a qualitative change. It became more 'integral', more power-oriented, more focused on culturally and even ethnically defined national communities.[112] Secondly, the 1840s witnessed the condensation of the national movement, which had hitherto been rather diffuse, into 'organised societal nationalism'.[113] The nation-wide process of politicization took place through the growth of ostensibly apolitical private associations (*Vereine*) of singers and gymnasts. By 1848 there existed some 1,100 associations of singers and 250 associations of gymnasts with a total membership of 100,000 and 90,000 respectively. These associations consciously acted in the public sphere and created a platform for themselves by organizing national festivals. The singers met in Würzburg (1845), Cologne (1846) and Lübeck (1847); the gymnasts organized festivals in Mainz (1842), Reutlingen (1845), Heilbronn (1846), Frankfurt and Heidelberg (both 1847). Great public gatherings took place to celebrate the unveiling of monuments like the ones for Bach in Leipzig (1843) and for Goethe in Frankfurt (1844). German scientists, academics and scholars started attending national congresses. Between 1840 and 1847 scientists and medics as well as classical philologists organized conventions every year; Germanists held meetings in Frankfurt in 1846 and in Lübeck the following year. By the eve of the revolution of 1848, the German national movement had developed into a 'powerful and effective force' whose existence has been described as a 'prerequisite for the outbreak of the Revolution in Germany.'[114]

In the early 1840s, when the 'Rhine Crisis' had passed and the passionately anti-French edge of popular nationalism had receded, British observers of German politics realized that the relationship between the German Diet and the governments on the one hand, and the liberal-national opposition on the other, was not marked by mutual support. The realization, however, that Germany's national movement constituted a destabilizing challenge to the status quo, noticeably influenced the way in which it was evaluated in British accounts. Although the importance of the national movement, its programmatic change and its organizational structure were still inadequately appreciated, the positive impression created by the 'Rhine Crisis' gave way to critical comments reminiscent of the early 1830s.

Accordingly, the few references to the German national movement of the 1840s were mostly hostile. In January 1843 Henry Richard Wellesley reported from Karlsruhe that 'throughout the country' there was a 'spirit of discontent [. . .] fomented by a set of intriguing lawyers, who ha[d] nothing else to do.' A fortnight later Henry George Kuper, chargé d'affaires at Frankfurt, echoed this analysis. He complained about publications 'of a blasphemous and revolutionary tendency. [. . .] Others replete with violent attacks upon the German Sovereigns, their governments, and the individuals in their service, all advocating revolutionary doctrines, are now inundating Germany.' He was not surprised that the 'opinions of the great mass of the population of the German states should have become more or less contaminated by the perusal of such publications' and lamented the 'effects of their baneful influence even upon the minds of the intelligent portion of the German community.' Westmorland, writing in 1845, warned of a 'liberal or revolutionary party throughout Germany.'[115] Travelling through Germany in the Queen's entourage in 1845, Aberdeen reported to Peel that there was 'undoubtedly a good deal of fermentation throughout Germany.' In the following year Forbes testified to a 'violent and democratical spirit' amongst the deputies of the Saxon chamber, and found the Duchy of Saxe-Gotha 'under the influence of a set of low Radicals' and 'becoming every day more democratical.'[116] Even more indicative than these familiar epithets is the complete absence from the reports by British diplomats of the associations of gymnasts, the complete silence about Germany's singers and the lack of any sort of analysis of the programme of German nationalism.[117]

The coverage the German national movement received in British newspapers and periodicals was similarly sparse and marked by hostility towards that 'incongruous mob of beardless boys and bearded pedagogues', which, according to the radical *Westminster Review*, had raised the cry for German unity. In 1843, the *Times* thundered against 'those revolutionary and subversive principles which are the bugbear of the petty courts of Germany' and deplored the 'plots and abomination of anarchists and secret societies.'[118] Although they were united in slighting the German national movement, both Britain's diplomats and her organs of published opinion nevertheless agreed that there was a need for reforms in Germany. In British journalistic and diplomatic discussions of German politics two issues were mentioned as in particular need of reform: the German Diet and the constitutional situation in Prussia.[119]

By the early 1840s British criticism of the German Diet was already a long-running theme. In June 1832 the *Times* had called the it 'powerless to do good, or to restrain folly.' Three years later the *Westminster Review* judged the Confederation a 'total failure' at bringing about a union of German states, while sarcastically pointing out that 'its utility as an instrument of despotism ha[d] been very considerable.' In the same year Cartwright reported from Frankfurt that there was 'such a dearth of matter for deliberation in the Diet, that the regular sittings [. . . had] been suspended for the present.' In September 1841 the *Times* asked if the Germanic Confederation was a 'nullity' and answered: 'in the present state of things it nearly is so.' John Ward, writing in the *Edinburgh Review* in 1844, argued that 'the kind of union obtained by means of this confederation was more formal than real', and believed that 'something more cogent than the federative diet was indispensable.' Two years on, Fox-Strangways echoed Cartwright's account of 11 years before, informing Aberdeen that on 12 February 1846 'the Diet did not hold its usual sitting literally from the total absence of business,' and adding that 'the gradual decline of business before the Diet, and the growing insignificance of that body, [were] becoming subjects of general remark.'[120]

In the eyes of British diplomats and politicians, Prussia's constitutional situation also gave rise to concern. Prussia, William Russell reminded Palmerston in December 1840, 'contains an enlightened population without a particle of civil liberty.' The envoy's reports on the Prussians' humbly formulated constitutional demands betrayed a noticeable degree of endorsement. 'The enlightened part of the Prussian people say: the late King promised us a constitution and signed the promise with his royal hand,' Russell wrote in 1841; 'for reasons unknown to us he deferred the execution. We respect his will and abided our time, – but now we ask from Your Majesty, if not a constitution, at least some concession, some control over our finances, some guarantee for our personal liberty.' According to Russell, the constitutional question had something inevitable about it. 'The struggle for more liberal institutions has begun,' he reported, 'and will probably be carried on with the slowness and tenacity, peculiar to the German character.' Two years later the question appeared to have become more urgent. Henry Kuper in Frankfurt described the Prussian public as 'clamorous in its demands for a representative constitution and for various changes in the organization and administration of the state.' By 1845 Aberdeen himself had come to believe that constitutional reforms on the part of the King of Prussia had become 'indispensable'.[121]

A number of authors writing in British periodicals shared the diplomats' and politicians' view that constitutional reform in Prussia was necessary. In 1842, in an article on 'Prussia and the Prussian System', the *Westminster Review* argued that of all European people the Germans, 'solid, sensible, and systematic in all things were the most fitted to exercise the important functions of self-government.' Francis Palgrave, writing in 1843, regarded it as highly probable that 'the seeds of great political changes, and of changes more than political, [were] now germinating in northern Germany.' The *Foreign Quarterly Review* entertained 'no doubt that a constitution resembling that of England, or perhaps that of France, [was] the only possible method of reconciling the continuance of monarchy in Germany with the feelings and opinions of the people.' To Richard Monckton Milnes the political state of Prussia posed many questions, but he was sure of the answer: 'What is still the unsatisfied desire that rankles at the heart of the nation – turning its kindliest feeling into gall, and blunting the edge of patriotism; changing the poet into the satirist, and the philosopher into the pamphleteer; making wise men foolish and wicked men mad [. . .]? What is the object of hopes so long delayed, of prayers so long neglected, now fast accumulating for the evil day of vengeance and despair? We answer, and they answer – political development under Liberal institutions.'[122]

British observers of Germany were thus agreed on two points: the need for certain political reforms, and the rejection of the German national movement as a possible agent of such changes. The British reaction to the personality and policies of the new King of Prussia, Frederick William IV, must be seen against this background. By introducing moderate constitutional reforms, the Prussian King seemed to provide an ideal solution to the perceived problem: the demands of the Prussian people would be met; through its leadership Prussia would provide direction and union to the whole of Germany; all this would serve to pre-empt the demands of the national movement and thereby defuse a potentially dangerous situation. Frederick William IV's first steps appeared to justify these high hopes. A number of liberal professors, who had been dismissed during the 1830s, were reinstated. Censorship was relaxed. The ultra-conservative Prussian ministers Rochow and Kamptz were replaced by the more liberal Bodelschwingh and Savigny. In 1842 the King summoned the 'United Committees' composed of members of the various provincial diets to discuss a range of political issues. These measures were widely – and, as it later turned out, falsely – regarded as a first steps along a path of liberal and constitutional development.[123]

In Britain they produced a favourable impression. Throughout the early 1840s the *Times* published a whole string of articles praising the course pursued by Frederick William IV which, according to a leading article in 1841, would 'speedily place him at the head of the great body of the German nation, and extend the influence of his government beyond the territorial limits of his kingdom.' A year later the paper found it 'impossible not to perceive, that whilst he [was] strong enough to concede nothing to ill-timed remonstrance, and [was] jealous of his own supreme power of improving the institutions of his kingdom, he [was] at the same time steadily advancing in a system which must greatly extend his own power throughout Germany, and increase the liberties of his subjects.' In 1843, the conservative *Fraser's Magazine* commended the 'patriotic energies of the present King of Prussia.' Summarizing British hopes for a German role of a reformed Prussia, Richard Monckton Milnes, writing in the *Edinburgh Review* in 1846, asked 'what better foundation could be laid for some great political future for united Germany, than a constitutional system working harmoniously through united Prussia.'[124]

Britain's diplomats and politicians commented on the issue in a similar way. In January 1842 George Hamilton, chargé d'affaires in Berlin, praised the King's 'conscientious intention of fulfilling the promise he has frequently made of gradually introducing the necessary improvements in the administration of his kingdom.' In a letter of February 1842 to the British ambassador in Vienna, Aberdeen sang the praises of Frederick William IV: 'his politics are so sound, he is so good a German. [. . .] I never met with more sincerity and patriotism. His great desire seems to be to unite and strengthen the German people.' Wellesley reported from Karlsruhe that in terms of constitutional progress Prussia had now replaced liberal Baden. 'The state of this country has become comparatively less interesting to Germany from the rapid strides that are making towards more liberal institutions in Prussia,' he wrote in January 1843. 'The hope of all German liberals [. . .] formerly centred in this small Duchy, are now turned towards that country.' In 1844, Palmerston, out of office and on a private visit to Berlin, was similarly impressed by the Prussian King. 'The King is a man of great acquirements, much natural talent, and enlightened views; and there can be no doubt that under his reign Prussia will make rapid advance in improvement of every kind. [. . .] In short, Prussia is taking the lead in German civilization.'[125]

British satisfaction with and optimism about the constitutional reforms undertaken by Frederick William IV peaked in February 1847 when the 'United Diet' assembled in Berlin.[126] British observers had waited increasingly impatiently for such a step, and expectations were high.[127] The news of the convocation of the 'United Diet', a body comprising deputies from all Prussia's provincial diets, was therefore greeted with joy. 'I have to desire,' Palmerston instructed Westmorland, 'that you will congratulate Baron Canitz upon this important event.' Palmerston viewed Prussia's constitutional reform as a measure 'calculated to strengthen the attachment of the Prussian nation to their sovereign and having a direct tendency to turn towards Prussia the sympathies of a large portion of the people of Germany, and thus to add to the internal strength and to the political influence of the Prussian monarchy.' The Foreign Secretary again expressed his optimism when he informed Malet on the eve of the opening of the 'United Diet' that Her Majesty's Government trusted that 'the enlightened views of the Prussian monarch on the one hand, and the good sense and intelligence of his subjects on the other, [would] combine to derive from the institutions which [had] been given, all the national benefits which the best friends of Prussia [could] desire to see realized.' The public reaction in Britain was equally positive. In February 1847, the Whig MP Philip Henry Howard drew the attention of the House of Commons to the fact that 'the enlightened Sovereign who ruled over the Prussian monarchy had given a constitution to his people, of which there could be no doubt they were worthy.' If anything, the *Times*, in a leading article in April 1847, proved even more jubilant: 'no one can for a moment doubt that the motives which have actuated the King of Prussia do honour to his throne; and we trust that these measures will throw a lasting glory on his reign.'[128]

The meeting of the 'United Diet' also provided the British Foreign Secretary with a welcome opportunity to lecture the Prussian parliamentary novice on sound constitutional practice. In February 1847 Palmerston instructed his envoy in Berlin to inform the Prussian Foreign Minister 'that both theory and experience show that two assemblies are far better and safer than one.' Assessing the session of the Diet, Palmerston wrote to the British chargé d'affaires in Berlin that it would have 'been better if the constitution given to the Prussians had been framed at once upon the usual modern model of two legislative houses, meeting periodically', and hoped that the Prussian government would now work towards such a solution.[129] In spite of these mild misgivings about the 'United Diet', British diplomats in Germany reported in favourable terms about its effect on the German political scene and the likely future of Prussia's constitution. John Ward wrote from Leipzig that Prussia's development had 'upon the whole excited a favourable impression in Saxony, and apparently in most of the German states.' He thought it 'pretty certain that the recent changes must, before the lapse of many years, place Prussia in the position of a constitutional state' and regarded them as 'undoubted indications of a liberal policy [. . .] dictated by a reforming spirit.' Prussia's 'influence over the other German states,' Ward predicted, 'cannot fail of being very considerably increased.' With regard to the 'future development of the constitutional liberties of this country,' Westmorland affirmed, 'there can now remain no doubt whatsoever.'[130] His chargé d'affaires agreed emphatically. 'The further development of the constitutional institutions of Prussia,' Henry Howard wrote in July 1847, 'appears only a question of time.' Fox-Strangways saw a great future for the Prussian parliament. 'It will throw into the shade the smaller parliaments of Saxony and Baden which can no longer claim to represent the popular feeling of the German nation, while the restless spirit of their opposition may take a lesson in habits of useful public business, as well as of sound constitutional principles from the conduct of the states of Prussia.' Looking back on the course of German history in May 1848, Lord John Russell argued that it was in 1847 that Prussia 'broke loose' from the 'despotic and dynastic forms of government' which had been established across Europe after Napoleon's defeat.[131]

British diplomats, journalists and politicians, like so many Germans, misunderstood the intentions and designs which motivated Frederick William IV's policies. The King, so regularly described as 'enlightened' in British accounts, was not pursuing a programme of liberal constitutionalism and improvement. The halting and recalcitrant manner in which his constitutional reforms were implemented was much more indicative of the King's real aims than the few concrete steps that were actually taken. His aim, in the words of a leading authority, was to '*create* a strong *counter*-revolutionary tradition, based both on popular support and on an affirmation of the divinely ordained nature of kingship as the only alternative to despotism.' His reforms, which apparently aimed at constitutional progress, really amounted to an experiment to put 'the relationship between King and people, between monarchy and society, on a new but non-constitutional footing.'[132] With their rejection of the German national movement of opposition and their awareness of Germany's need for reforms, however, British diplomats proved susceptible to Frederick William IV's dazzling policies.

All in all, three broad observations, which apply in equal measure to the Whig administrations of Grey, Melbourne and Russell and to Peel's Tory cabinets, emerge from an analysis of British perceptions of the *Zollverein*, the 'Rhine Crisis' and the policies of Frederick William IV: (i) the German national movement received only scant attention and was seen in a predominantly negative light. Only during the 'Rhine Crisis', when it was believed to support, rather than undermine, the status quo, did Britain's diplomats and politicians accord a constructive role to the German national movement; (ii) much-needed political reform measures initiated and controlled from above met with a largely positive reaction. In spite of the realization that there were problems associated with them, both the *Zollverein* and the constitutional steps taken by Frederick William IV were considered progressive and efficacious; (iii) through the favourable impression of the *Zollverein* and the expectation that Prussia's liberal course would greatly augment her influence in Germany, Prussia assumed a central position in the British evaluation of the German question.

2
British Perceptions of Revolutionary Germany, 1848–9

The European revolutions of 1848 inspired Palmerston to a moment of memorable rhetoric. 'We have no eternal allies, and we have no perpetual enemies,' he declared in the House of Commons a week after the abdication of Louis Philippe. 'Our interests are eternal and perpetual, and those interests it is our duty to follow.'[1] The revolutionary scenario which unfolded in Europe in the spring of 1848 confronted the Foreign Secretary with daunting challenges to what he regarded as Britain's eternal interests of peace on the continent and the maintenance of a balanced territorial order. The birth of a new French republic reawakened fears of Gallic aggression. The upheaval in Italy might spawn unstable new regimes, could provoke ideas of aggrandizement in France and trigger harsh Austrian reactions. The revolution in Hungary threatened to destroy the Habsburgs' multinational empire and thus jeopardized the very foundations of the European system.

Palmerston's response to these challenges turned out far more measured than his pugnacious reputation would suggest. The basic thrust of his foreign policy in 1848/9 was directed at de-escalating potentially explosive situations in order to shore up the European order. Unperturbed by the spectre of an aggressive French republic, he successfully involved the new regime in Paris in a cooperative dialogue to reassure it and guide it towards moderate paths. The Foreign Secretary's repeated attempts to find a solution to the Italian problem, by advocating the creation of a Piedmontese buffer state, were defeated by Charles Albert's unique blend of incompetence and obstinacy. In the face of Austria's strong military resurgence in Italy, Palmerston could only try to soften the blow for Piedmont. As for the Hungarian revolutionaries, the private sympathies he may have entertained for them did not induce Palmerston to lend them any tangible support. He denied them recognition of

Hungary's independence and may even have encouraged Russia – with whom he had pragmatically established an anti-revolutionary cooperative *modus vivendi* – to intervene on Vienna's behalf. Keen to maintain Austria as a great power, he only indulged in some public attacks on Russia and Austria once the Hungarians had been safely quashed.[2]

The German revolution of 1848–9 confronted British observers with a rapidly changing political scene marked by liberal and radical demands, revolutionary violence, royal concessions, the outbreak of war in Schleswig and governmental fightbacks.[3] In spite of the bewildering complexity of the revolutionary change, accounts of Britain's reaction to the German revolution have frequently been coloured by two simple, yet powerful, contemporary myths centring on the British Foreign Secretary. One myth, widespread amongst contemporary European conservatives and radicals alike, portrayed Palmerston as the champion of suppressed peoples, as the enemy of Metternich's dark despotism, as 'Lord *Feuerbrand*' ('Firebrand') challenging Prince '*Mitternacht*' ('Midnight' – a pun on Metternich's name). The King of Hanover, for instance, considered Palmerston 'the instigator of all the liberal movements now in progress.'[4] The second myth was born out of frustration. When the dreams of the German nationalists of 1848–9 had ended in failure, they were quick to blame the European powers who had allegedly vetoed Germany's unification. While autocratic Russia and reactionary Austria had only done what might have been expected, Palmerston was seen to have betrayed the liberal cause and became a *bête noire*. The bitterness caused by Britain's anti-German stance in the Schleswig-Holstein conflict and her refusal formally to recognize the government created by the National Assembly was reflected in the popular doggerel:

| *Hat der Teufel einen Sohn* | If the devil has a son |
| *so heißt er sicher Palmerston* | his name is surely Palmerston[5] |

In the following, an attempt will be made to question both these myths. The maker of Britain's foreign policy was neither a revolutionary firebrand nor was he diabolically opposed to the idea of a more closely united Germany. It will be argued instead that Palmerston and most British diplomats and journalists believed that revolution and German unity were two things which, in the best interests of Germany, Britain and Europe, ought to be kept strictly separate.

In spite of the complexity of the revolutionary events in Germany, British observers quickly identified the main thrust of the revolutionary process. 'Amid the struggling voices, that are able at first to achieve more distinct utterance,' an anonymous author wrote in *Tait's Edinburgh Magazine*, 'we discern above the rest, pre-eminent, these two – CONSTITUTIONAL FREEDOM *for the several members*; NATIONAL UNITY, *for the whole body*.'[6] The following discussion of British perceptions of German politics during the revolutionary period will, in turn, analyse these two 'voices' and the attempts made to answer their calls. Thus, a discussion of British reactions to the revolution in the separate German states will be followed by an analysis of British views on the central political institutions created at Frankfurt.

Reform, revolution and reaction in the German states

The direct conflict between the established order and the revolutionary challenge did not take place in the institutional centre of the revolution at Frankfurt, but in the individual German states. The revolutionary struggle here both predated and outlasted the new national bodies set up at Frankfurt. This suggests subdividing an analysis of the conflict into three chronological phases. During the first period, from the outbreak of the revolution in early March 1848 until the eve of the opening of the National Assembly in May, the revolutionaries confronted the separate governments with their demands for political change and were granted concessions. The second phase, from the opening of the National Assembly until the beginning of the states' reassertion of their role in national politics, saw the German governments in the shadow of the *Paulskirche* and reluctant to oppose the changes introduced in March. After January 1849, with the Frankfurt National Assembly on the wane, the focus of the revolutionary struggle returned to the level of the separate states. It was on this level that governmental forces defeated the revolution, state by state.

'Reasonable demands' and 'timely concessions': the German states, March–April 1848

By the time the revolutionary wildfire which swept Europe in 1848 reached the German states, British observers had already had plenty of notice of what was in the wind. Even before Louis Philippe's overthrow, Palmerston realized that the revolutions in Italy at the beginning of 1848 provided lessons which the German governments would do well to learn. On 22 February he instructed his envoy in Berlin to remind the Prussian foreign minister of the 'wisdom [of] yielding betimes to the reasonable demands of subjects' and to mention that 'if the King of

Naples had made timely concessions [. . .] the outbreak which subsequently happened would not have taken place.' Palmerston added that 'the late events in Naples and Sicily ought to serve as a useful warning.' If British perceptions and views of the first phase of the 1848 revolution in Germany in general, and of the course pursued by the German governments in particular, proved relatively favourable, this can be at least partially ascribed to the belief that in granting 'timely concessions' to 'reasonable demands' Germany's princes were heeding sound advice. It was believed that with both parties acting wisely, the movement of March 1848 offered an opportunity. 'If it be conducted with prudence and moderation on the part of the people, and met in a spirit of conciliation by their rulers,' Milbanke wrote from Munich on 7 March, 'its beneficial results to all classes of society can scarcely be overrated.'[7]

Measured against the strong anti-revolutionary feeling amongst Britain's foreign political establishment, and its derogatory attitude towards the German opposition since 1830, the accounts by British diplomats and journalists of the German revolutionaries in March 1848 were surprisingly calm. Though there was little actual praise for them, the German revolutionaries were frequently portrayed as loyal, and their political programme, the so-called 'March Demands' (liberty of the press, trial by jury, ministerial responsibility, reform of the German Diet), as relatively moderate. In one of the earliest despatches on the subject, Malet confirmed his and his colleague in Karlsruhe's 'strong conviction that there [would] not be an outbreak.' Ward in Leipzig expressed similarly reassuring opinions: 'I don't believe the people are republicans, but, on the contrary, attached to their Princes.' The coverage of the events of March 1848 in the *Times* was also sympathetic. 'The demands of the Germans,' a leading article declared on 13 March, 'are no more than the fulfilment of the pledges solemnly given at the peace.' Four days later the paper looked 'forward to the progress of Germany with the confident hope that the national movement of that great people will not degenerate into a democratic revolution, but that it will establish a solid barrier against destructive agitation and foreign aggression.'[8] However, three important reservations must be added to this favourable first impression. First, it was short-lived and turned sour as soon as the movement was seen to 'degenerate into a democratic revolution'. Secondly, British perceptions of the early phase of the revolution were dominated not by the revolutionaries, but by the much-praised German governments. Lastly, in concentrating on the political development, British diplomats all but ignored the social dimension of the revolution.

Only eight days after it had expressed 'confident hope' about the German national movement, the *Times* dramatically changed its tune. 'In truth, a democratic feeling is fast spreading among the people,' an alarmed correspondent observed. 'It is most lamentable, and it may in the result prove most disastrous.' By the middle of April, Germany had, according to the *Times*, descended into a 'perplexing scene of anarchy and confusion.' In May 1848 the conservative *Blackwood's Edinburgh Magazine* published an article by Professor John Blackie on the 'Revolutions in Europe'. The author anticipated 'no good from the revolution in Prussia [. . .]. Already all the usual and well-known effects of successful revolution are to be seen in Berlin. Extravagant ideas among the working classes, [. . .] expectations inconsistent with the first laws of society.' Professor William Aytoun, writing in the same journal, came to similar conclusions. 'Right sorry we were,' he reflected in September 1848, 'to learn that quiet Germany had lighted her revolutionary pipe from the French insurrectionary fires; that Mannheim, Heidelberg, and Hanau, those notorious nests of democracy, had succeeded in perverting the minds of many'. The *Annual Register* was also alarmed at the development in Germany, where 'political institutions had been gradually undermined by an undercurrent of agitation, of which the tendency was to establish democracy in its most dangerous form.'[9]

As the revolutionary change proceeded, British diplomats arrived at an equally negative judgement. Some of them even argued that there had been no justification whatsoever for the insurrection. 'When the first regular outbreak occurred in March last,' Lord Cowley, Britain's representative at Frankfurt, stated in August 1848, 'Germany laboured under no grievance which could really justify such violence. With the exception of Austria, there seemed to be a sincere desire among the sovereigns of the different states to grant such free institutions as they thought would be for the benefit of their subjects. [. . .] civil and religious liberty was everywhere guaranteed.' Revolutionary opposition to this idyllic state of things hardly merited British endorsement. The despatches by the conservative Westmorland on the events in Berlin expressed a strong dislike for the popular meetings composed of persons 'many of them strangers and others of the lowest class of society', and admiration for the military who had 'done their duty in dispersing the assemblage with exemplary patience and forbearance.' Amongst the Berlin revolutionaries Westmorland identified people 'who sought for the general overthrow of all order and the establishment of liberty, equality and communism.' On 30 March, Ward predicted that the 'principle of universal suffrage, or something very near it, will be established.

[. . .] It follows that the system of government in Germany will become highly democratic.'[10] Hanover was also affected. 'I am sorry to have to report,' John Duncan Bligh wrote from there a fortnight later, 'that even in this country, pernicious example and foreign emissaries have raised up a democratic spirit which threatens to dictate to the government and to upset all existing institutions which do not harmonize with that spirit.'[11]

While Britain's diplomats largely ignored the social dimension of the revolution,[12] the political impact of the process of democratic radicalization alone clearly sufficed to give cause for concern. 'The tractable disposition, the orderly habits, and sound sense of the German population have been greatly perverted by foreign incendiaries,' Stratford Canning, whom Palmerston had sent on a special mission to the German courts, reported from Vienna in April 1848; 'and the excitement of unexpected success has carried the national enthusiasm beyond those limits which are alike prescribed by a wise attention to the experience of others, and by the very nature of constitutional government. The most extreme right of suffrage, elections independent of property, and parliamentary peerages by election or life-appointment – added to the ordinary securities of liberty and the establishment of national guards, can hardly fail of producing so complete a transfer of power from the Crown to the populace, as to prove eventually incompatible with the maintenance and even with the name of monarchy.' Criticizing the German governments Canning argued that while 'there was danger stemming the torrent of democracy, there was also danger in yielding unreasonably to its violence.'[13]

Canning's suggestion that the German governments were lacking in resolve to withstand the revolutionary current came at the end of a period of almost unanimous British praise for Germany's princes. Indeed, the 'pre-March' pattern of focusing on governmental action continued throughout March and April 1848. Even after the outbreak of the revolution British accounts sidelined the national movement and painted a picture of reforming governments acquitting themselves well under difficult circumstances. The key term was 'concessions'. Faced with moderate popular demands, the governments speedily conceded changes which, British politicians and diplomats believed, would defuse the revolutionary crisis and at the same time establish an improved state of political affairs. Across the whole of the German Confederation 'March Ministries' were formed, headed by moderate liberals such as Friederich Römer, Paul Pfizer, August Hergenhahn, Bertram Stüve, Ludolf Camphausen and David Hansemann, and most of the

'March Demands' granted. As early as 7 March, Malet in Stuttgart proved optimistic: 'all southern Germany will in my opinion have made very great advances in constitutional liberty without any sacrifices of national principle or unsafe invasion of the power and influence of the respective governments.' On the same day, Orme in Frankfurt praised the Hessian Dukes because 'bloodshed has been spared in these immediate Duchies by the good sense of the Princes who have conceded the reforms most loudly demanded.' It almost appeared as if no British diplomat wanted 'his' government's prudence to remain unnoticed. Forbes believed that 'had every other government in Germany shown as much spirit and firmness as that of Saxony, the results would have been different – and sufficient praise [could] not be given to these ministers for the bold, constitutional line they ha[d] adopted and followed.' According to Canning, Frederick William IV had 'recognized the principle of looking to the advice of his responsible ministers in the spirit of a constitutional monarchy.'[14]

The Foreign Secretary shared the favourable impression conveyed by his diplomats. 'The present state of Germany must be a subject of great anxiety to all who wish well to that important portion of Europe, and who set a proper value upon the maintenance of general peace,' Palmerston wrote to Malet on 23 March, 'but the governments seem in general to be pursuing so wise a course and to be so sensible of the necessity of making reasonable concessions largely and promptly that the apprehensions which the first outbreak in France excited in one's mind has very much diminished.' Malet was instructed to congratulate the King of Württemberg, who had managed to 'unite courage with calmness, and firmness with enlightened liberality.' In a letter of the same date to Westmorland, Palmerston also welcomed the steps taken in Berlin. 'We are glad to find that the King of Prussia is making progress in his constitutional improvements.'[15]

Towards the end of the first phase of the revolution, however, the praise which British diplomats and politicians showered on the German governments gave way to more critical comments. The main thrust of this criticism was not that the princes' commitment to liberal change lacked sincerity but, on the contrary, that they were failing to uphold order. As early as 23 March, Canning observed from Cologne that the 'usual relations between the government and its subjects, and also between the military and civil portions of the population have undergone an ominous change. Should the regal authority and the ordinary means of enforcing respect continue in their present state of weakness [. . .] public tranquillity and the well-being of society must necessarily be exposed to imminent danger.' After his arrival in the Prussian capital, the special envoy was even more gloomy. Finding it 'very difficult to form a favourable opinion either of the King of Prussia's conduct or of his position,' Canning concluded on 26 March that 'Royal authority [was] at zero.' Five days later, he informed Palmerston that 'the revolutionary torrent threaten[ed] to hurry both [the King] and his ministers into a state of domestic confusion and war.' Everywhere order appeared to be collapsing. Strangways reported from Frankfurt that 'the effects of a continued suspension of government in the presence of a turbulent population [were] likely to prove a dangerous example to countries as yet removed from anarchy.' The newly appointed Saxon ministers proved no exception to this disquieting rule. Canning found them complacent with regard to the current 'precipitation towards extreme democratic principles'. The diplomat could only wish 'to find them more alive to the importance of combining a due respect for authority with the necessary degree of concessions to popular demands [. . .] and more determined to take part in providing some kind of barrier against the present exaggerated taste for institutions formed in the spirit [. . .] of republicanism.'[16]

In a letter to the Queen of 18 April 1848, Palmerston defined the role of the British government *vis-à-vis* the European revolutions as 'one rather of observation than of action'. This cautious line did not prevent the Foreign Office from making a somewhat futile attempt to address the problem of governmental weakness in Germany by giving unsolicited advice. During his audience with the Prussian King, Canning 'ventured to remark with due submission that next to reasonable concession and sincerity in acting on declared principles, firmness in resisting dangerous demands and judgement in resisting them so as to attain support from the more reflecting classes, were essential in the exercise of supreme authority.' Palmerston, characteristically, was more forward. 'I have to instruct you to exhort the Bavarian government,' he wrote to Milbanke on 20 April, 'to direct its effort to the maintenance of internal order and to imitate in this respect the example set by this country, where the active union and energetic demonstration of the upper and middle classes have prevented any disturbances of the public peace.'[17]

The brief period during which British observers regarded the political development of Germany with hope and optimism thus ended in disappointment. In the course of the first few weeks after the appointment of the 'March Ministries' British perceptions of German politics proved almost unanimously favourable. It seemed that through a carefully balanced interaction of moderate popular demands and well-timed governmental concessions the German states had been reformed, without compromising the monarchical principle. This evaluation was flawed in three respects: first, it was based on an incomplete perception of the revolutionary process which ignored the socially motivated uprisings of the peasantry and the urban lower classes. Secondly, it mistakenly assumed that the revolutionaries would be bought off by the concession of the 'March Demands'. The ensuing radicalization of the revolutionary movement repulsed British observers. Thirdly, the evaluation reflected an overestimation of the strength of the German governments. When it emerged that they were unable to defend the newly established status quo, their weakness attracted British criticism.

'Rash and weak precipitation': the German states to January 1849

The overwhelmingly negative assessment of the situation in Germany, to which the initial British optimism had given way, continued largely unchanged for another nine months. In their analyses and comments, British diplomats and politicians subjected the political developments of the German states in the shadow of the *Paulskirche* National Assembly to continued and fierce censure. The 'party of movement' was consistently portrayed as a set of 'low radicals' pursuing extremist and dangerous republican aims. Nor did the governments escape British criticism, which was principally directed at three different issues. First, there was general concern about the state of public order and governmental authority. British diplomats also deplored the franchise provisions of the newly-formulated electoral legislation and their effects on the exercise of strong government. Finally, when – as in Prussia in the autumn of 1848 – steps were taken to reassert monarchical authority, British politicians and diplomats wondered whether the salutary effects of these measures were compromised by the subsequently decreed constitutional settlement.

Even after the opening of the National Assembly in Frankfurt, the German states continued to display signs of revolutionary disorder which Britain's diplomats found deeply worrying. Reporting on the small Thuringian duchies in May 1848, Forbes was 'grieved to say that in all these smaller states the opinions [were] not only infinitely worse than in Saxony, but that republican principles and plans [were] avowed and discussed in the most undisguised manner. On the other hand the nobility and the higher classes [. . . did] not offer the slightest resistance to the attacks of their adversaries, but evince[d] a want of energy, nay of personal courage, which [could] not but lead to results as fatal to themselves as to their sovereigns. On this point the Saxon nobility [were] in no one degree better.' Milbanke's reports from Munich were similarly disheartening. 'We continue in the same state of weakness and helplessness, flattering ourselves that the spirit of the people is what is called *good* so long as no actual outbreak takes place,' he wrote on 29 May. 'Germany seems to be rotten to its very heart's core.'[18] The same applied to Austria. 'It is difficult to pass in review what has taken place here for these some months past, and what has just occurred,' Arthur Charles Magenis, chargé d'affaires at Vienna, wrote to Palmerston in July 1848, 'and not to perceive how completely the government has lost all power and energy and how that power has passed into other and irresponsible hands, who are likely to use it, to subvert almost everything.'[19]

In Berlin, royal authority was also seen to be at low ebb. After the storming of the city arsenal on 14 June, the capital appeared to continue in a highly combustible state. In his despatches to Palmerston, Westmorland mentioned 'Democratic Clubs' exerting themselves 'to keep up an agitation amongst the lower classes against the government and constituted authorities,' the 'mob' demonstrating 'in front of the prison where the persons implicated in storming the arsenal [were] confined,' and the 'extreme violence to which the republican party in this capital ha[d] lately had recourse.' At the end of October, public order in Berlin was seen to have broken down completely. On 1 November, Westmorland sent a detailed despatch describing a chaotic situation. There had been violent disturbances, the Prussian national assembly was under siege from the populace, the burgher guard had lost control and there had been numerous killings. Bligh in Hanover provided an explanation for the excesses which could be observed across the German states. 'One of the greatest difficulties with which Germany has to contend,' he observed on 29 June, 'has been the unlimited right of public meeting which, conceded at once to the popular demand by the different governments, prevents a calm consideration by these governments and by the representative bodies of the changes which are really required.' Malet endorsed this argument: it was 'generally felt and acknowledged that the lenity hitherto shown to the disturbers of the public peace in all the parts of Germany has had the effect of increasing their audacity.'[20] It is clear from the manner in which they reported on the political climate in the German states that Britain's diplomats strongly felt that the time for leniency was well and truly over.

The breakdown of public order across the German states was not the only criticism voiced by British observers, though. 'It is in the midst of this scene of danger, excitement, and tribulation that Prussia, without the least previous preparation for it, is to plunge at once into *universal suffrage*, equal electoral districts, and a deputy for every 50,000 souls,' John Blackie wrote in *Blackwood's Edinburgh Magazine* with alarmed consternation. 'England, with its freedom, cautious habits, realised wealth, and opulent middle classes, could not withstand such a constitution.' The German governments were not only criticized for their inability to impose their authority, but also for their acquiescence in the passing of electoral laws incorporating dangerously wide suffrages. British diplomats and politicians almost unanimously decried these inroads of democracy. In his final report, Canning condemned the German governments for making far-reaching decisions for the wrong reasons. 'Constitutions are formed or altered rather as concessions to popular clamour, than as the foundations of social improvements adapted to the real wants of the age,' he wrote from Munich in May 1848. The sudden appearance of democracy in revolutionary Germany left a lasting impression on the Foreign Secretary. As late as November 1850, he reminded the Queen of the 'rash and weak precipitation with which in 1848 and 1849 those governments which before had refused everything resolved in a moment of alarm to grant everything, and, passing from one extreme to the other, threw universal suffrage among people who had been [. . .] unaccustomed to the working of representative government.'[21]

A democratic tendency in Prussia was noticed as early as March 1848, when Westmorland reported that there was 'great opposition' to the re-assembly of the United Diet because it was 'looked upon by the movement party as too conservative in its opinions, and they would desire that the King should dissolve it, and himself promulgate a law of election on the basis of universal suffrage and call together a parliament elected upon that principle.' When, a week later, this demand had been met, Westmorland expressed serious apprehensions. 'The probable result of the law of election, according to which universal suffrage is established in its most extended form, corrected only by secondary election of the deputies, is entirely uncertain. [. . .] That this is a dangerous experiment is almost universally admitted.' In a private letter to Lord Aberdeen, his former chief, Westmorland was more open: 'What a chaos we have got into! it really is not to be described.'[22]

All across the German states, electoral provisions were introduced which were considered deplorably democratic. In September 1848, Forbes reported on the primary elections in Gotha and was 'sorry to say that the elections were generally speaking then of such liberal principles, that it is easy to foresee out of what class the deputies will be chosen.' Forbes also criticized 'the new law of election now before the second chamber' in Dresden, which, he argued, 'in its present shape is a forced concession to the democratic party, and which ought to be very much altered before it is passed.' Discussing the new Hanoverian constitution, Bligh argued that 'no advocate for constitutional guarantees ought to find fault with any of its provisions except those important ones which give so nearly universal right of suffrage for the election of members for both chambers. [. . .] Whether monarchy can long subsist under such circumstances is a problem still to be solved.' Bavaria was going down the same dangerous road. 'The widest possible extension short of universal suffrage was [. . .] given to this law,' Milbanke reported from Munich, 'and the consequence will in all probability be a most unmanageable lower chamber.'[23]

The results of the chamber elections in the various German states were seen to prove Milbanke's prediction right. 'Some persons of the most democratic opinions [. . .] have been returned with considerable majorities,' Westmorland wrote from Berlin in May 1848. 'In a number of places persons of the lowest class of day labourers have been returned and low shopkeepers such as retail bakers, butchers and haberdashers.' The electoral law which the Saxon government had granted, worked, in Forbes's view, as 'a means of selecting a set of either low radicals or avowed republicans.' The same predicament befell Bavaria, where 'the consequences of this new system [. . .] have fully justified the apprehensions entertained,' as Milbanke reported. In January 1849 he even found that he had 'underrated the numerical strength of the democratic fraction, – which however is formidable not so much by its numbers as by its activity and the oratorical talents possessed by many of its members. [. . .] Nearly the whole of them profess ultra-republican doctrines.'[24] In the eyes of Britain's diplomats, the calamity and its possible solution entirely hinged on the electoral laws. When discussing the problem of the radical chamber with the head of the Saxon ministry in January 1849, Forbes learned that the Saxon government was considering dissolving the chamber. 'I observed that with their present law of election, I did not see how they would be gainers, for that the same worthless set would be reelected and added "How are you to get rid of, or alter that law?" He admitted that there lay the difficulty.'[25] British hopes for an improvement of the political situation in the German states therefore focused on the possibility of reactionary *coups d'état* to reassert the monarchical principle and suppress democratic tendencies. As before 1848, but under profoundly different circumstances and with a very different objective, it was once again Prussia to which British observers looked to give sound political leadership to the German states.

Prussia had one asset, to which Westmorland frequently drew attention: her loyal army. As early as on 30 March 1848, having previously praised the military's conduct during the street fighting in Berlin, the British envoy was 'happy to say that troops to the number of 2,500 infantry have entered the town.' In September he commented on the army's 'exemplary conduct', its 'strict submission to discipline under very trying circumstances in which it has been placed since the revolution of March' and its 'remarkable patience'. For the successful completion of the *coup d'état* against the Prussian national assembly in early November 1848, the loyalty and discipline of the army was of the essence. Once again Westmorland was impressed, for 'all the military measures have been taken with great caution and without unnecessary display.'[26]

In the autumn of 1848, after months of prevarication and planning, Frederick William IV finally decided to carry out what his adviser Edwin von Manteuffel had called a 'carefully considered, carefully prepared restoration'. On 9 November, Count Brandenburg, the newly-appointed Minister-President, read a royal decree to the national assembly in Berlin, declaring it prorogued, and ordering its removal to the provincial town of Brandenburg. On 10 November the military occupied the capital, a state of siege was declared, the burgher guards were dissolved, political associations were banned and the right of assembly as well as the freedom of the press were restricted. The whole *coup* went smoothly and without bloodshed. The King was delighted and told his wife: 'Now I am honest again.'[27] Frederick William's particular kind of honesty was very favourably received by British diplomats. Westmorland offered his moral support to the King in 'the arduous task of re-establishing order where it has so long been wanting.' He affirmed Frederick William's complete acknowledgement 'of the obligation he is under to keep faith with the country, by the maintenance of his promise of a liberal constitution, but he is determined while doing so to establish order without which no liberty can exist.' Westmorland was also very positive about the 'first impressions produced in the country and at Berlin by the transfer of the national assembly to Brandenburg and by the measures taken by the government to restore order and the empire of the laws. Since that period the strongest feeling of attachment to the King and royal family and of confidence in His Majesty's constitutional intentions, as well as of gratitude for the course pursued by his ministers, have been manifested.'[28]

It was not only the conservative Westmorland who welcomed the recent changes. Cowley in Frankfurt was also clearly in favour of the Prussian government's course. 'We have followed all the proceedings at Berlin with the greatest of interest,' he wrote to Westmorland. 'The feeling of all those who dare speak out, with the exception of what is called the extrême gauche, is with the King. I wish that it had been shown in a more decided manner.'[29] The *Times* also approved the reactionary fightback which ended the revolutions in Berlin and Vienna.[30] 'If the Austrian and Prussian armies have intervened to restore the balance of power in their respective capitals, that result is attributable [. . .] to the popular excesses which provoked and demanded energetic repression,' a leading article argued in November 1848. A month later, the *Times* compared the continued revolutionary atmosphere at Frankfurt unfavourably with Vienna and Berlin, where 'a real force and a positive authority ha[d] happily succeeded to the cries of mobs and the decrees of conventions.'[31]

By the time the latter article appeared, the unanimously friendly reaction by Britain's diplomats and politicians to the King of Prussia's course in November 1848 had already been tinged by an element of disappointment and worry. On 5 December 1848 Frederick William IV completed the *coup d'état* by dissolving the national assembly. At the instance of the Brandenburg cabinet and against the wishes of his ultra-conservative advisers the King decreed a constitution on the same day. Thus, 'both Prussia and Frederick William IV had been brought once and for all into the constitutional age.'[32] Interestingly, for all the King's reluctance to grant a constitution at all, it was the liberal constitutional draft prepared by the Prussian national assembly, the so-called Charte Waldeck, on which the constitution of December 1848 was based. It was the liberalism and the democratic elements of this document which provoked British apprehensions.

The reaction of British diplomats and politicians to the Prussian constitution of 5 December 1848 was lively and unanimously critical. On the day of its promulgation Westmorland commented on its 'very liberal spirit' which left 'doubts with some persons [. . .] whether it [would] leave sufficient power in the executive to allow it to carry on the government of the country.' On 10 December, Cowley added his voice to the growing criticism, informing the Foreign Secretary that the more moderate politicians at Frankfurt were 'dismayed and embarrassed by the ultra-liberality of the royal charter, for they had hoped to pass here a constitution of less democratic tendencies.' Cowley found it 'consoling to think that there [were] leading men here who [saw] the dangers of giving the people too much power.' According to Westmorland, the Prussian constitutional guarantees led even Prussia's public opinion to voice 'distrust and alarm as to the extensive concessions contained in them to the principles put forward by the democratic and republican parties, who have lately proved themselves so dangerous to the liberties and prosperity of the country. The concession of universal suffrage as the basis of the law of election for the lower chamber [. . .] is looked upon with much alarm.' The government of the country, Westmorland continued, would 'be rendered extremely difficult by the concessions the King ha[d] made as to the almost unconditional liberty of the press, and the right of assembly in clubs and public meetings.'[33]

The critical stand taken by the diplomats in Germany was shared by observers in Britain. Richard Charles Mellish, a senior clerk at the Foreign Office, who was a specialist on German affairs and regularly corresponded with Cowley in Frankfurt,[34] was gloomy. 'The democratic nature of the constitution,' he wrote to the envoy on 13 December 1848, 'will in a very short time take from the executive all the power it still has got.' Palmerston was also worried. Four days after the constitutional decree, he mentioned the Prussian King's step in a letter to his brother, but regretted the constitution's 'many defects'. In January 1849, he subjected the Prussian envoy in London to a passionate tirade. 'They seem at Berlin to be "always in extremes and nothing long". But certainly the sooner they can get decently out of the extreme of democracy into which they last made their plunge, the better both for the King and for his people. Nothing good can come out of such a constitution.' Henry Reeve, a clerk at the Privy Council Office and journalist for the *Times* evaluated the situation similarly pessimistically. 'At Berlin I fear we shall now witness the meeting of another assembly not much wiser than the last,' he wrote in a letter to Prince Albert's secretary. 'The truth is that in most of the continental states they have adopted the representative system of government, with a complete absence of those innumerable checks and practical inconsistencies which alone render it possible and efficient in England.'[35]

The central theme in the British perception of the political situation in the German states between May 1848 and the beginning of 1849 was the fight against the threat which disorder and democracy posed to monarchical government. Against the background of the permanent danger emanating from the revolutionary 'party of movement', the

German governments were judged to be failing: they allowed a state of unrest to continue and permitted the passing of flawed electoral laws resulting in 'unmanageable' chambers full of radicals. Even the highly welcome reassertion of monarchical authority and good order brought about by the Prussian *coup d'état* was seen to have been compromised by a constitution embodying the 'extreme of democracy'. With British observers looking with sympathy and yet growing impatience at the attempts to contain republicanism and bring back order to the German states, the events of 1849 were to provide the German governments with a great, if hazardous, opportunity to prove their mettle.

'Utmost good sense': the German governments in 1849

On 23 February 1849 Lord Aberdeen wrote one of his many consoling letters to Metternich, whom the revolution of 1848 had driven into exile in England. Aberdeen conceded that 'the English press had materially contributed to promote the revolutionary movement which [. . .] afflicted Europe.' In the meantime, however, the press had improved and was now 'making full amends, at least the most respectable part of it. The articles in the "Chronicle" and "Times" both on Italian and German affairs are excellent, and well deserve your approbation.'[36] Aberdeen probably had a leading article in the *Times* in mind which had appeared some three weeks previously. While subjecting the Frankfurt National Assembly to harsh criticism, it praised the German governments for displaying 'the utmost good sense and tact whenever they ha[d] acted from their own convictions, and not under the direct or supposed pressure of popular agitation.'[37] This favourable evaluation of the German governments – endorsed by the conservative Aberdeen and, supposedly, the reactionary Metternich – was also shared more or less unanimously by Britain's diplomats in Germany and their Whig superiors, Palmerston and Lord John Russell. In 1849, in the course of their final, dramatic confrontation with the forces of revolution, the German governments in general and the Prussian government in particular won the respect of Britain's foreign political establishment.

Prussia's circular note to the German governments of 23 January 1849, in which the government in Berlin reclaimed the states' right to have their say in the deliberations on Germany's constitution, marked a turning point in the British perception of the conflict between the German governments and the revolutionaries. Cowley was impressed by this document. 'Your Lordship will, I think, consider this note one of the most important steps that has yet been taken in the affairs of Germany,' he wrote to Palmerston on 29 January 1849. From then onwards, British politicians and diplomats began to perceive a sense of direction and purpose in Prussia's policies. Although this never amounted to uncritical praise for her course, she emerged as the most agreeable party from the turmoil of 1848–9. In August 1849, after the victory of the reaction in Germany, Russell sent Palmerston some 'Notes on Foreign Affairs'. The aim of British foreign policy, the Prime Minister wrote, 'is the establishment of some solid basis for the future government of the states of Europe. This is not to be found in the riots, disorders and anarchy which have accompanied the attempts of the Red or Social Republicans in France, in Austria, in Prussia and in Italy.' For the provision of this 'solid basis' in Germany Russell looked to Prussia, where the King had meanwhile reduced the democratic component of the constitution through the imposition of the three-class franchise. 'In Prussia a representative government has been founded,' and this Russell considered 'still the best protection for all who wish to see Germany make a tranquil progress to free institutions.'[38]

Between the circular note of 23 January 1849 and Russell's confident memorandum of 16 August, however, the German governments were confronted with the most militant revolutionary challenge to date. During the spring and summer of 1849, Germany was swept by a second wave of insurrection. All over Germany, in Hanover, Württemberg, Saxony, Prussia, Bavaria and, above all, Baden, unrest and fighting broke out in an attempt to force the governments to adopt the German constitution passed by the Frankfurt National Assembly on 28 March 1849. This revolutionary *Reichsverfassungskampagne* ('Campaign for the Imperial Constitution') evoked memories of the March Revolution of the previous year, but differed in several respects. It was supported and organized by political associations like the people's and workers' associations while the *Zentralmärzverein* ('Central March Association') provided coordination on a national level. Whereas the movement of March 1848 had stopped short of the thrones, the *Reichsverfassungskampagne* was republican and forced a number of German sovereigns to flee their capitals. Unlike in 1848, the middle classes did not unequivocally support the revolutionary movement in 1849. These differences, together with the experiences of the past 14 months, led to a unanimous condemnation of the *Reichsverfassungskampagne* by British diplomats, politicians and journalists. There was no trace of the scant sympathy with which the revolutionaries of March 1848 had met in Britain. 'The real constitutional freedom in Germany must be established by supporting the governments,' the *Times* declared in May 1849, expressing the British consensus, and 'not by assailing them with all the weapons of anarchy.'[39]

From the beginning of 1849, Britain's diplomats had observed a worrying increase in the activity of the opposition in the German states. 'The Republican Party has by no means released in its activity in general, and has certainly gained considerable ground in some parts of Bavaria,' Milbanke wrote in January 1849. 'It is gradually and systematically organizing democratic clubs in which it has made astonishing progress during the last four months.' From the Hessian duchies Cowley reported a similar state of affairs: 'the republican feeling in this part of Germany runs very strong. The common feeling is "We want neither Austria nor Prussia but a united republic".' After Frederick William IV's rejection of the Imperial Crown offered to him by the National Assembly on 3 April 1849, the desire for national unity merged with republicanism, and the *Reichsverfassungskampagne* gained momentum. 'Certain is that renewed activity is observable among the leaders of the democratic or republican party who now range themselves unconditionally with the imperialists,' Milbanke reported from Munich. According to Malet the situation in Württemberg was equally ominous: 'popular meetings are being held in several places, all ostensibly with the same object, to further the adoption of the Frankfurt constitution.' He added that the constitution's 'democratic tendencies are sufficiently recognised by the men who direct the present agitation in this country.' In a letter to Cowley, the envoy to Württemberg was more open. 'One thing is very evident and cannot be questioned,' he wrote on 29 April, 'that the democratic principle is in the ascendant at Frankfurt and that there is imminent risk of the conflagration it seeks to light spreading in all directions.'[40]

Thus, when the German sovereigns at last took determined action against the unfolding revolution, they enjoyed the firm moral support of Britain's diplomats. On 27 April 1849, Frederick William dissolved the Prussian national assembly, which had declared the Frankfurt constitution valid. The Hanoverian chambers had already been dissolved on 25 April. 'A contest appears inevitable,' Cowley wrote from Frankfurt, 'but I firmly believe that that contest is preferable to an admission by the sovereigns of Germany of the unlimited sovereignty of the people.' The *Times* agreed, calling the struggle 'the last chance for the restoration of peace and order; if it fail, every throne and every government in Germany will be overturned, and the country consigned for a time to a boundless anarchy.' Milbanke also joined the chorus of well-wishers for Frederick William's counter-revolutionary course. 'Prussia will, I presume, make an effort to octroyer a new electoral law in a more conservative sense,' he wrote to Cowley, 'and if she can succeed she will do well.' Looking back on the 'Year of Reaction', the conservative historian Sir Archibald Alison came to a similarly positive evaluation of the Prussian course in 1849: 'anarchy has been extinguished in Prussia only to make room for the fair forms of order and liberty, which cannot exist but side by side; the revolutionists are overawed, but the lovers of real freedom are only the better confirmed in their hopes of the ultimate establishment of a constitutional monarchy.'[41]

British sympathy for the forces of order became even clearer once fighting had broken out. 'The situation in Leipzig has for the last three days been one of complete disorder,' Ward reported on 7 May, 'the mob moving about in masses calling for arms, and attacking several places where arms were thought of. Agitators were not wanting who excited the people to violence.' The atmosphere in Dresden was equally critical, but on 9 May Saxon and Prussian troops marched into the city and soon the capital was, as Forbes put it, 'in the peaceable possession of the military.' He remarked that 'the courage of the troops, and their behaviour throughout ha[d] been beyond all praise.' Extolling the newly-achieved public tranquillity and the mildness of martial law, Forbes found it 'impossible not to admire the government' for their courage and determination. All over Germany, order seemed threatened. 'The fermentation in the country is increasing daily,' Cowley reported on 8 May. 'The March Association (März-Verein) met here the day before yesterday, and has issued the most incendiary proclamation to the German people and the German army. In the neighbouring states, the people are arming, as they say, in defence of the constitution.'[42]

The hotbed of the *Reichsverfassungskampagne*, however, was the southwest of Germany. In Baden, Malet wrote on 15 May, one day after the Grand-Duke had fled to the fortress of Mainz, the government was now 'in the hands of a revolutionary party professing ultra republican opinions, and backed by the communist leaders of the former attempts at rebellion made last year.' According to Milbanke, 'all the reports from the Palatinate concur[red] in representing that province to be in a state of the most complete anarchy and confusion.' Meanwhile the insurrection in Baden was seen to grow even more threatening. It was, as Cowley wrote on 19 May, undoubtedly 'part of a widely organised plan emanating from Paris.' The next steps of the Badenese revolutionaries were believed to be 'to insurrectionize Württemberg and Darmstadt. If these two countries respond[ed] to the call made from Baden and the

Palatinate, an attempt [would] probably be made to declare a republic.' By appointing a 'dictatorial triumvirate', nominating a 'commissary with powers of nearly unlimited extent', declaring martial law and setting up military tribunals, the revolutionary government at Karlsruhe, Malet later explained, had used 'all the machinery of triumphant and tyrannous democracy.'[43]

There was no question in the minds of British observers that such revolutionary excesses had to be met by governmental force, and the very resolute intervention by Prussian troops to quell the insurrection in the south-western states of Germany provoked no British criticism. In May 1849, Bligh reckoned that it was owing to the 'salutary example of the defeat of the anarchists at Dresden' that public peace had not been disturbed in Hanover, and believed that the German governments were compelled to curtail 'the extravagant degree of liberty, which, in a moment of weakness, they allowed the people to extort from them.' The *Times* agreed. On 24 May, it rejected the notion that liberal government was a safeguard against revolution: 'the more resolute policy subsequently adopted by the Prussian army and Landwehr, now hold out better hopes for Germany.' Indeed, in Cowley's analysis, the Prussian military provided a solution even for Baden and the Palatinate. 'So long as Prussia can keep an imposing force on foot, tranquillity may be preserved,' he argued on 8 July 1849, 'but as soon as these countries are again abandoned to their own governments the same disorders are likely to recur, until a central authority is formed.' Thus, a connection was made between Prussia's defeating the *Reichsverfassungskampagne* and her ambitions to head a newly-formed federation of German states. The *Times* argued that 'the best claim which Prussia can prefer to the leading position she aspires to retain is that of having saved some of the minor states from the ruin and destruction which the democratic party had inflicted on the country.' Consequently, if the Prussian government planned, as Westmorland argued it did, to use the great extent of the power, recently gained 'by the successes of its arms against the anarchy with which Germany was threatened,'[44] to secure a commanding influence, it could expect a fair amount of British goodwill.

The way in which British diplomats, politicians and journalists commented on the struggle which took place between established order and revolutionary challenge in the German states in 1848–9 was in many respects a continuation of a pattern which can be observed from 1830. The challenge to the political and social status quo posed by the forces of revolution was seen in a critical or even condemnatory light. Gorged with dangerous ultra-liberal, democratic and republican doctrines, the radicals, insurrectionists and communists who were seen to make up the 'party of movement' constituted a lethal threat to peace and good order and therefore had to be contained. Only for a brief moment in the early phase of the revolution were they accorded a constructive role, when British observers considered their moderate demands instrumental in stimulating measured governmental reforms.

There was also continuity in the perception of the German governments. Even in a year of revolution and large-scale popular unrest it was they who dominated British analyses. Their task was considered to be twofold. In order to forestall further revolutionary unrest they should both implement measured reforms of the political system and resolutely impose public order and authority. Indirectly and directly both these tasks served the same end: containment of the opposition and consolidation of the established political system. The German governments' standing was a direct function of their success at fulfilling these twin tasks. They were hailed for the measured concessions granted in March and April 1848, but were bitterly criticized for their failure to stop the subsequent process of radicalization. The Prussian King was praised for his *coup* in November 1848, but the liberal constitution he decreed in December provoked censure. Through their determined reactionary policy in 1849, Prussia and the other German governments redeemed themselves and provided a basis for cautious British optimism. 'The only safety for Germany is making the best conditions the sovereigns can with Prussia and uniting to form a Central Power of which she should be the chief,'[45] Cowley wrote to Malet in June 1849. By then, Prussia was aiming at just that.

Revolution, constitution and nationalism in the Frankfurt centre

Because of the federalism of the Germanic Confederation, 'Pre-March' Germany had no real political centre. Decisions affecting the whole of Germany were made at the seat of the German Diet in Frankfurt, but also in Vienna, Karlsbad and Berlin. The revolution of 1848, however, with its demands for a reformed Diet, a German Parliament and a united constitutional Germany created a political focus for the entire country. As seat of the National Assembly, its preparatory bodies, the 'Imperial Vicar' (*Reichsverweser*) and the provisional central executive, Frankfurt became a political nerve-centre for the whole nation. Between May 1848 and the summer of 1849, these newly-established institutions provided the platform for national German politics of an unprecedented intensity. It was here that the tasks of giving Germany a constitution and a national government were addressed. It was here that German unity was to be forged. British perceptions of these issues will be analysed in three steps. First, there will be a discussion of Britain's reactions to the new political bodies and their aims until September 1848, when a marked shift of opinion took place. A second section will take the study of British attitudes towards the National Assembly to its dissolution in June 1849. Finally, there will be a discussion of British views on the connection between the nature of German unity and Germany's role in Europe.

'Alternately the cause of hope and apprehension': the political bodies at Frankfurt, March–September 1848

Among the different 'March Demands' with which the German governments found themselves confronted in the spring of 1848, one stood out in the eyes of British diplomats. 'All the other concessions,' Malet wrote to Palmerston on 16 March, 'are evidently secondary to this scheme, the consequences of which, if carried into effect, appear pregnant with change.' What the envoy referred to was the project of establishing a political representation of the German people to replace the Diet of the Germanic Confederation. From the very beginning of the revolutionary insurrection in Germany, British diplomats testified to the strength of this demand. Early in March, John Ward observed that in Saxony the forces of change strongly desired a reform of the Germanic Diet: 'they say that it has never had public confidence, and must be reconstituted, and composed of the representatives of the people, as well as of the deputies of the sovereigns. This is a point on which grave, moderate men agree with the radical mob. They want, in short, a kind of German parliament.' Ward's view of a broad consensus in favour of a national assembly was endorsed by the *Times*. 'What the people – meaning by that word all classes, high as well as low – wish to have,' one of the first articles on the German revolution argued, is 'a real united representation of the whole German race.'[46] Throughout March, the Foreign Office received despatches from Britain's diplomats in Germany indicating, as Frederick Orme, chargé d'affaires in Frankfurt, put it, 'that nothing short of a National Parliament on a very liberal scale [would] satisfy the popular cry, and [that] any opposition on the part of Austria and Prussia [would] either lead to civil war or a dissolution of the Confederation.'[47]

Prior to the opening of the Frankfurt National Assembly on 18 May 1848, British diplomats concentrated on two aspects in their discussion of the demands for a German parliament: the inadequacy of the existing German Diet, which triggered these demands, and the extremism of the plans for a national representation. Acknowledging the justification of the former point and regretting the dangers inherent in the latter, British observers of Germany addressed the question of how the revolutionary momentum could be restrained so as to produce a reformed, but not a revolutionized, state of affairs. They were particularly concerned with maintaining governmental control and with preventing an appropriation of the proposed national parliament by ultra-liberal or democratic forces.

As has been shown above, British criticisms of the Diet of the Germanic Confederation had been voiced throughout the *Vormärz* period. Calls for its reform in the spring of 1848 were therefore favourably received. 'One point appears to be generally felt,' Malet reported from Stuttgart, 'that the Diet as now constituted has forfeited general confidence and that it must be replaced by some analogous institution which instead of being obstructive of all progress, will at any rate have weight enough to sanction if not direct and guide the progressive political advance of the German people.' The inefficiency of the Diet 'in fulfilling the purposes for which it was created,' Malet declared four days later, 'has given sufficient ground for the desire of change.' Milbanke's discussion of the Diet came to similar conclusions. 'It would be needless for me to recall to notice,' he wrote to Palmerston, 'the reproaches which it has incurred for years past of apathy in all that might be conducive to the material interests of Germany in commercial matters, or the animadversions to which it has been exposed from the obstacles which it has invariably thrown in the way of all useful reforms and the attainment of more liberal institutions.' Even in March 1848, in the face of the revolutionary challenge, when most German princes were seen to be acquitting themselves with so much good sense, the Diet was found wanting. On 3 March, Orme criticized the feet-dragging which was going on with respect to the widely-demanded abolition of censorship and emphasized the 'dissatisfaction which [was] felt by almost all parties at the delay which ha[d] occurred in the Diet in its decision on the important question of the press.'[48]

Reform of the Diet was not only accepted as necessary but even appeared to offer a real opportunity for salutary change. In spite of their initial mystification at the myriad of new ideas, a number of British diplomats were rather optimistic as to what might be achieved. 'If then the German parliament is constituted in conformity with general expectation, of two chambers, the upper one composed of mediatised nobles, and a proportion of the members of the existing upper chambers in the various states, and of a second chamber of delegates from the respective second chambers,' Malet wrote to Palmerston on 22 March, 'there can be no doubt that assemblies so composed would offer guarantees for order, union and strength such as the most sanguine friends of these principles can desire.' In a despatch written one day later, Orme related some promising news about the liberal party in Germany which aimed 'to keep in view as much as possible the conformation of the English parliament, taking as a pattern for the second chamber, (or people's representation) the English House of Commons, with a form of election somewhat similar, though more liberal.'[49]

The last two words of Orme's despatch already indicate how the course of the German revolution was to put a damper on British optimism about the proposed German parliament. While hoping that this was the moment when Germany could at last become more like Britain, British observers were worried that the control over the reform process might slip from the hands of the governments into those of the democratic party. They were clearly aware of the potential consequences of the introduction of popular representation into the German Diet. 'The sovereign power would be ultimately transferred to the representatives of the people,' John Ward predicted on 15 March 1848.[50] Desirous to see the German governments remain in charge, British diplomats and politicians looked with distrust at the unofficial conventions and committees of liberal and radical politicians which met at Heidelberg and Frankfurt in March and April to prepare the meeting of the National Assembly.

Given that these self-elected bodies favoured universal suffrage and seemed to be threatening the independence of the individual states, Bligh in Hanover was astonished that the governments were not straining 'every nerve to stop them'. He later informed Palmerston that he had often urged 'something of this sort' which he believed the governments would have been perfectly justified in doing 'as they would have had to deal with a self-constituted and illegal body.'[51] On 11 March, Orme announced the proposed meeting at Frankfurt of the *Vorparlament* ('Pre-Parliament') and immediately suggested scuppering it. 'It is clear therefore that if any counter-proposition is intended by the Diet, to check this movement, no time is to be lost,' he wrote to Palmerston, 'for otherwise the important moment will have gone by, and the agitation have reached such a pitch, that any future measures of the Diet will be disregarded or violently opposed.' Orme's opposition to the 'Pre-Parliament', which had been convened by a meeting of 51 liberals at

Heidelberg to prepare the meeting of the National Assembly, was further fuelled by their ideas for a German parliament. On 18 March he informed the Foreign Office that the scheme was believed to be 'of a very liberal, not to say democratic character.' Milbanke came to similar conclusions. 'The proceedings of the recent meeting of deputies at Heidelberg may be looked upon as the commencement of an active system of agitation to carry out this project,' he observed. 'The clamour which has been raised on this subject throughout Germany has compelled the governments and the Diet to take the initiative in the hopes, I presume, of restraining the movement within reasonable bounds.'[52]

Having been briefed in this manner by Bligh, Orme and Milbanke, Palmerston proved alive to the idea of undermining the unofficial bodies in order to strengthen governmental initiatives. On 23 March, in two private letters to Malet and Westmorland, the Foreign Secretary suggested a way to weaken the 'Committee of Seven', which the Heidelberg group had set up to prepare the session of the *Vorparlament*. 'This self-constituted assembly at Heidelberg may give trouble,' Palmerston wrote to Westmorland. 'Would it not be possible for the German governments to appoint some of the leading men among them to be members of the subsidiary body which is to be added to the Diet at Frankfort? Such an arrangement would break up the Heidelberg assembly, and give additional influences to the Frankfort authority.'[53]

Palmerston's advice unheeded, the *Vorparlament* met at the end of March, and although the sovereigns had, in Orme's opinion, given 'ample proof of their good intentions,' the British diplomat had to report on 28 March that the popular movement had 'made such rapid strides and assumed that shape, that the initiative [could] no longer be said to remain in the hands of the Diet.' This eclipse of the legitimate governments as represented in the Diet was rendered even more regrettable by the aims expressed by the *Vorparlament* and its 'Committee of Fifty', which remained in Frankfurt until the opening of the National Assembly. 'Your Lordship will observe that the formation of the second chamber in the proposed parliament is on a republican scale as to qualification of voters,' Orme wrote to Palmerston, 'and it is not likely that any modification of this plan will be acceded to by the liberals, on the contrary, it will be a matter of congratulation, if [. . .] the project as it now exists is definitively adopted, for it is much feared that the ultra and republican Party who will be here in great force on the 30th will by agitation and outrage, endeavour to force into existence a parliament still more democratic.' John Ward also reported that 'a strong republican spirit ha[d] shown itself among the members' of the *Vorparlament*.[54]

All this meant that by early April, Strangways found the political scene at Frankfurt dramatically changed. 'The Diet, weak before the late events, is now absolutely powerless,' he reported on 8 April. It was ruled entirely by the 17 'Men of Public Confidence' who were in turn dominated by the 'Committee of Fifty' 'By the side of these anomalous and dangerous, though not ill-intentioned bodies,' Strangways explained, 'is another, small in number but desperate in character, and unscrupulous in its views, headed by the notorious demagogue Struve, who daily holds forth to the rabble that follow him, the most violent and revolutionary doctrines.' Bligh equally deplored the 'complete success of the self-constituted parliament at Frankfurt.' The governments, he claimed, could 'do no more than lament that fifty men, who have no possible right to call themselves the representatives of Germany, issue their decrees and dictate their will to almost as many millions of their countrymen. [. . .] Indeed all those who ought to govern Germany seem to be paralyzed and full sway is given to the people.' The attacks on the bodies at Frankfurt in the official accounts were echoed both by the press and the conservative opposition. On 18 April, the *Times* dismissed the *Vorparlament* as a 'self-elected club' and called Frankfurt 'a scene of permanent political excitement' where no parliament could meet 'in independence and security.' In the Commons the next day, Disraeli sarcastically referred to 'a curious body, a body itself in a state of reconstruction and revolution, calling itself the Germanic Diet, and assembling at Frankfort.' In his private correspondence, the Tory politician was more damning, arguing quite inaccurately that those 'fifty mad professors at Frankfort, calling themselves a Diet, self appointed, [would] not conclude their labours till they ha[d] established a federal republic like the U.S.' and labelling them 'the Jacobin Diet of Frankfort.'[55]

In spite of these inauspicious circumstances, the elections to the National Assembly held in April and May produced results which – on the whole – pleasantly surprised British diplomats. 'All those who have been elected are of decided monarchical principles,' Bligh reported from Hanover on 5 May. 'They are almost without exception lawyers and professors.' News from Bavaria was also reassuring. On 8 May, Milbanke informed Palmerston that the members chosen were 'remarkable for the moderation of their opinions.' In Württemberg, the elections had, according to Malet, 'fallen on individuals quite new to public life; the men of moderate opinion and monarchical principles form[ed] a majority.' Baden proved a more ambiguous case: 'out of twenty elections there are said to be ten conservative,' Malet wrote, 'but the tendency of public feeling is unequivocally shown by the return of Monsieur Itzstein, the friend and confederate of the declared republican Hecker for eight electoral districts.' In addition to its agreeably moderate political complexion, the Frankfurt National Assembly also enjoyed a legal status which set it apart from its unloved preparatory bodies. 'The National Assembly,' Bligh explained, 'was elected, and sits by the authority of the sovereigns.'[56]

The relatively positive first impression thus produced by the National Assembly was confirmed by the elections in May and June of Heinrich von Gagern as its speaker and Archduke Johann of Austria to the office of *Reichsverweser* ('Imperial Vicar'). However, throughout the summer of 1848 a process took place in which this impression was steadily eroded by doubts, disappointment and growing disregard, resulting in an extended period of ambivalence and prevarication. For Milbanke, the proceedings at Frankfurt were 'alternately the cause of hope and apprehension.'[57] British perceptions and opinions, especially those of Lord Cowley, who was soon to occupy a central position,[58] oscillated between the wish that the National Assembly would make a beneficial – though never clearly specified – contribution to the process of reforming Germany on the one hand and growing disenchantment with this body on the other. By September 1848, this ambivalence was resolved in favour of the legitimate governments and above all that of Prussia.

The National Assembly, which convened in May 1848, came to be known by the name of the building in which it met, Frankfurt's *Paulskirche* (St Paul's Church). To begin with, British reactions to this assembly were broadly favourable. Sir Alexander Downie, the physician to the British mission at Frankfurt, commented on the election of Gagern, formerly head of the Grand Ducal government of Hesse, as speaker. It was regarded 'by the friends of order and constitutional government as a happy omen, foreshadowing [. . .] the tone likely to be observed in the future deliberations of the assembly.' The *Times* was also impressed by the early steps of the *Paulskirche* assembly. On 30 May, a correspondent praised the talent and devotion of the deputies. 'Nothing,' he continued, 'will be required for a good settlement upon the great questions of constitution but time.' A month later, the *Spectator* expressed similar optimism about the German Parliament. 'It includes among its members many experienced officials, and some of the most tried and practical statesmen of Germany. The sagacity and moderation which has hitherto characterized its deliberations are also of favourable augury.'[59]

By the time the latter article appeared, the *Paulskirche* had taken a further step which was received with approbation in Britain. On 29 June, the National Assembly voted for the Austrian Archduke Johann to head its recently created executive. Britain's political leadership was pleased with this election. 'I am very glad to find that Archduke John has been chosen by the Frankfort Diet,' Palmerston wrote to Ponsonby on 3 July. A week later, in a letter to Lord John Russell, the Foreign Secretary called Johann's appointment 'a good and important thing.' The Prime Minister expressed similar satisfaction. 'I think it would be a good thing that Lord Beauvale should go specially to Frankfort to visit and congratulate the Archduke,' he suggested to Palmerston. 'The Archduke is a very worthy liberal man, and would be very sensible to such a compliment.'[60] The politicians' warmth was shared by the *Times*, which called Johann the 'best possible choice' and praised Gagern for his great services to the cause of monarchy and order.[61]

During the early weeks of its existence, British politicians and diplomats as well as journalists viewed the *Paulskirche* with a fair portion of goodwill and optimism. This still shone through the instructions which Palmerston issued to Cowley on 29 July 1848. 'You will express the deep interest which the British government takes in the welfare of Germany, and the sincere and earnest wish which the British government forms that the deliberations in which the representatives of Germany at Frankfort are now engaged, may lead to results conducive to the prosperity, the happiness, the strength, and independence of the German nation.'[62] In retrospect, the Foreign Secretary's 'sincere and earnest wish' for Germany's future appears almost as the swansong of British confidence in the Frankfurt National Assembly. As time went on, concerns and disagreements, which had existed from the beginning, became increasingly prominent and led British observers of Germany to conclude that the *Paulskirche*'s deliberations were unlikely to give Germany prosperity, happiness, strength or independence. The growing British disaffection with the Frankfurt National Assembly sprang mainly from three sources: the German politicians appeared to lack ability and practical sense; there were also apprehensions about the *Paulskirche*'s protectionism; most importantly, it was the parliament's stand on the Schleswig-Holstein issue which caused Britain's foreign political opinion to turn sharply against it.

A permanent source of irritation for British observers of the *Paulskirche* was the allegedly foolish way in which the affairs of the National Assembly and the Central Power were conducted. The problem was perceived to be one both of organization and of personalities. 'The proceedings of that assembly,' Malet complained on 18 June, are 'so dilatory and so evidently impeded by counteracting influences, that it is much to be apprehended no genuine accord will be arrived at.' A fortnight later, Milbanke predicted that 'in so numerous an assembly containing so many discordant elements, the confusion and diversity of views and interests would oppose an insurmountable barrier' to proper decision-making. Moreover, as Cowley informed Palmerston on 20 August, 'the National Assembly, in the transaction of business, ha[d] taken that of France as its model, and the members ha[d] adopted the French expressions of centre, right and left centre et cetera to express the different grades of opinion in which the assembly [was] divided.' Coming from the pen of a British diplomat in 1848, this was hardly meant as a compliment. The account of the state of affairs which Cowley gave in a letter to Ponsonby on 14 August, was accordingly laced with condescension. 'We are here in a sad condition,' he complained. 'A chamber which chooses to be constitutive and executive at the same time – a government with nothing to govern. A Vice-Emperor without an Empire. What children's play! But how often does children's play end in tears?' In the above-mentioned despatch of 20 August, Cowley completed his analysis of the woeful state of the political institutions at Frankfurt. 'If we descend to particulars,' he wrote to Palmerston, 'we find a Minister for Foreign Affairs without agents to correspond with, a Minister of the Interior, who has not even power in Frankfort, a Minister of Finance with no treasury to superintend, a Minister of Justice with no laws to guide him. [. . .] Such is the state of the Frankfort government. Add to it that neither the Archduke nor any of its members receive any stipend from the state, and the picture is complete.'[63]

The situation was seen as being exacerbated by the personalities of the Frankfurt politicians. Within a week of his arrival Cowley had formed a clear opinion, which he shared with his colleague in Berlin: 'I never met with such a set of impracticable men as there are here,' he informed Westmorland. 'They will listen to nothing but their own theories.' The new German Foreign Minister, Johann Heckscher, Cowley wrote to Palmerston on 21 August, was 'so obstinate and at the same time so hot-headed, that he [was] a dangerous man for a post that require[d] coolness and moderation.' Cowley found it 'a great trial of patience to converse with him. The other ministers [were] quite as incapable.' He traced the inadequacies of the Frankfurt politicians back to their professional origins. 'Men that would be possible as ministers under the present system are confined chiefly to such classes as advocates, professors and men of letters and science,' he explained to the Foreign Secretary on 20 August, 'but such persons are necessarily mere theorists – the practical working of a constitution, the machinery of state government they are entirely unacquainted with.' Concluding his analysis of the political institutions created at the Frankfurt centre, Britain's leading diplomat in revolutionary Germany arrived at a bleak outlook. 'If, my Lord, I saw among the patriots assembled at Frankfort, men of tact, moderation and firmness, into whose hands the government was likely to fall, I should have better hopes for the future. Far be it from me to say that they do not exist, but it is certain that they have not appeared in the political arena as yet.' Cowley's apprehensions did not end there. 'While these conflicting interests, these hopes and fears are in array against each other,' he warned Palmerston, 'the fire of democracy is smouldering beneath them. Let princes and senators look to it, as it may yet destroy them all.'[64]

The process of Britain's growing disenchantment was not only fuelled by the manner in which the Frankfurt politicians went about their business, but also by some of their policies. Britain had a lively interest in Germany's future tariffs. Even before the *Paulskirche* turned to this question and appointed a 'Committee for the National Economy' in July 1848, British diplomats had drawn attention to the potential connection between the National Assembly and protectionism. On 18 June, Malet reminded Palmerston of the 'doctrines professed in this portion of southern Germany on the subject of protecting domestic manufactures' and predicted that with the 'prospect now held out of approaching extensive changes in the fiscal administration of Germany, the greatest efforts [would] be made to justify the enforcement of protective principles.' Ten days later, Strangways proved Malet's prognosis right by reporting that a number of manufacturing towns had petitioned the assembly in favour of navigation laws and differential duties. Once the 'Committee for the National Economy' was established, its political complexion appeared to vindicate British apprehensions. 'There are many advocates for high protective duties both in the Assembly and in the Committee,' Ward informed Palmerston on 3 July, 'and the fact of the Committee having chosen two known protectionists [. . .] as their President and Secretary indicates a strong leaning.' By 20 July, the *Times* also raised the alarm. 'Under the disguise of a liberal policy and a popular revolution,' a leading article warned, the *Paulskirche* threatened to achieve what had eluded the *Zollverein*: the imposition of protectionist tariffs on the free-trading states of north Germany.[65]

These concerns about policies detrimental to Britain's commerce sufficiently impressed the Foreign Secretary to include a relevant passage in Cowley's instructions. 'When the time shall arrive for discussing the commercial arrangements which may be proposed for Germany,' Cowley should recommend a 'liberal and enlightened system of commercial policy.' The politicians at Frankfurt were unimpressed by Palmerston's lecture. On 5 August, Ward reported that a motion had been introduced to increase tariffs on imported manufactures and commented on the strength of the protectionists both in the Assembly and in the Committee. Lobbied by the Bradford Chamber of Commerce, Palmerston instructed Cowley to step up his opposition to the *Paulskirche*'s commercial plans: 'you will avail yourself of all fitting opportunities to recommend to the Central Power at Frankfort not to adopt measures calculated to be injurious to trade generally.' British irritation about the trade policies pursued at Frankfurt heightened when the new German Minister for Trade unveiled a plan for a 'German Commercial System'. On 26 October, the Board of Trade rejected the proposal as 'wholly at variance with the declared principle of this country upon this branch of national policy.' In an increasingly hostile climate of opinion, there were even suggestions of retaliatory tariffs and punitive charges. It is fair to argue that the *Paulskirche*'s commercial policies, which compared unfavourably with Prussia's assurance not to raise duties, contributed substantially to the erosion of British sympathy for the German parliament.[66]

Above anything else, it was the stand the Frankfurt bodies took on the war in Schleswig-Holstein, which frustrated and infuriated British politicians, diplomats and journalists.[67] For several reasons, mainly to do with maintaining the equilibrium established in 1815, honouring treaty obligations, keeping strategic key points out of the hands of great powers, preventing the emergence of maritime rivals and sympathy for the underdog, Britain's government and public opinion – though not the Germanophile Court – opposed the German side in the Dano-German conflict. While generally backing Denmark, Palmerston did his utmost to prevent the outbreak of a European war over the Schleswig-Holstein issue and fulfilled the unenviable task of mediator with near-inexhaustible patience. From April 1848 he doggedly negotiated with both Denmark and Prussia, whose troops bore the brunt of the fighting on the German side, to draw up armistice conditions acceptable to both parties. He therefore reacted angrily when it was suggested that the *Paulskirche* would not ratify the planned armistice. 'I have to instruct you plainly,' Palmerston wrote to Cowley on 8 August with undisguised sarcasm, 'to represent to that government and to individual members of the assembly, that if a general war in Europe is their object, they are setting to work the right way to achieve it.' Cowley's reply was anything but encouraging. 'They all know that they are in the wrong, 'he wrote on 21 August, 'but there are not above half a dozen men in Frankfort, who have the courage to *avow* it. The rest rave about German honour, German independence and German determination to a degree, that would be amusing, were it not dangerous. [. . .] In short they are a parcel of children who want whipping and caressing alternately.'[68]

Affairs came to a head in September. On 26 August, the Prussian government, after months of negotiations, signed an armistice without consulting Frankfurt. On 4 September the *Paulskirche* voted to cancel this agreement by a majority of 238 to 221. The British reaction was unanimous. This 'unfortunate decision of the National Assembly,' Bligh predicted, 'will hasten a crisis of which the catastrophe will either be the entire breakdown of the ill-founded fabric of German unity, or complications leading almost inevitably to a general war.' Mellish found it 'really too abominable that a set of harebrained students should thus thrust all Europe into a war.' Palmerston was equally outraged. 'I cannot allow a day to pass,' he wrote to Cowley, 'without requesting you to ask the members of the Frankfort assembly with whom you may be acquainted, to ask them, I say, in civil terms whether they are mad and really intend to disavow the Slesvig Holstein armistice. If they are deliberately determined to rush into conflict with all Europe, including, as it seems, Prussia, well and good, let them take the consequences.' For the *Times*, the decision of 4 September settled the question of how to view the *Paulskirche*. 'The conduct of the assembly on the first important practical question of European policy in which it has been called upon to act,' the paper wrote on 13 September, 'has demonstrated its unfitness for the task it had assumed.'[69]

On 16 September, after almost a fortnight of hectic negotiations, the Frankfurt parliament yielded and accepted the armistice by a majority of 21 votes, overturning its earlier decision. When this triggered an outbreak of revolutionary violence in the city, necessitating troop deployment and leaving more than 200 dead and wounded, the Frankfurt institutions finally lost the little credit which they still might have enjoyed in the minds of British diplomats, politicians and journalists. 'The demoralisation of the German character seems to be complete. The worst pages of history do not contain a more horrible plot, than that which providentially failed last week in this town,' Cowley concluded on 25 September. 'Why, my Lord, do I refer to these painful facts, but that Your Lordship may see the dangers that menace this country, so long famed for its love of order, its sobriety, its temperance. It is now

ruined to its foundations. [. . .] Where are we to look for eventual reme-
dies to such great evil? Surely not in the decrees of national assemblies
elected by universal suffrage.'[70]

Between March and September 1848, British perceptions of and judge-
ments on the bodies which concerned themselves with reforming or
even revolutionizing Germany's political organization went full circle.
Initially, the widespread calls for a reform of the Diet were approved as
triggering salutary governmental reform measures. When unofficial,
self-elected political committees, products of the revolution and apparently tinged with democracy, threatened to hijack the reform process,
they met with fierce British criticism. In contrast to these preparatory
bodies, the National Assembly with its initial promise of moderation,
its governmental sanction, and Gagern and Archduke Johann as its
respectable heads appeared to offer a second, if less reliable, chance for
moderate reform. However, through its inadequate organization and
personnel, its commercial policies and – most of all – its stand on the
Schleswig-Holstein issue, the National Assembly lost its initial British
goodwill. By the end of September, British observers found themselves
again where they had started: looking to the legitimate governments
for a reform of Germany's central political institutions while worrying
about the dangers of democracy.

'Weak to do good, it is powerful to do harm': the *Paulskirche* until June 1849

There are few more damning, more condescending and more vitriolic
testimonies to the depths to which the *Paulskirche* had plunged in the
estimation of some British observers by the autumn of 1848 than the
article which Professor William Aytoun published in the conservative
Blackwood's Edinburgh Magazine in November 1848. Having witnessed
the street-fighting in Frankfurt, Aytoun declared 'that the supreme
authority had fallen into the hands of men utterly incapable of dis-
charging the duty of legislators.' He pitied Germany for what had
befallen her. 'Here is a nation [. . .] about to be plunged into irretriev-
able misery and ruin, by a set of selfish hounds who look to nothing
beyond their stipend of five florins a day! Heaven help the idiots!'[71]

Similar feelings were shared by many British diplomats. 'I am unable
to expect the least good to arise from your Diet,' Ponsonby wrote to
Cowley on 30 September. 'I have seen so much folly in its conduct and
read so much nonsense in the reported speeches of its members, as to
make me think that the most illiterate men [. . .] would be vastly better
fitted to direct affairs of state than your congregated philosophers, pro-

fessors and pedants.' Early in November, Cowley informed Palmerston that the National Assembly indulged in 'differences of opinions and principles, which degenerate into the most disgraceful squabbles and have led to riot and murder,' while the Central Power was bent on 'keeping the administration in the hands of a certain set, who promulgate ordinances and issue commissions which receive but uncertain execution or unwilling reverence.' By mid-November, Mellish had already given up on the *Paulskirche*. 'Your accounts of the Central Power convince me more than ever that its days are numbered,' he wrote to Cowley. 'It is my conviction that the central authority as now constituted and imagined, will disappear. [. . .] I look to great struggles and uproar.'[72]

The disgrace of the National Assembly led British observers of German politics to resolve a question which they had hitherto treated with ambivalence. They had quickly realized that the central institutions at Frankfurt and the German governments would clash over who was to lead the reorganization of Germany. Throughout the summer, with the *Paulskirche* still retaining some of its initial prestige and the governments disorganized and weak, British diplomats had noted this conflict but expressed no unanimous preference. The more conservative Bligh and Westmorland sided with the Hanoverian and Prussian governments. The German princes, Bligh reported in July, 'are beginning to feel what bad taskmasters they have imposed upon themselves by having allowed [. . .] the election, by universal suffrage, of a constituent assembly whose tendencies must naturally be republican.' From Berlin, Westmorland testified to 'a very strong feeling in favour of the maintenance of the individuality and independence of Prussia and in opposition to the tendency of the German parliament at Frankfort' which had the 'effect of essentially strengthening the hands of the government and producing a reaction against the agitation of the Ultra Democratic Party.' John Ward disagreed. 'The leading object of the reformers [!] has all along been to establish an effective central government in Germany,' he wrote to Palmerston on 11 August, 'but in Prussia as well as in Hanover, some difficulties have unfortunately arisen which have not yet been overcome.' Ward was not too concerned about this opposition: 'it is a reactionary spirit which will ultimately be put down by the national voice of Germany.' Cowley, who knew the weaknesses of the *Paulskirche* better than anyone else but nevertheless retained some sympathy for it, especially for Gagern, sat on the fence. 'The Central Power and Prussia are watching each other like two tigers, each hoping the other will make a false move,' he wrote to Ponsonby on 22 August.

'The King of Prussia must take care. He has helped to raise the storm, and because he cannot govern it, he wants to upset those who attempt it.' Three weeks later, in a letter to Britain's ambassador in Paris, Cowley was still rather cautious. 'The great internal question of the day is, who is to be the leading power in Germany,' he informed to Normanby. 'Prussia has the best chances but she will not succeed, *I think*, without a severe struggle.'[73]

By the end of September 1848, this period of indecision was coming to an end. Even before the much-applauded *coup d'état* profoundly changed the political scene in Prussia, British observers went over to the Prussian camp and looked to Berlin for political leadership for Germany. Cowley informed Palmerston on 25 September that he had always believed 'that if Prussia was desirous of seeing herself at the head of the present movement in Germany, she must do nothing to force public opinion but must wait to see what time and events would do for her. I little thought however that a few weeks could work such a change in her favour. [. . .] The explanation of this change is to be found in the fact that men of sense are [. . .] beginning to find out that a central government without power to govern, is a delusion, and that that power can only be derived from the larger states of Germany.' Five days later, the envoy was even more openly pro-Prussian. 'The reaction in favour of Prussia is progressing daily,' he observed. 'The necessity of Prussia's taking the lead and putting herself at the head of Germany is in everyone's mouth. [. . .] I believe that sensible men feel that their choice is between Prussia and anarchy, and they are willing to accept the one in order to save themselves from the other.'[74]

For all this disregard for the Frankfurt institutions, Cowley's analysis of the political situation in Germany initially led him to advocate cooperation between Prussia and the National Assembly. It is important to realize, though, that Cowley did so for preventative reasons and not because he expected the *Paulskirche* to make a positive contribution to the political process. 'The Central Power, supported by Prussia, may do much good during the present crisis in Germany,' he wrote to Westmorland on 29 September. 'Alone, it can do nothing but harm, for it has neither power nor prestige within itself, and must fall back on the democrats for assistance.' By supporting a Prusso-Frankfurt partnership, Cowley was aiming to prevent a renewed outbreak of revolution. The cooperation between the *Paulskirche* and the Prussian government was designed both to discipline the National Assembly itself and to placate and pacify the radical forces outside it. In suggesting this argument, Cowley agreed with the Saxon head of government, von der Pfordten, who, according to Forbes, believed that 'if the Central Power were not there, a republic would be proclaimed throughout Germany.' In a despatch to the Foreign Secretary of 23 November, Cowley clarified his argument. 'I would not, however, that your Lordship should think, that in urging so constantly as I have done the necessity of an understanding between Berlin and Frankfort, I have been advocating the cause of the Central Power against Prussia,' he wrote to Palmerston. 'Nobody can be more alive to the faults and follies of that so-called power, nobody can blame its arrogance or pity more than myself, but I cannot shut my eyes to the fact that if weak to do good, it is powerful to do harm, and that the best chance of making it strong for good and weak for harm is to guide and not to oppose it, and that Prussia is [. . .] the only power capable of so guiding it.'[75]

Cowley's argument that the *Paulskirche* should continue to play a role in German politics, albeit a much-reduced and essentially conservative one, depended on three conditions. First, it was crucial that the *Paulskirche* served to prevent democratic radicalization. This involved the difficult task of avoiding both its own drift to the left, and the appearance of being a reactionary force which might trigger risings against it such as the one of September 1848. Secondly, Prussia had to continue in a state of relative political weakness. As soon as the Prussian government was strong enough to defeat the forces of revolution unaided, the *Paulskirche* would be redundant. Finally, Prussia had to agree to cooperate with the National Assembly, because 'unguided' the National Assembly was only 'powerful to do harm.' The history of British perceptions of the National Assembly and the Central Power between November 1848 and the Assembly's dissolution in June 1849 is principally the history of the non-fulfilment of these conditions. With Prussia reasserting herself and rejecting the advances from Frankfurt and with the National Assembly going down a spiral of left-wing radicalization, British diplomats and politicians joined ranks with the forces of reaction. Eventually, a British diplomat, with the approval of his Whig Foreign Secretary, called upon a German government to put an end to the German parliament.

The bitter wording which Cowley chose for his despatch of 19 November indicates that the *Paulskirche* had defaulted on the first condition of abstaining from radicalism even sooner than he had anticipated. 'To denounce what I conceive to be a dishonour and a crime in a government and in a parliament,' he admitted to Palmerston, 'is a task from which I should shrink did not my duty impose it on me.' Cowley's anger was caused by the National Assembly's unanimous acceptance of a motion decreeing the punishment of all persons involved in the execution of Robert Blum.[76] 'A resolution has been passed,' the envoy fumed, 'that has rendered the assembly which was to purify and regenerate Germany, a fraterniser with the aula of Vienna, a vindicator of barricades, and an assertor of the rights of its members to combat with impunity wherever the red flag of the republic is raised against the sovereigns of Germany. [. . .] The course now adopted can have no other result than that of irritating the Austrian government while it excites the bad passions of Germany, and places the Central Government in a most humiliating position.'[77]

At the same time, after its successful *coup d'état*, the Prussian government was growing in strength, thus undermining the second precondition for the National Assembly's continued role. Cowley, who welcomed the steps taken by Prussia, was worried that the *Paulskirche* might side with the prorogued Prussian National Assembly to oppose the King, and tried hard to win over influential members of the Central Power to the cause of order. 'I said that if Germany was not to be given over to anarchy,' he informed Palmerston on 20 November, 'they must in some way or other support the King of Prussia, that it was not a question of Prussia alone but of all Germany for whatever happened in Prussia would find its re-echo throughout the land: in short, My Lord, I made use of every argument I could think of.' A fortnight later and having received 'a far more favourable account of affairs' from Prussia, Mellish, who had been sceptical about the notion of a Prusso-Frankfurt cooperation all along, flatly contradicted Cowley's argument: 'the only hope of quiet and order for Germany is to be found in the consolidation of Prussian power *independent* of the Central Power.'[78]

Another nail in the *Paulskirche*'s coffin was its plan for a German constitution. Given that it was the central task of the National Assembly to draw up an all-German constitution, British diplomats had surprisingly little to say about it. In August 1848 Ward had predicted that 'the new German constitution [would] be much more democratic than the fundamental laws of England'; but apart from some general comments about the deputies' penchant for theorizing, the lengthy debates on fundamental rights, which occupied the National Assembly until 20 December 1848, provoked little response. By the time the fundamental rights bill was nearing completion, the Assembly's influence had so weakened that even conservative British observers were not too concerned about its effects. 'The Diet [!] will conclude its ridiculous constitution for Germany in a few weeks,' Ponsonby wrote to Palmerston on 4 December. 'It will then expire having done its work, and probably its constitution will follow it to nonentity.' Observers less blasé than the ambassador to Austria were more critical. On 10 December, Cowley reported on the second reading of the fundamental rights and was 'sorry to say that all amendments proposed to diminish their democratical tendency [had been] rejected.' Milbanke drew Palmerston's attention to the damaging effects of the *Paulskirche*'s legislation on the social and commercial situation in the German states. 'The ignorance of the social peculiarism of the separate states which characterizes the proceedings of the Frankfort legislators,' he wrote on 15 January 1849, 'is likely to occasion very serious inconveniences in some countries.' Some of the fundamental laws would 'operate in a manner most prejudiced to many vested interests.' In Bavaria, Milbanke predicted, the new legislation would be rejected because it would bring about a 'complete revolution of property.'[79]

By the end of 1848, a broad consensus in favour of Prussian leadership in Germany had emerged amongst British observers. On 10 December, Cowley reported that 'the wisest thing the sovereigns can do, is to call in Prussia to take the reins of the Central Government.' The same feeling was expressed in the press. 'The headship of Germany in the hands of the King of PRUSSIA, supported by a powerful army, and by the pride of its own subjects, would be a very different thing from the mere abstraction which now affects to reign at Frankfort,' the *Times* argued ten days later. For the *Paulskirche* to retain some British goodwill, it would have to be seen to aid Prussia in assuming that leading role, which, as the Prussian circular of 23 January 1849 indicated, Prussia was now prepared to accept. Instead and much to Cowley's disgust, the National Assembly became bogged down in a lengthy and inconclusive dispute over the constitutional form of the proposed head of Germany. In the course of January the *Paulskirche* debated and rejected each of the following options: a republican presidency, a directorate, an elected head for one term of office, a headship alternating between Austria and Prussia, a hereditary Emperor, an elected Emperor, an Emperor for life, an Emperor for 12, for 6 years and for 3 years. Only two motions found majorities: the new head of state (who was to be neither elected nor hereditary) should be one of the German princes, and he should bear the title 'Emperor of the Germans'. Cowley was appalled by such tomfoolery. 'It is impossible to exaggerate the state of discredit into which these last proceedings of the national assembly have brought it,' he commented to Palmerston on 29 January 1849. 'The deputies themselves ridicule its conduct openly, but they do not seem

to understand the more damaging effect, which such palpable incon-
sistency is likely to produce.'[80]

When the *Paulskirche* proceeded to debate further elements of the
constitution, Cowley became even more dismissive. In February 1849
the National Assembly discussed the electoral law. 'By its provision,'
Britain's envoy in Frankfurt reported with despair, 'every person calling
himself a German, and not actually in prison, has the right of voting
at elections. Nothing in fact can be more democratic than its whole tendency. Every attempt to introduce a qualification for voters failed.' In
Cowley's judgement, the labours of the National Assembly had produced a constitutional cul-de-sac. The *Paulskirche* had decided to place
an Emperor at the head of the new Germany, 'but,' as Cowley wrote to
Palmerston on 28 March, 'he never can govern Germany with such a
fundamental law, constitution, and electoral law as has been voted by
the National Assembly.' A fortnight later, he reiterated his rejection of
the German constitution in even stronger terms: 'a pure and simple
acceptation of the constitution would be an abandonment of every
sovereign right.' In Cowley's eyes, the National Assembly's decision in
favour of a hereditary Emperor on 27 March 1849 and the election of
Frederick William IV on the subsequent day was therefore more or less
irrelevant. On the day of the election, Cowley informed Palmerston that
– according to the Prussian representative at Frankfurt – the King would
have refused the imperial crown if deputy Welcker's motion of 12 March
to confer it on him had been carried. Cowley calmly added: 'I presume
that His Majesty will do the same now.'[81]

Frederick William's renunciation of the imperial crown offered to him
by the National Assembly on 3 April 1849 meant that the third and last
of the conditions for a justifiable continuation of the *Paulskirche*'s political role, Prussia's willingness to cooperate with it, had come to nought.
Unguided by Prussia, Cowley had predicted, the German Parliament
was only powerful for harm. In the eyes of many British observers, the
Paulskirche's subsequent decisions to support the *Reichsverfassungskampagne* vindicated Cowley's prediction. A damning leader in the *Times*,
published on 4 May, the very day on which the National Assembly
called on the German governments, parliaments, local communities
and the whole German people to enact the constitution and ensure its
application, captured a widespread mood. 'The contest with which
Germany is now threatened,' the article explained, 'is one between the
rights of sovereignty, the freedom of established government, and the
faith of treaties on the one hand, and the arbitrary authority of a lawless
popular convention on the other.' Two days later, Cowley endorsed this

characterization by attacking the *Paulskirche*'s 'usurpation of authority, which ha[d] already caused blood to flow, and which [. . . would] not be put an end to without a direful struggle.' The National Assembly's dwindling moral authority was further undermined by the steady departure of the moderate deputies leaving behind an ever more radical Rump-Parliament. 'It is to be feared,' Cowley wrote on 12 May, 'that within a few days the left will have the church of St Paul entirely to themselves.' On 21 May, nine days before the remnant of the National Assembly decided to flee from the approaching Prussian troops by adjourning to Stuttgart, Cowley's patience finally ran out. 'The National Assembly,' he wrote to Palmerston, 'may, I think, be considered as defunct.'[82]

Predictably, the German Parliament's decision to transfer its sittings to Stuttgart did not meet with much enthusiasm on the part of Malet. 'Reduced as they are to the representatives of one party,' Britain's envoy to Württemberg wrote to Palmerston on 2 June, 'it is very certain they can do nothing but mischief wherever they meet.' Cowley's predictions about the course which the Rump Parliament would pursue were unlikely to alleviate the alarm of the good people of Stuttgart: 'an attempt will no doubt be made to overturn the government, to fraternise with Baden and the Palatinate, and to spread the insurrection into Franconia.' Malet watched the proceedings of the National Assembly for nine days and then decided, without prior authorization, to call on the Württemberg Foreign Minister. 'Considering the critical position of affairs in Württemberg, and weighing the consequences which the presence and action of the fraction of the late National Assembly of Frankfort, which has fixed itself here, may entail,' he explained to Palmerston on 15 June 1849, 'I have thought it my duty, in conjunction with Monsieur de Fontenay, my French Colleague, [. . .] to impress on Monsieur Roser the necessity of getting rid of the so-called National Parliament.' Three days later, Württemberg cavalry dissolved the last meeting of the Rump Parliament and Germany's revolutionary National Assembly came to an end. A further four days on, Palmerston replied to Malet. As the envoy had been 'encouraging the Württemberg government to resist a party who are endeavouring to obtain assistance from France in support of their revolutionary and anarchical schemes,' the Foreign Secretary wrote, 'Her Majesty's Government approve[d] the step.'[83]

The British perception of revolutionary Germany's central political institutions between the autumn of 1848 and the summer of 1849 was thus marked by a comprehensive rejection of their politics and policies. The process of disenchantment, which had characterized British reactions to the political bodies at Frankfurt throughout the summer and early autumn of 1848, led many British observers to turn to the German states for a reorganization of Germany. As early as 18 August 1848, Palmerston argued that the vision pursued at Frankfurt was 'fast dissolving, but probably the efforts made to realize that phantom may lead to a reconstruction of the Confederation in some form better adapted to the present state of Germany.'[84] A unanimous decision against Frankfurt was, however, delayed by the argument proposed by Britain's best-informed, most prolific and most intelligent diplomatic representative. Throughout the autumn of 1848, Lord Cowley advocated – both towards the Foreign Office and towards his contacts in Frankfurt – a particular kind of cooperation between the Frankfurt institutions and the Prussian government. This cooperation, it is argued, was not designed to provide a framework in which the ideas of the *Paulskirche* could inform the process of Germany's reorganization. Rather, it was meant to restrain the German Parliament from taking radical steps and to provide a safety-valve to prevent a new revolutionary outbreak by the radical forces outside the National Assembly. The coalition advocated by Cowley was an anti-revolutionary instrument. When – because of Prussia's recovery and its own turn to more radical positions – the *Paulskirche* lost the little usefulness it might have retained, Cowley's carefully balanced argument broke down and he eventually joined the majority of British diplomats in calling for an end of the Frankfurt institutions.

'Large republics seem to be essentially and inherently aggressive': German unity and German nationalism in Europe, 1848–9

British observers of Germany soon realized that the revolution of 1848 involved more than issues of freedom and reform. 'The great aim of the Liberal party throughout Germany,' the *Times* reported as early as 6 March 1848, is 'to fuse her into one great nation, instead of being, as she is at present, an aggregate of disjointed units.' Ten days later, a correspondent writing for the same paper emphatically reiterated this point: 'no words of mine can convey to you the ardent longings of all classes for an united Germany.'[85] Having treated the demands for German unity somewhat perfunctorily for so many years, the strength of this feeling must have astonished British diplomats and journalists. During the years of the *Vormärz* British perceptions of the German national movement, its structure and aims, had mainly consisted of a series of dismissive comments expressing distaste, but failing to engage in a probing analysis. After March 1848, though, with German unity no longer the programme of a disdained movement of opposition, but the dominant ideology shaping events, British politicians, diplomats and journalists finally tackled the phenomenon and its consequences intensively and incisively. Although this marked a clear change from their earlier practice, there was also considerable continuity in the manner in which British observers characterized German nationalism.

In July 1822, Frederick Lamb, who was then based at Frankfurt, sent a despatch to Castlereagh, in which he outlined the history and character of the German national movement. Even as early as 1806, Lamb argued, 'many of the secondary leaders of these associations had embraced the notion of an union of all Germany under a republican government.' After 1815, he continued, 'the direction of the party fell entirely into the hands of demagogues, consisting principally of professors, lawyers and literary men. These addressed themselves with success to the perversion of the youth of the nation.' As has been shown, the attitude reflected in Lamb's despatch was endorsed by the majority of Britain's politicians, diplomats and journalists throughout the 1830s and 1840s. 1848 and 1849 saw a continuation of these negative clichés. In September 1848, for instance, Cowley informed Palmerston that 'a strong democratic spirit' had been at work ever since 1815. Six weeks later, the envoy explained how the principle 'of communism and socialism, which pervades not only the lower classes, but [. . .] the middling to a great extent', had been disseminated before 1848. His explanation implicated the whole national movement. 'It is a common practice in Germany to form associations for any object the development of which is desired,' he wrote to the Foreign Secretary. 'There exist accordingly religious associations, associations for the advancement of music, shooting, gymnastic exercises, and so on. It appears that the meetings which these associations brought about were the vehicles for spreading these new lights. That of the gymnasiums has been the most active and continues to be the most dangerous for in them are enrolled all the youth of Germany, and the members of them (Turners as they are called) are the terror of the peaceable and well disposed.'[86]

At the same time, similarly dismissive views on the national movement of *Vormärz* Germany were repeated in Britain's conservative periodicals. German unity, the playwright John Palgrave Simpson wrote in *Blackwood's Edinburgh Magazine* in September 1848, 'has been, in truth, long since the watchword of the German student, when, in the recesses of his beer-cellar at the university, he collected a set of fellow fancied enthusiasts around the beer-jugs, [. . .] and deemed himself a notable and formidable conspirator, because he drank off his *Krug* of beer to the cry of "Perish all Princes – long live the German Fatherland".' William

Aytoun, writing for the same monthly, shared Simpson's feelings. He regretted that 'studentism, once comparatively harmless, had become utterly rampant throughout the land.' Not even in his younger years, he went on, had he taken 'any deep pleasure in cultivating the society of the Burschenschaft, but, on the contrary, [had] rather regarded them as a race to be eschewed by all who had a wholesome reverence for soap and a horror for Kantean philosophy.'[87]

This distaste for the national movement contributed to spurring British diplomats and writers on to engage in a lively discussion of the desirability and consequences of German unity. The mainspring of their interest in the question of Germany's future organization, however, was the realization that the German revolution might profoundly alter the structure of the European system, and thus substantially affect British interests. To British observers of Germany the events of 1848–9 suggested two possible outcomes: a centralized German republic embodying the ideas of revolution and threatening peace on the continent, or a reformed and more close-knit union of German states safeguarding European peace. In their discussion of German unity, British diplomats were motivated by the hope of aiding the creation of the latter, or at least contributing towards the prevention of the former.

Throughout 1848 and 1849, British politicians, diplomats and writers repeatedly defined Britain's interest in Germany's political shape. This interest was not of a bilateral nature but concerned the function which Germany was allocated within the British concept of a larger European order. Germany, Palmerston informed Strangways on 25 March 1848, ought to be 'productive of additional security to the balance of power in Europe' and contribute 'to the preservation of general peace.' On the same day, Russell defined Britain's main foreign policy aim as maintaining peace 'by enacting and not by forgoing our influence in Europe.' Britain should therefore support 'the formation of a German power, or two German powers, combined in favour of their independence against any attack in Germany from France and Russia.' More than a year later, with the revolution all but over, Palmerston reiterated this idea. 'It would be advantageous for the peace and general interests of Europe, and therefore conducive to the interests of England,' he wrote to Prince Albert, 'that the various fragments into which Germany is now politically split should as far as possible be brought together into one body politic as regards at least [. . .] the system of German defence against foreign aggression.' The British press endorsed the politicians' belief in the importance for Europe of Germany's cohesion. 'As far as [. . .] the continental interests of this country are concerned, the independence and union of Germany [. . .] cannot but prove beneficial,' the *Times* wrote on 23 March 1848. 'There lies the huge and impassable barrier against the inroads of both Russia and France.' In September 1848, *Tait's Edinburgh Magazine* reminded its readers that 'for the maintenance of the peace of Europe and the quieting of restless France, England has nothing better to wish than a strong and a united Germany.'[88]

Germany's positive, stabilizing role in Europe, which deserved British goodwill and support, was not seen to be the automatic consequence of *any* form of German unity, though. On the contrary, British observers feared that the revolutionaries of 1848–9 might establish a form of German unity which would seriously endanger the general peace of Europe. The efforts to unite Germany undertaken by the Frankfurt National Assembly and later through the *Reichsverfassungskampagne* were perceived to be fatally flawed on two levels: internally, with respect to the proposed constitution, and externally, regarding the policies towards Germany's neighbours. On the level of the constitutional arrangements for Germany, British diplomats and politicians rejected the National Assembly's unity project for two related reasons: its democratic character and its centralism. Externally, the *Paulskirche's* policies regarding Schleswig-Holstein earned German nationalism as represented by the National Assembly a reputation for recklessness and aggression. While approving of Germany's union in principle and welcoming reforming steps in that direction, Britain was thus deeply and comprehensively opposed to the work and aims of the National Assembly.

As has been shown above, in the eyes of British observers both its various preparatory bodies – the Heidelberg meeting, the 'Pre-Parliament' and the 'Committee of 50' – and the National Assembly itself bore the blemish of 'ultra-liberal' and democratic doctrines. The constitution drawn up by the *Paulskirche* with its provision for universal suffrage and fundamental rights was dismissed as democratic and incompatible with the existence of sovereign princes. British diplomats and politicians soon suspected that the National Assembly, for all its talk of Reich and Kaiser, was pursuing a plan which, as Bligh predicted in September 1848, 'if it resolves itself at all will probably be in a republican shape.' This view was shared by Mellish. 'The unity of Germany in the shape hitherto dreamt of by the people at Frankfort,' he wrote to Cowley in December 1848, 'is only practicable through the republic.' Studying the *Paulskirche's* constitution in April 1849, Malet found it 'impossible not to recognize such pervading principles of democratic ascendancy as must render their practical application to the forms of government of constitutional sovereignties extremely perilous, if not wholly impracticable.' The envoy to Württemberg interpreted Gagern's recent speech in favour of adopting the constitution as 'an appeal to the principle of the sovereignty of the people, as established on the basis of universal suffrage.'[89]

Apart from British Whigs' and Tories' almost innate distaste for democracy, the *Paulskirche*'s constitution was rejected for two further reasons concerning the role which Germany was expected to play within the European system. On the one hand, Palmerston considered democracies incapable of pursuing a peaceful course. 'Large republics,' the Foreign Secretary wrote to the British ambassador in Paris in February 1848, 'seem to be essentially and inherently aggressive.' On the other hand, there was a widespread belief amongst British diplomats that a German republic would quickly form an unholy alliance with republican France and thereby destroy the European balance. 'It cannot be indifferent to us,' Canning wrote in his final report to Palmerston in May 1848, 'whether Germany may succeed or fail in establishing the forms of constitutional monarchy. Great as our means would be in an event of a war with France, we could ill afford to see Germany leagued with that power against us in consequence [. . .] of its new democratic affinities.' Strangways endorsed these apprehensions. 'A republic, once proclaimed in this part of Germany,' he warned Palmerston in June, 'would be instantly recognised by France, and if need were, assisted by her.'[90]

The second important constitutional aspect of the *Paulskirche*'s project which British diplomats and journalists resolutely opposed, was the danger it was seen to pose to the continued existence of the individual German states. 'Almost all who think,' Bligh informed Palmerston in July 1848, 'see in a Central Power, with ministers responsible to a parliament, which is to be based upon regulations to be enacted by a constitutional assembly elected by universal suffrage, the rapid absorption of all other inferior and local authority.' Both conservative and liberal commentators agreed that the united and centralized Germany planned in Frankfurt was unprecedented. 'There is no record, within the last six centuries, of any such Germany as it is now proposed to summon into life,' the journalist Harry Woodham wrote in the liberal *Edinburgh Review* in March 1848. 'No such unity as is at present contemplated, can be detected by the most anxious scrutineer of Germanic history.' For the *British Quarterly Review* the 'creation of such an Empire' as desired by the National Assembly was 'indeed a creation, and not a restoration.' Travers Twiss, an Oxford law don, writing in the conservative *Quarterly*

Review in December 1848 and March 1849, came to an almost identical assessment: 'Germany, indeed, has never known unity in the sense of indivisibility; her unity has always reposed upon certain conditions of division, not hypothetical but real and practical.' Germany, he declared in 1849, is 'essentially anti-Unitarian in its nature.'[91]

Palmerston, who had reacted so passionately when he saw the independence of the German states threatened by Metternich's allegedly centralizing measures in 1832, strongly disapproved of the same tendency inherent in the National Assembly's policies. 'It appears to me that the scheme of German organization proposed at Frankfort cannot be carried into effect without overthrowing many existing sovereignties, and crushing some separate nationalities,' the Foreign Secretary wrote to Prince Albert in May 1849; that this 'is not likely to be carried out with the willing consent of the separate governments; and that the Frankfort party have taken for their motto "If I cannot sway the gods, I will move hell" [. . .]. I conceive that what Monsieur Gagern and his party aim at, is to apply to Germany the political organization of the United States of America.' Palmerston's letter to Prince Albert makes clear why he rejected a centralized Germany and supported a federal solution based on the independence and inviolability of the German states. He wanted to frustrate what Malet had described as the 'aim and object' of Germany's ultra-liberal party: 'the destruction of the existing sovereignties – the creation of a German republic or republican federation.' Centralization, it was believed, constituted a decisive step towards the dreaded German republic, whereas 'the vast number of small principalities into which the country is divided,' as the journalist Percy Bolingbroke St John put it in *Tait's Edinburgh Magazine* in July 1848, acted 'much against republican principles taking root.'[92]

Paradoxically, the interpretation that Britain championed German federalism because of its anti-republican effect is also supported by Cowley's suggestions that certain tiny German states ought to be amalgamated or mediatized. 'There is no inherent strength in them,' he reported to the Foreign Secretary on 15 October 1848. 'If left to themselves they would become the theatre of continual outbreaks.' In a private letter to Palmerston written on the following day, Cowley argued his case more forcefully. 'I certainly have my doubts whether in the end it will be possible to preserve monarchies in Germany. Sure I am that the last chance is to make them as strong as possible by fusing the smaller states into them.'[93] Besides, in many cases the small German states were seen as the breeding ground for democracy and republicanism. Forbes reported repeatedly that republican principles were rife in Meiningen, Altenburg, Weimar, Coburg, Gotha, Schwarzburg-Rudolstadt and Reuss. 'Nothing can be more pernicious to general order and tranquillity,' he argued on 1 August 1848, 'than these very small states, where the governments do not possess sufficient military force to be able to repress tumults.'[94] Britain's support for the independence of the separate German states was not granted indiscriminately but depended on their ability to play their allocated anti-republican role.

British opposition to the republicanism and the centralism of the National Assembly's project for German unity and the expected consequences for the role Germany would play within Europe was heightened by a profound and widespread uneasiness about the external policies which a revolutionary Germany might pursue. The press quickly drew attention to the potentially immense power of the new centralized Germany, a power which might prove perilous if exercised by the wrong people. As early as 13 March, the *Times* realized that 'the Prince or President who should so wield the national forces of 40 millions of Germans would be one of the greatest potentates in Europe. [. . .] It is evident that such a change implies a total revolution in the balance of power.' Commenting on the constitutional plans discussed in Frankfurt, the *Edinburgh Review* argued in July 1848 that 'a mightier or more imposing revolution was never projected.' The conservative *Fraser's Magazine* was openly sceptical. 'If this reorganization of Germany under the influence of the theory of unity is, in reality, what it assumes and appears to be,' the monthly predicted in August 1848, 'then will a revolution have been effected far more important and dangerous than any of those made by the arms of Napoleon.' Three months later, the *British Quarterly Review* also highlighted the enormous weight of the new Germany: 'as a unity, a great federal state, it possesses within itself an aggregate mass of material power, of intellectual resources, and of political activity, unknown probably to the history of the world.' While being more low-key about the power-political potential of the proposed Germany, British diplomats also drew attention to its international implications. The proposed reform of the Diet, Ward observed on 15 March 1848, 'may alter the principles of the Confederation very materially, and therefore well deserves the attention of those powers which are guaranteeing parties to the General Act of the Congress of Vienna.' A week later, Malet informed Palmerston of the far-reaching political changes in Germany which 'may affect the established balance of power in Europe.'[95]

In spite of their early awareness of the potentially problematic role which a united Germany might play in European politics, British observers appear to have been prepared to give the nascent German state the benefit of the doubt. On 17 March, the *Times* optimistically expressed its 'conviction that whatever tend[ed] to strengthen an imperial or federal power in Germany, [was] an auspicious event for the peace and prosperity of Europe and [was] in all respects conformable to the permanent continental interests and policy of Great Britain.' On 15 April, Strangways reported the incorporation of Eastern and Western Prussia into the Germanic Confederation without adding any critical comment. In May, he discussed current plans to incorporate Denmark, the Netherlands and the German cantons of Switzerland, and concluded that they had plenty to recommend them. Far from being outraged, Palmerston reacted calmly to these ideas. He considered the inclusion of the Netherlands a 'scheme upon which much might be said both ways' and expressed concern that the addition of the Swiss-German cantons to the Confederation might lead to results which meant that 'Germany would lose one way in security and comparative power, as much as she would gain in the other.'[96] This unexcitable attitude towards the *Paulskirche*'s foreign political ambitions, however, soon gave way to fierce condemnation and opposition. British observers came to see German nationalism and its political representation in Frankfurt as aggressive and irresponsible forces, which Europe could ill afford to ignore. More than by anything else, this dramatic change was caused by the Schleswig-Holstein conflict.

British repulsion at the German role in this conflict was expressed most forcefully in the public sphere. In the House of Commons on 19 April 1848, Benjamin Disraeli launched a scathing attack on German nationalism. 'It is actually laid down as a principle by men now occupying seats in the cabinets of Europe,' he exclaimed, 'that wheresoever the German language is spoken, there the German flag ought to wave.' The actual motivation for the attack on Denmark was alleged to be Germany's craving for naval power. For Disraeli, German nationality was nothing but 'dreamy and dangerous nonsense'. On the following day, the *Times* opened its columns to Orla Lehmann, a Danish politician, who anonymously castigated the German position: 'the hidden *vis motrix* of the German revolution is a wild sentiment of nationality [. . .], the unrestricted violence of which is likely to overwhelm the whole social state of Europe and merge all states in a common deluge.' On 8 July, the *Times* explained that Germany had paid dearly for its aggression. 'At the moment when the sympathy of this country was most strongly excited by the efforts of the greatest nation of central Europe to establish its unity and to consolidate its liberties, that cause was tarnished by an act of supreme injustice.' By September 1848, a leading article clearly identified the *Paulskirche* as responsible for the ongoing hostilities. 'We have nothing to do with the extravagant language and pretensions of the Frankfort Assembly,' the article read. 'If their powers are indefinite and their relations with the sovereign states of Germany are unsettled, that is no reason why the rest of Europe is to be duped by false negotiations or exposed to the inconvenience and loss occasioned by an unprovoked war.'[97]

Leading British periodicals, both conservative and liberal, condemned the role of German nationalism in international politics. Harry Woodham, writing in the liberal *Edinburgh Review* in July 1848, deplored 'the invidious and repulsive character of its rudimentary essays, directed against a comparatively defenceless state, for questionable purposes, and under circumstances suggestive of most equivocal motives.' Three months later, he accused the Frankfurt deputies of aiming at 'the consolidation of the German race by all requisite institutions, and the extension of the national frontiers by a somewhat unscrupulous interpretation of public law. They ha[d] laid resolute hands on Danish Schleswig and Polish Posen.' The conservative *Fraser's Magazine* attacked the 'so-called German Parliament' more openly: 'its arrogant assumption of an authority incompatible with the existing European system had been observed by all thinking men with a contempt not altogether unmixed with fear.' In his incisive analysis of German nationalism in the Tory *Quarterly Review*, Travers Twiss argued that the language-based nationalism pursued in Frankfurt clashed with 'received standards of political nationality,' and was 'inconsistent with the maintenance of peaceful relations towards foreign states.' Nationalism based on a common language, Twiss continued, was 'from the nature of that basis, aggressive in its tendencies.'[98]

The treatment of the new Germany's foreign political aggressiveness by British diplomats and politicians was less dramatic in style but equally clear in content. As has been shown above, the *Paulskirche*'s stand on the Schleswig-Holstein question deeply frustrated and infuriated Palmerston and his diplomats. The 'unreasonable pretensions and the groundless assumptions of Gagern and his Frankfort revolutionists,' as Palmerston called them in a letter to Westmorland in May 1849, eventually led the makers of and contributors to Britain's foreign policy to draw two conclusions. The first was outlined by John Ward as early as August 1848. The National Assembly, he wrote to Palmerston, 'has shown some signs of a disposition to extend the German territory where practicable, by annexing German races who are the subjects of other states. This tendency requires to be matched by foreign powers.' Through its firm stand on the Danish question Britain did just that. The second conclusion was formulated by Palmerston himself. In a confidential letter of 25 May 1849, the Foreign Secretary told the Prussian envoy in London that British hopes for a successful mediation in the Schleswig-Holstein controversy, had 'long been kept up by the belief that the violence and injustice of Frankfort would be counteracted by the moderation and equity of Berlin.'[99] The National Assembly was not only to be vigorously opposed in its expansionist designs, it also had to be considered unfit for its assumed task of conducting Germany's foreign affairs. For sound leadership of Germany in European international politics Britain had to look once more to the sovereign states.

An analysis of British reactions to the attempted national unification of Germany in 1848–9 reveals an apparent contradiction between the sympathy which British observers expressed for a reformed and more close-knit Germany acting as a stabilizing force in Europe and their rejection of the National Assembly's efforts to achieve it. Contemporaries and a number of historians have ignored or underestimated this contradiction. They consequently confused British hostility to both the *Paulskirche* and the revolutionaries in the German states with a fundamental opposition to the idea of greater German unity, or underrated Britain's rejection of the plans pursued at Frankfurt.[100] To do this means distorting a crucial point: British observers did not dismiss German unity. On the contrary, they thought it far too important an issue to be left in the hands of amateurs, doctrinaires and revolutionaries. The contradiction can be resolved by noting the central position accorded to the German states. British hopes for a reformed German nation state rested squarely on them. All positive statements by British observers about the kind of Germany they would like to see emerging from the upheaval of the revolutionary years reflect the importance allocated to the legitimate governments and contained at least one of the following key characteristics: The new political organization of Germany should be firmly monarchical. This was seen only to be possible through the establishment of a federal union of independent states and not of a centralised unitary state.[101] There were also, as has been shown above, growing calls for Prussian leadership of the new Germany.

On 25 March 1848, with plans for a reform of the old Diet abounding, Palmerston informed Strangways that he welcomed 'any arrangement which would tend to strengthen Germany by more closely uniting and consolidating the separate states of which it is composed.' Nine months later, when the National Assembly had already lost most of the little credit it had once enjoyed, Cowley argued that 'the best means of rendering Germany strong and respected, and that for the sovereigns the best hopes of reinstating themselves in some degree in their former power, [was] by seeking the protection of Prussia, and making their cause hers.' The Foreign Secretary was taken by this reasoning. 'If indeed the several states of Germany were to be joined in a general league of separate states, and Prussia were to be the chief and directing member of such a league,' he replied to Cowley on 22 December 1848, 'such an arrangement would be simple and practicable.' In a carefully worded leading article, the *Times* came to similar conclusions. In January 1849, the paper welcomed an 'increased union in Germany as an additional guarantee of the maintenance of peace' provided that 'there be no encroachments on the established rights and the traditional influence of other states – provided also these changes can be effected by negotiation between free and independent states, and not by the arbitrary decrees of a more or less revolutionary convention.' By late June 1849, Cowley privately informed Malet that he had 'many unofficial reasons for believing that we are desirous to see Prussia at the head of Germany.'[102]

By the summer of 1849 the revolutionary attempt to establish constitutional liberty in the separate German states and to forge a united Germany had ended in failure. The major German states had experienced successful reactionary *coups d'état*, the Frankfurt National Assembly was dissolved and the *Reichsverfassungskampagne* defeated. British politicians, diplomats and journalists welcomed the collapse of the revolutions. They had rejected the revolutionary project on three different levels. On the level of the separate states, they had sided with the governments, advocated measured reforms from above, condemned democracy, welcomed governmental fightbacks and applauded the victory of the reaction. British observers also dismissed the central political institutions which the revolution had created at Frankfurt. The National Assembly, as well as its unofficial precursors, were perceived as dangerous, extremist and revolutionary conventions full of incompetent, excitable and dogmatic men. Their main achievement, the German constitution, was dismissed on account of its centralism, its republicanism and its impracticability. On the European level, Britain feared an unholy alliance of the French and German republics; they fiercely opposed the aggressive nature of the *Paulskirche*'s nationalism and despaired of its irresponsible course on the Schleswig-Holstein issue.

In spite, or rather because of, their satisfaction about the failure of the revolution, British observers were more hopeful about the possibility of a reformed and more closely united Germany in the summer of 1849 than at any time before. For them, the question of bringing about salutary reforms in Germany had always lain with the sovereign German states and their legitimate governments. Having ridden out the problems of 1848–9 and even emerged with a constitution, Prussia now devoted herself to reorganizing Germany. British observers wished her well.

3
British Perceptions of the Austro-Prussian Struggle for Supremacy, 1848–51

Between the defeat of the revolutions of 1848/9 and Palmerston's dismissal in December 1851, foreign affairs probably attracted more attention among a wider British public than at any period previously considered. However, while the fate of Hungarian and Polish refugees and the Don Pacifico affair aroused a great deal of excitement, they were in themselves relatively minor issues whose appeal owed much to Palmerston's penchant for playing to the gallery. In the Hungarian refugees' affair, he skilfully rode the crest of popular Russophobia and Austrophobia. Having refused to support the Hungarian revolution before it was crushed, Palmerston was quick to profit from Britain's public outrage at Austria's harsh treatment of the vanquished revolutionaries. In the autumn of 1849, Britain and France stiffened the Sultan's resistance to Russian and Austrian demands for the extradition of the Polish and Hungarian refugees who had fled to Turkey. Keen to boost British influence at the Porte, Palmerston even breached the Straits Convention of 1841 by ordering a naval demonstration in the Dardanelles. In 1850, the Foreign Secretary found himself again in line with popular Austrophobia, when he all but endorsed the manhandling of an Austrian general by a London mob. In the following year Palmerston planned to extend a private invitation to Lajos Kossuth, the exiled leader of the Hungarian revolution, during the latter's triumphant visit to Britain.[1]

The Don Pacifico affair of 1850 provided Palmerston with yet another opportunity to enhance his popularity. Don Pacifico, a somewhat shady Athens businessman, had suffered some damage when his property had been attacked by a crowd. Born in Gibraltar, he claimed British citizenship and appealed to London to support his vastly exaggerated demands for compensation from the Greek government. In January

1850 Palmerston employed the sledgehammer of a naval blockade of Athens to crack the nut of Pacifico's claim, thereby alienating France and Russia, co-guarantors with Britain of Greece's independence, and inviting fierce criticism from his political opponents in Britain. Popular opinion, however, warmly approved of Palmerston's robust style, and he emerged from the affair, as Greville noted in July 1850, 'so great in the Cabinet and so popular in the country [. . . that if he . . .] renounces his offensive manners and changes his mode of proceeding abroad, he may consider his tenure of office perfectly secure.'[2] Subsequent developments justified Greville's careful use of conditional clauses, and after a further 17 months of alienating the Court and violating Cabinet procedure, Palmerston found himself dismissed over his unauthorized recognition of Louis Napoleon's *coup d'état*.

Obscured by the pyrotechnics of the Pacifico affair and noisy Austrophobia, lay the much more substantial question of Germany's political future. The failure of the *Paulskirche* to implement the imperial constitution left behind a political vacuum. The revolution had swept away the Diet of the German Confederation but did not succeed in putting anything of durability in its place. Austria and Prussia reacted to this situation by formulating their own plans for Germany's political reorganization. Although both plans were aimed at overcoming the revolutionary challenge and shared a firmly monarchical basis, it quickly became clear that they were mutually exclusive. The pursuit of their respective projects soon involved the two German great powers in heightening antagonism. Since Prussia and Austria aimed at profound political change in Germany and raised questions of European importance, British observers followed these developments with keen interest.[3]

The project of a Prussian-led *Kleindeutschland*, May 1848–April 1850

Determining the nature of the relationship between the proposed German nation-state and the Habsburg Empire proved one of the most divisive problems faced by the Frankfurt National Assembly. Following the earlier draft constitution submitted by the 17 'Men of Public Confidence', the *Paulskirche*'s constitutional committee proposed that only the German provinces of the Austrian Empire be included in the future German state. Since the link between them and the Habsburgs' non-German provinces was to consist merely of a personal union, the proposal amounted to a partial dissolution of the Austrian Empire. On

27 October 1848, this *großdeutsch* ('greater German' – greater because it aimed to include German Austria and Bohemia) motion was carried in the National Assembly. One month later the greater-German project met with an insurmountable obstacle when Prince Schwarzenberg, the new Austrian Minister-President, ruled out any splitting up of the Habsburg monarchy.

This gave a boost to the advocates of the rival *kleindeutsch* ('small-German') programme, which its main protagonist, Heinrich von Gagern, outlined to the National Assembly on 18 December: a Prussian-led Germany without Austria's German provinces was to be formed. International treaties were to connect this 'Small Germany' with a Habsburg Empire which would no longer form an integral part of Germany. Soon a bitter conflict developed between the anti-Prussian supporters of the unattainable *großdeutsch* solution and the advocates of Gagern's *kleindeutsch* programme. Eventually, as the governments of the German states reasserted their authority and regained the political initiative, Prussia adopted the Gagern scheme for her own purposes.[4]

A 'sound and wise' plan: the *kleindeutsch* solution, May 1848–July 1849

There can be no doubt as to which side British diplomats took in the *großdeutsch–kleindeutsch* controversy. Their support for a small-German scheme to provide a framework for Prussian leadership in Germany predated Gagern's speech in the *Paulskirche* by more than half a year. As early as 1 May 1848, Stratford Canning privately informed Palmerston that he would support the idea 'of making Austria independent in all essential matters of Germany. This might possibly leave more room for the development of Prussian influence in Germany.' Five months later, Cowley referred to the same idea. 'It is generally supposed that Austria will separate herself entirely from Germany and endeavour to reconstruct her ancient Empire,' he informed Palmerston in October 1848. Cowley added that there could be 'no doubt that if such a scheme [could] be executed it [would] greatly add to the strength, perhaps also to the happiness of Germany.' The Foreign Secretary agreed with these suggestions. The 'plan for establishing Austria as an independent Empire united to Germany by treaties,' Palmerston told Cowley on 18 December, seemed 'sound and wise'. Encouraged by this, the envoy in Frankfurt continued to advocate support for the Gagern programme, calling it 'the simplest plan' and 'the happiest thing for Germany' in letters to Ponsonby and Prince Albert's secretary. By the end of the year, Britain's official opinion appeared settled. 'Gagern's plan seems to be approved in London,' Ward wrote to Westmorland on 1 January 1849; 'and indeed no time ought to be lost in reconstructing Germany in the best practicable way.'[5]

Palmerston's, Cowley's, Canning's and Ward's clear preference for a *kleindeutsch* Germany allied to a reconstituted Austria was somewhat surprising in view of the absence until January 1849 of any political initiative, acceptable to British observers, to form the narrower federation which was to be the core of Gagern's scheme. The aspirations of the *Paulskirche* and Gagern's own ideas for this had been consistently rejected on the grounds of their unfeasibility, their democratic centralism and their aggressive nationalism. Prussia, on the other hand, to which British diplomats, politicians and journalists had increasingly been looking for sound monarchical leadership in Germany, had so far disappointed them by remaining inactive. Before Prussia's return to German politics, Britain's sympathy for a Prussian-led *Kleindeutschland* remained wholly theoretical. This ended when Prussia re-entered the arena of national politics by sending the circular despatch of 23 January to the German governments. 'The position which Prussia has taken with reference to Austria can hardly be mistaken,' Cowley observed in his discussion of the circular. 'In fact, she adopts M. de Gagern's plan.'[6] The despatch of 23 January therefore inaugurated a second, more intensive phase of discussion of the 'small-German' plan which ended when the plan for the German 'Union' was published in May 1849.

Following the Prussian circular, Cowley stepped up his campaign for the adoption of the *kleindeutsch* project. 'In the course of my correspondence with Your Lordship,' he wrote to Palmerston in February 1849, 'I have more than once taken the liberty of expressing my individual opinion, that the plan of M. de Gagern was, generally speaking, that best calculated to satisfy the exigencies of the times. It appeared to me to be simple and comprehensible.' Since Austria's opposition to Prussia had made the peaceful adoption of Gagern's plan impossible, Cowley feared that a collision might take place between the two great German powers, 'the one as the opponent, the other as the champion of constitutional liberties. On which side Germany will rally,' the envoy predicted with unconcealed partisanship, 'there can be but little doubt, and the day may yet come when united Germany, finding the impossibility of bringing Austria within its constitutional pale, will itself pronounce the sentence of her expulsion.' One month later, Cowley reiterated that Austria could not 'offer such terms to Germany as [would] satisfy the latter, and that the double federation must be attempted.' On 30 March, he pushed the same idea by informing his colleague in Vienna of what he claimed were Austria's real interests. She should leave Germany alone and 'had better not burn her fingers with the constitutional questions and theories which have unfortunately become inevitable in this part of the world,' he wrote, cleverly appealing to Ponsonby's conservatism.[7]

The King of Prussia's refusal of the *Paulskirche*'s imperial crown on 3 April 1849, together with his simultaneous invitation to the other German governments to join Prussia in the formation of a federal, Prussian-led German state, further fuelled Palmerston's and Cowley's optimism. Prussia 'looks to be the leading power of independent Germany,' he confidently wrote to Russell on 9 April 1849. Five days later, Cowley sent Palmerston a detailed outline of a proposal aired by the Prussian representative in Frankfurt pre-formulating the Prussian project. While praising the plan as 'in reality so reasonable, in appearance so practicable,' Cowley also emphasized the 'great, perhaps insuperable difficulties in the execution.' On 28 April 1849, the Prussian government finally rejected the Frankfurt constitution and pressed on with its own *kleindeutsch* ambitions by inviting the other German governments to a conference. On 6 May 1849, Cowley welcomed this 'noble, manly and straightforward' step. He believed that in spite of the many obstacles, Prussia now had to act. 'The best chance for Germany,' Cowley advised Westmorland on 7 May 1849, is that the King of Prussia 'should at once declare what parts of the [Frankfurt] constitution he accepts, or else octroyer a new one with such of the sovereigns as will go with him.'[8] Although it had tried and failed to win Austria's endorsement for its plan,[9] the Prussian government resolutely opted for the second of Cowley's options. On 17 May 1849, representatives from Prussia, Bavaria, Württemberg, Hanover and Saxony convened in Berlin to draw up a new constitution for Germany.[10]

During the run-up to the Berlin conference and after its opening, British interest in the emerging 'Union' project became more widespread. No longer confined to the realm of professional diplomacy, the topic attracted comments in the periodical and daily press. In March 1849, Travers Twiss attacked the Prussian project in the Tory *Quarterly Review*. Germany, Twiss believed, 'would be mutilated in a very inconvenient manner' if she were to be separated from Austria. He further observed that the *kleindeutsch* project of creating a 'north German unitarian state, with Prussia at its head, [was] inadmissible on the part of France.' Any power acting with such disregard for the 'established international landmarks of Europe,' Twiss predicted, 'would justly be regarded as the common enemy of the whole European family.' Twiss's anti-Prussian Austrophilia was not representative of the broader climate of public opinion, though. In the following month, Richard Monckton Milnes expressed an opposite view in the liberal *Edinburgh Review*. Gagern's plan, he argued, contained 'so many advantages, otherwise unattainable, that [. . .] we incline to believe that it, or some scheme very similar, will at last prevail.' On 22 May 1849, five days into the Berlin conference, the *Times* published its first detailed article on the subject. An anonymous correspondent welcomed 'the formation of a closer union of the several states' with which Austria would 'enter into certain federal relations. Such an event would prove the greatest political act effected since 1815,' he argued. 'Europe would see a complete and active union separating France from Austria and from the Moscovite Empire.'[11] It is important to note, though, that the correspondent's optimism was based on the erroneous assumption that Austria had approved the plan. This already indicated the limits of British support for the Prussian plan, which were to become more obvious in the course of the following year.

The Berlin conference resulted in a partial success for Prussia. While Bavaria and Württemberg refused to be drawn into the Prussian orbit, Hanover and Saxony yielded to a mixture of pressure and persuasion. On 26 May 1849 they and Prussia concluded the so-called 'Three Kings Alliance' to establish the monarchical and federal yet constitutional small-German 'Union'. Two days later, Prussia and her allies published the provisional constitution of the 'Union' which incorporated the plan for a German-Austrian alliance. Given that some British observers had been leaning towards a Prussian-led *Kleindeutschland* for more than a year, it is not surprising that the news from Berlin was received with some optimism. 'I am disposed, upon the whole, to think,' Cowley informed Palmerston on 2 June 1849, 'that this project will be accepted by the majority of the 29 states who have declared in favour of the constitution of the assembly.' Reassuringly, the 'Union' also had the 'right' enemies, as John Ward pointed out on 10 July 1849. 'The republican party,' he informed Palmerston, 'do what they can to prevent the constitution of the three Kings, as it is called, from being carried into execution.' Besides, the formation of the 'Union' also promised to be beneficial from a commercial point of view. 'Considering the strong bias of Hanover in favour of low duties,' Ward explained in the same despatch, 'the accession of that state to the customs union [of the proposed 'Union', not the *Zollverein*] appears likely to operate strongly for a reduction of the tariff.' The permanent exclusion of Austria would further strengthen this tendency.[12]

In view of the long-standing support for a two-tier solution to the Austro-German problem by several British politicians and diplomats, though, the 'Union' plan met with surprising reservations. Unanimous in their rejection of the *Paulskirche*'s constitution, British diplomats considered a new constitutional settlement a prerequisite for the re-organization of Germany. 'The arrangements, as far as they have gone,' Westmorland reported from the Berlin conference on 24 May 1849, 'have tended to the reform of the constitution promulgated by the National Assembly of Frankfort and of the law of election [. . .] in a very liberal spirit.'[13] It was the liberality of some elements of the constitution of the 'Union' which attracted British criticisms. Reflecting their deep-seated fear of democracy, British diplomats focused on the pro-posed electoral law which provided for universal suffrage, even though the elections were to be indirect and heavily weighed against the poor through the inclusion of the Prussian three-class franchise. Against the background of the ongoing *Reichsverfassungskampagne* such electoral provisions struck British diplomats as both dangerously democratic and likely to produce unrest because of their stark inequality.

'Until by some means or other the electoral laws be changed,' Forbes wrote on 1 June 1849, 'I cannot see how much essential advantage can accrue from it.' The envoy to Saxony hoped that the planned constituent assembly would 'frame and issue a new law of elections for those states who consent to this constitution.' Cowley was equally concerned about the proposed franchise. 'I am told that in the duchy of Nassau while the first class will hardly include 300 persons, the third will comprise about 80,000,' he wrote to Malet on 13 June; 'such machinery can never work.' Six days later, Palmerston expressed his opinion in a letter to Prince Albert, who had complained about Britain's diplomats' hostility towards the 'Union' project. 'The principle of uni-versal suffrage on which that constitution is founded,' the Foreign Secretary wrote in his spirited defence of Forbes and Bligh, 'is scarcely compatible with the permanent existence of monarchical institutions; and the complicated contrivance [. . .] by which the evils of universal suffrage are proposed to be mitigated, is far, I think, from removing the objection to the principle. The fact is that universal suffrage is essentially a republican institution.' Similar fears were expressed in the columns of the *Times*. On 4 June 1849, a leading article expressed concern about the planned 'introduction of a form of government based on universal suffrage.' Recent experience indicated that Germans were ill-suited for parliamentary politics. 'The world has now had some ex-perience of German popular assemblies,' the paper observed, 'and we have no reason to suppose that the diet of the new league will differ materially from those which have preceded it.' The Prussian project, the paper dramatically concluded, 'once more evokes and enthrones the evil powers of uncontrolled democracy and anarchy.'[14]

Further British misgivings concerned the relationship between the centre and the individual states within the planned 'Union'. 'You will have seen the new German project of constitution by Berlin & Co. before this reaches you,' Cowley wrote to Malet on 2 June. 'What say you to it? My humble opinion is that it cannot work with Landtags [= diets] in the independent states. They will certainly come into collision with each other.' Milbanke at Munich echoed Cowley's views. 'The vox populi will call for a popular representation at the seat of the central government,' he predicted on 9 July 1849, 'but how on earth is such a parliament to keep time or agree with the chambers of the half independent states which would still drag on a miserable existence. The central government would be thwarted from above and below – real sympathy or good faith there would be none on any side, and the end would be confusion and chaos.' Malet's worries pointed in the opposite direction and probably reflected opinions in Württemberg, which had refused to accede to the 'Union'. 'I shall never be brought to believe in the possible coexistence of minor states with major ones, or rather *a* major one,' he replied to Cowley. 'All independent action in foreign relations being necessarily surrendered, all real control of military means given up – a constant tendency *above all* to central absorption of authority in judicial proceedings [. . .] I think any state which adopts the constitution thinking to maintain its independence beyond the name is wilfully blind and thoroughly mistaken.'[15]

Irrespective of their pronounced views on the planned 'Union', Britain's diplomats in Germany agreed that the Prussian initiative was significant and wondered as to what line they should follow in response. 'I wish very much I knew more than I do of the tone *our Chief* would wish to be taken in the démêlé between Austria and Prussia,' Malet wrote to Cowley on 26 June, 'and if, as is probable, you have had any hint on the subject and would inform me, you would render me a great service.' By that time, Palmerston had not decided himself which tone he wanted adopted, and advocated strict neutrality. In his letter to Prince Albert of 19 June, the Foreign Secretary claimed somewhat facetiously that he had 'never been able distinctly to comprehend the plans for German unity.' He declared that Her Majesty's Government would be 'stepping beyond its legitimate or its safe ground if it were to become the partisan or the advocate of any particular scheme'. Consequently,

Palmerston sent Malet what the latter sulkily called 'a very *curt* answer to my query as to Austrian and Prussian *rivalry*, viz. "Her Majesty's Government have no wish to interfere in any questions which may arise therefrom." '[16]

It would be misleading, though, to conclude from these statements that the Foreign Secretary had no interest in the Prussian project or intended to remain in a position of mere observation. During the first half of July 1849, Palmerston must have been engaged in a process of intensive evaluation of the information he received from Germany and Austria, for on 13 July, the Foreign Secretary finally sent a long despatch to the British envoy in Berlin. In this document, which was printed and circulated to all British missions on the continent,[17] Palmerston, far from refraining from any partisan position, firmly committed the British government to supporting one of the rivalling parties in Germany. Fourteen months after Stratford Canning had first recommended a two-tier organization for Germany and Austria, the makers of Britain's foreign policy were now confronted with a credible effort to implement it. It will be argued that the decision about how Britain was to react to this effort was influenced by a careful reading of the political situation in the summer of 1849, as well as by the experiences since the outbreak of the revolution in March 1848 and by an even longer established pattern of analysing the question of reform in German politics.

A 'practical measure . . . advantageous to Europe': supporting the 'Union', July–October 1849

Palmerston's despatch to the Earl of Westmorland of 13 July 1849 marked a significant departure from Britain's previous diplomatic practice. While expressing clear preferences concerning Germany's domestic politics in internal correspondence, the Foreign Secretary had insisted throughout 1848–9 that both the British government and the diplomatic service adhere to a neutral position in their external communications. He had told the Queen as much in April 1848 and repeated this line in January 1849 to the Bavarian envoy. As late as 19 June 1849, Palmerston wrote to Prince Albert that Britain's diplomats had best remain 'passive but observant spectators of events.' Even his despatch of 13 July 1849 retained some of the same rhetoric. The Foreign Secretary pointed out that 'even now, though these matters ha[d] been much simplified by the course of events, Her Majesty's Government would not wish to take any direct and active part.'[18] These comments turned out to have been little more than rhetorical convention. The core of Palmerston's despatch to Westmorland was new and unmistakable.

'The Central Power at Frankfort, which was to have been the nucleus around which German unity was to have been formed,' Palmerston observed, 'seems to have crumbled to pieces. [. . .] The scheme of German unity which has led to no result at Frankfort has been taken up at Berlin and [. . .] has, provisionally at least, been worked into a practical measure. Prussia, Hanover, Saxony, and many of the smaller states appear to have united together by formal engagements. [. . .] Such an extensive organization of Germany,' the Foreign Secretary continued, 'would no doubt be advantageous to the German people, with reference both to their internal interests, and to their foreign relations, and it would consequently on that account be advantageous to Europe at large.' The despatch made also perfectly clear that only Prussia could lead such a league because 'the peculiar condition of Austria, past, present, and future, seem to oppose obstacles of a grave character, to prevent that power from being the head of united Germany.' Palmerston's circulating an official communication to call the 'Union' a 'practical measure' benefiting both Germany and Europe amounted to an unequivocal declaration of support. This was precisely what Count Colloredo, the Austrian chargé d'affaires in London, understood the attitude of the British government to be. Palmerston, he reported to Schwarzenberg on 5 August 1849, favoured the Prussian plans and looked for ways to support them.[19]

In view of the comments and reports of Britain's diplomats in Germany since the official launch of the 'Union' project in late May, Palmerston's despatch of 13 July 1849 appears somewhat surprising. As has been shown above, serious misgivings had been expressed about the proposed constitution of the 'Union'. Moreover, although most of the smaller German states soon joined, some British diplomats remained rather pessimistic about the feasibility of the project. 'The general feeling amongst those in authority here,' Bligh reported from Hanover, one of the signatory states of the 'Three Kings Alliance', on 14 June, 'appears to be that the proposed constitution will come to nothing.' Predictably, the view from Württemberg, which had refused to enter the alliance, was even bleaker. 'As to the unity dream,' Malet wrote to Cowley on 26 June, 'very few continue to indulge in it, but the dislike and fear of Prussian determination are very general.' In Mellish's opinion the Prussian project was 'as great a force as the Frankfort one, and [would] like its predecessor end in smoke.' On 2 July 1849, Westmorland predicted to Palmerston that Austria 'as well as Bavaria, and probably Wurtemberg, [would] decline to agree to the great extension of a power which would go far to annihilate their own, and to which their people are generally understood to be disinclined.' This view was shared by Milbanke. In a letter to Cowley of 9 July, he called it 'downright madness to expect to shoulder Austria out of Germany without a struggle.'[20]

A more than year-long position of neutral observation of Germany, serious misgivings about its constitution and numerous gloomy predictions for the future of the 'Union': all this meant that Palmerston's sudden and unprecedentedly clear declaration in favour of the Prussian plan requires an explanation. 'What do you think of our German despatch,' the ever-sceptical Mellish asked Cowley at the end of July. 'We look upon it here as a mistake into which the German influence in high places has forced the chief.' Given Palmerston's unflinching defence of Bligh and Forbes against Prince Albert's accusations in June and the stubbornness with which he defied the Court's wishes over the Schleswig-Holstein question, Mellish's suspicion is not particularly convincing.[21] While mentioning Palmerston's support for the 'Union' plan in 1849, several relevant studies similarly fail to provide an adequate answer to the question why the Foreign Secretary and the Prime Minister made this decision in July 1849.[22] It will be argued here that the British Foreign Secretary decided to support the Prussian plan for the 'Erfurt Union' because it offered a cluster of attractive features, which can only be fully appreciated when seen against the background of British perceptions of Germany not just in the summer of 1849, or since the outbreak of the revolution in March 1848, but throughout the whole of the *Vormärz*. On the highest level, the Prussian project appeared conducive to establishing a particular distribution of power on the continent which corresponded with British security interests. On the level of German politics, the 'Union' offered a governmental counter-proposal to the *Paulskirche*'s project with its unacceptable democratic, centralist and protectionist characteristics. Supporting Prussia and her reform proposal also promised to have a strong anti-revolutionary effect. Thus, in the summer of 1849, for the first time since the July Revolution of 1830, a significant reform of Germany's political organization appeared possible which fully conformed with British interests. This opportunity might have escaped the attention of Britain's diplomats,[23] but not Palmerston's, who had been dealing with German affairs since 1830.

It was the level of international relations which probably triggered Palmerston's open declaration of support for the 'Union' project. On 10 July 1849, Prussia yielded to heavy international pressure and signed peace preliminaries to halt the war in Schleswig, which had flared up again in the spring.[24] Once this irritation was removed, the benefits which would result from the establishment of a small-German state became more obvious. During the spring and summer of 1849, Palmerston and Russell expressed concern about the close cooperation between Austria and Russia which threatened another 'Holy Alliance'. Prussia's determination to steer her own course, though, alleviated these fears. 'There is evidently a close connection between Austria and Russia,' Palmerston informed the Prime Minister in April 1849, but 'we are so far better off than we have hitherto been, that there are only two powers linked together instead of three, as Prussia has broken off' and was no longer 'the kettle tied to the tail of her two great military neighbours.'[25]

The Austro-Russian agreement of May 1849 to cooperate in the defeat of the Hungarian revolutionaries made the need to balance the emerging autocratic block in central Europe appear even more pressing. On 30 June 1849 Palmerston explained to Viscount Normanby, Britain's ambassador to France, that after their victory in Hungary Russia and Austria would 'occupy a very strong military and political position.' It was 'not unnatural that in anticipation of such a contingency, and considering that there [were] points of difference between Prussia and Austria, the Prussian government should [...] endeavour upon defensive principles to place its military establishments upon an efficient footing; and it [was] probable that considerations of this kind ha[d] also led to the conclusion of the treaty of defensive alliance which ha[d] lately been signed between Prussia, Saxony and Hanover.'[26] Although the Foreign Secretary was wrong about the reason for Prussia's military preparations, which were caused by the revolution in Baden, and over-emphasized the defensive element of the 'Three Kings Alliance', this despatch indicates that Palmerston perceived the 'Union' as a means to counter Austro-Russian dominance. According to Anselm Doering-Manteuffel's interpretation, this attempt to allocate to Prussia the role of a liberal counterweight to the autocratic Austro-Russian alliance, constituted a major, if not the main, reason for Palmerston's decision to support the 'Union' plan.[27]

The first and most obvious asset of the 'Union' project was thus that it aimed at the creation of a German state under *Prussian* leadership. This not only conformed with British predilections expressed since the foundation of the *Zollverein* and more frequently since the autumn of 1848, but was particularly relevant *vis-à-vis* Austria's entanglements in Hungary and Italy, which suggested that an Austrian-led Germany could never play an independent role in Europe. 'The head of such a German league,' Palmerston argued in his despatch of 13 July, 'should not only be a substantively powerful state, but should also be heart and soul German; it should be biased by no foreign interests, and should be swayed by no foreign influences. [. . .] The larger proportion of the territories and races which formed that aggregate mass, which has been called the Austrian Empire, were not German, and therefore the government which ruled that aggregate mass, was bound in duty to be biased by interests foreign to, and possibly, in some cases, at variance with the interests of Germany.'[28]

This interpretation is further borne out by the observation that in his support of the 'Union' plan, Palmerston played down the importance of the proposed 'wider federation' between the planned 'Union' and the Austrian monarchy. In his despatch to Westmorland of 13 July, he approved a political alliance between the 'Union' and Austria merely 'for all purposes of common defence', while arguing that 'their joint action in cases in which their common interests might be concerned would probably not be the less sincere and effectual because the two bodies politic had mutually abstained from interfering with each other in regard to matters belonging to internal organization and to administrative details.' Prussia's rejected proposal of 9 May 1849, however, had gone much further towards creating an integrated Austro-German league. When, on 20 July, Baron Bunsen brought this document to Palmerston's attention, the reaction was telling. 'The tendency towards a German Union was laudable,' the Foreign Secretary replied; 'could it be realised, it would be beneficial and would entirely suit the policy of this country. But the plan to erect such a monster of an Empire [as proposed by Prussia on 9 May 1849] is another thing. That would be a public nuisance.'[29] Clearly, the 'Union' plan for Germany's reorganization was welcomed only as a strictly *kleindeutsch* and essentially anti-Austrian measure. By July 1849, through Schwarzenberg's intransigent opposition and Prussian determination, that was what it had become. In view of this and because of Austria's weakness in the summer of 1849,[30] Palmerston could indulge in a little optimism. 'I believe that all this will end in a closer union of the German powers (perhaps with the exception of Austria, Württemberg and Bavaria) under Prussia's patronage,' he told the French envoy in London on 22 July; 'perhaps this would be for the best. Germany, thus organised, will form a solid barrier between the great states of the continent.'[31]

Seen through British eyes, the 'Union' was not only a beneficial addition to the European states system, it also provided an agreeable answer to the question of how Germany was to be organized internally. Like the *Paulskirche* constitution, the 'Union' provided a response to the powerful popular desire for German unity. However, as the Prussian government had commendably 'entered upon a course [. . .] by which it aim[ed] at a middle point between despotism on the one hand and republicanism on the other,' as Palmerston explained to Normanby on 30 June 1849, the 'Union' differed from the rejected project of the National Assembly in a number of important respects. First, the 'Union' was a constitutional reform project initiated and implemented by legitimate monarchical governments and not by elected assemblies with their democratic tendencies. As such the 'Union' incorporated a strong federal element and avoided the centralism of the *Paulskirche*. 'The difference between this scheme and the plan proposed at Frankfort is obvious and great,' Palmerston explained in the despatch of 13 July. 'The constitution makers at Frankfort proposed a scheme which, if adopted, must have resulted in the extinction of all the separate sovereignties of Germany, and in the welding of all Germany into one general mass, to be governed by the Frankfort parliament [. . .] By the Prussian plan it would seem that separate nationalities would, to a certain degree, be preserved, while Prussia, retaining her position as a European power, would be the head of a German Confederation combining in its organization many of the advantages of unity without destroying those moral springs of action which derive their strength and elasticity from feelings of local nationality.' By now, with the last embers of the revolution in Baden almost stamped out, Palmerston's earlier apprehensions about the wide franchise of the 'Union's' electoral law had clearly abated.[32]

Yet another strong argument in favour of the 'Union' plan was its expected anti-revolutionary effect. It is important to remember that the last bastion of the German revolution, the fortress of Rastatt, did not fall until 23 July 1849. As has been shown, British observers had been unanimous in their alarmed condemnation of the forces of democracy. Prussia had greatly risen in their estimation, because of the role she played in the suppression of the *Reichsverfassungskampagne*. The usefulness of the 'Union' in this respect was commented on from a relatively early date. On 24 March 1849, Cowley sent Palmerston a sympathetic account of the first unofficial airing of the plan for Prussian leadership by the Prussian representative at Frankfurt. The smaller German states, he argued, 'have no means within themselves of repressing disorder, they must look for protection elsewhere.' Once the 'Union' plan had taken on a more concrete form, this notion resurfaced in British observations of Germany. 'Whatever may be thought of the policy of the

Prussian government and of the highly artificial system by which it proposes to construct the constitutional unity of Germany,' the *Times* grudgingly conceded on 7 June 1849, 'it can hardly admit of a doubt that [. . .] Prussia, alone has the ability and the power to surmount the dangers which threaten it.' On 2 July 1849, Westmorland referred to 'the altered position of many of the smaller German states, in consequence of the late revolutionary movements during which the inability of their governments to maintain their authority has been proved.' People therefore welcomed 'the formation and extension of the Prussian league by which the influence of their country will be increased and the better government of those states secured.' Ten days later, Bligh reported that the results which the Hanoverian court party desired from the recent negotiations at Berlin were 'the maintenance or re-establishment of public tranquillity, and the overthrow of the revolutionary party.'[33]

On 29 July 1849, Palmerston told Bunsen that there was nothing to be said against the idea of a German Empire but that nobody seemed capable of making it happen.[34] Having said that, the Foreign Secretary was certainly not indiscriminate in his endorsement of the 'idea of a German Empire'. His despatch of 13 July 1849 welcomed a monarchical, constitutional, Prussian-led, federal *Kleindeutschland* established from above. Such a Germany would be safe against popular revolution and democracy, promise liberal trade policies and play an independent, balancing role in Europe. A careful investigation of which features of the 'Union' project were attractive to the British government, and induced Palmerston to take the unusual step of publicly supporting Prussia's policy, thus yields an outline of the kind of united Germany their analysis of *Vormärz* and revolutionary Germany had led British diplomats and politicians to approve.

With Austria returning to Germany's political stage, though, the second half of Palmerston's half flippant, half wishful comment to Bunsen gained a painfully prophetic quality. Throughout July, August and September, British diplomats in Germany unanimously predicted that the 'Union' project was doomed to failure and viewed Prussia's course with little favour.[35] While Palmerston largely abstained from further interventions, the few instructions which he sent to his diplomats between his July despatch and Austria's formal re-establishment in German politics at the end of September 1849 suggest that he continued to believe that the 'Union' project ought to be given a chance.

The hopes for the political development in Germany expressed by Palmerston in July 1849 met with a first disappointment when

Westmorland communicated the substance of the Foreign Secretary's despatch to Count Brandenburg. The Prussian Minister-President was quick to notice the anti-Austrian slant of Palmerston's statement. Westmorland outlined Brandenburg's reply that the plan of a 'narrower and a wider federation' originally proposed by Gagern 'would be acceptable to Prussia and would offer the advantages observed by Your Lordship; but that the Prussian Government would not attempt to obtain it by driving Austria out of the connection she had maintained for centuries with Germany.' In spite of Brandenburg's caution, fierce opposition against Prussia's plans was forming. On 24 July 1849, Milbanke informed Palmerston of the great bitterness against Prussia which prevailed in Bavaria, a country which would sooner fight than fall under Prussian supremacy. This alarming report induced Palmerston to make a further cautious yet clear appeal for the 'Union' project. He instructed Milbanke to express 'the sincere regret with which Her Majesty's Government have observed the growing dissensions which prevail between the governments of Germany upon questions deeply affecting the feelings and interests of the German people, but Her Majesty's Government still hope that fuller explanations may lead to understandings and arrangements by which a due regard for the honour and the interests of the several states may be made compatible with an organization which may cement together for common purposes the different states into which the country is divided.'[36]

In the late summer of 1849, with the surrender of the main Hungarian army on 13 August and Schwarzenberg's continuing opposition to the 'Union' plan, it became clear that Palmerston's hopes would remain unfulfilled. On 9 August 1849, Bligh wrote to the Foreign Secretary that the 'Union' project 'must be a very imperfect one without the cordial co-operation of Austria, and that that co-operation [was] unattainable under the exclusive leadership of Prussia.' News from Vienna was hardly more promising. 'Austria will continue the policy of declining to concur in the plans of Prussia,' Ponsonby predicted on 28 August 1849. 'I have reason to believe,' the ambassador continued, 'that those Kings on whose support the Prussians appear to rely are not likely to side with Prussia, if things are actually pushed to the extremity of military contest.' Doubts about the feasibility of the 'Union' plan were also expressed by Howard at Berlin, Ward at Leipzig and Bligh at Hanover, who all also accused Prussia of selfish designs of 'aggrandizement'. The greatest doom-monger was the British envoy at Dresden. On 5 September, Forbes reported that the continued opposition of Bavaria and Württemberg meant that the 'Union' project had collapsed. 'Some other project must now be invented, which may afford a semblance of union in Germany,' he declared. 'With Austria now free to speak and act, it appears to me, that they must all soon return to something like the former Germanic Confederation.'[37]

All these pessimistic reports must have dampened Palmerston's hopes for a Germany in the 'Union' mould. In his readiness to return to the Austrian-dominated *status quo ante*, however, the envoy in Dresden had gone too far. 'I have to state that you should continue to observe attentively [. . .] all that passes upon the subject to which your despatch relates,' the Foreign Secretary reprimanded Forbes, 'but you should of course be careful, as you no doubt have been, not to say anything on these matters which could tend to convey the impression that Her Majesty's government have formed any opinions, or specific wishes in regard to these complicated matters. Her Majesty's government are sincerely desirous that the discussions now going on between the various German governments on the subject of the future organization of Germany should lead to that result which may be the best adapted to promote the welfare and prosperity of the German nation.' Although the tone of this instruction was markedly more guarded than that of Palmerston's July despatch, Britain was still perceived to be supporting the 'Union'. Count Rechberg, for instance, the Austrian envoy at Frankfurt, harboured a 'great suspicion that the policy of Great Britain [was] in favour of Prussian supremacy in Germany.'[38]

At the end of September 1849, the framework of German politics underwent a significant change which compromised two elements crucial for Palmerston's approval of the 'Union' project: the chance of the 'Union' being established while Austria was kept outside the German political arena and the expectation that the connection between the proposed 'Union' and Austria would be little more than a defensive alliance. On 30 September, after several weeks of negotiation, Austria and Prussia agreed to form a joint commission to take over, for a period of 7 months, the responsibilities of Archduke Johann, who had still been clinging on to a powerless office. The declared aim of this so-called 'Interim' was the maintenance of the German Confederation.[39] After 30 September, it was clear that Prussia would pursue the 'Union' project only within a wider constitutional framework which included Austria and would lead to a much closer integration than a mere international treaty. Besides, since Schwarzenberg had continually denied the legality of the 'Union' project, the 'Interim' was a major Prussian climbdown which further reduced the 'Union's' chances of success. While marking neither the end of the 'Union' project nor the re-establishment of the old German Diet, the setting up of the 'Interim' nevertheless concluded the brief period during which the British government cautiously supported Prussia's plan for the political reorganization of Germany.

'Complicated political manoeuvres . . . abortive in their results': the failure of the 'Union', October 1849–April 1850

The Prussian government and British observers of German politics differed sharply in assessing the consequences of the 'Interim'. Joseph von Radowitz, Frederick William IV's most influential adviser, hoped that placating Austria by joining an essentially *großdeutsch* supervisory commission with a (somewhat spurious) link to the old German Confederation would give Prussia more leeway to pursue her *kleindeutsch* ambitions.[40] Yet Britain's diplomats now rang the death knell for the 'Union' with renewed vigour. On 7 October 1849, the British chargé d'affaires at Stuttgart reported that Württemberg had officially declared its non-adherence to the 'Union' because of Austria's and Bavaria's continued opposition. Hanover and Saxony laid down their membership of the 'Union' on 20 October. The following week, Milbanke informed Palmerston that Bavaria, Württemberg, Hanover and Saxony were 'in confidential communication on the subject of the formation of a separate union among themselves.'[41] On 22 November 1849, Howard, Westmorland's chargé d'affaires, confirmed that Schwarzenberg had sent a despatch to Berlin insisting on the continued legal validity of the German arrangements of 1815 and 1820 and declaring their incompatibility with the 'Union' project. This view, Howard reminded Palmerston a week later, was shared by Russia. On the same day, Bligh predicted from Hanover that as public feeling there was 'so strongly against any scheme calculated [. . .] for the exclusive benefit and aggrandizement of Prussia, it [would] necessarily fall to the ground as relate[d] to Hanover.' Westmorland endorsed these bleak prognoses. 'I am afraid,' he wrote to Prince Albert on 8 December 1849, 'that at present the people still less than their governments, in some part of Germany, are inclined to join the Prussian League as is likely to be established, this is the case in Hanover, and, I am told, it is much the same in Saxony.'[42]

In view of these developments, British diplomats could not but condemn the decision of the Prussian government to continue with the 'Union' project by setting the elections for the constituent assembly for 15 January 1850. 'I would submit to you,' John Ward wrote to Bunsen on 16 October 1849, 'that *now* it is really against the King's interest to proceed with this plan.' One month later, Malet called it 'unwise on the part of Prussia to persist in a parliament at Erfurt, after assenting to the execution of her convention with Austria, which establish[ed] a central authority at Frankfort,' and prophesied 10 days later that 'each step made by Prussia in securing what seem[ed] her own separate interests, [would] have the effect of detaching more decidedly from her those governments which ha[d] in them any possible elements of independence.' He could not help fearing that the Erfurt parliament might trigger 'a very dangerous crisis'. Ponsonby shared Malet's alarm. 'The state of things with Prussia is very disagreeable,' he informed the Prime Minister on 27 November 1849. 'I am told that it is the fixed intention at Berlin to proceed with measures of which the result is to be the annexation to the monarchy of Prussia of some of the minor states of Germany. I have some reason to think that such an addition to the power of Prussia would be ill-seen in France.'[43]

It is interesting to note that during the phase of uncertainty which followed the establishment of the 'Interim', the General Act of Vienna of 1815 and the Final Act of 1820, which rarely featured in earlier British accounts, suddenly entered the discussion. As Schwarzenberg had consistently opposed the Prussian plan on the basis of its alleged violation of these two treaties, this development was an Austrian success. With the Prussian project failing and military conflict threatening between the Prussian and Austrian camps, a return to a modified German Confederation seemed a sensible option. After all, as the *Times* pointed out on 29 October 1849, 'the old Confederation, that worked, however imperfectly, for 30 years, owed its existence to the influence of French, Russian, and English diplomatists.' Milbanke criticized Prussia for aiming at 'so flagrant a violation of the federal Act as would be involved in the change of the present order of things in Germany by an assembly illegally constituted if the treaties of 1815 continue to have any value.' The *Times* took up the same idea. While dismissing the 'Union' as 'vague and dangerous theories', a leading article declared on 19 November 1849 that 'to renew the principles of the confederation of 1815, [. . .] and to cement that league by more active and popular measures for the union of the material interests of the whole nation, [was] therefore the primary interest of all Germany.' Ten days on, even the Cabinet considered 'whether the German Diet of Erfurt might be considered a violation of the treaties of 1815. Lord Palmerston thought not, but had not examined the question.'[44]

The question of the compatibility of the Erfurt parliament with the treaty of 1815 did not receive a clear answer. Instead, in his reply to Howard, who had reported the Russian government's conviction that

the 'Union' violated the Vienna treaty which was guaranteed by its signatory powers, Palmerston drew a distinction between signing and guaranteeing. Only a few specific clauses of the Vienna treaty were actually
guaranteed by the Great Powers, he informed Westmorland on 26
December 1849. 'The arrangements respecting the German Confederation were, it is true, guaranteed by the several German states forming
that Confederation,' the Foreign Secretary continued, 'but the guarantee so given by those states was only recorded by the other powers
[...] and those powers did not thereby become parties to that guarantee.'[45] While this cautious answer denied that Britain was treaty-bound
to intervene against the 'Union', it failed to affirm the legality of
Prussia's policy and noticeably lacked any expression of support for it.
This change of opinion among the makers of British foreign policy, who
no longer contradicted the diplomats' negative accounts, can also be
traced in Russell's letters to the Queen and Prince Albert. 'The affairs of
Germany are in a critical position,' he wrote on 29 November 1849;
'Austria will oppose anything which tends to aggrandize Prussia; Russia
will oppose anything which tends to free government; and France will
oppose anything which tends to strengthen Germany. Still these powers
might be disregarded were Germany united, but it is obvious that
Bavaria and Wirtemberg look to Austria and France for support, while
Hanover and Saxony will give a very faint assistance to the Prussian
League.' In a letter to the Prince, Russell was similarly gloomy about
Germany's political future. 'Some power must take the lead in these
changes,' he wrote on 1 December 1849. 'Austria is disqualified by her
Hungarian and Italian possessions, even were she disposed to adopt sincerely liberal views of government; Prussia seems to awaken so much
jealousy of her superiority that it is not probable she will be allowed
without war or revolution to sway the futures of Germany.'[46]

There was, however, one member of Britain's diplomatic corps who
even as late as December 1849 appeared to take a more positive view of
the 'Union' plan. In a long letter of 14 December 1849 to Prince Albert's
secretary, Cowley explained his views on Germany. While avoiding
actually mentioning the 'Union' project, Cowley, unlike the Prime
Minister and his colleagues in Stuttgart, Munich, Berlin, Hanover and
Vienna, seemed to have retained some optimism. 'Unless great faults
are committed by its advocates, such faults as marred their cause last
year,' he wrote, 'I am more inclined to believe than to doubt, that the
world will still see a free united, constitutional Germany. There wants
no other proof to show that it is the policy of England to encourage
such a work, than the efforts made by France and Russia to counteract

it.' A week later, Cowley wrote an official despatch expressing hopes for reformed political institutions to give greater cohesion to the German states.[47]

It is important to realize, though, that, as had been the case with his support for a cooperation between Prussia and the *Paulskirche* in late 1848, Cowley's pro-Erfurt leanings were at least partially motivated by anti-revolutionary considerations. Towards the end of 1849, the envoy at Frankfurt worried about what might happen if the popular desire for German unity were once again frustrated. With the *Reichsverfassungskampagne* still fresh in their memories, some British diplomats kept a wary eye on the danger of unrest. 'The revolutionary feeling,' Ponsonby wrote to Russell on 27 November 1849, 'is alive but not kicking.' Analysing the situation in Saxony, Ward distinguished three contending parties: the reactionary, the constitutional and the democratic party. The latter, he informed Palmerston on 2 January 1850, was 'far stronger in point of numbers than the other two. [. . .] Throughout the country, democratic principles are universally entertained by the middle of lower classes of society.' Cowley was equally impressed with the power of popular opinion. 'I see also,' he wrote in his letter to Meyer of 14 December 1849, 'that no government dares put forward a public document, which has not German unity as its basis, no newspaper ventures to raise any other standard, no orator takes upon himself the necessity to refute it.' In a long despatch of 22 December 1849, Cowley was more alarmist: 'the revolution of 1848 is checked but not stopped. The democratic party is held at bay, but is not crushed.' A short glance at Germany made clear, he argued, 'that tranquillity is alone maintained by the enormous forces which Austria and Prussia are enabled to dispose.' Liberal institutions, Cowley argued, would make internal peace less precarious, for they would win over to the side of order those politically active, liberal men who had hitherto against their will sided with the democrats. Only then could a broad front of the friends of proper constitutional freedom be formed to defeat those who were bent on terror and communism.[48]

Palmerston was unperturbed by the worries expressed by Cowley, Ward and Ponsonby. 'I am inclined to hope well for the tranquillity of Europe this year,' he wrote to the Prime Minister on 29 January 1850, 'and I do not feel as much alarm as some seem to do, of revolutionary outbursts in Germany.' Russell took these warnings more seriously. 'What Prussia intends I can tell as little as you,' he wrote to Ponsonby on the same day, 'but I conclude that the German unity party will not easily let her slip out of the engagements she has taken.' Two months later, when the failure of the Erfurt parliament had become apparent, Russell shared his concerns about Prussia with Prince Albert: 'I hope however she will be strong enough to keep down the republican spirit, which will probably arise upon the ruins of German unity.'[49] The demise of the 'Union' project thus raised the very fears of revolution which, in its auspicious days in the summer of 1849, its success had promised to allay. This highlights once again how, in the British perception of German politics since 1830, the question of improving Germany's political institutions was inextricably connected to preventing revolutionary outbursts with republican or democratic aims.

By early 1850, hardly any British observer still believed in Prussia's 'Union' project. 'It has long been clear to me,' Russell wrote to Prince Albert on 9 April 1850, 'that Prussia having to contend against the open hostility of Russia and Austria, the covert hostility of France and the jealousy of the principal German sovereigns [. . .] would not succeed.'[50] The session of the 'Union's' constituent assembly at Erfurt in March and April 1850 therefore attracted little attention and no support. With Bavaria, Württemberg, Saxony, Hanover and some smaller states refusing to hold elections for the Erfurt parliament and the turnout low in Oldenburg, Brunswick, and the Thuringian duchies, the authority of the Erfurt parliament was considerably diminished before it even assembled. Britain's diplomats agreed that nothing good could come of the parliament. 'It is expected here to be a complete failure,' Forbes reported from Dresden on 7 February 1850, and added that 'people already ridicule it.' Ward believed that 'the object of German unity [was] rather retarded than advanced by the formation of the Prussian nucleus.' Even after the opening of the Erfurt parliament, interest in it did not pick up. It 'does not appear likely to call forth much observation at present,' Cowley commented on 25 March 1850.[51] It was consequently considered sufficient to despatch the undistinguished vice-consul Robert Koch to Erfurt to cover the proceedings. Koch's reports were devoid of any interest and only attracted a characteristically brusque reprimand from Palmerston. Koch was instructed to 'enlarge his handwriting or to save himself the trouble of writing that which it is too much trouble to decipher.'[52]

Britain's published opinion was less homogenous in its coverage of the Erfurt project. In January 1850, the conservative *Fraser's Magazine* printed an article on the German question which argued that any Austrian influence in Germany 'serve[d] in reality to extend the dominion of Russia over Europe. There [could] be no question, but that such a result [was] alike hostile to the interests of the people in Germany,

Prussia and England.' This realization almost forced the author to end on an optimistic note: 'our anticipations of success go with the Prussian League, and constitutionally, with the parliament of Erfurt.' Three months later, Richard Monckton Milnes contributed a similarly encouraging article to the liberal *Edinburgh Review*. It may be concluded, he argued, 'that the political influence of Prussian predominance would not, in the long run, be adverse to the constitutional liberties of Germany.' The majority of the press, however, echoed the diplomats' disapproving attitude. The *Times*, in particular, which had argued as early as 22 October that the Erfurt parliament deserved to become the 'laughing-stock of Europe', now came out strongly in favour of Austria. Throughout the early months of 1850 the paper ran a string of leading articles criticizing the Erfurt plan. 'The greatness and union of the nation have nothing in common with the league formed by Prussia on the 26th of May,' the paper declared on 25 March 1850. 'That project has no claim to popular sympathy, and is a mere artificial attempt [. . .], calculated to produce the political suicide of Germany.' In its summary of the year's events, the 'Annual Register' probably came closest to catching the mood prevalent among Britain's diplomats: 'the ill-concealed ambition of the King of Prussia led to a series of complicated political manoeuvres which were abortive in their results, and which are as uninteresting to the reader as they are embarrassing to the historian.'[53]

The political developments in Germany since the agreement of the 'Interim' at the end of September 1849 left most British observers wearied, a little perplexed, but unexcited. 'I confess I do not see my way as to the future organization of Germany,' Russell told Prince Albert on 24 April 1850. 'If it is declared at Erfurt that Austria cannot by her constitution enter into the confederation, and at Vienna that she must enter with all her states, there appears no room for negotiation.' Since Palmerston furthermore believed that there was no serious risk of military conflict between the two camps, a general readiness prevailed calmly to watch Cowley's prognosis of 27 February 1850 come true. 'All the attempted coalitions among the German states seem to be on the eve of failure,' the envoy had written to Ponsonby, 'and I begin to think that ere long we shall have something like the Old Diet renewed.' On 30 April, one day after the closure of the Erfurt parliament, Cowley had the satisfaction of seeing his prophecy realized. 'Austria,' he reported, 'in her capacity of president of the ancient Diet, convokes a full meeting (Plenarversammlung) of that body, for the 10th of May next.'[54]

'On the German question,' the Prime Minister wrote, defending himself against Prince Albert's criticisms on 9 April 1850, 'the only opinion we have forwarded, and that some twelvemonth ago, was favourable to Prussia.'[55] While the Prince certainly welcomed that British support had been given to Prussia, rather than to the *Paulskirche* or Austria, Russell's implicit admission that a public endorsement of the Prussian course had only been given once, namely for a short period in the summer of 1849, vindicated Albert's complaints. It is because of its singularity and short duration, however, that Britain's support for a Prussian-led *Kleindeutschland* offers a valuable insight into British perceptions of the larger questions of political reform and national unity in Germany. The idea of a Prussian-led 'narrower federation' complemented by a loose 'wider federation' with Austria had found favour with British observers from the very beginning of the revolution. This plan appeared to offer the opportunity of creating a reformed, constitutional, small-German federation of monarchs which was immune against revolution and retained the German Confederation's essentially defensive European function.

In order to translate this basic inclination on the part of Britain into even as little as a public declaration of approval of the 'Union' project, two crucial conditions had to be met. First, the project had to be practically feasible, which meant that Prussia had to champion a plan which enjoyed the willing cooperation of a clear majority of the other German governments. Secondly, since Britain's interest in peace on the continent always remained paramount, Austria had to be either unwilling or unable to oppose her exclusion from Germany in any substantial way. Only for a short span of time, about a 'twelvemonth ago' as Lord John Russell put it somewhat inaccurately in April 1850, did these two conditions appear fulfilled, and then Britain expressed a 'favourable opinion'. When, in the autumn of 1849, Prussia's opportunity had passed and the forces of revolution had withered away, British politicians, diplomats and journalists showed little or no attachment to the 'Union' scheme and calmly acquiesced in the return to the devil they knew, the old German Confederation.

Austria's campaign to recover her role in Germany, 1848–51

The revolutions of 1848–9 threw the Austrian Empire into three concentric crises. With Vienna in the hands of the revolutionaries and the court forced to flee, the nerve-centre of the monarchy was out of the control of the imperial government. Beyond the capital, the existence of the Habsburgs' multinational empire was threatened by the revolutions which erupted amongst the peoples of Italy, Hungary, Bohemia, Croatia and Galicia. Thirdly, by the summer of 1849, the developments at Frankfurt, together with the policies pursued by the Prussian government, had all but destroyed the pre-eminent position which Austria had enjoyed in the German Confederation before 1848. In March 1849, after its original *großdeutsch* constitutional draft had been rejected by Schwarzenberg, the Frankfurt National Assembly passed an effectively *kleindeutsch* constitution and offered the imperial crown to the King of Prussia. Frederick William IV refused the *Paulskirche's* offer but pursued his own version of the *kleindeutsch* project. The success of any small-German plan, though, would have resulted in a reduction of Austria's formerly integral role within Germany to one more or less alongside her.

For the Austrian imperial government, to recover completely from these crises meant to reassert its authority in all three of these spheres. The governmental fightback began in earnest in November 1848 with the military reconquest of Vienna by Windisch-Grätz and the appointment of Prince Schwarzenberg as Minister-President. In March 1849 the new Emperor Francis Joseph decreed a unitary constitution for the entire empire. From then on, Austrian troops – partly assisted by Russian forces – were engaged in fighting in Italy and Hungary. On 22 August 1849, Venice, the last place in Italy to resist Austria, surrendered, and little more than a week later the Austrian commander-in-chief in Hungary declared the Hungarian 'rebellion' at an end.[56]

Reconquering Austria's political position in Germany required a more subtle approach. Within a few weeks of his coming to power, Schwarzenberg had clearly defined the aims of his German policy. On 27 November 1848 he reacted to the *Paulskirche's* 'greater-German' plans by making the 'Kremsier Declaration', in which he insisted that the Austrian Empire would continue to exist as a unitary state. One month later, in a letter to the Austrian plenipotentiary at Frankfurt, Schwarzenberg countered Gagern's plan of a 'narrower and a wider federation'. He declared that Austria as a 'German federal power' (*deutsche Bundesmacht*) had a right both to participate in the constitutional deliberations at Frankfurt and to be a part of the resultant body politic. In January 1849, Schwarzenberg expressed his aim more robustly: 'we won't be thrown out of Germany.'[57] Determined to recover or even enhance Austria's position in German politics, Schwarzenberg addressed three different questions. How should the Austrian Empire be linked with the German Confederation? Should Germany and the Austrian Empire form a tariff union? Lastly, by which institutions should a reorganized Germany be coordinated and governed? Thus, at various stages between the autumn of 1848 and the spring of 1851, the Austrian Minister-President pressed for the admission to the German Confederation of the entire Habsburg Empire, the formation of an Austro-German customs union and the re-establishment of a revised Diet of the German Confederation.[58] All three of these objectives attracted the lively interest of British observers.

'Endless German bickerings': Schwarzenberg's German policy, November 1848–September 1850

Throughout 1848 and most of 1849, Schwarzenberg's determination to restore Austria's position in Germany attracted few British comments. This was mainly due to the inaction of the Austrian government, which was pinned down by the revolutions in Vienna and the constituent nations of the Habsburg Empire. British observers simply had little on which to comment. Moreover, as has been outlined above, there was a broad consensus of opinion amongst British diplomats, shared by the Foreign Secretary, that Austria ought to be relieved of her German commitment and be left to reorganize her own affairs outside Germany. As was indicated by the scarcity of British despatches on German affairs to and from Vienna, throughout the revolution of 1848–9, British diplomats barely considered Austria a relevant player on the German stage.

In spite of this, Schwarzenberg's statements on Germany's future political organization did not go unnoticed. A fortnight after the 'Kremsier Declaration', Cowley sent Palmerston an analysis of Austria's options and laid his finger on an issue which would continue to cause Britain's objection to the Austrian course. 'If the various component parts of that diversified empire, the German provinces with the rest are united under one federal bond,' Cowley concluded from Schwarzenberg's statement, 'it is clear that the same provinces cannot enter into another league with Germany, nor does it appear possible, as it has been proposed by some, to admit the non-German [. . .] within the German federal state. [. . .] Many of the governments of Europe would not consent to see such an overwhelming power established in its very centre.' However, since the 'Kremsier Declaration' could be misread as indicating Schwarzenberg's acceptance of the Gagern-plan, widely favoured by British observers, there appeared to be no grounds for concern yet. 'Austria ought to be reconstituted as an empire by itself, separate and independent,' Palmerston confidently replied to Cowley on 18 December 1848, 'and its connection with the rest of Germany would best be determined by treaty arrangements to be settled after the reconstruction of the Austrian Empire is completed and when it shall be seen what shape the organization of Germany is to assume.'[59]

On 7 March 1849, Emperor Francis Joseph dissolved the imperial parliament, decreed a unitary constitution for the Austrian Empire and thereby sealed the fate of the last lingering *großdeutsch* hopes. Cowley welcomed this step and informed Palmerston on 15 March 1849 that Austria's new constitution was 'greatly admired on all sides.' The favourable impression created by Schwarzenberg's *coup d'état* was some-what marred, though, by the simultaneous statement with which the Austrian government reacted to the *kleindeutsch* decisions of the Frankfurt National Assembly. It made clear that Austria would not consent to her being in any way excluded from Germany. In a note to the Provisional Central Power dated 9 March 1849, Schwarzenberg demanded the admission of the entire Austrian Empire to a future German federation, the creation of a seven-member executive and the establishment of a federal chamber made up of deputies chosen by the chambers of the individual states. Cowley was baffled by this proposal, which ended all hopes that Austria would accept a solution based on the model of a 'narrower and a wider federation.' 'What will Europe, what above all will Russia say to the gigantic empire revealed in Schwarzenberg's note?' he asked Palmerston. A fortnight later, the envoy at Frankfurt expressed his disappointment in a letter to his col-league in Vienna. 'I think that Austria has been very unwise in her conduct towards Germany,' he wrote to Ponsonby on 30 March 1849. 'She ought to feel [. . .] that the less she has to do with *regenerated* Germany, the better for her.'[60]

The Foreign Office was left in no doubt that Austria was as im-placably opposed to Prussia's 'Union' project as she had been to the *kleindeutsch* plan proposed by the *Paulskirche*. On 22 May 1849, Arthur Charles Magenis, Ponsonby's chargé d'affaires, reported that Prussia's proposal had been 'at once rejected by this government on the ground that Austria formed a part of the German Confederation founded by the treaty of Vienna [. . .] and that she could not forgo the rights conferred on her by that act.' Two months later, Ponsonby reiterated that Austria would 'not yield the right she asserts, to be a German power.'[61] Considering the Foreign Secretary's support for the 'Union' and his op-position to an integrated Austro-German federation, British reactions to these reports were surprisingly calm. This equanimity probably re-sulted from two considerations. As long as the revolutions in Italy and Hungary had not been quelled, Schwarzenberg seemed little more than a paper tiger in German politics. For all his imperious declarations, he might helplessly have to watch Prussia succeed.[62] Secondly, Schwarzenberg's reliance on the legal framework of 1815 must have had a reassuring effect, for it appeared to limit Austria's ambitions to a proposition which was acceptable to Britain, namely the return to the *status quo ante* 1848. As will be seen later, both Britain and France insisted that the treaty of 1815 ruled out the creation of an integrated Austro-German Empire. With Austria's commitment to the arrangements of 1815 remaining strong – as was apparently proved by the establishment of the Prusso-Austrian 'Interim' in September 1849[63] – and Schwarzenberg's prolonged silence about the formation of the Austro-German league, even Austria's resurgence following her victories in Italy and Hungary did not provoke British worries.

Throughout the summer and autumn of 1849, Schwarzenberg appeared to lack both the means and the ideas to take effective steps against the 'Union' project. Since May 1849, the Austrian Minister-President had sent several protests to the Prussian government, culminating in his note of 28 November 1849, in which he once again asserted that the 'Union' plan threatened the treaties of 1815. He even went so far as to hint at Austria's preparedness to use military force. Schwarzenberg also encouraged Bavarian plans for an anti-Prussian 'Four Kings Alliance' of Bavaria, Saxony, Württemberg and Hanover in February 1850. However, this counter-league proved inconsequential and Schwarzenberg himself was unconvinced by its aims and prospects.[64] Having failed to stop Prussia from pursuing her 'Union' project by these means, Schwarzenberg resorted to a 'propaganda coup'[65] in the shape of the plan for an Austro-German tariff union, championed by the Austrian Minister of Commerce, Baron Bruck.

Karl Friedrich von Bruck, the son of a bookbinder from the Rhineland and a follower of the economic ideas of Friedrich, represented the city of Trieste in the *Paulskirche* before Schwarzenberg appointed him Minister of Commerce in November 1848.[66] Bruck aimed at the establishment of a customs union comprising Germany and the Austrian Empire. Protected by high tariffs, it was designed to withstand British competition. This vision of an economic world power both reflected and appealed to German nationalism, but to Schwarzenberg it offered the chance to regain some of the political initiative. While removing the commercial predominance which Prussia had acquired through the *Zollverein*, the Bruck plan also gave the German Confederation a boost by complementing its political level with a commercial one. It further suggested the complete admission of the Austrian Empire without immediately raising difficult political questions. Finally, it shrouded the added security risks arising from the admission of Venetia and Galicia, and sweetened this step with high commercial hopes.[67] On 26 October 1849, Schwarzenberg launched the Bruck plan by giving it a semi-official airing in the *Wiener Zeitung*. Two months later, the Austrian Minister of Commerce detailed his project in a memorandum for the German governments. On 26 January 1850, Schwarzenberg invited them to attend a congress in Frankfurt to discuss questions arising from the project of an Austro-German customs union.

The plan for an Austro-German *Mitteleuropa* united on the basis of protective tariffs was anathema to Britain's trading interests. It threatened to set up what John Ward later called 'an equivalent to a continental blockade against some of the leading articles of British manufactures.' Palmerston shared this view. When Bligh informed him on 8 February 1850 that the Hanoverian government 'seemed quite prepared to further' the Austrian project, the Foreign Secretary reacted with some vigour. 'The Customs tariffs to be proposed by the government of Vienna,' he replied on 19 February 1850, 'will probably be founded upon the principle of excessively high import duties [. . .] practically having the effect of greatly restricting foreign commerce.'[68] Cowley even came up with a practical measure to oppose the Austrian scheme. He had been approached by Friedrich von Blittersdorf, Baden's former Foreign Minister, who was now 'in some distress'. On 7 January 1850, Cowley informed Palmerston that he 'been indirectly asked whether [. . .] the British government would be disposed to employ him to write for them in the German papers.' Blittersdorf, Cowley explained, was a powerful writer, but there were doubts about 'his moral character when politically engaged.' These doubts cannot have weighed too heavily, for one month later Cowley argued that 'should the commercial congress proposed by Austria assemble at Frankfort [. . .] we should do well to secure him on our side, not only as a writer, but as a talker.' Palmerston was persuaded and instructed Cowley 'to make an arrangement for securing the services of Monsieur Blittersdorf upon reasonable terms.'[69]

While the opinions on the Bruck plan expressed by British observers were hostile, they treated it as a non-event and referred to it only occasionally. As early as 26 November 1849, Ward calmly predicted that 'the proposed commercial union between Austria and the Zollverein, except in some minor matters, [was] reserved for accomplishment to a more distant day than the Vienna officials appear[ed] to anticipate.' This prognosis seemed vindicated by what Baron Kübeck, the Austrian member of the 'Interim' commission, told Cowley in January 1850: 'the Austrian government hesitates at making any direct proposals for the moment, because there is a large class of persons embarked in commerce in Austria, who [. . .] oppose a change which they are afraid might be disastrous to them.' As was unsurprising given this halting approach, Austria, while making some headway at the South German courts, was soon bogged down by Prussia's delaying tactics. The planned customs conference never met. Bruck had to content himself with publishing a second, more detailed memorandum in June 1850, designed to influence the deliberations at the *Zollverein* conference which opened in Kassel on 7 July 1850. Cowley was unimpressed. 'The Memorandum itself,' he informed Palmerston on 15 July 1850, 'does not appear to have excited much attention.'[70]

The course which the British government pursued towards the Kassel conference further demonstrated their lack of concern about the Bruck plan. In order to win back the South German states which had been tempted by Austria's protectionist offer, and thus to prevent the dissolution of *Zollverein*, Prussia suggested a temporary rise of certain tariffs. Unmoved by the stratagem behind this decision, Britain reacted angrily. Palmerston instructed Howard to protest to the Prussian government. 'Great Britain has now abolished the duty on foreign corn, and has placed foreign shipping [. . .] upon a footing of perfect equality with British shipping,' he explained, 'and Her Majesty's government think they are fairly entitled to expect that the same principles of enlightened policy [. . .] shall be manifested in the regulations to be established by the Zoll Verein.' The British government's aim, Palmerston declared in the Commons on 15 July 1850, was simply to dissuade the German governments from increasing the tariffs.[71]

Thus, John Ward, who represented British interests at Kassel, advocated free trade and reciprocity. At the conference, he lectured the Prussian commissioner on the baneful economic consequences of increased duties, but also employed more direct means to prevent the adoption of higher tariffs. Ward knew that the *Zollverein* could only make decisions unanimously and that the commercially liberal northern states would never accept a protectionist tariff. Ward therefore encouraged Leipzig merchants to press for a high tariff, a demand which would produce a stalemate, leaving the tariffs unchanged. In a further attempt to scupper the proceedings, Ward asked Cowley to persuade Hesse-Kassel's fiercely anti-Prussian minister Hassenpflug to withdraw his commissioner and thereby to disable the conference. In the end Brunswick blocked the introduction of higher tariffs. Since no changes had been introduced and the Bruck plan had been shelved, both Prussia and Britain had reason to congratulate themselves at the outcome.[72] Instead of supporting the Prussian strategy which aimed at maintaining the *Zollverein* and preventing the formation of Bruck's *Mitteleuropa* with its far-reaching political and commercial consequences, Britain had employed every means at her disposal to stave off the imposition of tariffs inimical to her trading interests. Given that Austria's inability to make tariff concessions to the more free trading German states rendered Bruck's project stillborn, and with Prussia still bent on a 'Union' plan which British observers had long since considered a dangerous liability, this decision made sense both politically and commercially.

The third and most successful element of Schwarzenberg's German policy concerned the institutions through which the German states were to be given political cohesion and coordination. On 26 April 1850, Schwarzenberg invited the German governments to a conference at Frankfurt to reconstruct the old 'Federal Assembly' (*Bundesversammlung*). It opened on 10 May 1850, but as Prussia still clung to what was by then the carcass of the 'Union' project, only ten German states were represented.[73] On 2 September 1850, the Frankfurt conference constituted itself as the 'Federal Assembly' and assumed all the responsibilities of this body. Some British diplomats backed the course by which Schwarzenberg was trying to regain Austria's old rights as president of the Diet. On 30 April 1850, Ponsonby hoped that 'the Prussian government [might] quietly submit to that which there may be no means in its power to resist with success.' Four months later, Bligh ventured 'respectfully to suggest that the time may possibly have arrived when the influence of Her Majesty's government may be used indirectly at Berlin, if not directly at Frankfort as suggested by Prince Schwarzenberg.' On 1 September 1850, Forbes informed Palmerston of his conviction that the moment was not far distant, 'when Prussia must join Austria with regard to Germany.'[74] However, this support for the Austrian Minister-President by some of Britain's diplomats was significantly qualified by others who realized that Schwarzenberg's course was anything but unproblematic.

Throughout the summer and early autumn of 1850, Cowley, Ward and Milbanke raised several criticisms. On 21 May 1850, Cowley pointed out that the proceedings of Austria were '*strictly speaking* illegal. [. . .] The President has no power of convoking the plenum [. . .] and the plenum when convoked cannot deliberate or discuss as is now proposed by Austria.' In addition to attacking the illegality of the proceedings, Cowley further argued on 18 June 1850 that it was 'useless to discuss any project for a central government of Germany, whether provisional or permanent, while Prussia holds aloof.' Milbanke was similarly unimpressed with the Frankfurt meeting. 'As for the endless German bickerings, I am perfectly sick of them. [. . .] Your plenum at Frankfort has a strong appearance of dying of atrophy,' he wrote to Cowley on 21 June 1850. The simple truth was, as Palmerston informed Russell on 23 June 1850 that there was 'no existing authority at Frankfort acknowledged by the whole of Germany.' Further misgivings concerned the direction of Austria's policy. 'In its opposition to the revival of the old Diet,' Ward informed Palmerston on 3 June 1850, 'the Prussian government carries public opinion decidedly with it. The liberal party in Germany, though they have no great confidence in the Berlin cabinet, will naturally support it in a struggle against the return of that Austrian domination of Germany which was exercised for so many years through the instrumentality of the old Diet, with so unfortunate results.' Cowley also reminded Palmerston that the Federal Diet had been 'the main point of attack in the beginning of the revolution. Its proceedings had been reprobated by the liberal party in Germany for years before. It was looked upon as the incarnation of everything despotic, as the bar to the development of liberal institutions.'[75]

Palmerston decided to pursue a course *vis-à-vis* Austria's rump diet at Frankfurt which proved highly frustrating to Schwarzenberg. As it turned out, Britain had an important trump card to play. In July 1850, Count Buol, the Austrian envoy to Russia, paid a visit to Cowley, who assured him that Britain had a sincere interest in Austria's strength. 'Buol then said "Well! You will soon have an opportunity of proving this. [. . .] You can render an immense service to Austria by taking her part in this German question."' On the basis of this informal conversation, Cowley predicted to Palmerston on 18 August 1850 that 'in all probability the demand of recognising under the treaties of 1815 the Diet about to be opened by a part of Germany at Frankfort [would] shortly be made on Her Majesty's Government.'[76] Cowley was right: international recognition for the Frankfurt body turned out to be a major aim of Schwarzenberg's. On at least five further occasions between July and September 1850, the Austrian Minister-President urged Britain formally to recognize the Frankfurt assembly by accrediting a diplomatic representative.[77]

In order to make his demand for recognition of the Frankfurt body more difficult to refuse, Schwarzenberg cleverly linked it to an issue which was important to Palmerston: the Schleswig-Holstein conflict. In

January 1850, the Austro-Prussian 'Interim' commission had delegated Prussia to negotiate with Denmark. On 2 July 1850, after months of patient British mediation, Prussia concluded a peace treaty. Eighteen days later, however, very much to Palmerston's chagrin, Schwarzenberg insisted that this treaty be ratified by the 'Plenary Assembly' of the German Federal Diet. Schwarzenberg's reasoning soon became obvious. 'I received the assurance of his Highness,' Magenis informed Palmerston on 6 August 1850, 'that upon the constitution of the inner council [at Frankfurt], the first question to be submitted to their consideration would be the ratification of the treaty of the 2nd of July.' A fortnight later, Schwarzenberg was more direct. 'The best means to establish peace in the duchies,' he told Magenis, is 'to strengthen the organ of the German Confederation about to be established [. . .] by accrediting to it a diplomatic agent.'[78] There was a second connection between Austria's rump diet at Frankfurt and peace in Holstein. After the withdrawal of the Prussian troops, irregular Holstein forces continued their fight against Denmark. When, upon the reconstitution of the 'Federal Assembly', the Danish King applied for a 'federal intervention' to subdue the Holstein rebellion, the Frankfurt assembly agreed to consider the request. Schwarzenberg regularly reminded Magenis 'that the only means of arriving at the pacification of Holstein was through the German Confederation.' The newly-constituted diet would act, Schwarzenberg promised Magenis on 24 September 1850, 'but not until we are formally recognised by foreign powers.'[79]

Cowley's understanding of the question of formal recognition was clear. 'The object of Austria and her allies,' he wrote on 18 August 1850, 'is to coerce Prussia morally to submission, and no doubt if they could obtain of the powers of Europe to recognise them as the representatives of the German Confederation of 1815, a great part of their cause would be gained.'[80] There was no need for Cowley to worry. In spite of the skilful use of the Schleswig-Holstein argument, Palmerston stubbornly refused to oblige Schwarzenberg. On 30 September 1850, the Foreign Secretary repeated more or less verbatim what he had written to Schwarzenberg on two former occasions, namely that the British government would not formally accredit a diplomatic representative 'till it [could] see at Frankfort some regular organ which foreign governments may be justified in considering as permanently established by the general consent and concurrence of Germany.'[81] This demonstrates that even at the high price of delaying a settlement of the Schleswig-Holstein problem Palmerston refused to endorse a political reorganization of Germany which amounted to an Austrian triumph. To

Palmerston, restoring the *status quo ante* 1848 meant returning to an arrangement to which *all* German states, but above all Austria and Prussia, consented.

It is also noticeable that in his communications to the Austrian Minister-President, Palmerston did not refer to Cowley's and Ward's misgivings about returning to an unreformed Diet. Rather, the Foreign Secretary refused Schwarzenberg's demands purely on the basis of a strict interpretation of the stipulations of the 1815 treaty.[82] In view of a number of reports indicating Schwarzenberg's continued intention to push through Austria's complete admission to the German Confederation,[83] Palmerston's insistence on the stipulations of 1815 might well have been designed to prepare a powerful legal argument against Austria's plan. This interpretation is supported by an 'Addendum' to an anonymous Foreign Office memorandum filed among the despatches from Vienna. It calls the idea of admitting the entire Austrian Empire a principle 'to which Great Britain, as an acceding power to the General Treaty of the congress of Vienna ha[d] not assented', and asks how Britain could be expected 'to accredit a representative to such a confederation, at all events without some previous arrangement with respect to the novel principle now introduced.'[84]

British perceptions of Austria's policies to recover her position in Germany since September 1849 can thus be said to reflect a preference for a restoration of the *status quo ante* 1848. British observers were inimical to the creation of an Austro-German federation through the complete admission of the Austrian Empire to the German Confederation. They rejected Bruck's plans for a protectionist *Mitteleuropa* and Palmerston actively obstructed the reconstitution of the federal institution in a way which would replace the old Austro-Prussian dualism with an Austrian hegemony. As it turned out, the return to a consensual solution was to lead dangerously along the edge of the abyss.

Giving 'peaceful counsels': the Autumn crisis of 1850

On 8 November 1850, Prussian and Bavarian troops exchanged shots near the village of Bronzell in Hesse-Kassel. Although the skirmish was hardly a significant military encounter – allegedly only five Bavarian riflemen and one Prussian horse were wounded – it marked the climax of a serious crisis.[85] For a few weeks in the autumn of 1850, Germany stood on the brink of civil war. Britain watched the escalation of the Austro-Prussian struggle with a mixture of shocked disbelief and helpless apprehension. 'The Cabinet had nothing to resolve,' Sir John Hobhouse, the President of the Board of Control, wrote in his diary on

6 November 1850, 'but only to wait for events and give peaceful counsels.'[86] While this was a realistic description of Britain's actual means of
influencing the course of events in Germany, British observers nevertheless took a keen interest in the 'Autumn crisis' of 1850.[87]

The conflict between Prussia and Austria over the political organization of Germany had been simmering since Schwarzenberg's rejection
of the Prussian proposals in May 1849. In the autumn of 1850 two
smaller issues arose which acted as catalysts and exacerbated the
contest: yet another act of the interminable Schleswig-Holstein saga and
a constitutional crisis in Hesse-Kassel. On 2 September 1850, the King
of Denmark, unable to assert his authority in Holstein against the irregular German government there, applied to the Frankfurt assembly
for a federal intervention. The Prussian government understood that by
being seen to aid the crushing of the Holstein rebels, it would lose the
support of the liberal-national party for the 'Union' project. Nor was
it prepared implicitly to recognize the Austrian-dominated body at
Frankfurt by acquiescing in the federal intervention. Frederick William
IV, influenced by Radowitz, his newly-appointed Foreign Minister,
therefore continued in his refusal to sign the London Protocol, which
acknowledged the complete integrity of the Danish monarchy, and
declared he considered all resolutions of the Frankfurt assembly void.
He also threatened to oppose a federal intervention in Holstein by
military means. Undaunted, the Frankfurt assembly initiated the federal
intervention on 25 October 1850.

The second catalyst also arose from the 1848 revolution. In February
1850, the Elector of Hesse-Kassel replaced his liberal ministry, which
had adhered to the 'Union', with the notorious reactionary Ludwig
Hassenpflug. His illiberal, pro-Austrian course soon brought him into
conflict with the chamber, which countered the government's policies
by throwing out the budget. In September 1850, the Elector dissolved
the chamber, unconstitutionally decreed the budget and declared
martial law. These measures provoked the so-called 'Renitence', an
extraordinary act of constitutional loyalty by the chamber, the civil
service, the army and the courts of Hesse-Kassel. Faced with this united
opposition, the Elector appealed to the rump diet in Frankfurt which
eventually promised him support and prepared an intervention.[88]
Prussia's opposition to this decision was, if anything, even more uncompromising than in the case of Holstein. Besides defying the rump diet
and supporting the pro-'Union' forces of the 'Renitence', the Prussian
government was determined not to let the strategically important
military roads, which connected Rhenish Prussia with Berlin and ran
through Hesse-Kassel, fall into Austrian hands. Prussia vowed to prevent

the occupation of Hesse-Kassel by troops acting for the Frankfurt assembly, and began to mobilize her army.

For all the drama of the Holstein and Hesse-Kassel questions, British politicians and diplomats did not miss the wood for the trees. 'Behind the two questions of Holstein and Hesse, about which neither party very much cares, except with reference to ulterior matters,' Palmerston informed Russell in December 1850, 'lies the real question at issue and that is how the relative preponderance of Austria and Prussia as members of the German Confederation is to be adjusted.'[89] British observers correctly identified and concentrated on the national and European dimension of the 'Autumn crisis'. Their analyses of and comments on the two catalyst conflicts themselves nevertheless offer an illuminating perspective on British perceptions of German politics. They were not only determined by the specific political situation of the autumn of 1850 but reflect the importance of older criteria.

With regard to Prussia's stand towards the rebellion in Schleswig-Holstein, for instance, the Foreign Office unwaveringly stuck to its pro-Danish line, and showed no sympathy for Prussia's specific motivation. In late September 1850, Magenis tried to induce Schwarzenberg to intervene in Holstein by intimating that the Frankfurt assembly would be more likely to receive international acknowledgement if it proved its effectiveness. As he had done consistently since March 1848, Palmerston considered the suppression of the Holstein insurgency necessary because of its potentially catastrophic consequences. 'I think it highly probable,' he told Russell in October 1850, 'that if the Holsteiners do not leave off their aggressive operations, [. . .] a French army may be assembled in a threatening posture in the frontier of the Rhenish province, while the Russians are stationed in force on her Polish frontier.' The outcome threatened to be 'a fearful conflict attended with much disaster.' Less than a fortnight later, Palmerston told the Prime Minister that on this issue Prussia stood alone 'against all Europe' and that it 'would therefore be wise for her to get the Schleswig Holstein question settled as soon as possible and upon any fair terms.' Russell endorsed this view. 'I do not think it reasonable of the Prussians to pretend to interfere by force to prevent the execution of the treaty of July 2. Europe has a right to see it executed,' he wrote to Prince Albert on 4 November 1850. 'Prussia ought therefore rather to agree with Austria in this subject than to thwart her.' For Cowley, Prussia's conduct in this affair showed that she was 'unfit for the high station to which she aspired.'[90] These comments on the Holstein question showed clearly that Britain considered a policy which jeopardized European peace an unacceptable means to any end in German politics.

British diplomats' reactions to the Hesse-Kassel question in 1850 paralleled their attitude towards the 'Six Articles' in 1832 and indicate once more that after the failure of the 'Union', they were determined to see a faithful re-establishment of the political *status quo ante* 1848. British diplomats and politicians opposed both the Elector and the actions of the Austrian-led assembly in Frankfurt. On 18 September 1850, Cowley called the Elector's policy 'most unwarrantable' and hoped for the resignation of Hassenpflug, 'the prime mover of these, what may be termed ridiculous, if they do not prove unfortunate measures'. A fortnight later, Magenis informed Schwarzenberg of his regret that it was not 'in support of a worthier cause than that of Hesse-Kassel' that Austrian help was offered. When federal troops eventually entered Hessian territory, British opposition to this step was unequivocal. 'The march of the Bavarian army to put down the constitution in Hesse-Kassel,' Russell wrote to Palmerston on 29 October 1850, 'appears to me the greatest outrage which has been committed in Europe since the partition of Poland.' The Prime Minister and his Foreign Secretary decided to respond by making the intervention in the Electorate 'an additional reason for our non-recognition' of the Frankfurt assembly, as Russell put it on 16 November 1850. Two days later, Magenis was instructed to inform Schwarzenberg of this decision.[91]

As in 1832, the condemnation of the one party did not mean supporting the other.[92] The actual constitution which the Elector's renitent subjects were defending attracted much British criticism. In March 1850, Cowley had welcomed Hassenpflug's policy as 'the first attempt made on the part of one of the smaller German states to make head against the revolution of 1848, and to assert the principle of the rights of the sovereign.' On 8 September 1850 Cowley wrote about Hesse-Kassel that 'not even the states of Germany [could] be governed under such constitutions as the late revolution has been the means of producing', and called it 'far preferable to suspend constitutions altogether.' Ten days later, he explained that a decision by the Frankfurt assembly against the Elector would be 'a triumph for the democratical party.' In a similar vein, Forbes argued that Prussia's support for a constitution 'infinitely more liberal than the one which was abrogated at home, [could] not stand a moment's reflection' and would leave her 'with no other allies than the extreme liberal party, whose final aim is to overturn every government and throw Germany into all the miseries of anarchy and revolution.' Palmerston shared these views. He could not 'persuade himself,' he informed the Queen on 18 November 1850, when federal troops had occupied Hesse-Kassel, that 'rational and sound constitutional government [was] at present in danger in Germany.' The Hessian constitution apparently lacked both soundness and rationality.[93]

Rather than being caused by support for the Hessian constitution, British opposition to the federal measures – in 1850 as in 1832 – appears to have been motivated by the desire to maintain the original structure of the German Confederation. On 20 November 1850, Russell discussed the 'interference of the so-called Diet in Hesse' and concluded: 'it appears clear that the laws of the confederation does not justify it.'[94] This short passage contained the pith of the British government's reading of the Hesse-Kassel conflict. The Austrian-dominated 'so-called Diet' at Frankfurt did not comply with the stipulations of the 1815 treaty because it was not supported by all German states. The British government therefore refused to recognize this body and did not accept that it was authorized to initiate any federal measures, let alone the intervention in Hesse-Kassel, which violated federal law.[95] Their perception of the Hesse-Kassel conflict thus illustrates once again that British observers opposed the prospect of an Austrian-dominated German Diet riding roughshod over the independence of the German states guaranteed in 1815, and despatching troops at will to suppress opposition.[96]

In spite of their interest in the questions of Holstein and Hesse-Kassel, British observers of Germany naturally focused on the war which threatened between Prussia and Austria in the autumn of 1850. British politicians, diplomats and journalists unanimously condemned what they regarded as a dangerous and futile calamity. 'Great Britain as a European power must ever feel the liveliest interest in the welfare of Germany,' the Foreign Secretary wrote to Howard in Berlin on 5 November 1850, 'and must deeply deplore any events which would place the states of Germany in hostile conflict with each other.' In a private letter to Cowley of 22 November 1850, Palmerston was more candid. 'Enormous armies have been put into the field on both sides [. . .] without any intelligible question to fight about. [. . .] In the meanwhile Russia on the one side and France on the other [. . .] must be inwardly chuckling at seeing Germany come down in so short a time from *Einheit* to intense exasperation, and to the brink of civil war.' In a leading article on 14 November 1850 the *Times* expressed what was probably the national consensus. 'We as Englishmen [. . .] can take no sides in this unnatural and deplorable contest. Our enemy is the war itself.'[97]

As was the case with their perceptions of the conflicts in Holstein and Hesse-Kassel, the reasons for British opposition to a threatening Austro-

Prussian war, and the strategy which the Foreign Office adopted in order to prevent it, also indicated which political organization of Germany was favoured. In the first place, Russell and Palmerston rejected such a war as a dangerous folly which might lead to an invasion of Germany by French and Russian troops and thus upset the European system. However, if fighting were to break out after all, Palmerston wrote to Russell on 26 November 1850, 'the interests of England and, I should say, of Europe generally, would be that out of such a war Prussia should come unscathed, and if possible, enlarged and strengthened. For when in 1814 and 1815 the members of the Congress were dealing out territories like cards in a pack, it was a mistake not to have given Prussia a better hand.' If Prussian influence in Germany were increased 'through the consent of the other members of the Confederation,' Palmerston explained the following day, 'well and good, we would be glad of it, and Germany would be better for it.' He also believed that the 'sympathies of this nation would be in favour of Prussia, Protestant and liberal', but thought it impossible that Britain would prove either willing or able to assist her militarily.[98] However, since the Foreign Secretary feared that Prussia would be defeated by Austria and her allies, who – as Palmerston knew[99] – also enjoyed Russian backing, Britain's interest in Prussian strength meant that she had to try to preserve peace. Britain's German policy during the 'Autumn Crisis' thus aimed at preventing two things: war, which would result in an Austrian victory, and a Prussian defeat without war. The British government's 'peaceful counsels', which constituted its only political tool, were therefore carefully targeted to induce Prussia, to make concessions in order to defuse the situation and to persuade Austria to show moderation in victory.

By the autumn of 1850, Palmerston appears to have lost all his sympathy with the German powers in general and with Prussia's stubbornness in particular. 'The only thing which seems pretty clear,' he privately wrote to Cowley on 22 November 1850, 'is that all parties are more or less in the wrong. But Prussia seems to bear away the palm in this respect.' The Foreign Secretary repeated that the 'Union' would have been 'a very good European arrangement', but when it failed 'Prussia ought to have taken at once the only other possible course and to have come to an arrangement with Austria for reconstructing the German Confederation on the principle of the treaty of 1815.' In order to prevent Prussia's defeat by Austria and Russia and to prevail upon her to do what he believed she should have done more than a year before, Palmerston insisted that he would not support Prussian intransigence, and strongly advised her to yield. On 5 November 1850, Howard was instructed to tell Radowitz that Palmerston could not but feel 'that any reasonable concessions made by either party in the spirit of peace [. . .] would be highly honourable.' Cowley was also trying to bring about a *détente* by reminding Prussia 'that there is greater dishonour in pursuing a false course, than in relinquishing it,' as he wrote to Palmerston on 18 November 1850. When Howard informed him that the democratic party in Germany believed Britain would support Prussia in a war against Austria, Palmerston was quick to dash such hopes. On 26 November 1850, he instructed his envoy in Berlin 'to lose no opportunity of saying that [. . .] Her Majesty's government ha[d] held out to no party in Germany any hopes or expectation of support.' Nor was Radowitz given any encouragement when he went to England to conclude a defensive alliance in late November 1850.[100]

Palmerston did not share Queen Victoria's and Prince Albert's apprehensions that Austria was aiming to establish despotic government all over Germany. 'This notion,' he wrote to Russell in November 1850, 'has it seems to me been inspired into their minds by Bunsen and Stockmar and the German Unity Clique [. . .] in order to make out a plausible ground for Prussia.'[101] This did not mean, however, that Palmerston supported Austria. He proved alive to what Cowley called 'the danger of humiliating Prussia unnecessarily'[102] and made it clear that he would not recognize any political solution for Germany which was not endorsed by all German states. On 30 September 1850, he cuttingly reminded the Austrian Minister-President that it was 'impossible for anybody to shut their eyes to the fact this so much desired union has not yet been effected', and refused yet another of Schwarzenberg's demands for Britain's recognition of the Frankfurt assembly. A fortnight later, Cowley described how he had tried to dissuade the French envoy at Frankfurt from recognizing the rump diet by arguing that Palmerston's course was 'the only safe one'. On 15 October 1850, Palmerston refused the Austrian demand again and added quite superfluously that 'the Diet of the treaty of 1815 represented the whole of the states named in that treaty' and that it was 'a notorious fact that a portion of those states [. . . had] refused to send representatives to the present Frankfort Diet.' On 18 November 1850, the Foreign Secretary turned down yet another Austrian request for recognition and added the rump diet's policy in the Hesse-Kassel question to his list of grievances.[103]

On 2 November 1850, after it had become clear that Frederick William IV, by backing his moderate Minister-President Count Brandenburg, sought a compromise with Austria, the hawkish Radowitz resigned. Following Brandenburg's death on 6 November 1850, the *détente* was continued by Otto von Manteuffel. Malet warmly welcomed these developments. 'Common sense and sound interests of the country seem at length to be in a fair way prevailing both over the dogmas of theorists and revolutionary intrigue,' he wrote to Palmerston on 4 November 1850. Magenis was also quick to pick up on the changes in the Prussian cabinet. He told Schwarzenberg that 'the present government at Berlin, of which M. Manteuffel was the head, was sincerely desirous of maintaining peace, but that their difficulties would be greatly increased, if not rendered insurmountable, were moderation not shown.' He was happy to say, Magenis wrote to Palmerston on 12 November 1850, that he had found Schwarzenberg 'very moderate'.[104] On 29 November 1850, after almost a month of military stand-off, Manteuffel and Schwarzenberg drew up the 'Olmütz Agreement' which ended the crisis. The 'Union' project and the Frankfurt assembly were abandoned, and both parties agreed that Germany's new political organization was to be negotiated by all German states at 'Free Conferences' in Dresden. Prussia accepted the occupation of Hesse-Kassel and took joint steps with Austria for the pacification of Holstein.

It is difficult to gauge the extent to which British diplomacy helped to bring about the Olmütz compromise. There had been a strong anti-war party in Prussia all along, and Russia had been leaning heavily on Berlin. Besides, Schwarzenberg's relative moderation in victory was also influenced by domestic considerations. Nevertheless, according to Baron Meyendorff, the Russian envoy at Berlin and Schwarzenberg's adviser at Olmütz, Britain's de-escalating influence had been considerable. Indeed, he thought that the importance of Palmerston's 'ambiguous language' was of 'first rank'.[105] Irrespective of how it was brought about, though, the makers of Britain's foreign policy had reason to be pleased with the resolution of the Autumn Crisis. Russell was 'happy to see [. . .] that all look[ed] well for peace, on terms honourable to Prussia.' Palmerston's welcome was more guarded. 'We may trust that the arrangement agreed upon at Olmütz will for the present time at least secure peace,' he wrote to the Prime Minister, 'and we must hope that the conferences at Dresden will improve the organisation of Germany without violation of any treaty engagements.'[106] The Foreign Secretary's caution was justified. While complying with the British demands for a renegotiation of Germany's political bond by all German states, Schwarzenberg was determined to use the Dresden Conferences to bring about a revision of the German Confederation which would benefit Austria. Thus, while Prussia's defeat in war had been avoided, Austria's victory still threatened.

Towards a 'miserable consummation': the Dresden Conferences, 1850–1

Of all the plenipotentiaries attending the Dresden Conferences, which opened on 23 December 1850, the Austrian delegation was the best prepared. Prince Schwarzenberg and Count Buol-Schauenstein could rely on comprehensive instructions which clearly outlined Austria's objectives. While committed to the old federal constitution, they were aiming at modifications of the German Confederation which would strengthen the power of the executive and frustrate Prussian demands for parity. Keen to establish a Federal Diet dominated by Austria and her allies and able to stamp out opposition, the Austrian Minister-President pressed for three crucial changes: an executive commission of no more than five members; abolishing the veto of the smaller states; and facilitating federal interventions. Austria's dominant role in German politics was to be further buttressed by the admission of the entire Austrian Empire to the confederation, clearly outweighing Prussia. As soon became apparent, these aims were not only opposed by Prussia and the other German states but were also rejected by France, Britain and, eventually, Russia.[107]

In a letter to Russell of 27 November 1850, Palmerston strongly emphasized the importance of the settlement of 1815. The constitutional arrangements of Germany, he wrote, 'are part and parcel of the treaty of Vienna, to which all the great powers of Europe [. . .] were parties; and that treaty [. . .] is still the great title deed by which almost every state on the continent of Europe holds some essential rights or some important territory.'[108] By the end of 1850, the Foreign Secretary fully appreciated the usefulness of the 1815 treaty as a political tool. Throughout the summer and autumn he had used its stipulations to refuse the recognition of the rump diet at Frankfurt. Now, the legal framework provided by the Congress of Vienna proved helpful in three different ways. By offering the prospect of a stable and tested arrangement for Germany, the 1815 settlement gave Britain's German policy a clearer sense of direction. Secondly, because of their ring of legitimacy, demands based on the 1815 treaty were difficult for Austria to refuse. Finally, approaching the question of a revision of the German constitution as a signatory of the treaty of Vienna with a legal right to be consulted, gave the British government additional leverage. In view of these tactical advantages, Palmerston and Russell decided to formulate their attack on Schwarzenberg's plans for a revision of the federal executive and Austria's complete admission in strictly legal terms. It is not without irony that in 1851, Britain and France used the treaty of 1815, the very means of Schwarzenberg's victory in 1850, to scupper the plans he was pursuing at Dresden.

The 1815 argument was not, however, a panacea. A useful spanner to be thrown into the works of Schwarzenberg's reactionary plans, it also reduced the chances of liberal reform by suggesting a simple return to the *status quo ante*. In many ways, that was precisely what British observers wanted. The German Confederation should return to its stabilizing European role, guarantee the independence of its members and rest on their willing participation. In other respects, though, some British diplomats considered reforms necessary to prevent another 1848. On 7 October 1850, Cowley informed Palmerston of his concerns caused by 'the fixed determination which appears to animate the more con-siderable of the sovereigns to return to the ancient Diet.' He believed that if they went ahead with this plan there would be no tranquillity in Germany, for it would provide 'a handle of discontent for all the disaffected.' Russell agreed with Cowley's analysis. 'If the Emperor of Austria and the King of Prussia will seriously betake themselves to the work of reforming the confederation,' he wrote to the King of the Belgians on 5 December 1850, 'I shall have no fears for the peace of Europe or for the future welfare of the German states.' If, on the other hand, 'ambitious projects were to be indulged,' the Prime Minister pre-dicted 'sad scenes of anarchy and revolution.' On 16 December 1850, Palmerston, in a despatch to Lord Bloomfield, the British envoy at St Petersburg, also suggested that the German Confederation, while pro-viding a 'starting point and guide' for the Dresden Conferences, would benefit from 'considerable improvement'.[109]

It is important to remember in this context that Russell and Palmerston only advocated carefully measured reforms. The passage between the Scylla of despotism with its threat of triggering revolutions and the Charybdis of democracy seemed a narrow one indeed. The limits of their support for political change in Germany were strikingly illustrated by Russell's and Palmerston's reaction to the letter which Prince Albert sent to Frederick William IV in reply to the Radowitz mission. Having rejected Prussia's alliance offer, Albert merely assured the King that 'a Prussia prepared to come forward as the genuine pattern of constitutional monarchy on the continent and with unself-seeking patriotism to protect the constitutional union and foster the devel-opment of the states of Germany [. . . would] meet with England's sympathy and support.' Russell and Palmerston objected to the word 'support', and the Foreign Secretary added that Prussia should only be exhorted to maintain 'reasonable constitutional government in each separate state', and warned against creating the impression 'that the English public would take much interest in favour of a single parliament for all Germany, or for the maintenance of universal suffrage.'[110] Thus, wary of weakening their legal argument and worried that the Germans might overshoot the limits set by moderation, the British government refrained from advocating liberal reforms and concentrated on frustrating Schwarzenberg's ambitions.

'Nice people these Germans. One year the red republic, the next the Holy Alliance,' Mellish sarcastically wrote to Cowley on January 1851. 'Will the people swallow all the reactionary measures in progress? I am inclined to think they will.'[111] The Foreign Secretary and the Prime Minister shared Mellish's opinion. They were suspicious that Austria and Prussia were conniving to set up a reactionary machine to stamp out liberalism and threatening the independence of the separate German states. The Austrian plans for a stronger federal executive were perceived as a counter-revolutionary and centralizing scheme. Schwarzenberg had first suggested the establishment of a Prusso-Austrian executive to govern a federation including all Austrian provinces as part of a 'Six Point Programme' in July 1850. It was not until the Autumn Crisis, however, that Prussia accepted this idea. At the end of October 1850, Brandenburg and Schwarzenberg met at Warsaw to resolve the escalating crisis. Prussia offered to acquiesce in the complete admission of the Austrian Empire in return for a co-equal role in a strengthened Prusso-Austrian executive. Schwarzenberg, however, now felt strong enough to refuse. While still committed to a powerful executive, he demanded a more numerous body where Prussia could be outvoted.[112] What emerged from these negotiations fuelled Russell's darkest suspicions. 'We ought to have serious elucidation of the project, on which Austria and Prussia seem to concur, for the admission of Hungary, Croatia and Galicia into the Germanic Confederation,' he wrote to Palmerston on 18 November 1850. 'Coupled with the present proceedings in Hesse, this fact would seem to imply that Bavarian or Prussian troops may be called upon to put down constitutional resistance in Hungary, and Hungarian troops to suppress insurrections on the Rhine.'[113]

As soon as news of the Olmütz agreement reached London, Palmerston informed Vienna and Berlin of his misgivings about the planned revision of the federal constitution. On 3 December 1850, Magenis was instructed to remind Schwarzenberg that the German Confederation was 'the result and creation of a European treaty' and that therefore 'no important change [could] properly be made in the character and composition of the Confederation without the consent and concurrence of the powers who were parties to the treaty of Vienna of 1815.' Palmerston especially demanded information 'as to the degree, if any, of interference which is in any case proposed to be exercised by one over the other members of the Confederation, or by the aggregate body, in the internal affairs of any state belonging thereto, and in any differences which may arise between sovereigns and subjects.' Two months later, Russell's and Palmerston's concern for the independence of the separate German states found its way into the Queen's speech which mentioned the hope that 'the affairs of Germany may be arranged by mutual agreement in such a manner as to preserve the strength of the Confederation and to maintain the freedom of its separate states.' During the subsequent debate, the Prime Minister took this point still further. 'We hope that while that great Empire maintains its power, the various states that form the confederacy may not only preserve those constitutional liberties which they have now held for a long period of years, but that their institutions may be rendered still more favourable to liberty.'[114]

On 7 March 1851, in his next major despatch to Vienna, Palmerston repeated almost verbatim his query about the 'interference [...] in the internal affairs of any state' which he had raised in December 1850. By now, Schwarzenberg was seriously annoyed by Britain's persistence. 'This paragraph,' Magenis reported, 'appeared to particularly displease H[is] H[ighness].'[115] Schwarzenberg's irritability was probably caused by the problems he was encountering at Dresden, where Prussia and the other German states had stalled Austria's plans for a revision of the federal constitution. On 27 March 1851, Prussia torpedoed the Austrian scheme by calling upon the former members of the 'Union' to return to the old federal law. Thus, while any hopes of moderate liberal change which Russell or Palmerston may still have silently entertained were disappointed, they could congratulate themselves at seeing Austria's plans checked. This attitude was captured in the pragmatic despatch which Forbes wrote from Dresden on the day after the negotiations ended. 'These conferences from which at first so much was said to be expected, have now terminated with little good result, but they have postponed a war in Germany and have paved the way for the re-establishment of the Diet, which is now fully proved to be the only means of getting on at all.'[116]

For the makers of British foreign policy, Austria's attempt to create a powerful, central executive threatening to intervene in the internal affairs of the separate German states constituted only the intra-German dimension of the reactionary backlash. The plans for the admission of Austria's and Prussia's non-German provinces to the confederation and Russia's backing of this step gave rise to serious concerns in the field of international relations. Whenever, in the course of the previous 20 months, the distant spectre of an integrated Austro-German federation had been mentioned, British observers had rejected it as 'monstrous' or 'gigantic' but had not pursued the matter further. On the eve of the Dresden Conferences, however, with Austria resurgent and enjoying Russian support, Schwarzenberg's ambitions had to be taken more seriously. Russell and Palmerston saw in these plans the attempt both to destroy the European balance by forming an overpowering empire and to revive the Holy Alliance. Over the next few months these two fears featured prominently in British accounts.

Schwarzenberg's Austro-German Empire was portrayed as an aggressive state posing a threat to Europe. 'The whole mass might in the name of the Confederation be employed against France or Belgium,' Russell wrote to Palmerston on 18 November 1850. 'This is a serious matter [. . .] inconsistent with the balance of power in Europe.' On 5 March 1851, Britain's ambassador in St Petersburg, keen to undermine Russian support for Austria, told the Russian Foreign Minister Nesselrode that though 'the German Confederation had not, up to the present time, shown itself to be an aggressive body, still if it obtained such an accession of strength as was proposed, and if such men as Prince Schwarzenberg continued to direct the destinies of Austria, it was impossible to predict the consequences.' In his despatch to Vienna of 7 March 1851, Palmerston anticipated the possible incorporation of Denmark and the Netherlands into the German Confederation which would have the effect of 'deranging the general balance of power' and might lead 'to consequences of a very serious nature.' The next day, Palmerston described an even more aggressive scenario. 'The Diet,' he wrote to Westmorland, 'might by its own authority take into the confederation Courland, Livonia et cetera, because the people therein speak German.' Mellish joined in this scaremongering. 'Holland, Denmark and the German coasts of the North and the Baltic Sea, once united on a federal bond,' he wrote to Cowley on 19 March 1851, 'would give us an additional, decidedly inconvenient maritime neighbour.'[117]

Lord Bloomfield in St Petersburg regarded all this as part of a larger strategy. 'I become daily more confirmed in the impression,' he wrote to Palmerston on 26 November 1850, 'that the re-establishment of the principles of the Holy Alliance is the point at which Russian policy now aims.' On 10 January 1851, Bligh confirmed that Russia 'owing to the unhappy differences which ha[d] lately agitated Germans, exercise[d] predominant influence in Germany.' In April 1851, Bloomfield explained that Russia supported Schwarzenberg's project so consistently because she considered it 'the best means of carrying out her conservative policy [. . .] and because she hope[d] thereby to re-establish the good understanding and close alliance which had formerly existed between the three Northern powers.' In addition to disturbing the European balance of power, it was also feared that this development would complicate the Eastern Question. From Constantinople, Stratford Canning predicted that a revival of the Holy Alliance would encourage Russia to turn against Turkey. Such was the perceived magnitude of this threat to the European balance that in April 1851 even the House of Commons became aware of the problem. The Radical Thomas Anstey demanded to know if the government would insist on the 'maintenance of those stipulations of the Treaty of Vienna, by which the integrity of Germany and the liberty of Europe is guarded.' If Anstey, who was a notorious critic of Palmerston, had planned to embarrass the Foreign Secretary with this interpellation, he failed. Insisting on the arrangements of 1815 was exactly what the government had been doing since December 1850.[118]

In their efforts to prevent the admission of the entire Austrian Empire, Russell and Palmerston used the Final Act of the Congress of Vienna in two different ways. On the one hand, they employed a strictly legal argument based on the 1815 treaty. Palmerston first resorted to this step in his despatch of 3 December 1850, when he reminded Schwarzenberg and Manteuffel that the German Confederation formed 'part of the general settlement of Europe.' The principle on which the Germanic Confederation was based, he continued, 'was that [. . .] it should be a purely German body, and be composed of purely German elements.' The Foreign Secretary insisted that Austria's plans violated this principle and that this could only be done with the agreement of all contracting parties to the 1815 settlement. Palmerston reiterated this argument in his despatch to Magenis of 7 March 1851. 'The whole of these proposed arrangements are objectionable in principle, and likely to be injurious in their consequences,' he wrote. They could 'not consistently with the stipulations of the Vienna Treaty of 1815, be carried into effect without the concurrence of all the powers who are parties to that treaty.' This point was again repeated on 18 March 1851 in a despatch to all minor German courts. In order to add a little bite to his legal objections, Palmerston once more raised the question of international recognition. On 15 March 1851, Magenis bluntly told

Schwarzenberg that he did not believe that either Britain or France would recognize the confederation 'such as Austria and Prussia proposed to extend and found it.' When Schwarzenberg replied that patience was necessary, Magenis retorted that Schwarzenberg 'would require a larger dose of that quality [. . .] than what he had, to attain the end he proposed.'[119]

The other way in which Britain employed the 1815 treaty was to use it to unite the signatory powers France, Britain and eventually Russia to isolate Schwarzenberg. Russell suggested a coordinated effort as early as 18 November 1850. 'We ought to concert with France our policy on those continental affairs,' he wrote to the Foreign Secretary, for she was also keen to prevent 'the erection of a new Austro-German state.' This strategy succeeded, and on 20 February 1851, the British chargé d'affaires at Paris could report that the French government desired 'that some simultaneous step should be taken by England and France without delay for the purpose of preventing the realization of that project.' In his sustained attempts to dissuade Russia from backing Schwarzenberg, Palmerston again resorted to the legal argument, asking Nesselrode on 19 March 1851 if it was wise to allow Austria and Prussia 'to set aside and disregard the stipulations and engagements of the Treaty of Vienna [. . .] which forms the barrier of rights, which would arrest ambitious projects.' At the end of March 1851 the Tsar finally withdrew his support from Austria. Completely isolated, Schwarzenberg now silently dropped his plan. British diplomats sensed this change with satisfaction. 'I have done everything in a quiet way towards furthering your intentions as to the non entry of the Austrian provinces,' Westmorland wrote to Palmerston on 6 April 1851; 'my impression is most decidedly that it will not take place.' According to Manteuffel, he continued, 'a return to the Frankfurt Diet, without any additions to the German territory is the most likely solution.'[120]

British opposition to a strong federal executive and the admission to the German Confederation of all Austrian provinces was not, of course, motivated by a disinterested concern for the sanctity of treaties. There was doubt and even dissent amongst Britain's diplomatic establishment as to the validity of the legal argument.[121] Rather, the frequent references to the stipulations of the 1815 settlement were a means to an eminently political end. The British government was firmly opposed to Schwarzenberg's plans because ever since March 1849 and culminating at the Dresden Conferences, Austria had been seeking to create a Germany at odds with British interests.[122] Schwarzenberg pressed for the establishment of an Austro-German state of 70 million people which was considered incompatible with a peaceful and balanced European system. Even though Schwarzenberg's plans for a strengthened federal executive were designed to provide the means for an effective anti-revolutionary policy, they also suggested Austria's predominance in Germany and were perceived as a threat to the independence of the German states. The notion of a reactionary, Austrian-dominated, centralized Germany – possibly allied with Russia – was not only in itself anathema to Britain, but also carried the risk of triggering new revolutions. Lastly, the Austrian scheme included unacceptably protectionist commercial plans. British diplomats sent frequent reports on the tariff plans pursued at Dresden,[123] but rather than become active themselves, Palmerston and Russell relied on Prussia and the *Zollverein* to defeat these proposals. This was probably because protesting against the commercial arrangements of the German Confederation could not have been incorporated into Britain's strictly legalistic opposition to Schwarzenberg's plans.

Having witnessed the failure of both the Prussian 'Union' project and Schwarzenberg's plans, the first with regret, the second with relief, British observers were resigned to a return to the *status quo ante* in German politics. There was some disappointment at the 'miserable consummation' of the Dresden Conferences, as John Ward called the return to an unchanged German Diet in April 1851, but the British government did not hesitate to accept this outcome. After the potentially calamitous developments of the past three years, the old order – with its weak central element, its guarantee of the independence of the small German states, its crippling Austro-Prussian dualism, its anti-revolutionary consensus and the *Zollverein* holding out a promise of free trade – did not strike British observers as a disagreeable option. Thus, on 14 May 1851 Palmerston took a step which Schwarzenberg had probably concluded would never happen. Thirty-three months after he sent his first despatch from Frankfurt, Lord Cowley was accredited to the German Diet, which was thus formally recognized by Britain.[124]

4
British Perceptions of the 'Reaction' and the Struggle for Federal Reform, 1851–63

During the dozen years between the Dresden Conferences and the final failure of the attempts at federal reform, the issues confronting Britain's foreign political establishment were increasingly closely linked to German politics. Apart from the Indian Mutiny and the American Civil War, all major foreign political challenges faced by Britain from 1851 to 1863 had discernible German dimensions which will be explored more fully below. During the Crimean War the German Confederation was an important arena for diplomatic manoeuvre: the Foreign Office made every effort to enlist Austria, Prussia and the smaller German states as allies against Russia. The Italian war of 1859 not only saw Austria directly involved in the fighting but was contained by the attitude taken by the other German powers. Germany's importance – both as a vulnerable target and as a potential ally – was further highlighted by the Anglo-French antagonism of the late 1850s which culminated in the invasion scare of 1859. Even the Cobden–Chevalier Treaty of the following year, which went some way towards mending relations with France, was found to have a powerful impact on German politics. When Prussia followed Britain's example and concluded a commercial agreement with France, a conflict erupted amongst the members of the *Zollverein* in which Britain openly took sides. German powers were directly involved in the suppression of the Polish rising of 1863 and in the rumblings in Schleswig-Holstein. On both issues the British public and – in a somewhat more differentiated way – Britain's foreign political establishment held strong views. Thus, between 1851 and 1863 German politics consistently featured on Britain's foreign political agenda.

After three years of revolutionary upheaval, Germany was heading for an era of relative political calm. During the so-called 'Reaction' period governmental policy was guided by the 'attempt firmly to re-establish the conservative, bureaucratic and authoritarian state of order and to shield it from all kinds of liberalism and all the tendencies which had led to the revolution.'[1] With the liberal-national opposition kept in check by an elaborate police network, the governments of the 1850s presided over a decade of relative uneventfulness in the domestic sphere. The 'Reaction' took different forms in the various German states. The Prussian constitution remained in force but the Manteuffel ministry could rely on large conservative majorities to support an authoritarian course. Austria turned back the clock. Having revoked its constitution, the Habsburg Empire entered a period of neo-absolutism. Under Minister Alexander Bach, it became synonymous with police informers, centralization and governmental control of religious and educational matters. In some of the smaller German states the 'Reaction' took even harsher forms.[2]

Between the re-establishment of the Federal Diet in 1851 and the beginning of the Prussian regency seven years later, the liberal-national movement played a more subdued role. The opposition found it difficult openly and vigorously to address the questions of political reform and national unity which had dominated the public discussion of German politics since 1830. Nevertheless, the period was less rigid and witnessed more political movement than is suggested by the monolithic label 'Age of Reaction'. There were significant differences between – and even within – the different German states in the degree to which reactionary forces could assert themselves. Because of its strong liberal tradition, 'a real reaction in Baden was unthinkable.'[3] In Bavaria, a more conciliatory system of governmental cooperation with the chamber continued until the mid-1850s. The political complexion of the Prussian Rhine-Province differed markedly from that of Prussia's East Elbian heartlands. Austria's Neo-Absolutism was not merely backward-looking but also effected a partial modernization.[4] The limits of the 'Reaction' were further revealed by the re-emergence of oppositional voices after 1854. At public gatherings, celebrations and during Carnival festivities, in newspaper articles, pamphlets and several parliamentary motions dissatisfaction was expressed with the political situation in the states and particularly with Germany's federal institutions.[5]

This ambivalence, which was reflected by the unevenness and incompleteness of the 'Reaction' in the different states, can also be found at its institutional centre, the re-established Federal Diet. On the one hand, the unreformed diet served as the basis for a nation-wide policy of oppressive legislation and illiberal interference. Federal troops were stationed in Frankfurt, Hamburg, Electoral Hesse and Holstein. The diet annulled the basic rights granted in 1848/9. A 'Reactionary Committee' (*Reaktionsausschuß*) was set up to monitor if individual states complied with federal law. Constitutional revisions were imposed in no fewer than nine states. In 1854 the diet restricted the liberties of the press and of free association. Although some of these measures could not be effectively implemented and the federal system of political repression of the 1850s lacked the stringency of the Metternich era,[6] it is this oppressive dimension which has come to dominate perceptions of a 'decade of unbridled police-state activity'.[7] On the other hand, recent research has highlighted a different aspect. From the Dresden conferences of 1850/1 onwards, leading politicians and diplomats mainly from the German Middle States were engaged in an ongoing debate about federal reform. Numerous memoranda and governmental initiatives reflected an appreciation of the sources of popular discontent, addressing core issues such as the weak executive, the absence of a representative body and the need for a federal court.[8]

Like much of the later literature on the 1850s, though, British observers of the time failed to appreciate the ambivalence of a decade between reaction and reform. Two things above all appear to have caused British diplomats and politicians to produce rather clichéd and prejudiced appraisals of German politics during those years: an overestimation of the success of reactionary policies; and the impact of the Crimean War, which conditioned British perceptions of Germany between 1853 and 1856. It was therefore not before 1858, when the end of Frederick William IV's reign ushered in a new departure in Prussia and Germany, that British observers returned to giving more illuminating analyses of the process of political reform in the German Confederation.

In August 1851, Cowley sent Palmerston a despatch outlining a truly awesome course of reactionary regression on which the two German Great Powers seemed to have embarked. Prussia and Austria planned 'nothing but the annihilation [. . .] of the development of constitutional institutions which they [could] not characterise by any other term than the progress of democracy. The object therefore of the two governments [. . . was], by employing a large military force, by depriving parliamentary assemblies of any power, by restricting the press and such like measures, to enable the governments to act in defiance of public opinion.' A month later, the envoy was stunned by the 'reactionary drama now enacting in Germany.' German constitutionalism was a sham, Milbanke observed in July 1856. 'The notion that parliamentary government is the basis of these so-called constitutional countries is altogether erroneous,' he explained. 'Most of the ministers are mere promoted employés whose education has been confined to administrative matter [. . .] Whatever authority they possess, [. . .] is derived entirely from the sovereign, and they are more powerful in proportion as they succeed in identifying themselves with his will and opinion.'[9]

Generally, British diplomats seemed agreed as to the efficacy of this policy in quelling the forces of opposition. 'The last three years have served to establish the ascendancy of the reactionary party so completely,' Ward reported in February 1853, 'that the democrats have retired completely from the political field, and the middle party [. . .] have also come to the conclusion that they can do nothing.' At the height of the Crimean War, Malet dampened Clarendon's hopes for Anglophile liberals. 'As to what is called the national party in Germany,' he informed the Foreign Secretary in July 1855, 'you can have no idea how low it has fallen. [. . .] In short the party is for the present moment utterly down, and as such gives scarcely a sign of life.' Clarendon had to agree: 'the people of Germany are too submissive, and their governments are too watchful and brutal to permit of opinions being resolved into acts.' Milbanke, while noting 'opposition tendencies in nearly all classes,' shared the Foreign Secretary's view. 'Owing to the total absence of all organisation it [would] in all probability be long before they assume[d] an aspect of danger to the present unsatisfactory system of government.'[10]

Even more than by their exaggerated belief in the effectiveness of reactionary policies, British observers' appreciation of the reforming potential of the 1850s was distorted by the conflict with Russia.[11] 'When once the war begins,' Clarendon predicted to his envoy in Berlin in February 1854, 'whoever is not with us will be against us.'[12] He bitterly condemned Prussia's strict neutrality and took the unusual step of urging the other German governments to follow the lead of the Austrian government which was leaning towards Britain and France. The Foreign Secretary told Malet in March 1855 that 'now would be a really good moment for the German Courts to ally themselves with Austria instead of being dragged through the mud by such a double-dealing treacherous cowardly court [. . .] as that of Prussia.' In the following year Clarendon blamed 'the craven King of Prussia' for the continued suffering in the Crimea. Prussia was merely 'a Russian province' and he accused Frederick William of 'neutralising Germany in the interest of his suzerain.'[13]

Because of this attitude British diplomats and politicians found it practically impossible calmly to assess the moves by the neutral German powers. Unfortunately, the governments of the German Middle States, whose dynastic links with Russia and lack of interest in the Eastern Question led them to remain strictly neutral, were also the most active proponents of federal reform. In May 1854, Baron Beust, Saxony's Foreign Minister, who had been airing ideas about federal reform and the enhancement of the role of the smaller German states since June 1853, organized a conference of seven of them.[14] The Middle States' concern that by accepting Austria's and Prussia's invitation to join their recently concluded alliance they could jeopardize their neutrality certainly helped Beust to persuade his colleagues to attend the conference at Bamberg. However, the neutrality issue did not completely eclipse the original reform agenda and it was understood that the Bamberg Conference was to be the first of a series of meetings of the governments of the 'Third Germany'.[15]

British diplomats and politicians brushed all this aside in one ill-tempered Russophobe sweep. 'The representatives of the secondary states felt that while they put forward the pretext of asserting independence, and the right of the confederation,' Malet explained in June 1854, 'they were in reality serving in an underhand way the very unpopular cause of Russia.'[16] The Foreign Secretary's reaction was more forceful. 'I have seldom read anything with greater disgust than the state paper proposed by M. von der Pfordten [the Bavarian Minister-President] for the Bamberg Conference, but it was worthy of the man and the occasion and the people for whom it was intended,' Clarendon exploded in a letter to Milbanke of 21 June 1854. 'The idolatry of Russia [. . .] has made these little powers blind to their own true interests [. . .] but *it will be remembered*, and in the event of a general war being followed by a general congress the position of Bavaria may not be improved. You can *intimate this* to M. de Pfordten in any way you think best.' Similarly dark warnings were despatched to Saxony and Hanover. Forbes was instructed to inform Beust that Bamberg would be 'remembered hereafter, and [would] be found an impediment to that greater freedom of action which the minor German powers are naturally desirous of obtaining.' Six days later the Hanoverian government was sent the ominous reminder that the 'policy pursued by those [small German] courts at the present moment [might] hereafter be of vital importance to them.'[17] By October, these feelings had been cast into verse and – via the columns of the *Times* – afforded some grim satisfaction to a wide audience:

> With strings of apron basely tied,
> By means of sister or of bride
> Are those mere satraps of the Czar
> To their Imperial Master's Car.[18]

The preoccupation with the Crimean War which conditioned British observers' reactions to the Bamberg initiative also coloured their perceptions of the popular discontent with Germany's political status quo which re-emerged after 1854. Incited by the war against 'despotic' Russia and with the reactionary pressure weakened by Austria's and Prussia's disagreement over their policies *vis-à-vis* the Crimean War, democrats and moderate liberals once again dared to voice criticisms publicly. In 1855 and 1856 opposition deputies in Württemberg, the Grand-Duchy of Hesse, Bavaria, Saxe-Coburg-Gotha and Baden introduced motions calling for federal reform. Issues of reform and national unity were also raised in newspapers and pamphlets.[19]

Against the background of the attitude of the German governments, which seemed 'all Russian to the backbone',[20] this movement of opposition greatly interested the Foreign Office. Promising reports had been coming in for some time. 'There can be [. . .] no mistake as to the fact that public opinion throughout Germany is far from favourable to Russia,' Milbanke wrote in June 1853. Forbes, Ward and Jerningham endorsed this observation.[21] Consequently, in July 1855 Clarendon informed Malet and Milbanke of his desire to 'get on better terms with the national party in Germany, which though cowed and torpid still exists and is rather acquiring than losing vitality. [. . .] I would not disguise that we have an immediate and direct English interest in this,' he added, 'because Germany by its geographical position must be the principal bulwark against Russian aggression.'[22] The keenest observer of the anti-Russian effect of political reform in Germany was Consul-General Ward at Leipzig. The motion demanding federal reform recently discussed in the Württemberg chamber pointed 'in the right direction,' he argued in July 1855, for thereby 'the influence of Russia over the dynasties will be effectively paralysed.' A few days later he insisted that it could 'not be repeated too often that the constitutional party in Prussia and the smaller states are the true allies of the Western Powers in the present war.' Loftus in Berlin equally believed that the cry for reform 'certainly affords the best and only means of combating the advance of Russian influence.'[23]

On 23 August 1855 Ward drew Clarendon's attention to a pamphlet by the democrat Gustav Diezel which aimed 'to rouse the liberals of all shades of opinion into a union against Russia, and for the specific purpose of gradually drawing the German governments into an effective alliance with the Western Powers.' The Foreign Secretary was delighted. 'The importance of checking and if possible destroying the influence of Russia in Germany cannot be exaggerated,' he replied to Ward. 'Her Majesty's Government look with sincere satisfaction upon [...] the writings of men like M. Diezel.' Clarendon immediately informed all his diplomats in Germany about this 'very able pamphlet' and invited comments on the 'influence, if any, which it may be expected to have on the general feelings and opinions of the various classes of society.'[24] Bligh's, Malet's, Forbes's, Loftus's and Milbanke's analyses of the German political scene,[25] however, dashed the Foreign Secretary's optimism. Impressed by the power of the 'Reaction', Britain's diplomats emphasized the strength of the governments, the efficiency of the police, widespread political lethargy and the lack of suitable opposition leaders. Liberal reform of Germany's political system, Ward wearily concluded in November 1855, could only be achieved by unacceptable means. 'There is little chance of such a step being taken,' he wrote to the Foreign Secretary, 'until some sort of revolutionary movement shall show itself.'[26]

Towards the end of the 1850s, though, a number of developments took place in Prussia, amongst German liberalism, and in international politics which ended the stalemate of the years since 1851. A 'New Era' was believed to be dawning. As it turned out, neither Britain's condemnation of neutral Prussia, nor her championing of Austria's leadership in Germany, nor the unprecedented British sympathies for German democrats outlasted the specific constellation of the Crimean War.[27] When the question of reforming the federal institutions was again thrown open, British politicians, diplomats and journalists easily picked up the thread. At first, British observers' perceptions of the developments after 1858 led them strongly to endorse Prussia's course. At a later stage, however, changes took place which not only removed the basis of Britain's support for Prussia but even made them despair of the possibility of political progress in Germany altogether.

Suggesting Prussian leadership: perceptions of Germany, 1858–61

British perceptions of the developments between 1858 and 1861, which reopened the questions of political reform and national unity, did not merely register that new dynamism had been injected into German politics. Rather, Prussia's 'New Era', Germany's response to the challenge posed by Louis Napoleon's foreign policy and the reawakening of the German liberal-national movement confirmed Britain's pro-Prussian leanings. British politicians and diplomats reacted favourably to Prussia's promise of constitutional progress and to what they regarded as her prudent response to France in 1859. They also proved hopeful about Prussia's potential for giving greater union to Germany and her ability to lead and control the groundswell of national feeling. By 1861, more than a decade after the failure of the 'Union' plan, a majority of British observers once again believed that the time was ripe for Prussia to lead Germany.

'A constitutional, intelligent, progressive and peaceful state': Prussia during the 'New Era', 1858–61

Having deputized for his mentally unstable brother for almost a year, Prince William of Prussia formally assumed the full powers of regent on 9 October 1858. Frederick William IV's ultra-conservative court camarilla, which backed Minister-President Manteuffel's reactionary government, had staved off the inevitable for as long as possible. Now they saw their worst fears realized. Interior Minister Ferdinand von Westphalen, the fiercest reactionary in the cabinet, was dismissed immediately. The rest of the ministry had to go within weeks. Against his brother's express advice the regent swore an oath on the constitution. Less than a fortnight later, Prince William appointed a new liberal-conservative cabinet headed by Prince Anton von Hohenzollern-Sigmaringen and Rudolf von Auerswald. On 8 November 1858, in a speech to the new ministry, the regent expounded the programme of what was soon perceived to be a 'New Era' in Prussian politics. By outlining a break with the reactionaries' educational and ecclesiastical policies, criticizing their over-reliance on Russia and Austria in foreign politics and promising 'moral conquests' in Germany, William delighted liberal and national circles in Prussia and beyond. The years of reaction seemed over.[28]

In Britain, the transition of power from Frederick William IV to his brother was watched with unusually keen interest. The marriage of the Queen's eldest daughter to Prince William's son, the Prussian heir presumptive, in January 1858 had met with a lively and favourable public reaction. Moreover, the Orsini affair, rumours about Napoleon III's Italian ambitions and the rapid expansion of the French navy caused a marked deterioration of Anglo-French relations in 1858. Thus, on 1 October, when the struggle between Prussia's reactionary camarilla and

Prince William was still undecided, the *Times* commented that 'no continental monarchy ha[d] now greater interest for the English people
than that of Prussia.'[29] British reactions to the political change in Prussia
were overwhelmingly favourable. The personality of the regent and the
steps taken by Prussia's new ministry were believed to augur well for
the future. British observers considered this development important
both for Anglo-Prussian relations and Prussia's role within the German
Confederation.

British diplomats in Berlin quickly sensed that the regency heralded a
significant departure in Prussian politics. On 23 October 1858, Augustus
Paget, Britain's chargé d'affaires, reported that there were reasons to hope
'that the constitution [was] no longer to remain the dead letter which it
ha[d] been almost since the period of its creation.' This optimism was
further fuelled by Paget's favourable view of the regent's personality and
by the new cabinet. On 6 November 1858 he applauded 'the honesty,
high principles and firmness of the Prince Regent' and called William's
popularity 'a just tribute' to his 'eminent qualities and virtues.'[30] The
new ministry, which Paget discussed on 13 November 1858, looked
equally attractive: Prince Hohenzollern-Sigmaringen professed 'constitutional and liberal principles,' Schleinitz, the Foreign Minister, was
'moderately liberal,' while Auerswald was 'a decided liberal [. . .] but
moderate and practical in his views.' Moreover, the welcome change in
Prussian politics did not only extend to the sovereign and the executive
but also to the legislature. In November 1858 elections were held for the
Prussian diet. They 'appear to be going on very satisfactorily,' Paget
informed the Foreign Secretary, Malmesbury, on 18 November. 'By this
I mean that men of moderate views will probably be elected [. . .]. The
whole thing appears to have got into a steady constitutional course,
there is no improper interference, and every one seems satisfied and
hopeful for the future.' Paget's prediction proved correct. Without
governmental support the Conservatives suffered a devastating defeat,
and a large majority of moderate liberals was returned. Shortly after-
wards, the Prussian ministry relaxed press censorship. This step, Lord
Bloomfield, the British envoy at Berlin, reported on 18 December 1858,
was received 'with much satisfaction on the part of the public.'[31]

In Britain, the encouraging news from Berlin did not fall on deaf ears.
Only a few weeks into the Prussian regency, there was broad agreement
that Prussia had undergone a profound and beneficial transformation.
'The change of the ministry in Prussia,' Lord Augustus Loftus, the British
envoy in Vienna recalled in his memoirs, 'was viewed in England with
great satisfaction.' On 1 December 1858, the Foreign Secretary told Lord

Bloomfield that it was 'very necessary that you as English minister should take fitting opportunities to fortify and encourage the Prince Regent in his liberal policy.' In a printed memorandum at the end of the year Malmesbury concluded that Prussia had seen 'the inauguration of a new order of things under the administration of the Prince Regent.'[32] The *Times*, which, on 1 October 1858, had merely hoped that Prussia's constitution would 'be made a reality', declared on 12 November that this 'change ha[d] come at last, and promise[d] to be complete.'[33]

During the following months, Prussia's 'New Era' continued to find favour. The new liberal administration under Palmerston and Russell proved as ready as their conservative predecessors to believe that Prussia was now committed to moderate liberalism and constitutional progress. In the summer of 1859, when the crisis caused by the Italian war had abated and British diplomats returned to discussing Germany's domestic politics, this continuity of opinion became clear. On 30 July 1859, Bloomfield wrote to Russell, the new Foreign Secretary, that over the past year the Prussian government had been 'steadily advancing in a liberal sense.' Five months later, John Ward reviewed the regent's recent speech from the throne and came to similar conclusions. 'The present administration in Prussia appears to be pursuing its reformatory course cautiously, but surely,' he wrote to Russell on 18 January 1860. No one 'can doubt that it is doing its best to effect practical improvements at home, or that its foreign policy leans towards the establishment of constitutional rights, and rational liberty, in other countries.' The Foreign Secretary agreed with Ward's evaluation and marked the despatch 'very fair and impartial'. Such views were not confined to the narrow circles of official diplomacy. The *Times* also discussed the regent's speech and found it so progressive that it seemed more fitting for an American President than for a European sovereign. In a Commons debate on 19 April 1860, the right-wing Liberal Edward Horsman praised Prussia as 'a kindred state, a constitutional, intelligent, progressive and peaceful state.'[34]

Britain's high opinion of Prussia during the 'New Era' was reinforced by the Prussian stand on the Hesse question. In 1859 the conflict between the Elector of Hesse-Kassel and the Hessian chambers erupted again. The issue, which hinged on whether the country's liberal constitution of 1831 had been replaced or merely suspended by the reactionary charter of 1852, was brought before the Federal Diet. When the Austrian-led majority declared the 1831 constitution invalid, Prussia registered a formal protest implying that she would resist federal measures against a renewed 'Renitence' in Hesse-Kassel. 'No unbiased examination of the provisions of the Federal Constitution,' Bloomfield informed Russell on 2 April 1860, 'can lead to any other conclusion than that at which the Prussian Cabinet has arrived.' The Foreign Secretary's reaction was unequivocal. 'In so far as Her Majesty's Government can judge of the question respecting Hesse,' he replied, 'Prussia appears to them to be entirely in the right.'[35]

Although some disappointment was beginning to be expressed at the slow pace of Prussia's change, British trust in the regent's commitment to sound constitutional government was still fundamentally unshaken when Prince William succeeded to the throne in January 1861. In his critical review of Frederick William IV's reign, William Lowther, chargé d'affaires at Berlin, singled out the Prussian constitution as the King's one notable achievement. Lowther believed that the constitution was safe under the new King who was 'far too honourable a man to wish to put it aside.' Two days later, Lowther called King William 'honest, straightforward and courageous.' Russell shared these feelings. 'I rejoice in the manly and courageous character of the present King of Prussia,' the Foreign Secretary told Bloomfield in a private letter of 9 January 1861. 'I shall look to him to defeat intrigue and the liberal party in Prussia to support a national policy.'[36] In this short passage, Russell summarized the double impact which the advent of the 'New Era' had on British perceptions of Prussia's political role. On the one hand, King William's perceived commitment to liberal change and constitutional government improved the relationship between Prussia and Britain. On the other, it also confirmed and strengthened a belief which had been prevalent among many British observers since the *Vormärz*: that Prussia ought to play a leading role in a reformed Germany. It is, however, important to note that these developments were the result of and therefore strictly dependent on Prussia's liberal and constitutional development.

Once the 'New Era' had begun, British commentators were quick to observe that the change in Prussia's political complexion had turned her into a partner and even a potential ally. As early as 1 January 1859, in his 'Memorandum on the State of Foreign Relations at the close of the year 1858', Malmesbury observed that the political change in Prussia bid 'fair to the promotion of more friendly and cordial relations with ourselves than have of late existed.' William E. Aytoun, writing in June 1859, went even further. 'The interests of Prussia seem to be in all respects the same as ours,' he observed in the conservative *Blackwood's Edinburgh Magazine*. 'Liberal in her tendencies and Protestant in her

faith, Prussia is our natural ally.'[37] British Liberals expressed similar incli-
nations. In a letter of 1 August 1859, Russell informed Bloomfield
that Britain 'desire[d] to be well with Prussia.' In February 1860 Russell
was still confident. 'I trust we shall go on well with Prussia,' he wrote
to Bloomfield. She 'might at this moment make a move in advance, and
promote liberal principles in Germany, as well as elsewhere.' On 26
March 1860, the popular *Daily Telegraph* even declared that Prussia was
'the continental parallel of England and should advance side by side
with us as the only first class Protestant state of the Old World, Great
Britain excepted.' Between Prussia and England there should be a
'perpetual and intimate alliance.'[38]

In April 1860, the prominent liberal MP Edward Horsman raised
a debate on Britain's foreign relations in the House of Commons.
Commenting on recent developments in Italy, France and Germany,
Horsman attacked the government's inaction and strongly advocated
an alliance with Prussia. 'Allied with Prussia, we stand firm and pursue
a policy of our own,' he declared. 'We stand forward as inculcating
certain great principles, and upholding great English influences.' Russell
gave the mutinous backbencher a dressing down. While refuting many
of Horsman's comments on France and Italy, however, the Foreign
Secretary appears to have shared – at least partially – Horsman's views
on Prussia. Four days later, Russell sent a despatch to the British envoy
in Frankfurt. 'Her Majesty's Government are desirous of supporting
Prussia as one of the strongest and most efficient members of the
German body,' Russell wrote to Malet, 'and I have to direct you to make
your language conform to this policy.'[39]

This despatch illustrates the second effect of the 'New Era' on the
British perception of Prussia. Guided by moderately liberal and constitutional principles, Prussia was viewed as worthy of playing a leading
role in Germany and beyond. As early as 6 November 1858, Paget commented that the new ministry was 'calculated to raise Prussia to that
high position which her intelligence, her resources and her power
entitle[d] her to occupy in Europe.' British diplomats soon agreed that
Prussia's political change was also designed to strengthen her relative
position in Germany. 'One of the great objects she now has in view,'
Bloomfield informed Malmesbury in March 1859, 'is to re-establish her
influence in Germany.' In the context of Prussia's bid to enhance her
position in Germany, Britain was seen to have an important role to play.
Bloomfield believed that Britain and the 'New Era' formed a virtuous
circle. On 5 May 1859, he explained to the Foreign Secretary that Prussia
was 'the government to which the lovers of constitutional liberty in

Germany look for guidance.' He believed that it was the 'supposed friendship with England which add[ed] strength to the position of the present advisers of the Prince Regent, and [. . . that] if there was any appearance of that friendship diminishing the consequences might be regretted.'[40] The more she progressed along a constitutional path, the more Prussia qualified for British support, which, according to Bloomfield, would in turn strengthen both the regent's liberal advisers and Prussia's position in Germany.

The diplomats' favourable assessment of Prussia's German role found a wider echo in the British press. Throughout the 'New Era', the *Times* ran a series of pro-Prussian articles. 'The hope of progressive improvement in Germany depends on Prussia,' a correspondent observed in July 1859. Prussia now had 'an opportunity for putting herself at the head of Germany. If she miss it, we must bid adieu for long years to all expectation or real constitutional government in Germany.' In November 1860, the *Times* drew a parallel between what Sardinia had achieved for Italy, and Prussia's future. 'Prussia might even yet become that saviour of Germany which her traditions and her wishes alike call on her to make herself.' In 1861, the paper's optimism was still strong: 'Let Prussia lay down any principle of action which is once liberal and intelligible, and the German nation desires nothing better than to enlist under her standard,' a leader argued on 23 January. 'She might obtain without bloodshed and without offence an empire, vast, solid, and enduring.' The *Saturday Review* took a similar line. Sound judgement dictated, the paper argued on 28 April 1860, that Prussia 'assume the championship of Germany.' For this, the German Confederation would have to be modified and the 'direct power of Prussia increased.'[41]

Their reading of Germany's political scene confirmed many British diplomats, politicians and journalists in their Prussian sympathies. By the end of 1859 Russell believed that the developments in Austria and Prussia as well as the strength of public opinion in Germany all 'point[ed] to Prussia as the future representative of Germany.' Few, however, agreed with John Ward, who argued in September 1859 that Germany needed military and diplomatic centralization under the leadership of Prussia. Instead, the British government continued to insist on the federal structure of the German body politic. In June 1860, this was made clear in a despatch to Vienna. 'Her Majesty's Government wish to be allied [. . .] with all Germany,' Russell wrote to Loftus, 'and this union of Germany is only to be obtained by respecting the independence of each, and by conciliating the national feeling of every German state.' On 13 August 1860, Russell expressly warned against 'absorbing all the smaller states in one German monarchy' and declared that it was 'by the maintenance of the existing territorial distribution in Germany, the improvement of the institutions of the separate states, and the strengthening of the bond which [held] them all together, that the material and moral power of Germany [were] to be sustained and increased.'[42]

It is important to note that the inviolability of the separate German states was not perceived to be in any way at odds with Prussia's German policy. Alarmed by the agitation of the national movement and unsure about the intentions of Napoleon III, the small German states had come to the 'common resolution to sink their differences [. . .] with Prussia,' as Britain's envoy in Hanover put it on 31 May 1860. Prussia's reputation among the small German states improved further when at a meeting between the German sovereigns and Napoleon III at Baden-Baden on 18 June 1860, Prince William declared that he would defend the territorial integrity of all the German states. The regent's line at Baden-Baden, Milbanke reported on 27 June 1860, 'produced the best possible effect even among those who have been heretofore most hostile to Prussia.'[43] Robert Morier, attaché in Berlin and already a widely acknowledged authority on German politics,[44] also confirmed that William had no intention of violating the independence of the smaller states. 'The Princekins therefore (as Carlyle calls them) need have no fears,' he informed Bloomfield on 30 June 1860. Prussia had declared at Baden-Baden that she regarded 'the territorial arrangements within the confederation' as 'sacred rights.' This did not mean that Prussia was content with the status quo, though. 'The present constitution of the Diet is hateful to her and she will use her best endeavours to bring about a reform therein.'[45]

Thus, Britain's support for Prussia once again proved very discerning. British observers welcomed what they believed was the regent's sincere commitment to moderately liberal and constitutional principles. Such a Prussia deserved to enhance her position within Germany by addressing the question of federal reform. While championing constitutional liberty, though, Prussia was neither to undermine Germany's federal structure nor to endanger the peaceful co-existence of the two great German powers.[46]

'In the best sense of the word a conservative force': Prussia and French aggression, 1859–60

It is probably fair to say that in the years following 1858 no single individual did more to change British perceptions of Prussia's role in German politics and of German unity, than Napoleon III. The European crisis caused by France's involvement in the war between Austria and Sardinia, as well as her alleged ambitions on the Rhineland, forcefully reminded the makers of British foreign policy of the international importance of the German Confederation. On the one hand, their analysis of the specific crisis arising from the Italian war confirmed the British belief that sound political leadership in Germany was most likely to come from Prussia. German fears about possible French aggression, on the other hand, provided a powerful argument in favour of a more closely united Germany capable of mounting a credible self-defence.

Britain's attitude towards the war which France and Sardinia fought against Austria in the early summer of 1859 was fraught with contradictions. Widespread support for the cause of Italian nationalism and opposition to Austrian rule in Italy amongst Britain's élites co-existed uneasily with the Court's pro-Austrian feelings and a general interest in Austria's continuing to play a defensive role as a great power. Palmerston explained his attitude rather tortuously as 'very Austrian north of the Alps, but very anti-Austrian south of the Alps.'[47] The situation was further complicated by the Gallophobic invasion scare which swept Britain in 1859. It was to repulse Sardinia's French ally that Tennyson's 'Riflemen, Riflemen, Riflemen' formed.[48] With regard to the German Confederation's role in the Italian crisis, however, British interests were far less contradictory. Eager to keep the conflict as short and localized as possible, Britain wanted the German states to assume a position of armed neutrality.[49] Avoiding the twin dangers of appearing to be easy prey for French aggression and provoking France to attack by taking too martial a stand, the German states should leave Austria to her fate. Prussia's role in bringing this about was considered pivotal.

Throughout the Italian crisis, British observers of Germany were struck by the strength of the anti-French feeling among the German population. 'Nothing can be much keener than the angry feeling expressed against the Emperor of the French,' Malet reported from Frankfurt in January 1859; 'I should say that the whole of Southern Germany was ready to take arms against France.' Ward confirmed Malet's impression. 'The sympathies of all classes of people and of all parties in Germany are strongly with Austria,' he wrote on 23 February 1859, 'and the general fear and hatred of France, and of Bonapartism (as it is called) are more openly expressed than they have been in Germany for many years.' On the following day, Loftus wrote from Vienna that 'the public opinion throughout all Germany [was] expressing itself very strongly against France' and predicted that 'if the armaments in that country continue[d] and the hopes of peace diminish[ed], it [would] be impossible for the German governments to prevent some defensive military measures being taken by the Diet at Frankfort.'[50] This groundswell of popular feeling together with Austria's appeal for help from her German confederates led to calls for the mobilization of the federal army against France.

While never condemning the public outburst of anti-French feelings, the Foreign Office reacted with alarm to the steps considered by the German states. Three months before the war in Italy, Malmesbury had declared that Britain wanted to contain the conflict. 'It is very essential to us that Prussia should be neutral at first and not go beyond strengthening her army on her frontier,' the Foreign Secretary informed Bloomfield on 2 February 1859. 'If Prussia joins Austria in defence of Italy it will be a war with France on the Rhine, war in Belgium, and that draws us into it inevitably.' Britain therefore tried to dampen the bellicosity of the German states. In March 1859, Milbanke and Gordon were instructed to inform Bavaria and Hanover that Britain regretted their attempts 'to force Prussia to take an active part in support of Austria and to make an appeal to the Diet with regard to the necessity of making preparations for war.' On 9 March 1859, Loftus in Vienna was told to 'take every opportunity if necessary of urging Count Buol to avoid proceedings which might induce the German Powers to act precipitately.' On 2 May 1859, Malmesbury rushed out a telegram in reaction to Malet's report that at the next session of the Diet, Württemberg would advocate joint action with Austria: 'protest strongly against the insane policy proposed by Wurtemberg.' At the request of the Prussian Foreign Minister, Malmesbury sent instructions to Britain's representatives at the small German courts. They were 'to state explicitly,' he informed Bloomfield on 4 May 1859, 'that if Germany should [. . .] provoke a war with France, [. . .] Her Majesty's Government [. . .] could give Germany no assistance.' The liberal administration under Palmerston and Russell, which assumed office towards the end of the Italian war, continued their predecessors' efforts to contain the conflict.[51]

British politicians regarded cooling the warlike tempers of the German states and assisting Prussia to maintain her armed neutrality as two sides of the same coin. 'The Prussian government has shown so much caution and moderation, in regard to the Italian war,' Ward observed on 9 June 1859, 'that, so long as the other German states submit to be guided by the discernment of Prussia, it may be confidently assumed that the enthusiasm of the nation will be restrained within reasonable bounds.' In his telegram of 1 May 1859, Malmesbury explicitly instructed Malet to support Prussia at the Diet. On 5 May 1859, Bloomfield informed the

Foreign Office that in his recent conversations with the envoys of the other German states he had 'advocated the propriety of their [. . .] placing confidence in the watchfulness of the Prince Regent and his government over the interests of Germany, and being guided by the more pacific policy of Prussia.'[52] Backing Prussia's moderate line and restraining the more pugnacious German states did not, however, mean that the Foreign Office condemned Germany's Gallophobia. On 11 May 1859, worried that he might have counselled too much restraint, Malmesbury sent two despatches to Berlin, Frankfurt, Paris, Vienna, Dresden, Hanover, Munich, Stuttgart and Hamburg. He was 'most anxious not to be hereafter open to the reproach on the part of Germany for having restrained her from adopting a stout national policy,' he declared in the first. 'In suggesting to Germany a cautious and moderate line of policy,' the Foreign Secretary clarified in his second circular, 'Her Majesty's government had no desire to repress either natural feelings of patriotism or devotion to a national cause.' After all, as the *Times* observed in October 1859, Germany's current national movement was different from that of 1848: 'it was then quickened by the contagion of democracy; it now apparently obeys the instincts of self defence.'[53]

It is also important to note that knowledge of Prussia's ulterior motives did not diminish Britain's endorsement of the Prussian course in 1859. It was well understood that the government in Berlin, by remaining neutral and thus de-escalating the conflict between France and the German Confederation, aimed at reducing Austria's German position. On 5 March 1859, Bloomfield informed Malmesbury that Prussia was 'inclined to turn the present opportunity to advantage by showing the German states that out of selfish motives Austria has been urging them to adopt measures [. . .] which might draw hostilities on Germany.' Two months later, Malet predicted to the Foreign Secretary that 'Prussia [would] not only in no case be a cordial ally of Austria, but that she threaten[ed] to become a very serious obstacle in her way.' Prussia's German stratagem was believed to cover even the eventuality of war. 'There can be no doubt that the object of Prussia is to take the direction of the war, if there is to be war in Germany, out of the hands of Austria, and thus establish her supremacy over the smaller states,' Bloomfield reported on 28 May 1859. 'The policy pursued by Prussia,' the envoy concluded in July 1859, 'was mainly inspired by the desire to wrest the direction of affairs at the Diet from the hands of Austria and place herself at the head of Germany.'[54] Amongst the German public, Prussia's calculated inaction made her deeply unpopular.

'Instead of rejoicing at having, in great part owing to the prudent conduct of Prussia, escaped the dire calamity of war,' Milbanke decried the public reaction to the treaty of Villafranca, 'the German press [. . .] has taken the line of angry invective and recrimination [. . .] against Prussia.'[55] The Foreign Secretary, on the other hand, who was keen to see Prussia's give sound constitutional and peaceful leadership to Germany, treated her more favourably. On 3 August 1859, Russell instructed Bloomfield to 'take some opportunity of saying in general terms that we wish to remain closely united with Prussia.'[56]

While Prussia's commitment to *détente* in 1859 recommended her for a leading role in Germany, the continuing fear of French expansionism drove home the importance of a closely-united Germany capable of deterring foreign attacks. Throughout 1859–60, Germany was abuzz with rumours about France's aggressive plans. Being similarly suspicious of Louis Napoleon's intentions, British observers discussed these fears frequently and in considerable detail. Between June 1859 and the German princes' meeting with Louis Napoleon a year later, the risk of a direct French invasion of Germany was mentioned by Malmesbury, Murray, Howard and the *Times*.[57] A French conquest of the Rhineland was discussed by Milbanke, Malet, Murray and Bloomfield.[58] The subversive activity of French agents in the Palatinate and French plans for the formation of another 'Confederation of the Rhine' featured in despatches by Milbanke, Gordon, Malet, Bloomfield and Murray.[59] 'I think that L[ouis] N[apoleon] means simply to be Master of Europe – if we let him, well – if not, by force,' Russell wrote to Palmerston in July 1859.[60] German fears during the subsequent year appeared to vindicate the Foreign Secretary.

British observers agreed as to how the problem of Germany's weakness and disunion, which destabilized Europe by inviting French aggression, should be addressed. 'In view of the jealousies, suspicions and rivalries which divide the Courts of Germany,' Russell advised Malet in February 1860, 'it appears to Her Majesty's Government that the best chance of maintaining German independence is by cultivating the national spirit.' The *Times*, in a number of leading articles, exhorted the Germans to do the same. 'A powerful and warlike nation is concentrated on their frontier,' the newspaper wrote on 2 April 1860, 'and now, if ever, it is necessary to rouse once more to the aid of German nationality that national enthusiasm which her Princes knew so well how to call forth and how to deceive in 1813.' On 13 April 1860, another leading article reminded the readers of the *Times* that it was 'an object of great and immediate importance to us that Germany should be united.'

Germany, a leader-writer argued, 'is in the best sense of the word a conservative force. [. . .] It is to our interest that this conservative element
of an European society should be powerful, and therefore it should be
united.' Ten days later, Russell instructed Malet in the same vein: 'I have
to observe that it will be desirable that you should endeavour to counteract the disunion of Germany which is fostered by exaggerated suspicion of Prussia.'[61]

'Rather to be led than opposed': Germany's national movement after 1858

The 1850s had been a period of hibernation for Germany's liberal-
national movement. When, as a result of the 'New Era', the Italian war
and the popular reaction to Napoleon III's allegedly aggressive aims,
the movement reawoke in 1859, it proved impressively energetic. The
demands for greater national cohesion, political liberalization and constitutional progress manifested themselves in forms which harked back
to the *Vormärz*: associations of singers, gymnasts and riflemen flour-
ished; public celebrations were organized; newspaper articles and poems
addressed the question of national unity. In the shape of the *Nationalverein* ('National Association'), a political pressure group was formed
to agitate for a Prussian-led, small-German nation-state based on the
Frankfurt constitution of 1849.[62] For British observers of Germany, the
reawakening of the German national movement proved an ambiguous
issue. British diplomats and journalists noted the desire for substantial
constitutional and institutional change accompanying the anti-French
feelings of 1859–60. They paid attention to the public gatherings of
singers and riflemen and sensed their underlying political motivation.
However, while they found more to praise in the German national
movement in the years following 1858 than they had ever done before,
British diplomats retained a great deal of suspicion and innate aversion
to its aims and methods.

Britain's representatives in Germany were quick to identify the factors
which had brought about the renewed activity of Germany's national
movement. Within weeks of the beginning of Prince William's regency,
they noticed that Prussia's 'New Era' produced a positive reaction in
many parts of Germany. 'At this place and in other places of Saxony
a lively feeling of satisfaction prevails in consequence of the change
which has just taken place in the government of Prussia,' Ward reported
from Leipzig on 14 October 1858, and added that 'the announcement
of the regency ha[d] been received with gratification and confidence
throughout Germany.' Gordon in Hanover, though more cautious than

his colleague, made similar observations. 'The accession to the government of Prussia by the Prince Regent, and the composition of the administration which has been appointed [. . .] are exciting, as elsewhere in Germany, so here [. . .] very grave speculations amongst men of all parties: inspiring Liberals with probably exaggerated hopes, and exciting corresponding alarm in the Court and Government party.'[63]

British diplomats also realized that the political fluidity caused by Prussia's apparently liberal departure was channelled into a more definite direction by the Italian war. Members of Germany's liberal-national movement felt that Austria's defeat and the formation of an Italian nation-state had taught them a lesson. The failure of the German governments to stand up to France and Sardinia, Milbanke reported in April 1859, had 'once more aroused the national tendencies in the direction of unity, and little pains [were] taken to mask the opinion, that had a powerful central government based on popular representation been in existence, not only would Germany have been safe from attack, but all danger of war in Italy or elsewhere would have been averted.' Writing in September 1859, John Ward confirmed that 'the political excitement which prevailed in Germany during the late war in Italy ha[d] given rise to a strong and general desire in most parts of the country for a reform of the Germanic Federal Constitution.' The Oxford don Mark Pattison, who, in 1858, had spent three months in Berlin reporting for the *Times*, echoed the diplomats' assessment. 'The renewed agitation for reform of the federal constitution,' he wrote in the radical *Westminster Review* in July 1860, 'commenced under the impulse of the Italian war.'[64] As has been shown, Britain supported both Prussia's liberal course and the notion of a more closely united German Confederation containing French ambitions. The German national movement was thus seen to have been reawakened by two issues which British observers endorsed: Prussia's 'New Era' and self-defence against France.

British interest in Germany's post-1859 national movement was reflected in an increased awareness of the different ways in which nationalism manifested itself. When preparations were made all over Germany to celebrate the centenary of Schiller's birth on 10 November 1859, Britain's diplomats sensed the politics behind this apparently literary endeavour. William Lowther in Berlin regarded the plans as designed 'to get up a demonstration in an ultra liberal sense.' With the 'Schillerites being chiefly of the liberal party,' Lowther wrote after the celebrations, the festival necessarily had a 'semi-political' character. Loftus in Vienna called the celebration 'a great national demonstration' and Ward predicted that the Schiller commemoration 'on account of the national enthusiasm which it ha[d] called forth [. . . would] tend very much to strengthen the hopes of national unity that pervades the minds of the German people.'[65] The role of gymnasts' and riflemen's clubs was assessed in a similar manner. The people would soon proceed to action, Loftus predicted to Russell in July 1861: 'it is in this light that I view the institution of the *"Turner Vereins"* which are forming all over Germany under the auspices of the National *Verein*.' According to the British envoy at Dresden the national convention of riflemen held at Gotha in July 1861 was 'accompanied with some political demonstrations of interest.' In October 1861, *Cornhill Magazine* devoted an entire article to this meeting. 'The political dream' of the German people was to make Germany 'one powerful consolidated empire,' the article argued. 'In the convention of Riflemen (*Schützenfest*) at Gotha, as well as in the *Sängerfest* at Nuremberg, and the *Turnerfest* at Berlin, this was the deep underlying idea.'[66]

Understanding the political significance of these ostensibly cultural and sporting activities tied in with an appreciation of the increasing importance of the national movement. The agitation 'in favour of national unity,' Ward observed in September 1859, 'has been steadily increasing.' The success of the national movement could best be measured in terms of the growth of the 'National Association'. According to Malet, its foundation in September 1859 had met with little public interest and attracted no one of name. Three months later, Ward reported that it had grown in strength. By March 1860, Bloomfield informed Russell, the association was still expanding steadily. Within a year of its foundation, the 'National Association' had made considerable progress, having enrolled 5,262 members, as Ward reported from his new post in Hamburg in September 1860. Another six months on, the association had become a thorn in the flesh of the authorities. 'The National Society is attaining a development which gives much disquietude to the constituted governments,' Malet observed on 1 March 1861. 'The society gains adherents and consistency and it may be predicted that the agitation will not cease as long as the sources in which it originates subsist.' In October 1861, Loftus informed Lord Clarendon about 'the immense progress' which the National Association had made in Germany. It had 'infiltrated itself with the great mass of the thinking classes; and its fibres ha[d] spread throughout all Germany.' By March 1862, Malet declared that it was 'impossible to shut one's eyes to the fact that considerable political agitation subsists in Germany, by which the existence of the Diet may be affected, or considerable changes wrought in its constitution.'[67]

The perceived perfusion of German society by the growing national movement changed the way British observers analysed Germany's political scene. Giving evidence to a Parliamentary Select Committee on the Diplomatic Service in May 1861, Lord Clarendon explicitly drew attention to the importance of obtaining information 'from the middle classes of society in Germany, which [were] very important.'[68] For the first time a real interest was taken in the aims pursued and the methods employed by Germany's middle-class national movement. There was also an unprecedented degree of approval in British accounts of the post-1859 national movement. In many instances, British diplomats suggested that the German national movement had the right aims and pursued them by acceptable means.

The logical complement to the outburst of Gallophobia in Germany in 1859 was the call to reform the German Confederation. Ever since the *Vormärz*, the inefficiency of the German Diet had been a continuous theme in British comments on German politics. On this point they clearly agreed with the national movement. 'The Diet has fallen into great and general discredit,' Ward reported on 13 October 1859. 'It has shown itself to be worse than useless when Germany was threatened with foreign aggression. [. . .] Sooner or later the Diet must be replaced by a more efficient central power, and it is to this end that the labours of the national party still continue to be earnestly directed.' Even more damningly, Morier, in a long memorandum on the Hessian question, concluded on 25 February 1860 that 'the central organ of a confederation when composed exclusively of the diplomatic representatives of cabinets and uncontrolled by the action of a representative assembly, must sooner or later degenerate into a secret dynastic society in a state of chronic conspiracy against the liberties of the several states.' In March 1861, even Malet, who was accredited to the Diet, could not help registering 'the disgust and irritation prevailing in the minds of all reflecting Germans at the political feebleness of the Confederation.'[69] These views were amplified by the *Times*, which, throughout the 'New Era', castigated the 'incompetency' of the Diet and the 'utter worthlessness of the Confederation as a bond of union in times of emergency.' In February 1858, even before the beginning of the 'New Era', the newspaper had already dismissed the German Confederation as a 'mysterious, half-fabulous phenomenon' and, employing ominously eastern similes, had likened it to 'the last Urus in his Lithuanian forest – the last Mammoth splashing about in his Siberian mud-bath.'[70] When Germany's national-minded public argued that it was time for this beast to go, British observers could not but agree.

A second perceived area of agreement between Britain and the national movement concerned the question of who was to lead Germany. The German public was seen to look to Prussia to play a dominant role in a reformed Germany. Prussian leadership was the declared aim of the *Nationalverein* and was reported to be favoured by the national movement at large. 'Prussia holds a powerful and commanding position,' Loftus informed Malmesbury on 12 May 1859, 'and the German nation looks to her to fulfil her high calling.' All parties apart from the ultra-conservatives, Lowther confirmed in September 1859, were anxious to see 'an acknowledged and recognised supremacy of Prussia.' Consul-General Joseph Crowe, Ward's successor at Leipzig, came to the same conclusion. 'The hopes and aspirations of all liberal men in Germany,' he wrote on 7 December 1860 in a despatch which Russell marked 'Interesting', 'lie in the ultimate supremacy of Prussia.'[71] On 27 August 1859, the *Spectator* had put the same observation somewhat more robustly. 'There is no doubt that should a German parliament be once more assembled at Frankfurt,' the weekly asserted, 'the imperial purple would again be offered to a Hohenzollern.' A few days later, the *Times* also declared that the national movement was evidently to Prussia's advantage.[72] Twice before, during the 'Rhine Crisis' and in the early days of the March Revolution, British diplomats and politicians had expressed favourable opinions on the German national movement. On both occasions the popular national feeling was seen to be buttressing or enhancing legitimate authority. During the 'New Era', this condition was again met.

From the very beginning of its agitation for a united, constitutional Germany, the 'National Association' renounced illegal means. The failure of 1848–9 had taught the German liberal-national movement that national unity could only be achieved in alliance with the established order and not by threatening to overturn it. British observers noted this change with gratification. 'It is satisfactory to observe,' Ward wrote on 8 September 1859 about one of the groups preparing the launch of the *Nationalverein*, 'that the Eisenach committee, and their adherents disclaim all revolutionary designs, and seek to realize their objects by legal and peaceable means only.' In March 1860, Bloomfield portrayed the association as dedicated to 'keeping alive by all lawful means the national aspiration for Germany' and as restricting 'their programme to means of moral influence.' The *Nationalverein*, Milbanke confirmed a year later, 'repudiates all illegal attempts to overthrow existing arrangements, and limits its programme to intellectual preparation for a reform of the constitutional arrangements of the common

"Fatherland".' Loftus was confident that the association would make 'no attempt to carry out their views by physical force. [. . .] The course which it is intended to pursue,' he informed Clarendon on 17 October 1861, 'is a strictly legal and constitutional one.' In the same month, *Cornhill Magazine* also highlighted that 'the great popular movement which prevail[ed] throughout Germany' sought national unity not by revolutionary means but 'through all permitted channels.'[73]

British accounts of the German national movement thus noted the following characteristics: the movement was growing in importance and exerted a powerful hold on German society; it was motivated by self-defence against French aggression and by the prospect of reform in Prussia; it was committed to improving the inadequate Diet and to giving political leadership in Germany to a liberal Prussia; relying on legal means it abjured revolution. If this had been an exhaustive description of Germany's national movement after 1859, the makers of Britain's foreign policy would probably have encouraged the *Nationalverein* in the same way they supported Prussia. However, the German national movement was seen to pursue further aims which prevented British observers of Germany from abandoning their traditional reserve. As always, they were concerned that what the members of the national movement were really aiming at was to revolutionize Germany by turning her into a centralized republic.

Several British diplomats drew attention to the element of centralism in the national movement's programme, which jeopardized the federal principle. By opposing the national movement, Gordon reported from Hanover on 1 July 1859, the small German states were trying to protect the Confederation against 'the numerous party who are desirous of [. . .] abolishing the present territorial divisions of Germany entirely.' The majority of the *Nationalverein*, Gordon reported from his new post in Stuttgart in January 1861, believed 'that the constitution of the German Empire of 1849 should be upheld in all future efforts.' The association was promoting 'the absorption of Germany by Prussia.' On 12 December 1861, Henry Howard, Britain's new envoy in Hanover, feared that the liberal victory in the recent Prussian elections would produce 'pressure upon the government to adopt a course towards the secondary German governments inconsistent with the sovereignty and independence of the latter, with a view to carrying out the programme of the party in favour of German unity.'[74] The Germany of the national movement's dreams not only threatened to be centralized but also democratic. 'The first great change which the leaders of that party insist upon,' Malet told Russell in July 1859, 'is a national representation as an adjunct to the Diet.' Ward also mentioned the reformers' demand for 'a representation of the people in the federal government.' The *Nationalverein*, Milbanke observed in April 1861, had 'been joined by earlier republicans.' Malet kept reminding the Foreign Secretary that 'the leading democrats of Germany' and the 'most prominent leaders of the ultra-democratic party' were to be found amongst the ranks of the 'National Association.'[75]

All this went far beyond the federal, moderately liberal Germany which Britain wanted to see Prussia form. Moreover, a number of British diplomats believed that despite the *Nationalverein's* protestations to the contrary, such a programme could only be implemented through revolution or war – if it could be implemented at all. As early as April 1859, Milbanke warned that the political developments in Germany bore 'an ominous resemblance to those which preceded the troublous year 1848.' The political change desired by the national movement, he declared four months later, could only by brought about by violent means. Even Ward, who had a great deal of sympathy for the cause of political reform in Germany, could not help thinking 'that the realization of the plans of the national party [would] be attended with the greatest difficulties [. . .] unless some impulse or excitement should come from without (such as a war with France or another revolution in that country).' Less sympathetic commentators were more outspoken. 'Those self-constituted regulators of the mode in which Germany is to be effected will not admit the feasibleness of any plans but their own,' Malet attacked the *Nationalverein* in October 1862. 'Plans,' he added, 'which nothing but violence and revolution can realise.'[76]

While many British diplomats endorsed the national movement's diagnosis of Germany's political problems and respected its powerful impact, they remained uneasy about its methods and aims when left to its own devices. Their analysis of the German national movement confirmed Britain's diplomats and politicians in their belief that Prussia should head the process of political reform in Germany. 'The spirit of the German nation is roused,' Loftus observed in May 1859. 'Any attempt to repress it will only tend the more to inflame it [. . .]. Prussia may now lead and control the movement. If she fails to do so, she will later be dragged in its wake.' Loftus repeated his advice for Prussia in a private letter to Clarendon. 'By placing herself at the head of the movement,' he wrote in October 1861, 'she can alone hope to stem the tide of revolution.' In August 1863, Crowe stated that the 'movement in favour of unity' was now too strong to be checked. His conclusion echoed Loftus's: it was 'rather to be led than opposed.' According to the

Foreign Office, the future of Germany depended on Prussia. In his instructions for Clarendon, who was to attend King William's coronation in October 1861, Russell outlined what role Prussia should play. 'It is clear that the course for Prussia, tho' not easy, is grand and glorious,' he declared. 'But she must avoid on the one hand the delusions of the *Nationalverein*, and on the other the feudal dreams of his late Prussian Majesty. She must not attempt to dethrone actually or virtually the four Kings. [. . .] She must comply with the demand for a free government in Prussia. But not assume stiffly, harshly, pedantically and prematurely the supremacy in Germany. The pear will fall when it is ripe.'[77]

Spanners in the Prussian works: adversaries, reaction and conflict, 1859–63

The years between 1858 and 1861 left many British observers of Germany convinced that the time had finally come for Prussia to assume the leadership of a reformed German Confederation. Her domestic development, her role in international politics and the groundswell of popular feeling were perceived to pre-ordain Prussia to establish a new order in German politics. By the end of 1863, however, a reformed, Prussian-led Germany seemed as unattainable as ever, and British politicians were as loath to back Prussia's German policy as they were to support that of any other German state. In the run-up to 1863 three principal obstacles in the path to a Prussian-led Germany were registered: the German Middle States and Austria; Prussia's return to reactionism; and the acrimonious conflict over the various plans for federal reform. While the British perception of Prussia's German adversaries was such that their opposition indirectly boosted Prussia's policy, Berlin greatly harmed its own cause. King William's resorting to unconstitutional and reactionary measures gravely disenchanted British diplomats, politicians and journalists. Lastly, during the cacophonous argument over federal reform, which poisoned intra-German relations between 1861 and 1863, most British observers all but abandoned hope for reforms in the German Confederation.

'Kinglings' and a 'sick man': the 'Third Germany' and Austria, 1859–61

Between 1858 and 1860, Prussia, Napoleon III and the re-energized liberal-national movement profoundly challenged Germany's political status quo. By either demanding reforms in the German Confederation or demonstrating their necessity, they set in motion a process which proved impossible to ignore. There were, however, more players on Germany's political stage. The challenge was taken up by the forces which had so far proved content with the federal system re-established in 1851: the states of the 'Third Germany' and Austria. While these powers appeared to respond to the widespread calls for reform, it soon became clear that their objectives differed significantly from those of Prussia and of the liberal-national movement. The attention which British observers dedicated to the reform measures considered by the 'Third Germany' and backed by Austria reflected their interest in political change in Germany. Their attitude to them revealed a clear preference for Prussia. Although Britain had championed the principle of Germany's federal diversity consistently since the 'Six Articles' of 1832, British accounts of the political reality of the smaller German states had often been less than flattering. In the context of the 'New Era' and the renewed agitation for federal reform, these misgivings increased in frequency and intensified in tone. Three different criticisms were voiced with some regularity. The rulers and governments of the small German states were portrayed as incorrigibly retrograde and reactionary. There were also some doubts about their patriotic loyalty. Finally, the reforms discussed by the 'Third Germany' were dismissed as inadequate and ill-intentioned.

From the start of the 'New Era', many smaller German states were seen to be hostile to Prussia. The motives which British diplomats imputed to this opposition showed how much they despaired of finding good political sense among the German Princes. According to Malet's analysis of November 1858, most of them were trying 'to re-establish their systems of internal governments as nearly as possible as they were before 1848.' Writing in May 1859, Bloomfield came to the same conclusion: the rulers of the 'Third Germany' were hoping to abolish their constitutions. Any effort towards liberal progress would incur their inveterate hostility. Ward was equally dismissive about the politicians in charge of the German Middle States. They were the same men who, at the Bamberg Conference in 1854, had worked 'to prevent the Germanic body from joining England and France in the war against Russia,' he reminded Russell in November 1859. 'This fact may suffice as an index to the political tendencies of the ministers.' The most passionate outburst against these governments came from the pen of the Foreign Office's most trusted specialist on German politics. 'I have no wish to [. . .] be too hard upon the individual Kinglings, most of whom are insignificant enough,' Robert Morier wrote to Russell on 26 January 1861, 'but of the class of statesmen who *rule* in these minor German courts [. . .] it is impossible to have too hard an opinion. For ten years they have used the protectorate of Austria to secure impunity to their own execrable misgovernment and to emasculate the national spirit of Germany.'[78]

The governments of the German Middle States were not only described as reactionary and incompetent. There were also persistent rumours testifying to Britain's lack of faith in the national loyalty of some German courts. On 1 July 1859, Malet argued that Austria's defeat in Italy had deprived the small German states of their protector. 'It is not to be wondered at that they cast about for means of preserving their existence,' he wrote to Russell, 'and France (for some of them at least) is an apparent ready supporter.' From then on the ghost of a revived Confederation of the Rhine haunted the Foreign Office. In November 1859, Lowther informed Russell of fears that 'the minor states of Germany [. . .] should form a league too favourable to France.' Just over a month later, Russell underlined a passage in a despatch from Gordon informing him that Bavaria and Württemberg 'would prefer French to Prussian supremacy, and would be inclined, therefore, rather than submit to this latter, to appeal to France for protection, and be willing to agree to her taking compensation for the same by extending her frontiers to the left bank of the Rhine.' Between February 1860 and May 1861, the notion of a French protectorate on the Rhine was discussed in numerous further despatches by Bloomfield, Howard, Morier and Crowe.[79] By the summer of 1861, with the *Spectator* publicly wondering whether the German princes might 'throw themselves into the arms of France,' the question could no longer be ignored. On 22 May 1861, Russell sent despatches to Munich, Stuttgart, Dresden and Hanover enquiring if there was any truth in these rumours. The replies must have come as a relief. Cowley, Milbanke, Gordon and Howard reported that no such plans were seriously being considered. Russell nevertheless decided to make Britain's view absolutely clear. On 21 June 1861, he wrote to Stuttgart explicitly sanctioning Gordon's 'allowing it to be inferred that Great Britain could not approve of the formation of another Confederation of the Rhine.' In a despatch of the same day to Britain's representatives in Munich, Dresden, Stuttgart and Frankfurt, the Foreign Secretary praised the King of Prussia as a 'true and loyal Prince, devoted to the interest of Germany' and warned that 'if any of the German Kings should [. . .] seek refuge [. . .] in the protection of France, such Kings would be hurled from their thrones by popular revolution.'[80]

Against the background of these attitudes towards the German Middle

States, it is hardly surprising that their decision to consider federal reforms was greeted with a great deal of scepticism. On the initiative of the Saxon Minister, Beust, representatives from Saxony, Bavaria, Württemberg, the Hessian states, the Mecklenburgs and a number of smaller states met in Würzburg in November 1859 to discuss reform measures.[81] British diplomats reacted to the news with a mixture of pessimism and suspicion. 'There can be small hope that the labours of the present congress will yield more practical results than were attained at Dresden', Milbanke observed on 18 November 1859. Ward was even more negative. 'The ministers now sitting at Würzburg,' he wrote on 24 November 1859, 'are in reality averse from all federal reform, and have brought forward their proposals merely as palliatives, and to prevent the progress of the movement for the establishment of an effective central power.' Even Malet, who had more sympathy than many for the cause of the 'Third Germany', was anything but hopeful about the Würzburg initiative. 'I do not find,' he wrote to the Foreign Secretary on 26 November, 'that even those who participate in this movement, are very sanguine as to its beneficial results.'[82]

The governments represented at Würzburg eventually agreed on a number of recommendations concerning the harmonization of law codes, military organization and common weights as well as other technical questions. British reactions to this outcome were harsh. Having spoken to Beust after the conference, both Malet and Murray agreed that Prussophobia rather than any positive aims had been the basis of the proceedings. Ward repeated his characterization of the Würzburgers as anti-reformers. Having studied the meagre yield of the conference, Bloomfield censured 'the extreme frivolity of the practical results arrived by a coalition so solemnly inaugurated.' There was, however, he informed Russell on 24 December 1859, 'more system in this apparent frivolity' than appeared at first sight. Too weak to oppose Prussia outright, and not daring to try to out-liberalize her for fear of being outbid, the anti-Prussian camp had initiated a 'competition of mediocrity' to 'tire out the present universal feeling for large and comprehensive reforms by putting forward small and unmeaning ones.' The Foreign Secretary endorsed his diplomats' conclusions. 'Those conferences have ended, as might have been expected, in nothing,' he replied to Bloomfield on 28 December 1859. 'To represent futile resolutions as a result of a deep and refined policy is but a shallow artifice.' Eight weeks later, he told Loftus that 'this buzzing cabal of a Third Party in Germany [could] only do mischief.'[83]

The first Würzburg Conference made British diplomats and politicians unwilling to countenance further such efforts. When, in the summer of 1860, the Würzburg governments convened again to discuss military matters, Russell was openly hostile. 'I have to observe to you,' he wrote to Howard, who had reported that more meetings were planned, 'that in the opinion of Her Majesty's Government such conferences at the present time would not be likely to lead to any good result, and on the contrary would be calculated to affect injuriously the general interests of Germany.' On 13 August 1860, Russell replied to Milbanke's summary of the Würzburgers' agenda, which included plans for the creation of an independent military contingent. 'Her Majesty's Government are of opinion,' he declared, 'that no good effect could follow from an attempt by the secondary states in Germany to create a separate position for themselves.'[84] In Britain's diplomatic correspondence, the last Würzburg Conference in May 1861 was drowned out by the rumours about plans for a new Confederation of the Rhine, and failed to attract any comment.

The slight regard with which British observers treated the Würzburg Conferences was not only the result of their attitude towards the Middle States of Germany. It also reflected the British perception of Austria, their traditional protector, who, as Milbanke and Lowther believed,[85] was backing the conferences. British accounts of Austria's role in Germany between 1859 and 1861 were negative in three different ways. Absorbed by the internal reforms triggered by her defeat in 1859, Austria all but disappeared from British accounts of German politics. On the few occasions when they broke their silence on the Habsburg monarchy, British diplomats and politicians focused on its weakness and lack of influence in Germany. Lastly, these comments were laced with an arrogant dislike, which seriously undermined the credibility of Palmerston's protestation that he was 'very Austrian north of the Alps.'[86] Thus, as had been the case in the summer of 1849, the background to British support for Prussian leadership in Germany was Austria's perceived weakness.

As early as November 1859, Malet observed that Austria had lost 'ground in public estimation.' In December, Russell concluded from 'the losses of Austria in the war, both material and moral' and her 'inability to proceed in the reform she was beginning' that Prussia was now likely to lead Germany. Five weeks later, Malet confirmed that Austria's influence in Frankfurt was waning, and reported that the Austria envoy's 'tranquil attitude accredit[ed] an opinion that his government [was] resigning itself to the loss of their German supremacy with a sort of sleepy indifference.' In March 1860, Howard argued that Austria was 'so crippled by the late war and by the state of her internal affairs' that she could not 'render any very efficient assistance for the general defence of Germany'. Over the subsequent 18 months, these unfavourable appraisals of Austria continued. In September 1860, Russell called her 'too weak and too retrograde to lead.' Morier observed on 26 January 1861 that Austria had become 'wholly impotent in regard to the internal politics of Germany.' According to Crowe, she was 'a state crippled in finance and menaced at once by external and internal foes.' On 7 November 1861, Palmerston called Austria 'weak and disorganized.'[87]

British politicians and diplomats accompanied these pessimistic accounts of Austria's capabilities with comments which betrayed disregard and dislike. As early as September 1859, Palmerston called the 'Austrian leaning on the part of the Prince and urged on us by him through the Queen [. . .] very tiresome' and vowed not to give way to it. By January 1861, Russell was 'willing to leave Austria to go to the devil her own way.' The Habsburgs' salvation, Russell told Clarendon, hinged on Britain's advice. 'The stolid Austrian mind begins to let in some light,' the Foreign Secretary observed in October 1861. 'Poor dear man! He has enemies on all sides, and few real friends. The Italians wish him out of Italy, and the Germans out of Germany; the Hungarians out of Hungary, and the Poles out of Poland.' Two months later, Russell treated Bloomfield, who had been promoted to the embassy in Vienna, to another dose of sarcasm. 'The Austrian vitality is wonderful,' he wrote, 'especially its financial existence. It is now not much worse off than Turkey.' The *Times* shared and amplified these views, deploring Austria's repressive influence and calling her the centre of old, crusty and inert Germany and a 'dismembered, half-bankrupt state with millions of discontented subjects and a first-rate power threatening her on either sides.'[88]

British perceptions of the German Middle States and of Austria, both obstacles on the road to a Prussian-led Germany, thus reflected and reinforced a preference for the course which the cabinet in Berlin was believed to pursue. On 15 April 1861, Bloomfield reported to Russell that Count Rechberg, the Austrian Foreign Minister, had expressed dissatisfaction with Britain's attitude. 'England is exercising her influence in Germany at this moment to the disadvantage of Austria, and with a view to extend the power of Prussia,' he had remarked, 'and the embarrassments of Austria are turned to account in an unfriendly manner.'[89] Although Bloomfield, as a dutiful diplomat, denied these accusations, there can be little doubt that Rechberg had good grounds for complaint.

Measures 'of an abnormal and despotic character': Prussia's turn to reaction, 1861–3

Seen through British eyes, Prussia was her own worst enemy. While the opposition to Prussia on the part of the German Middle States and Austria only served to reinforce Britain's pro-Prussian leanings, Prussia's own political development after 1861 gravely damaged her reputation. The limits of William I's commitment to liberal government were revealed by his clash with the Prussian chamber over military reforms proposed by the crown. The linchpins of the planned reorganization were an increase in the size of the standing army, a three-year term of military service and a reduction in the importance of the militia-type *Landwehr* with its predominantly bourgeois officer corps. These measures were designed to strengthen Prussia's military muscle and cement the army's loyalty. The liberal majority in the lower chamber of the Prussian parliament, however, refused to authorize funds to maintain the unloved three-year term and to reduce the *Landwehr*. British perception of the increasingly reactionary policies to which King William and his governments resorted during their conflict with the chamber clearly indicated that British approval of the Prussian course depended on the liberal promise of the 'New Era'.[90]

Even before the clash between crown and parliament, doubts about Prussia's commitment to liberal progress had occasionally been expressed. In December 1859, Bloomfield reported that War Minister Bonin, a confirmed liberal, had been replaced by the conservative Roon. He wondered whether this meant that the Regent was now less inclined to listen to liberal counsels. Prussia 'somehow acquires all the hatred due to taking a liberal course,' Palmerston remarked two months later, 'and does nothing liberal after all.' Bloomfield had to agree. British perceptions of the early phase of the parliamentary conflict were nevertheless marked by approval of the army project and a willingness to give the Regent the benefit of the doubt. In March 1860, Bloomfield regretted that a conflict was unfolding between a well-meaning sovereign, adamant about his military prerogative, and the 'trustees of the public purse.' In a letter to Prince Albert of 21 March 1860, Russell called it 'unfortunate that the liberal opposition should identify itself with resistance to a law, which tends to increase the military strength of Prussia.' On the same day he wrote to Bloomfield that he would be 'very sorry if the army plan were rejected.' Ten days later, the Foreign Secretary instructed his envoy to 'communicate with some of the leading liberals in the Prussian chambers and ask them to suspend their opposition to the army project.'[91] The conflict was temporarily defused on 15 May 1860, when the chamber passed an extraordinary finance bill funding the military reforms for one year.

This compromise, however, did not halt William's growing disenchantment with parliamentary politics, which, in turn, disappointed Britain. On 7 December 1860, Crowe noted reactionary and illiberal tendencies in Prussia. In January 1861, Lowther reported that the King's replies to two civic deputations had 'given great offence' and regretted that he appeared 'to show a want of confidence in the good intentions of his subjects.' William's address on opening the chamber in January 1861 was not encouraging either. 'There is unfortunately very little in that speech that can give pleasure to the country,' Crowe commented. Lord Augustus Loftus, Britain's new envoy in Berlin, was not optimistic. 'From what I can learn, the present government is the *maximum* of liberalism to be expected here,' he informed Russell on 9 February 1861. 'If any change should take place it will be rather in a reactionary than in a progressive sense.' With the additional army budget having again passed parliament only as a one-year measure and by a much reduced majority, the King's drift to the right continued. By June 1861, Loftus feared that 'under the influence of reactionary councils, he [would] enter upon a retrograde course.' Already then, there were some British voices linking Prussia's constitutional conflict with her role in Germany. 'The national question [. . .] is closely bound up with the Prussian constitutional question,' the *Times* argued on 22 June 1861. 'As long as the attitude and policy of the Prussian government are irresolute, vacillating, and [. . .] anti-liberal, this country cannot command in Germany that degree of confidence and respect which would win partisans for her supremacy.'[92]

These doubts about King William's commitment to constitutional government were confirmed by Lord Clarendon, the former and future Foreign Secretary, who represented Britain at William's coronation in October 1861. Even before his departure, Clarendon had none too high an opinion of the Prussian monarch. 'He is thought to be an honest gentleman and a good drill sergeant,' he wrote to Russell on 11 September 1861, 'but unable or unwilling to comprehend the rudiments of constitutional government.' Having witnessed the coronation, Clarendon saw no need to change his opinion. 'As a constitutional sovereign he does not inspire confidence,' he reported to the Queen, 'as people [. . .] justly think, that His Majesty neither likes or understands the representative system and that he is determined never to let it encroach upon the rights of a crown which he himself has publicly declared here that he holds from God.' Loftus's despatches on the government's plans for the case of an unfavourable outcome of the chamber elections on 6 December 1861 vindicated Clarendon's appraisal. 'It is generally reported,' Loftus wrote on 23 November 1861, 'that in the event of a hostile majority the King will dissolve the chambers and again appeal to the country.' On 21 December 1861, Loftus regretted that the King had 'on several occasions of late expressed [. . .] the disfavour with which he should regard the choice of persons of extreme political opinions.'[93] All this failed to prevent a landslide victory for the liberals.

The huge new liberal majority in the chamber soon clashed with the government. The chamber refused to vote for a third provisional finance bill, and defeated the government on 6 March 1862 on a motion calling for itemization of the budget. The King's subsequent dissolution of parliament was, according to Loftus, 'generally looked upon as an "unnecessary" step [. . .]. For the new chamber [would] most certainly be as liberal if not more so than the one dissolved.' King William also appointed a less liberal cabinet and addressed it with a royal rescript which, according to Loftus, 'savour[ed] much of absolute power.' Within days, measures were taken offering 'incontestable evidence of the reactionary spirit of the new cabinet,' as Loftus observed on 5 April 1862. However, not even the massive governmental manipulation of the elections, which Morier criticized in a detailed memorandum, could prevent an even greater liberal triumph on 6 May 1862. In a chamber of 352 deputies, a mere 11 conservatives faced 248 liberals, 133 of which belonged to the left-liberal 'Progress Party'. By then, however, Loftus believed that the King no longer accepted the political meaning of elections. 'I am led to believe,' he wrote to Russell on 10 May 1862, 'that in the event of the present chamber offering any factious opposition to the King's government, it is the intention of His Majesty to dissolve it and to appeal again to the country. It is rumoured that in such an event, certain changes will be introduced into the electoral divisions – if not in the electoral law itself.'[94]

Undaunted by such threats, the new chamber took up the fight against the government. As early as June, three months before the all-important question of military reform was to be debated, Russell concluded from the government's continuing in office that 'no constitutional rule can be said to be established in Prussia.' With more than 80 per cent of the deputies committed to opposing the King's plans, the outcome of the budget debate, which commenced on 11 September 1862, was beyond doubt. 'I imagine the King's ministers will then resign,' Russell speculated in a letter to Palmerston on 14 September, 'but no one knows what the King will do. He says he will rather die than agree to dismount his hobby. [. . .] If he abdicates it will be a great mercy.'[95] Four days later, on the eve of the government's dramatic defeat in the chamber, the King indeed drafted his letter of abdication. Yet, at the eleventh hour, William denied Russell this 'great mercy' and appointed Otto von Bismarck Minister-President. On 13 October 1862, the rebellious chamber was prorogued.

Bismarck's appointment marked a new dimension in Britain's repugnance at Prussia's betrayal of the 'New Era'. Even in the first steps of the new cabinet, Loftus recognized 'the precursor of a system by which the reactionary party look to regain their former influence.' On 1 November 1862, the envoy observed that 'a spirit of passive resistance to the political measures of the government [was] manifesting itself daily here.' As soon as the chamber was reopened in January 1863, the conflict reignited. The disagreements over Bismarck's decision to collect taxes without a budget and his contention that ministers of the crown were not subject to the disciplinary powers of the speaker when addressing the chamber, quickly escalated. 'The King of Prussia, acting by one or two complaisant servants – we cannot call them counsellors,' the *Times* observed on 7 March 1863, 'has succeeded in bringing the great kingdom which he governs into a state of confusion [. . .]. All the hopes that were conceived at the beginning of his reign have passed away, and been followed by despondency and anger.'[96] By May 1863, Sir Andrew Buchanan, Britain's new ambassador in Berlin, believed that the revolution, which Russell had been anticipating since the spring of 1862, was now imminent. In his private correspondence with Loftus, the Foreign Secretary had frequently compared King William's policy to that of Charles X of France. On 25 June 1862, he had even jokingly offered to book rooms at London's Claridge's Hotel for the soon-to-be-exiled Prussian King. Almost a year later, these fears seemed close to becoming reality. Bismarck 'makes no secret of his intention [. . .] to dissolve the second chamber in the course of the autumn or early in the winter,' Buchanan reported on 23 May 1863. He anticipated that the government would take measures 'of an abnormal and despotic character' before the next election. This might have calamitous consequences: 'the country cannot be expected to see with indifference the complete nullification of its constitutional rights by almost the same process which was punished in France in 1830 by the expulsion of a dynasty.' Palmerston agreed. 'It is painful to see the unconstitutional course pursued by the King of Prussia,' he wrote to the Queen on 29 May 1863. 'It resembles the career of Charles I of England and of Charles X of France and it must if pursued in be ruinous.'[97]

King William's reactionary throwback was seen to manifest itself not only in domestic affairs but also in the sphere of international politics. In February 1863, Bismarck concluded a convention with Russia to facilitate the cross-border pursuit of insurgents involved in the Polish rising which had broken out in January. In Britain, the negative effect of Prussia's association with autocratic Russia was compounded by a widely-felt sympathy for the Poles. With tempers rising to boiling point in pro-Polish France, a serious international conflict threatened. Lord Granville, the former and future liberal Foreign Secretary, believed that the conduct of the Prussian government was 'suicidal and expose[d] the peace of Europe to the greatest danger.' Moreover, Russell was suspicious that this step might herald a revived reactionary alliance. 'Is it not possible,' he asked Buchanan in February 1863, 'that in this convention with Russia, Monsieur de Bismarck looks to the contingency of his requiring the aid of Russian troops to put down the liberal majority in Prussia?' The issue was eventually resolved without open rupture between the great powers, but the animosity created between Berlin and London lingered on for several months.[98]

While Prussia's role in the Polish issue was condemned as reactionary and unnecessarily harsh towards an oppressed nation, she also attracted criticism for supporting a national group. In the late 1850s, very much to the Foreign Office's chagrin, the Schleswig-Holstein issue once again set Germans against Danes. With Denmark reneging on her pledges to guarantee the special status of the Elbe duchies and the German Diet threatening to intervene, the Schleswig-Holstein issue soon excited the passions of the German public. Prussia's 'national' stand on this question greatly irritated Russell and Palmerston, who were mediating between the two parties. In March 1861, Russell bluntly reminded the Prussian Foreign Secretary 'that while French ambition appear[ed] to be directed towards the Rhine, it [was] an essential interest of Prussia, not to raise up enemies in her rear.' Undeterred by such warnings, the Prussian government persisted in pressuring Denmark. Britain's strongly Danophile published opinion quickly offered sinister explanations for Prussia's stance. 'She has a strong hankering after a German fleet,' the *Times* declared on 2 April 1861, 'and an idea that the harbour of Kiel would be just the place for it to assemble.' In October 1861, Palmerston confirmed that Prussia's 'aggressive policy against Denmark' set Britain's public opinion against her. Although their sustained efforts to broker a peaceful solution to the Schleswig-Holstein issue eventually led British politicians and diplomats – though not her public opinion – to conclude that all the parties involved were more or less in the wrong, Prussia was considered particularly unhelpful. In a letter to Russell of 27 June 1863, Palmerston called her the 'main instigator' of German aggression against Denmark.'[99]

After 1858, British politicians and diplomats had proved ready both to encourage Prussia's domestic development and to support her bid for leadership in Germany. This positive attitude, however, had not been unconditional. It was a Prussia progressing along moderately liberal, constitutional lines that British observers wanted to see head a reformed, more closely united Germany. A liberal and constitutional Prussia did not merely correspond with widely held British views as to what characterized sound political development. Through her calm yet strong leadership of Germany she was expected to help secure European peace against French aggression. Moreover, a liberal Prussia was considered the only legitimate political force capable of leading, and thus controlling, Germany's resurgent national movement. Prussia's return to authoritarian and reactionary policies and her embarking on potentially dangerous foreign political ventures thus removed the very reasons for which British politicians had decided to support her. Furthermore, by creating a domestic situation which was believed to threaten a revolutionary outbreak, the Prussian monarch and his governments had committed what was to British eyes a cardinal sin. On 29 May 1863, Palmerston summed up his disappointment in a letter to the Queen: 'The whole course of Prussian policy is unfortunate.'[100]

Princes 'making a mess of it': the struggle for federal reform, 1861–3

In October 1861, the Saxon Foreign Minister, Beust, responded to the widely voiced demands for reform by submitting a plan for a comprehensive remodelling of the German Confederation. Beust's initiative, which provoked Austrian and Prussian counter-proposals, triggered a two-year controversy over federal reform. Naturally, this struggle was motivated more by the question of the relative power of Prussia, Austria and the 'Third Germany' within the Confederation, than by a disinterested commitment to political improvement. British politicians, diplomats and journalists closely followed the complicated diplomatic intrigues to which Germany's politicians resorted in the name of reform. Prussia's reactionary development had left Britain with a bleak outlook. With Prussia, Austria and Germany's Middle States considered unfit to head the reform process in Germany, British diplomats commented on the barren schemes leading up to the *Fürstentag* congress of German princes in August 1863 with weary scepticism. 'It is impossible to form any calculations as to the future of the question,' Bloomfield sighed in January 1863, 'and of all complications a German one is the most difficult to unravel.'[101]

While making a number of gestures towards satisfying both the demands for popular representation and Prussia's desire for parity with Austria, Beust's proposal of 15 October 1861 hinged on the idea of giving executive power in the German Confederation to a triumvirate. A representative of the smaller German states was to hold the balance between those of Prussia and Austria.[102] British comments on this proposal reflected an unwillingness to see the 'Third Germany' play an independent role. Milbanke, Britain's long-standing envoy in Munich, was more than sceptical. 'Supposing this plan to be feasible, which I am by no means prepared to admit,' he wrote to Russell on 4 November 1861, 'the leadership [of the 'Third Germany'] would alternate annually between the Kings of Bavaria, Württemberg, Saxony and Hanover, but it is impossible even for the wildest German theorists to imagine that such an arrangement could be of long duration.'[103] Even Malet, who was less hostile towards the German Middle States than many, was scathing. 'It is generally said that Monsieur de Beust himself never meant to concoct a project of serious reform,' the envoy reported to Russell on 29 November 1861, 'but has redeemed a pledge incautiously made to the Saxon Chambers by purposely bringing forward an impracticable plan.' Beust's initiative was spectacularly unsuccessful. It was rejected not only by Prussia, but also by Austria and Bavaria. In February 1862, the Saxon Minister even had his knuckles rapped by Britain. 'Her Majesty's Government consider that Baron de Beust has no reason to congratulate himself,' Russell wrote to the British envoy in Dresden. 'His Excellency's unfortunate overture on the subject of German reform has excited bitterness and animosity among the German courts, which Her Majesty's Government deeply regret.'[104]

Count Bernstorff, Prussia's new Foreign Minister, did not merely reject the Saxon plan. In his reply to Beust's initiative, he outlined a Prussian counter-proposal based on Radowitz's idea of a small-German, Prussian-led 'Union' allied to Austria. Britain's reaction to this move was more muted than it had been to the Beust plan, but was clearly not supportive. Loftus reminded Bernstorff in January 1862 that the Prussian government had to 'be prepared to adopt and carry into practice a liberal policy at home' if it wanted to win support in Germany. On 1

February 1862, Howard reported that Prussia's overture was 'viewed with great disfavour by the Middle States of Germany, as, were it carried out, they would be reduced to mere vassals of Prussia, and Austria would be virtually excluded from Germany.' A few days later, Howard reiterated that Bernstorff's plan could not 'find favour with the numerous party, particularly in the South of Germany, which [. . . was] not willing to accept the supremacy of Prussia.' According to Malet, the 'Wurzburgher coalitionists' were convinced that the Prussian plan could 'only be carried out by civil war, as it [was] not to be expected that any but the weaker states [would] give up their military force, and the direction of the diplomatic, political, mercantile affairs, as sought by that power.'[105]

Thus aided by Bernstorff, Austria succeeded in forging an anti-Prussian coalition. In February 1862, Austria, Bavaria, Württemberg, Hanover, Hessen-Darmstadt, Saxony, Nassau and Saxe-Meiningen handed identical notes to the Prussian government. In them, they registered their protest against Bernstorff's plan, reminded Prussia of her climbdown at Olmütz and announced reform proposals of their own. This step, Loftus argued on 8 February 1862, confronted the Prussian government with a dangerous choice. Either it had to 'side with the liberal party at the risk of an open breach with Austria and the minor states or adopt a reactionary policy which may lead to a crisis here.' Such a crisis, Loftus emphasized in another despatch of the same date, might produce consequences 'more grave than even an external war.' While Loftus blamed Austria for this disquieting development and called the identical notes 'a cabal suddenly and secretly got up by Austria,' the Foreign Secretary took against the Prussian proposal and refused to support it. 'I think of the Prussian plan of a smaller confederation much as the Austrians think,' Russell informed Loftus on 19 February 1862. Bloomfield in Vienna was similarly disapproving. 'Bernstorff ought to have known that Prussia is thoroughly detested by the Wurzburghers,' the ambassador wrote on 20 February 1862, 'and that Austria always has them in her pocket, and that they are only too glad to seize the opportunity of showing their teeth at Prussia.'[106]

Nor were British observers at all sanguine about the Austrian-inspired reforms announced in February 1862. When, in August 1862, after months of tortuous negotiations, Austria and her satellites presented a reform plan whereby delegates from the German chambers should participate in federal legislation,[107] the British reaction was wholly negative. 'The project of federal reform submitted by Austria and the Würzburgers to the Diet is really too ridiculous,' Loftus wrote to Russell on 16 August. Rather than its pusillanimity, however, the fatal flaw of the proposal was Prussia's opposition to it. 'Any plan of union in which Prussia should refuse to join,' Russell told the British chargé d'affaires in Vienna on 17 September 1862, 'is an unmixed mischief.'[108] Alarmed by Bismarck's uncompromising opposition to the Austrian proposal,[109] British diplomats worked hard to defuse the situation. On 20 December 1862, Howard told the Hanoverian government 'that it would be vain for Austria and the German states acting with her to endeavour to carry out any plans of federal reform without the concurrence of Prussia.' Eleven days later, Russell wrote an urgent letter to Bloomfield in Vienna: 'Pray check this rash spirit of innovation which is rising up in Austria. Seriously the peace of Germany must be preserved.' The Foreign Secretary did not believe, though, that this was an easy task. 'I fear it will be very difficult to get Austria to give up the prospect of humiliating Prussia,' he admitted to Bloomfield on 14 January 1863. Thus, when, in January 1863, Russell received reports – misleading reports, as it turned out – that Hanover intended to vote against the Austrian proposal, he immediately praised the Hanoverian course.[110] At the same time, Buchanan in Berlin was busy dampening down Prussia's bellicosity. As instructed, the ambassador pointed out the great dangers of withdrawing from the Confederation and resorting to military means. He counselled moderation to both Bismarck and the King.[111] Eventually, open rupture was avoided on 22 January 1863, when the Frankfurt Diet narrowly voted against the Austrian proposal.

Undeterred by this setback, Austria secretly prepared a comprehensive proposal for federal reform to be submitted to a congress of German princes at Frankfurt. British diplomats first learned of the impending *Fürstentag* congress on 7 August 1863 a mere 9 days before its opening. Even without having seen the reform plan, their reaction was unfavourable. Howard immediately reminded Russell that 'no reform of the federal constitution [could] be carried out without the consent of Prussia.' Bloomfield was similarly glum. 'What is to come out of this meeting I know not, certainly not unity in Germany as Prussia keeps away,' he wrote to Russell on 13 August; 'therefore the result may be nothing more than a show of hands in which all will be in favour of Austria.' Loftus, now envoy in Munich, agreed that no significant change of the federal constitution could be undertaken without Prussian support. The British government thus approached the *Fürstentag* with a great deal of pessimism. 'The absence of Prussia,' Russell concluded on 15 August 1863 in his instructions for Clarendon, who was to report from Frankfurt, 'will be a serious, perhaps a fatal impediment to any real agreement.'[112]

While strengthening the central element, the Austrian reform proposal fell short of turning the confederation of German states into a
German federal state. It suggested the introduction of a federal executive (*Bundesdirektorium*), an assembly of princes (*Fürstenversammlung*), a
federal council (*Bundesrat*), an indirectly elected federal assembly (*Bundesversammlung*) and a federal court (*Bundesgericht*). While the assembly
of princes was to sanction laws passed by the federal assembly, the
federal council's remit was to be the ratification of international treaties.
The federal court would arbitrate between members and resolve constitutional conflicts within individual states.[113] These details did not
induce British diplomats to give up their sceptical stance. 'I wish I
thought that the Emperor's project was likely to be useful or rather that
it would not make matters worse and increase the evils that it desires
to abate,' Clarendon wrote on 20 August 1863 after a meeting with the
Austrian Foreign Minister. However, he could not help considering it
overcomplicated and unworkable. Malet's account of the same day was
no more encouraging. 'The project complicates instead of simplifying
the machinery of the central organ of the Germanic Confederation,' he
informed Russell. In a detailed discussion of the Austrian proposal,
Morier endorsed Malet's view. 'I have been unable to come to any other
conclusion than that the Austrian plan is totally unfeasible,' he wrote
to Russell on 6 September 1863, 'and that [. . .] it not only does not offer
to the German nation what the latter desires, but something diametrically opposed to its wishes.'[114]

The *Fürstentag* took place amid great splendour. Four kings, six grand-
dukes, six dukes, six princes and three governing mayors had accepted
Emperor Francis Joseph's invitation. Thirty of the 35 governments
of the German Confederation were represented, with only Prussia,
Denmark and three tiny states abstaining. British diplomats agreed,
however, that Prussia's implacable opposition condemned the Austrian
initiative to failure. 'It is not to be expected that the step taken by the
Emperor of Austria can lead to any immediate practical results, as it
is not believed that the opposition of Prussia [. . .] can be overcome,'
Howard reported on 22 August 1863. Russell was more flippant. 'Among
themselves the German princes seem to be making a mess of it,' he told
Palmerston on 26 August 1863. Reports from Munich corroborated this
view. According to the British chargé d'affaires, the Bavarian Minister-
President 'had left Munich a fortnight ago [. . .] little sanguine of any
result' and had returned with the conviction that 'the late meeting at
Frankfort ha[d] been of little or no advantage.' None of this surprised
or disappointed the Foreign Secretary: 'The matter has ended as we

might have expected,' he wrote to Clarendon on 13 September. 'The courts of Bavaria and Hanover say that their Sovereigns never meant to enter into an alliance with Austria, if Prussia did not adhere. So the old Diet lives on.'[115]

British observers' distinct lack of enthusiasm for Austria's *Fürstentag* initiative corresponded with their partisanship on another divisive issue. In the wake of the Cobden–Chevalier treaty of January 1860, the governments of France and Prussia began negotiations about a commercial treaty. In spite of the opposition from Austria and the German states, Prussia pressed on with the talks. On 29 March 1862 a treaty was initialled, which – through its low tariffs and the inclusion of the most-favoured-nation clause – all but established free trade between the two contracting parties. There followed a fierce conflict between Prussia and some of the other member states of the *Zollverein*. While the government in Berlin pressed for the acceptance of the treaty, the more protectionist German Middle States remained reluctant. Its liberal stipulations making the treaty tantamount to a permanent exclusion of Austria from the German customs union, both the championing of and the opposition to the treaty were influenced by political considerations. Against the background of the increasingly antagonistic politics of federal reform, the negotiations over the adoption of the French treaty soon reached a stalemate, throwing the *Zollverein* into a deep crisis.[116]

Since Britain had secured from the Prussian government the status of most-favoured-nation in the event of a Franco-Prussian treaty being concluded, she did not view this conflict disinterestedly. A detailed memorandum which Morier sent to the Foreign Secretary in December 1862 lucidly summarized the British attitude to this question. 'The revivification of the *Zollverein* by a liberal tariff and a continuance of the union in its present extent exactly coincides on the field of industry and commerce with what the party of "Little Germany" desires on the field of politics. On the other hand the inclusion of Austria with all her non-German provinces into the *Zollverein* exactly tallies with the views of the "Great German" party,' Morier explained. His conclusion was unequivocal: 'Whatever may be the political objects of Prussia in the matter, they run side by side with sound commercial principles, whereas the exact converse is the case as regards Austria.' It was believed that a success of the *Fürstentag* project would be commercially deplorable. On the day after the opening of the *Fürstentag* congress, the Board of Trade wrote to the Foreign Office warning that the fusion of Prussia and Austria 'into a common system, [. . .] would inevitably retard, if not altogether arrest, all liberal progress.'[117]

With the British case against the *Fürstentag* project so strong, an explanation is required why on at least two occasions the Foreign Secretary officially criticized Prussia's refusal to participate in the Frankfurt meeting. On 26 August 1863, and again on 30 September 1863, Russell informed Bismarck that 'Her Majesty's government greatly regret[ted] the King of Prussia's reluctance to go to Frankfort.' The explanation for this exhortation, which amounted to asking Prussia to give up the very means by which she ensured the failure of the *Fürstentag*, can be found in the next sentence. 'Has Monsieur de Bismarck reflected,' Russell asked, 'that the Prussian lower chamber may send deputies to the German parliament without the consent of the King, and thus if the Prussian nation adheres to the Austrian plan, it will be very difficult for the Royal Family to stand alone.'[118] Russell thus returned to an issue which had played a consistently important role in British perceptions of German politics since 1830: the connection between political reform and the threat of revolution. If Germany's Princes were not seen to be working towards delivering what the people wanted, the people might rise up and take it by force.

As soon as he learned of the planned *Fürstentag*, Howard in Hanover referred to the link between this project and the threat of insurrection. The princes had to respond to the general desire for federal reform, Howard summarized the conviction of Count Platen, the Hanoverian Minister-President, on 7 August 1863; 'otherwise the people would some time or other take the matter into their own hands.' In August, Russell received reports from Bloomfield, Clarendon and Bonar, Britain's chargé d'affaires in Munich, which confirmed that several German statesmen shared Platen's fears. The Foreign Secretary appears to have been impressed by this argument. 'I do not see how the German Confederation can work without Prussia. Prussia has therefore now a golden opportunity of throwing every thing into confusion; of reviving the follies of 1848, and of raising the cry of revolution against all the Princes of Germany,' Russell sarcastically replied to Clarendon on 4 September 1849. Ten days later, he told the Prime Minister that what he intended to say to Austria and Prussia was: 'If you don't agree, the democrats will supplant you both.'[119]

Fear of revolution was also the central concern in Russell's despatch to Berlin of 30 September 1863. The Foreign Secretary was particularly worried about the demand for a directly elected German national assembly, which Bismarck had recently adopted in order to outflank the Austrian reform plan. 'The first question to be asked is "What is to be the franchise?",' Russell began. 'If high it will not satisfy the great liberal party of Germany. If low it will be pretty sure to lead to a revolution by which the hereditary sovereigns of Germany would be reduced to insignificance. [. . .] In short the liberals of Germany would probably follow closely the footsteps of the liberals of France in 1791.' The fiercely anti-Prussian course, which the Austrian Foreign Minister, pursued after the *Fürstentag*, was criticized for the same reason. 'I fear he is going to bring upon us a democratic revolution in Germany,' Russell wrote to Bloomfield in October 1863, 'and that would be an awful thing.'[120]

British perceptions of the proposals for the reform of the German Confederation and of the ensuing struggle between the German powers between 1861 and 1863 thus confirm older patterns of evaluating the questions of political reform and national unity. The hostile reactions to Bernstorff's proposal, the Austrian delegates proposal and the *Fürstentag* project show that in British eyes the existence of vigorous opposition to a reform project within the German Confederation disqualified such a project. However, peaceful implementation was not the only important parameter in British evaluations of the halting process of political reform in Germany. The direction and aims of this process were also crucial. After 1861, with Prussia going back on its earlier promise of constitutional progress, British support for Prussian leadership in Germany soon faded. Reform projects like the Beust, delegates and *Fürstentag* plans, which were perceived to fail at rendering Germany more efficient, more coherent and more commercially liberal, also attracted British censure. At the same time, the proposed changes should not result in overly democratic forms of government. This was the reason why Bismarck's tactical call for a directly elected German parliament caused alarm, and why the German princes had to be committed or at least seen to be committed to reform. There were fears that the popular desire for political change might otherwise erupt into a revolution which would wrest control out of the hands of the legitimate authorities and establish a German republic.

Between 1858 and 1863, British observers of Germany proved a very discerning, difficult-to-please audience. Prussia, Austria, the German Middle States and Germany's liberal-national movement all disappointed them. To British eyes, the endless manoeuvres of German politicians were frustrating and threatened even more deplorable developments. 'They agree about nothing but firing into the Danes,' Russell wrote to Palmerston on 4 September 1863.[121]

Conclusion

The years following the *Fürstentag* proved Russell's gloomy prediction right. Circulars, conferences and constitutional drafts – the useless tools of Germany's barren politics since 1849 – were swept away by gunfire. By 1863, British diplomats and journalists had observed, analysed and commented on political reforms and the question of national unity in Germany for more than three decades. Now they had to widen their briefs and take on the duties of war correspondents. While many older British criteria and convictions remained important, the advent of war marked the beginning of a qualitatively new phase in German politics. 1863 therefore provides a good vantage point from which to review a distinct period of British perceptions of the German question. This concluding discussion will consider British views on the *necessity* and *direction* of political change in Germany, on its different *agents*, and lastly on the *manner* of its implementation.

Article 2 of the Federal Act of 1815 defined the *raison d'être* of the German Confederation as maintaining both the external and internal security of Germany and the independence and inviolability of the individual German states. This study of British politicians', diplomats' and journalists' perceptions of German politics has indicated that throughout the second third of the nineteenth century they retained a strong interest in this original core objective. From 1830 onwards, however, they were increasingly convinced that Germany's political organization failed to deliver these twin aims. There were doubts about the Confederation's ability to deter and, if necessary, repulse foreign aggression. In the early 1830s, in 1840, in 1849–50 and in 1859–60, Europe experienced the kinds of war scares and incursions which the Confederation had originally been designed to prevent. The Confederation was also found wanting in the domestic sphere. The German governments were held responsible for a latent crisis threatening to erupt into revolution at any time. They were jeopardizing internal stability by failing to placate a potentially dangerous popular movement demanding liberal progress and improved government. To win British approval, the actions of German politicians had to be seen to render the German states safer against revolution, and Germany as a whole more able to play a stabilizing role in Europe.

In view of the existence of a powerful challenge to Germany's political status quo in the shape of a popular liberal-national movement, British politicians and diplomats broadly agreed that reform in the German states had to take the form of measured concessions. In order to defuse the revolutionary situation, the German sovereigns should transfer power to representative assemblies elected on narrow franchises, introduce responsible monarchical government and grant moderate civil liberties. Moves perceived to be well-measured responses to popular grievances were welcomed. The *Zollverein*, Frederick William IV's course in the 1840s, the concession of the 'March Demands', the Prussian 'Union' and the 'New Era' were all interpreted in this light. Deviations from this golden way were deplored. The reactionary steps taken by the Diet in 1832 and by Prussia after 1861 were condemned as likely to trigger revolutionary outbreaks. When, on the other hand, as seemed to be the case in the summer of 1848, governments conceded too much and appeared to acquiesce in the establishment of the very kind of democracy which careful reforms should forestall, British reactions were equally negative. The broad consensus in Britain was that the German states should develop in a moderately liberal, constitutional direction, following, if possible, the British model. On various occasions – during the session of the Prussian 'United Diet' in 1847, in early March 1848 and during the 'New Era' – British politicians and diplomats either explicitly advised Germans to heed the British example or were pleased to report that it was already being aspired to.

Similar considerations applied to Germany's federal arrangements. Throughout the period under discussion, British views on the German Diet were consistently damning. Unable and unwilling to represent the common interests of the federated states efficiently, the Diet was portrayed as meaningless or worse. On the few occasions when its inaction was interrupted, the Diet's step were seen to be harmful. The 'Six Articles' of 1832, the measures against Hesse-Kassel in 1850 and 1859 and its involvement in the Schleswig-Holstein question after 1858 seemed to indicate that the Diet's only capacity was that of a reactionary instrument violating the rights of the individual states. Instead of merely failing to be part of the solution to Germany's domestic difficulties, the Confederation was considered a central part of the problem. It denied the German people the material advantages of closer national union and impeded sound progress. So deep was British dissatisfaction with the German Diet that the demand for its complete reform was welcomed even when it was voiced by revolutionaries, as was the case in 1848.

The question of Germany's internal tranquillity was perceived to have a bearing on her ability to play a stabilizing role in Europe. In the early 1830s, and again in 1849, British diplomats expressed fears that German revolutionaries might join their brethren in France and thus cause a European conflagration. Preventing revolutions through improving the domestic arrangements of the German states was thus seen to be a first indirect step towards enhancing Germany's contribution to European peace. On the level of Germany's federal arrangements, the internal and external dimensions were directly linked and reforms were thus doubly useful. Measures which seemed apt to enhance the cooperation of the states, such as the *Zollverein*, or the military talks triggered by the 'Rhine Crisis', were warmly welcomed. Such steps not only pacified the liberal-national opposition but strengthened Germany, making her safer against revolution and foreign aggression. Reactionary, divisive or cumbersome proposals such as the 'Six Articles', the plans for a separate 'Third Germany' or the *Fürstentag* proposal, on the other hand, would, it was argued, increase the risk of insurrection and weaken Germany internationally.

Although British politicians and diplomats remained vague as to what changes to Germany's federal organization they wanted to see implemented, they clearly favoured a closer union with a more efficient coordinating authority. They also attached great importance to Germany's federalism. In 1832–3, in 1848–9 and again in 1850–1, British observers strongly rejected attempts at centralization. Given their disregard for the smaller states, this championing of German federalism hardly sprang from sympathy for the putative victims of centralization. The reasons for Britain's interest in the continued existence of the separate German states can be gleaned from British reactions to the centralizing efforts by Metternich, the *Paulskirche* and Schwarzenberg. First, as is suggested by their responses to the Schleswig-Holstein issue in 1848–9 and by their suspicions about Schwarzenberg's plans in 1850, British foreign politicians believed that both a German republic and a centralized reactionary Germany would pursue aggressive aims and threaten the peace of Europe. Secondly, the existence of several legitimate monarchical governments was believed to help prevent Germany's turning into a centralized republic. For, as John Acton argued in 1862, democracy was 'incompatible with the continued existence of separate states.'[1] The British perception of the 'Six Articles' and of Schwarzenberg's programme for a stronger central authority in 1850–1 suggests that this second argument equally applied to the opposite scenario: federal diversity also blocked reactionary centralization. Thus, as had been the case with the internal development of the German states, the reform of the federal arrangements had to steer a careful middle course. While the individual states had to shun despotism and democracy at home, their federation had to eschew disunity and centralism.

While there was a broad consensus about the desirability of Germany's federalism, the question of Germany's geographical extent was more controversial. Apart from the vexing problem of Schleswig-Holstein, it was Austria's role in Germany which proved most difficult to define. During 1848–9 and again during the Italian war of 1859, several British observers regretted that the Habsburg Empire, through its widespread interests in Italy, Hungary and the Balkans, threatened to involve the German Confederation in non-German questions and compromised its independent, stabilizing role in Europe. The inclusion of the entire Habsburg monarchy in the German Confederation was therefore ruled out. It was also clear that including the Habsburgs' illiberal, backward and disparate empire rendered the creation of a more liberal, more closely coordinated German Confederation very unlikely. Britain's foreign political establishment failed, however, to conceive of a way to effect a separation of Austria from the rest of the confederation, for war was considered as unthinkable as a voluntary Austrian withdrawal was improbable. As soon as Austria appeared weakened, as in 1848–9 and after her defeat in 1859, though, British support for Prussian leadership in Germany markedly increased.

The latent British hostility to Austria's German role also reflected a different agenda, which went beyond maintaining Germany's internal and external security. Britain, as a great commercial nation, had a keen interest in gaining unimpeded access to the German markets. With Prussia tending towards free trade and Austria dependent on high tariffs to protect her infant industries, the commercial argument weighed heavily in favour of Berlin. Against this background, the *Zollverein* became an important element in British analyses of the German question. British diplomats, politicians and economists praised the benefits accruing to Germany's economy from this large intra-German free trade zone. Headed by commercially liberal Prussia, the *Zollverein* presented

Britain with an attractive proposition. Joined by protectionist Austria, the same organization would turn into a threat to British commerce.

The claim that between 1830 and 1863 British politicians, diplomats and journalists considered political reforms in Germany necessary, and broadly agreed on their direction, is confirmed by a study of their perceptions of the principal actors on Germany's political stage: the liberal-national movement of opposition, Prussia, Austria and the German Middle States. Throughout the period under discussion, the German liberal-national movement never really succeeded in winning British sympathy or support. While hinting at the existence of moderate reformers in the early 1830s, acknowledging the reasonableness of the 'March Demands' and praising the *Nationalverein*'s renunciation of violence, Britain's foreign political establishment always remained suspicious of the German national movement. The members of Germany's 'ultra-liberal' party were consistently portrayed as extremists bent on revolution and republicanism. The revolutionary outbreaks they threatened had to be pre-empted by well-timed concessions; the political groundswell they produced had to be channelled by shrewd governmental action; their 'excesses' called for resolute repression. Thus, while the liberal-national opposition might induce Germany's legitimate governments to take the right steps, it was definitely seen as part of the problem.

In a letter to the arch-conservative courtier Leopold von Gerlach, Bismarck once remarked in 1857 that as for foreigners he had only ever liked the English and occasionally still felt that way. 'However,' he concluded wearily, 'these people just will not let themselves be loved by us.'[2] This letter would probably have elicited a bitter laugh from Palmerston and Russell, for the feeling was mutual. Prussia was the great vehicle of British hope for Germany. Time and again, the government in Berlin was seen to promise a departure in the right direction. Each of these occasions triggered an outburst of British optimism. The *Zollverein*, Frederick William IV's pseudo-constitutional measures during the 1840s, the 'Union' plan and the 'New Era' of 1858–60 were all viewed as steps towards securing a considerable improvement in Prussia's and Germany's government. It is interesting to note how readily Palmerston, Aberdeen, Russell and their diplomats trusted Prussia's monarchs and their governments to implement substantial reforms. With its perceived track record of constitutional improvement, sound administration, military strength and commercial liberality, Prussia appeared pre-ordained to head Germany.[3] However, while

Prussia earned more British praise than any other player on the German stage, she also caused most frustration. Frederick William's constitutional steps during the 1840s were followed by weakness and irresolution in 1848. The opportunity to realize the 'Union' in 1849 was frittered away and then followed by dangerous obstinacy. The hopes raised by the 'New Era' were soon buried by the constitutional conflict. For all the bitterness caused by these disappointments, it appears nevertheless clear that British observers could not imagine an acceptable solution to the German question which did not involve enhancing Prussia's role.

Austria can hardly be said to have played a constructive role in British perceptions of the process of reforming Germany at all. Every Austrian initiative considered in this study was rejected: the 'Six Articles', the Bruck plan, Schwarzenberg's project of an 'Empire of 70 Millions', the Delegates Proposal of 1862 and the *Fürstentag* initiative of the following year. With liberal progress in the separate states, a closer and more efficient federal union and free trade dominating British wishes for Germany's development, Austria's chances of winning British support for her German policy always looked bleak. Britain nevertheless appreciated that the Habsburg monarchy, a great power with a sizeable party in Germany, could not simply be pushed aside, and that Austria's contribution to Germany's defence was considerable. In spite of this, in British analyses of German politics, the Habsburg Empire never really recovered from the impact of the 1848 revolution, when a numerous body among Britain's foreign political establishment had agreed that it would be beneficial for both Germany and Austria if their integrated link were severed. From that time on, Austria remained marginalized.

The middle and small states of Germany occupied a curious position in British perceptions of the German question. While the principle of their existence was considered essential to prevent republican or reactionary centralism, the states themselves attracted little more than ridicule and exasperation. The weakness of the smaller states prevented good government, their obsession with their 'miserable independence' hampered federal reform, and their protectionism stood in the way of free trade. On various occasions, British diplomats advocated mediatizing the smaller states, but the notion of establishing an independent 'Third Germany' met with unalloyed British rejection. In British eyes, German federalism appears to have been merely a means to the end of avoiding different, yet similarly undesirable, varieties of a centralized Germany.

Having considered British views on the necessity, direction and agents of political change in Germany, it remains to discuss British opinions on the manner in which this change ought to be brought about. Given the anti-revolutionary motivation behind Britain's support for reforms in Germany, it is not surprising that British politicians and diplomats wanted to see them conceived, proposed and realized from above, by legitimate governments rather than by forces from below. The *Zollverein* and the 'Union' plan met this requirement, the *Reichsverfassungs-kampagne* of 1849 and the National Association of 1859 did not. A second condition for British approval was that the implementation of the proposed reforms had to be consensual or at least uncontested. For British observers, the existence of determined opposition – from either of the German Great Powers or from the majority of the German Middle States – disqualified any reform project. As British reactions to the Autumn Crisis of 1850 or to the Delegates Proposal of 1862–3 indicate, civil war was considered too dear a price to pay for political change in Germany.

British perceptions of the German Question between 1830 and 1863 can thus be summarized in terms of six desiderata concerning the manner and result of the process of political reform: change without war; reforms without a popular reform movement; constitutions without democracy; federal union without centralized unity; a tariff league without protectionist tariff walls; and great defensive power without foreign political ambition. It is interesting to note that with the obvious exception of the war-like manner of its creation, Bismarck's *Reich* of 1871 fulfilled all these desiderata.[4]

These perceptions and preferences suggest two broad conclusions concerning British attitudes towards Germany's political development and the nature of Anglo-German relations. First, there appears to have existed in the minds of many British politicians and diplomats an indis-soluble link between the structure of a political reform process and its results. It was assumed that only an élite of aristocratic reformers could be trusted to initiate and carry through moderate, non-democratic and anti-revolutionary reform measures.[5] Indeed, it has been suggested that Palmerston could only relate to continental liberalism, where – as in Italy or Hungary – its aristocratic structure bore a resemblance to Whig traditions.[6] Germany's middle-class liberalism on the other hand – led, as Cartwright disparagingly put it in 1832, by 'attorneys, professors, students, physicians, and persons of a similar stamp'[7] – stood little chance of winning support. With Germany lacking aristocratic reform-ers comparable to the Whigs,[8] British hopes for improvement and progress were pinned on Prussia. Such a misreading of Frederick William IV's and William I's intentions almost inevitably made German politics a frustrating subject for British observers. This stubborn yearning for Whig policies in a country without Whigs, suggests that British politicians and diplomats appreciated German liberalism, constitutionalism and nationalism not for their intrinsic tenets but for their potential for bringing about a process of approximation to the British model of Germany's political and social structures.

Secondly, there were no British interests which were specific to Germany or of exclusively bilateral relevance. Germany was analysed within a European or even wider framework: Germany's security role was defined *vis-à-vis* France and Russia. Her commercial role was seen as part of a global free-trading agenda. Her political and social development was analysed in the context of a pan-European strategy of preventing revolutions through defensive modernization, and thus avoiding both war and the creation of 'extreme' regimes. British attitudes to Germany were thus crucially determined by the degree to which Germany could be integrated more or less harmoniously into an international system sanctioned by Britain. There was little or no room for a separate bilateral Anglo-German relationship at odds with such a system.

British perceptions of the German Question between the July Revolution and the *Fürstentag* thus revolved around two core problems: Germany's internal development towards liberal, parliamentary government and her compatibility with the European system. Over the following century, these two problems came to shape the course of German and European history. While the spectre of German hegemony meant that the latter problem dominated British perceptions of Germany during the decades after 1871, fear of revolution made British politicians and diplomats focus on the former problem during the period considered here. As it turned out, a German nation-state fully acceptable to Britain had to solve both these problems.

Appendix: Long-standing British Diplomats in the German Confederation (1830–63)

[The appendix begins overleaf.]

Name	Total length of service	Years posted in the German Confederation	Postings in the German Confederation	Year of retirement and final post
Sir John Duncan Bligh (1798–1872)	36 yrs	21 yrs	Vienna (1820–3) Hanover (1838–56)	1856; envoy to Hanover
John Arthur Douglas, Baron Bloomfield (1802–79)	53 yrs	26 yrs	Vienna (1818–23, 1860–71) Stuttgart (1825–6) Berlin (1851–60)	1871, ambassador to Austria
Sir Thomas Cartwright (1795–1850)	ca. 35 yrs	16 yrs	Munich (1821–9) Frankfurt (1830–8)	1850; envoy to Sweden
Henry R. Wellesley, 1st Earl Cowley (1804–84)	43 yrs	20 yrs	Vienna (1832–43) Stuttgart (1832–43) Frankfurt (1848–52)	1867; ambassador to France
David Montagu, 2nd Baron Erskine (1776–1855)	21 yrs	18 yrs	Stuttgart (1825–8) Munich (1828–43)	1843; envoy to Bavaria
Francis Forbes (1791–1873)	47 yrs	38 yrs	Vienna (1814–22, 1828–32) Dresden (1832–58)	1859; envoy to Brazil
Sir Robert Gordon (1791–1847)	36 yrs	15 yrs	Vienna (1815–25, 1841–6)	1846; ambassador to Austria
Henry Francis Howard (1809–98)	44 yrs	38 yrs	Munich (1828–32, 1866–72) Berlin (1832–45, 1846–53) Hanover (1859–66)	1872; envoy to Bavaria
Sir Frederick Lamb (1782–1853)	ca. 41 yrs	21 yrs	Vienna (1813–15, 1831–41) Frankfurt (1817–23) Munich (1815–20)	1841; ambassador to Austria

Lord Augustus Loftus (1817–1904)	42 yrs	33 yrs	Berlin (1837–58, 1860–2, 1866–71), Stuttgart (1844–52), Vienna (1858–60), Munich (1862–6)	1879; ambassador to Russia
Sir Arthur Ch. Magenis (1801–67)	41 yrs	10 yrs	Berlin (1825–6), Vienna (1844–51), Stuttgart (1852–4)	1866; envoy to Portugal
Sir Alexander Malet (1800–86)	42 yrs	23 yrs	Vienna (1843–44), Stuttgart (1844–52), Frankfurt (1852–66)	1867; envoy to the Diet of the German Confederation
Sir John Ralph Milbanke (1800–68)	41 yrs	31 yrs	Frankfurt (1826–35), Vienna (1838–41), Munich (1843–62)	1867; envoy to the Netherlands
Sir Robert B. Morier (1826–93)	40 yrs	23 yrs	Vienna (1853–8), Berlin (1858–65), Frankfurt (1865–7), Stuttgart (1867–72), Munich (1872–6)	1893; ambassador to Russia
Lord William Russell (1790–1846)	10 yrs	7 yrs	Stuttgart (1834–5), Berlin (1834–41)	1841; envoy to Prussia
Sir John Ward (1805–90)	25 yrs	25 yrs	Leipzig (1845–60), Hamburg (1860–70)	1870; minister-resident to the Hanse Cities
John Fane, 11th Earl of Westmorland (1784–1859)	ca. 31 yrs	14 yrs	Berlin (1841–51), Vienna (1851–5)	1855; ambassador to Austria

Notes

Introduction

1 Bismarck to Johanna, 5.7.1862, quoted in: Gall (1986: i, 181); Bismarck's report to King William in: Bismarck (1925: 384–6).

2 Following Schieder (1962: 27) the term 'liberal-national' is used in contradistinction to the later National Liberalism.

3 Moreover, the years 1864 to 1871 are well-covered; see: Hildebrand (1980; 1997); Metzler (1997); Millman (1965); Sandiford (1975) and Schaarschmidt (1993).

4 See the bibliographies in: Kennedy (1980: 553–86) and Pommerin (1997: XXIII–XXXVIII).

5 Martin Vogt's unpublished dissertation [Vogt (1963)] only considers newspapers, periodicals and books.

6 Heydemann (1995).

7 Precht (1925); Scharff (1942); Valentin (1937b: 9–46).

8 Gillessen (1961); Mosse (1958: 13–48), while making numerous acute observations, is based on little archival research.

9 Gillessen (1961: 66–155); Doering-Manteuffel (1991: 106–85).

10 Valentin (1937b: 134–201). Matthew Adler's M. Litt. thesis [Adler (1986)] offers little. Gabriele Metzler's impressive study [Metzler (1997)] contains many insights into British attitudes towards the German Confederation, but has a different focus. On commercial questions consult: Davis (1997).

11 Quoted in: Southgate (1966: 549).

12 Calculated on the basis of Turner (1948: 873).

13 *Times* (15.9.1832: 3b).

14 In 1858 and 1863 the figures were 31:13:5 and 34:12:6 respectively; see: Foreign Office List (1852; January 1859; January 1864). These figures exclude the consular service.

15 Bright (1907: 284).

16 For their individual details see the Appendix.

17 Middleton (1977: 225).

18 Forbes and Milbanke lead the field with 38 years each; Magenis comes last with seven years; nine other diplomats totalled twenty or more years of service in Germany.

19 Gordon only knew Vienna; Morier served at Vienna, Berlin, Frankfurt, Darmstadt, Stuttgart and Munich. On British diplomats' work in nineteenth-century Germany see: Freitag (2000: ix–xvii); on the diplomatic service in general consult: Bindoff (1935); Jones (1983) and Middleton (1977); Hildebrand (1997: 66–83) offers a concise sketch of Britain's foreign political machinery.

20 Frederick Lamb, Melbourne's younger brother, was a career diplomat and received his first senior appointment (to Bavaria in 1815) and subsequent promotion (to Spain in 1825) from Tory governments. Palmerston kept the Tory Westmorland in Berlin in 1846 and subsequently promoted him.

21 Bloomfield, Cartwright, Erskine, Forbes, Lamb, Magenis, Malet, Milbanke, Morier, Ward and Westmorland received promotions from both parties; Cowley was promoted only by liberal Foreign Secretaries, but was kept at the important Paris embassy by subsequent Tory administrations.

22 Out of a possible 27 changes in Vienna, Berlin and Frankfurt between 1830 and 1863 (i.e. nine changes of government) only four recalls occurred: the 1st Baron Cowley was recalled from Vienna in 1831; Frederick Lamb from Vienna in 1841; Robert Gordon from Vienna in 1846; William Russell from Berlin in 1841.

23 Jones (1981: 50).

24 Cf. Steele (1987: 48); for more examples of this tension see ch. 2 n. 93, ch. 3 nn. 21, 46 and 101, and p. 187. Besides, Victoria's and Albert's German policies have already received considerable attention; see: Binder (1933), Eyck (1959) and Fischer-Aue (1953); on the limits of the Crown's influence of foreign policy see: Hildebrand (1997: 73–7).

25 British expectations that the German Confederation would stabilize Europe are discussed by Gruner (1977a & b; 1981a and 1986); see also: Heydemann (1995: 23–9).

26 See: Heydemann (1995: 43–66, 135–44).

27 Schroeder (1994a) has characterized this detached attitude as 'benign neglect'.

28 Hansard, 3rd ser., vol. 112: 228–444, 478–596, 609–739 (for Disraeli's comment see: 733–4).

29 Palmerston to Russell, priv., 13.9.1865, quoted in: Bourne (1970: 382).

Chapter 1

1 Wellington's memorandum in: Bourne (1970: 215–16); for Britain's reaction to the July Revolution see: Webster (1951: i, 79, 93–5); Gruner (1981b).

2 Palmerston to Sulivan, 1.8.1830, in: Airlie (1922: i, 173).

3 On the repercussions of the 1830 revolution in Germany see: Faber (1979: 136–48); Gruner (1983); Hardtwig (1995: 52–66); Huber (1968: ii, 30–91).

4 On German radicalism and the Hambach Festival see: Deuchert (1983: 39–66); Foerster (1982); Foerster (1988); Huber (1968: ii, 125–50, 164–7); Wende (1975: 23–31).

5 On the German national movement in the early 1830s see: Dann (1996: 111); Schulze (1991: 60–3); on the repressive measures employed by the diet see: Billinger (1991: 50–156); Huber (1968: ii, 151–63, 173–84).

6 On British foreign policy in the early 1830s see: Bourne (1970: 26–33); Bourne (1982: 332–407); Clarke (1989: 184–200) and Webster (1951: i, 89–369).

7 Webster (1951: i, 3); Southgate (1966: 43); Bourne (1982: 332); Gollwitzer (1965: 315 [author's trans.]).

8 Bell (1936: i, 158); Southgate (1966: 51); similarly: Webster (1951: i, 221–36); Ridley (1972: 215–18); Bourne (1982: 367–71).

9 Heydemann (1995: 227–36 [for the quotation: 268]).

10 Disbrowe to Aberdeen, no. 43, 29.8.1830 (FO/82/24); Chad to Aberdeen,

No. 57, 22.9.1830 (FO/30/31); Milbanke to Aberdeen, No. 25, 29.9.1830 (FO/30/32); Disbrowe to Aberdeen, no. 63, 29.10.1830 (FO/82/24).

11 Disbrowe to Aberdeen, no. 63, 29.10.1830 (FO/82/24); Cartwright to Palmerston, no. 116, 6.9.1831 (FO/30/35).

12 Disbrowe to Palmerston, no. 46, 1.12.1831 (FO/82/25).

13 Cartwright to Palmerston, no. 29, 22.2.1831 (FO/30/33); Disbrowe to Palmerston, no. 8, 15.2.1832 (FO/82/26); Disbrowe to Palmerston, no. 23, 22.5.1832 (FO/82/26)

14 Disbrowe to Aberdeen, no. 63, 29.10.1830 (FO/82/24); Disbrowe to Palmerston, no. 8, 15.2.1832 (FO/82/26); Cartwright to Palmerston, no. 33, 19.3.1832 (FO/30/37).

15 Cartwright to Palmerston, no. 143, 23.11.1831 (FO/30/35); Cartwright to Palmerston, no. 21, 19.2.1832 (FO/30/37); Cartwright to Palmerston, no. 27, 6.3.1832 (FO/30/37).

16 Disbrowe to Palmerston, no. 41, 20.10.1831 (FO/82/25); no. 46, 1.12.1831 (FO/82/25); Lamb to Palmerston, no. 59, 27.5.1832 (FO/7/234).

17 Cartwright to Palmerston, no. 131, 22.10.1831 (FO/30/35); Cartwright to Palmerston, no. 20, 18.2.1832 (FO/30/37); see also: Cartwright to Palmerston, no. 29, 6.3.1832 (FO/30/37) where the 'Ultra Liberals' Jordan, Welcker and Rotteck are reported to work towards an 'antifederal System'; Cartwright to Palmerston, no. 50, 26.5.1832 (FO/30/38); for a discussion of Cartwright's analysis of the tensions between liberal developments and federal duties of the individual states see: Heydemann (1995: 215–17).

18 Cartwright to Palmerston, no. 54, 2.6.1832 (FO/30/38); Cartwright to Palmerston, priv., 14.6.1832 (BP-GC/CA/535); Lamb to Palmerston, priv., 6.6.1832 (BP-GC/BE/42).

19 *Times* (5.6.1832: 3a–b); *Morning Chronicle* (11.6.1832: 2a; 12.6.1832: 2c); *Annual Register* 74 (1832: 372–3).

20 Cartwright to Palmerston, priv., 14.6.1832 (BP-GC/CA/535); Cartwright to Palmerston, copy, no. 104, 20.8.1832 (CaP-Box 95/6); Cartwright to Palmerston, no. 54, 20.4.1833 (FO/30/43).

21 See: Erskine to Palmerston, no. 30, 24.5.1831 (FO/9/61) and no. 11, 24.1.1832 (FO/9/64). Erskine's accounts of the Hambach festival were calmer than his colleagues' [see: Erskine to Palmerston, priv., 8.6.1832 (BP-GC/ER/9)]. This line did not ingratiate Erskine with William IV who regretted 'the continued observations of Lord Erskine in favour of revolution [to Palmerston, 16.6.1832 (BP-RC/A/98)].' Erskine's abilities were not generally regarded very highly; see: Webster (1951: i, 69, 225–6).

22 Chad to Palmerston, priv., 6.6.1832 (BP-GC/CH/26).

23 Cartwright to Palmerston, no. 29, 6.3.1832 (FO/30/37); Cartwright to Palmerston, no. 121, 21.9.1832 (FO/30/39).

24 Lamb to Palmerston, priv., 6.6.1832 (BP-GC/BE/42); Hansard, 3rd ser., vol. 14: 1047.

25 Cartwright to Palmerston, no. 73, 25.6.1832 (FO/30/38).

26 Cartwright to Palmerston, no. 121, 21.9.1832 (FO/30/39); Cartwright to Palmerston, no. 42, 5.4.1833 (FO/30/43); Cartwright to Palmerston, copy, priv., 5.4.1833, (CaP-Box 94/3); for Cartwright's views on the Wachensturm see also: Cartwright to Palmerston, no. 52, 17.4.1833 (FO/30/43); Cartwright to Palmerston, no. 54, 20.4.1833 (FO/30/43); Cartwright to

Palmerston, copy, priv., 20.4.1833 (CaP-Box 94/3); Cartwright to Palmerston, no. 103, 12.7.1833 (FO/30/44).

27 Cartwright to Palmerston, no. 81, 4.6.1833 (FO/30/44); *Times* (28.6.1833: 7b); the journalist Johann Wirth was one of the organizers of the Hambach festival.

28 Cartwright to Palmerston, no. 116, 6.9.1831 (FO/30/35); Palmerston to Durham, no. 2, 3.7.1832, draft (FO/65/200); Lamb to Palmerston, priv., 21.5.1833 (BP-GC/BE/96).

29 Disbrowe to Palmerston, no. 36, 7.8.1832 (FO/82/26); on the war scare of 1830–2 see: Billinger (1976: 205); Palmerston to Durham, copy, priv., 10.8.1832 (BP-GC/DU/82) [Palmerston copied this formulation from a despatch by Cartwright; see his markings in: Cartwright to Palmerston, no. 86, 16.7.1832 (FO/30/39)]; Palmerston to Lamb, draft, no. 83, 7.9.1832 (FO/7/233); for the genesis of Palmerston's despatch to Vienna and Berlin of 7 September 1832 see: Webster (1951: i, 231–3); Southgate (1966: 52–3) and Heydemann (1995: 230–6).

30 See: Introduction: n. 25.

31 Palmerston to Granville, copy, priv., 24.7.1832 (BP-GC/GR/1413); Palmerston to Cartwright, copy, priv., 3.8.1832 (BP-GC/CA/585); Palmerston to Erskine, draft, Aug. 1832 (BP-RC/AA/43/enc. 1); Palmerston to Lamb, draft, no. 83, 7.9.1832 (FO/7/233); for more examples of Palmerston's fear of a general revolution triggered by repression in Germany see: Palmerston to Durham, draft, no. 2, 2.7.1832 (FO/65/200), Palmerston to Erskine, copy, priv., 3.8.1832 (BP-GC/ER/189), Palmerston to Lamb, copy, priv., 3.8.1832 (BP-GC/BE/420), Palmerston to Minto, copy, priv., 18.6.1833 (BP-GC/MI/543).

32 Palmerston to Taylor, copy, priv., 30.10.1833 (BP-RC/CC/10).

33 These resolutions limited certain rights of the states (right of chambers to petition the sovereign; right of chambers to reject the budget; right to pass legislation detrimental to federal duties; right of free speech in the chambers). The right to interpret the Federal and Final Acts was reserved by the Diet and a federal supervisory commission was constituted. On 5 July 1832, the liberties of the press, of association and of public meeting were restricted; see: Huber (1968: 151–63).

34 *Times* (18.7.1832: 4c); *Morning Chronicle* (18.7.1832: 4a); *Spectator* (21.7.1832: 679)

35 *Times* (6.8.1832: 4b); [W. Weir,] 'The Despots' Challenge to Germany', *TEM* 1 (1832: 620); see also: [*idem*] 'On the State and Prospects of Germany', ibid., 689–703.

36 *Morning Chronicle* (10.8.1832: 2c; 15.8.1832: 2b).

37 According to the Austrian Ambassador, there were only eleven MPs present and Palmerston could have had the House counted out; see: Webster (1951: i, 230 n. 1). The debate was, however, published verbatim in the *Times* (2.8.1832: 1f–2f).

38 Hansard, 3rd ser., vol. 14: 1045, 1061, 1065, 1048–9.

39 Lamb to Palmerston, priv., 26.7.1832 (BP-GC/BE/49).

40 Lord Erskine in Munich again dissented and attacked the 'Six Articles'; see: Erskine to Palmerston, no. 35, 26.6.1832 and no. 38, 8.7.1832 (FO/9/65).

41 Cartwright to Palmerston, priv., 14.6.1832 and 16.7.1832 (BP-GC/CA/535,

540); Disbrowe to Palmerston, no. 32, 17.7.1832 (FO/82/26); Lamb to Palmerston, no. 119, 23.8.1832 (FO/7/235); Lamb to Palmerston, priv., 27.3.1833 (BP-GC/BE/84); Lamb was probably referring to an Irish Coercion Bill debated at that time; for this 'Act for the more Effectual Suppression of Local Disturbances and Dangerous Associations in Ireland' see: *Parliamentary Papers* (1833: 71–106).

42 The King and Palmerston (backed by the Cabinet) clashed over the Foreign Secretary's decision to confront Austria and Prussia. As a result, the despatches to Vienna and Berlin were delayed until September 1832. On this conflict see: Webster (1951: i, 231–2 and ii, 799–800, 828–31) and Heydemann (1995: 229–32); for Lord Holland's account see: Kriegel (1977: 199–202).

43 See: Bourne (1982: 370 and 1984: 35).

44 Palmerston to Lamb, copy, priv., no. 12, 30.6.1832 (BP-GC/BE/419); Palmerston to Granville, copy, priv., 24.7.1832 (BP-GC/GR/1413); Palmerston to Lamb, copy, priv, no. 13, 3.8.1832 (BP-GC/BE/420); Palmerston to Minto, copy, priv., no. 23, 18.6.1833 (BP-GC/MI/543).

45 Palmerston to Lamb, copy, priv., no. 12, 30.6.1832 (BP-GC/BE/419); Hansard, 3rd ser., vol. 14: 1047.

46 Disbrowe to Palmerston, no. 32, 17.7.1832 and no. 34, 26.7.1832 (FO/82/26); Cartwright to Palmerston, copy, no. 88, 23.7.1832 (CaP-Box 95/6); Barnard to Palmerston, no. 28, 29.7.1832 (FO/68/35); Abercrombie to Palmerston, priv., 6.8.1832 (BP-GC/AB/5).

47 Palmerston to Cartwright, copy, priv., no. 1, 3.8.1832 (BP-GC/CA/585); Palmerston to Earl Grey, copy, 3.8.1832 (BP-GC/GR/2372); Palmerston to Erskine, copy, priv., no. 5, 3.8.1832 (BP-GC/ER/189); Palmerston to Lamb, copy, priv., no. 13, 3.8.1832 (BP-GC/BE/420); Palmerston to William IV, draft, 5.8.1832 (BP-RC/AA/43); for Palmerston's fear of revolution see: n. 31 (ch. 1).

48 Palmerston to Lamb, draft, no. 83, 7.9.1832 (FO/7/233).

49 Palmerston to Lamb, copy, priv., no. 12, 30.6.1832 (BP-GC/BE/419); Palmerston to Chad, copy, priv., 22.6.1832 (BP-GC/CH/49).

50 Palmerston to Lamb, copy, priv., no. 12, 30.6.1832 (BP-GC/BE/419); Clarke (1989: 190); see also: Bourne (1982: 368).

51 Hansard, 3rd ser., vol. 14: 1046, 1045; this emphasis on the 'independence' of the separate German states was also echoed in the speeches by Lytton Bulwer (1031, 1033) and Colonel Evans (1060).

52 Palmerston to Lamb, draft, no. 83, 7.9.1832 (FO/7/233).

53 Palmerston to William IV, copy, no. 13, 16.6.1832 (BP-RC/AA/31); Palmerston to Earl Grey, copy, 3.8.1832 (BP-GC/GR/2372); Palmerston to Lamb, draft, no. 83, 7.9.1832 (FO/7/233).

54 Palmerston to Granville, copy, priv., 24.7.1832 (BP-GC/GR/1413); Palmerston to Lamb, copy, priv., no. 13, 3.8.1832 (BP-GC/BE/420); Palmerston to Erskine, draft, Aug. 1832 (BP-RC/AA/43/enc. 1).

55 See: Billinger (1991: chs 3–6).

56 For Palmerston's hostility towards centralization in Switzerland and Germany see: Webster (1951: i, 229).

57 Cartwright to Palmerston, copy, no. 104, 20.8.1832 (CaP-Box 95/6); Cartwright to Palmerston, priv., 20.8.1832 (BP-GC/CA/541); Cartwright

dismissed the idea 'that Austria and Prussia desired nothing better than a fair and favorable pretext for overthrowing the Constitutions altogether,' in his no. 86 to Palmerston of 16.7.1832 (FO/30/39); Minto to Cartwright, priv., 30.10.1832 (CaP-Box 91/58); Lamb to Palmerston, priv., 26.7.1832 (BP-GC/BE/49).

58 Palmerston to Taylor, copy, priv., 30.10.1833 (BP-RC/CC/10); Palmerston's concern for the independence of the small German states was again expressed when he challenged the Diet over the continued occupation of Frankfurt by federal troops in 1833–4; see: Heydemann (1995: 241–4).

59 Hansard, 3rd ser., vol. 14: 1045; Palmerston to Lamb, draft, no. 83, 7.9.1832 (FO/7/233).

60 Palmerston to Durham, draft, no. 2, 3.7.1832 (FO/65/200); Palmerston to Lamb, draft, no. 83, 7.9.1832 (FO/7/233).

61 Milbanke to Aberdeen, no. 25, 29.8.1830 (FO/30/32); Cartwright to Palmerston, no. 33, 19.3.1832 (FO/30/37); Lamb to Palmerston, no. 59, 27.5.1832 (FO/7/234); Milbanke to Lamb, priv., 16.6.1832 (BP-GC/BE/46/enc.)

62 Lamb to Palmerston, no. 119, 23.8.1832 (FO/7/235).

63 Granville to Palmerston, priv., 19.7.1832 (BP-GC/GR/315).

64 Southgate (1966: 108); Hansard, 3rd ser., vol. 14: 1048.

65 Palmerston to Lamb, priv., no. 14, 28–1832 (BP-GC/BE/421); Lamb to Palmerston, priv., 12.9.1832 (BP-GC/BE/54).

66 Ibid.

67 On Britain's involvement in China see: Fay (1975) and Graham (1978); the British role in North American affairs is covered thoroughly by Bourne (1967).

68 Palmerston to William Temple, 21.4.1834 (BP-GC/TE/219).

69 On Peninsular affairs and the Anglo-French entente see: Bullen (1974; 1978); Cunningham (1957) and Parry (1936); on the Eastern Crisis of 1840/1 see ch. 1: n. 97; Britain's role in the Swiss civil war is covered by Imlah (1966); for the Minto mission of 1847 see: Schroeder (1994b: 781–2); Syme (1964) and Taylor (1934).

70 Treitschke (1919: v, 461).

71 While the actual effects of the *Zollverein* on Germany's economy are still controversial, older intepretations which portrayed it as a forerunner of Bismarck's *Reich* have now been largely refuted. For discussions of the *Zollverein* see: Hahn (1984) and Wehler (1987: 125–39).

72 Strangways to Palmerston, no. 20, draft, 18.12.1840 (FO/208/28); on Britain's brief opposition to the *Zollverein* see: Hahn (1984: 71–2).

73 Treitschke (1919: v, 462–4); Schenk (1939: 98); Henderson (1959: 97); Vogt (1965: 407); similarly: Bourne (1982: 371); for a collection of reactions to the *Zollverein* in the British press see: Vogt (1962: 157–222); see also: Heydemann (1995: 251–266).

74 Hansard, 3rd ser., vol. 20: 695, 699; [J. McCulloch,] 'Prussian Commercial Policy', *FQR* 9 (1832: 470); see also: [*idem*] 'Prussian Commercial Policy', *FQR* 11 (1833: 403–6) and the absurd accusations in Cargill (1840: 25) where the Zollverein was portrayed as a threat to India; *Times* (21.8.1832: 2c; 30.8.1832: 3c; 31.8.1832: 2b–d); *Spectator* (4.1.1834: 2).

75 *BFR* 1 (1835:, 318–61, 544–61); *BEM* 39 (1836: 49–79, 145–55, 780–92); *FQR* 22 (1838/9: 299–324); *BFR* 13 (1842: 188–205); *ER* 75 (1842: 515–56); *ER*

79 (1844: 105–29); *ER* 83 (1846: 224–39); *TEM* 19 (1848: 594–600); *BEM* 64 (1848: 515–42); *BQR* 8 (1848: 516–53); *NBR* 10 (1848: 240–60).

76 [D. Urquhart,]'The Effect on England of the Prussian Commercial League', *BFR* 1 (1835: 321); [J. Austin,] 'List on the Principles of the German Customs Union', *ER* 75 (1842: 523).

77 Milbanke to Dudley, no. 7, 24.3.1828 (FO/30/28); similarly: Addington to Aberdeen, no. 14, 6.10.1829 (FO/30/29); Chad to Palmerston, priv., 28.11.1831 (FO/64/175); Erskine to Palmerston, no. 50, 4.12.1833 (FO/9/66); Palmerston to Lamb, no. 86, draft, 18.9.1832 (FO/7/233).

78 *Parliamentary Papers* (1843: 271–288); Peel to Aberdeen, 11.10.1843 (PeP-Add.Mss. 40453); on the iron duties issue see: Gordon (1969); Palmerston: Memorandum, 16.9.1847 (QVP: vol. I.1, doc. 43).

79 Aberdeen to Addington, no. 4, draft, 18.9.1829 (FO/30/29); Forbes to Palmerston, no. 10, 23.3.1833 (FO/68/36); Abercrombie to Palmerston, no. 22, 1.9.1833 (FO/64/190); Abercrombie to Wellington, no. 15, 4.3.1835 (FO/64/200); Hansard, 3rd ser., vol. 31: 648.

80 On MacGregor's reports from Germany see: Brown (1958: 104–5); Mac-Gregor to Palmerston, 14.7.1838 (FO/68/44); *Parliamentary Papers* (1840: 2); Aberdeen to Peel, copy, 4.10.1845 (AP-Add.Mss. 43065).

81 Erskine to Palmerston, no. 17, 18.4.1833 (FO/9/66); Abercrombie to Palmerston, no. 22, 1.9.1833 (FO/64/190); Russell to Palmerston, no. 61, 14.11.1838 (FO/64/216); *Parliamentary Papers* (1840: 3); Laing (1842: 152).

82 Hansard, 3rd ser., vol. 20: 700; Russell to Palmerston, no. 16, 12.2.1839 (FO/64/221); *Parliamentary Papers* (1840: 2–3 and 1842: 7); Palmerston: Memorandum, 8.9.1846 (QVP: vol. I.1, doc. 21); see Palmerston's similar observations in his memorandum of 16.9.1847 (QVP: vol. I.1, doc. 43).

83 On Bowring's use of the *Zollverein* report to push his free trading views see: Brown (1958: 106–10).

84 *Annual Register*, 78 (1836: 413–14); *FQR* 9 (1832: 470); *Times* (30.12.1833: 2b; similarly: 3.1.1834: 2b and 11.5.1846: 11c); [anon.,] 'Germany', *WR* 22 (1835: 140); [A. Mallalieu,] 'Foreign Policy, Foreign Commerce, and the Prusso-Germanic Custom-House League', *BEM* 39 (1836: 54); for more examples see: *FQR* 22 (1839: 31–314), *BFR* 13 (1842: 199), *ER* 79 (1844: 109–10), *ER* 83 (1846: 228), *QR* 88 (1850: 181).

85 Chad to Palmerston, priv., 28.11.1831 (FO/64/175); Erskine to Palmerston, no. 1, 11.1.1833 (FO/9/66); Bingham to Palmerston, no. 4, 20.2.1833 (FO/9/66); Abercrombie to Palmerston, no. 8, 31.7.1833 (FO/64/190); Cartwright to Palmerston, no. 135, 1.12.1834 (FO/30/53).

86 Wellesley to Palmerston, priv., 25.3.1838 (BP-GC/CO/77); Wm Russell to Palmerston, no. 16, 12.2.1839 (FO/64/221); *Parliamentary Papers* (1840: 7 and 1842: 2); see also the similar comments in the memoirs of Lord Loftus, chargé d'affaires in Karlsruhe: Loftus (1892: i, 32, 53–4).

87 *Times* (30.12.1833: 2a–b).

88 This was particularly true for Bavaria; see: Hahn (1984: 74).

89 Palmerston to Lamb, no. 86, draft, 18.9.1832 (FO/7/233); Forbes to Palmerston, no. 10, 23.3.1833 (FO/68/36); *Parliamentary Papers* (1842: 4). It is interesting to note that one of the motives for the repeal of the Corn Laws in Britain was that these measures were believed to have an anti-revolutionary effect; see: Blake (1966: 280).

90 *Times* (3.1.1834: 2b); *Parliamentary Papers* (1840: 1 and 1842: 1); *Times* (13.10.1842: 4a); similar views can also be found in: Times (13.9.1842: 4c); *ER* 79 (1844: 110) and *ER* 83 (1846: 228).

91 Strangways to Aberdeen, no. 5, 29.4.1843 (FO/30/82); Westmorland to Aberdeen, no. 120, 27.11.1844 (FO/64/251); Palmerston: Memorandum, 8.9.1846 (QVP: vol. I.1, doc. 21); Palmerston: Memorandum, 16.9.1847 (QVP: vol. I.1, doc. 43); this British reading of the salutary political effects of the *Zollverein* bears close resemblance to the aims expressed in 1829 by Friedrich von Motz, its main architect; see: *Vorgeschichte* (1934: iii, 534–7).

92 [A. Mallalieu,] 'Foreign Policy, Foreign Commerce and the Prusso-Germanic Custom-House League', *BEM* 39 (1836: 53, see also: 58–59); *Parliamentary Papers* (1840: 1).

93 Laing (1842: 161, 127); [J. Ward,] 'Commercial Tariffs – The German Zollverein', *ER* 79 (1844: 109).

94 For British praise of Prussia's tariff policy see: Bowring to Palmerston, no. 1, 7.8.1839 (FO/97/326); Westmorland to Gladstone, copy, priv., Sept. 1844 (AP-Add.Mss. 43142); Aberdeen to Peel, copy, 15.8.1845 (AP-Add.Mss. 43064); *Times* (15.9.1843: 4e; 20.8.1845: 4b–c).

95 Strangways to Palmerston, no. 20, draft, 18.12.1840 (FO/208/28).

96 This translation is by Francis Palgrave, see his: 'Victor Hugo's *Letters on the Rhine*', *QR* 71 (1843: 331); on the Rhine Song movement see: Buchner (1955: 315–333), Veit-Brause (1963: 125–35) and Schulze (1991: 65–6).

97 For a detailed account of the Eastern Crisis of 1839–41 see: Webster (1951: ii, 619–776); a short recent summary is Rich (1992: 69–74); for the French policy towards Germany in 1840–1 see: Roghé (1971: 204–17), Owsinska (1974: 39–63) and Poidevin (1977: 22–4).

98 Schulze (1996: 194); on the importance of the 'Rhine Crisis' for the development of German nationalism see: Buchner (1955), Veit-Brause (1963: 136–278); Püschner (1977), Gruner (1987: 551–3); Gruner (1990); Schulze (1991: 65–6); Dann (1996: 116–17) and Simms (1998: 158).

99 On federal military reform see: Lee (1987) and Angelow (1996: 109–25); on the Austro-Prussian negotiations see: Veit-Brause (1963: 47–61) and Billinger (1990); the sovereigns' attitude is characterized in: Püschner (1977: 110–11); Schulze (1991: 66) and Dann (1996: 116–17).

100 Erskine to Palmerston, no. 6, 19.2.1841 (FO/9/82).

101 Erskine to Palmerston, priv., 11.5.1840 (BP-GC/ER/161); Wm Russell to Palmerston, priv., 7/15.9.1840 (BP-GC/RU/1456); Erskine to Palmerston, no. 30, 9.11.1840 (FO/9/80).

102 Palmerston to Lytton Bulwer, copy, priv., 22.9.1840 (BP-GC/BU/503).

103 Russell to Palmerston, priv., 7/15.9.1840 (BP-GC/RU/1456); Strangways to Palmerston, priv., 23/26.10.1840 (BP-GC/FO/178); Beauvale to Palmerston, no. 170, 11.11.1840 (FO/7/291B); Erskine to Palmerston, no. 4, 2.2.1841 (FO/9/82); the only other references to an anti-French disposition or national spirit in the German public in the manuscripts examined are: Palmerston to Lytton Bulwer, copy, priv., 22.9.1840 (BP-GC/BU/503); Bligh to Palmerston, no. 42, 15.10.1840 (FO/34/32); Beauvale to Palmerston, no. 164, 1.11.1840 (FO/7/291B); Forbes to Palmerston, no. 26, 7.11.1840 (FO/68/48).

104 *Gesandtschaftsberichte* (1936/1937: iv, 216, 256, 213, 257 [author's trans.]); on the new picture of Germany in France see also: Owsinska (1974: 44).

105   *Times* (1.4.1841: 5d); Hansard, 3rd ser., vol. 52: 1223–1243; [H. Longueville Jones,] 'England and her European Allies', *BEM* 50 (1841: 457).

106   Schroeder (1994b: 749); see also: Bullen (1979: 127).

107   Forbes to Palmerston, no. 26, 7.11.1840 (FO/68/48).

108   Beauvale to Palmerston, no. 116, 29.8.1840 (FO/7/291A); Erskine to Palmerston, no. 27, 21.10.1840 (FO/9/80); Sulivan to Palmerston, priv., 21.11.1840 (BP-GC/SU/67); Palmerston to Wm Russell, no. 94, draft, 3.11.1840 (FO/64/227).

109   Palmerston to Victoria, 11.11.1840 (*QVL*: i, 247–8).

110   Beauvale to Palmerston, priv., 30–1/6.2.1841 (BP-GC/BE/372); Wm Russell to Palmerston, no. 64, 23.12.1840 (FO/64/229) and no. 50, 25.8.1841 (FO/64/233).

111   Siemann (1995: 353).

112   See: Meyer (1994: 177–229, 273–4) and Siemann (1995: 353–4).

113   This term was coined by Düding (1984).

114   Düding (1987: 41); on German nationalism during the 1840s see also: Thomas (1951), Düding (1984; 1987; 1988: 166–83); Schulze (1991: 64, 66–9); Dann (1996: 114–23).

115   Wellesley to Aberdeen, no. 3, 13.1.1843 (FO/82/42); Kuper to Aberdeen, no. 3, 27.1.1843 (FO/30/82); Westmorland to Aberdeen, no. 93, 28.5.1845 (FO/64/257).

116   Aberdeen to Peel, 1.9.1845 (AP-Add.Mss. 43064); Forbes to Aberdeen, no. 4, 7.1.1846 (FO/68/60) and no. 8, 31.1.1846 (FO/68/60).

117   Only once and then characteristically late did an association of gymnasts feature in a despatch. In January 1848 Frederick Orme, chargé d'affaires in Frankfurt, reported the city's decision to ban the 'Gymnastic Association' which had 'latterly assumed a political character' [Orme to Palmerston, no. 5, 22.1.1848 (FO/30/104)] As before, Bourgoing showed a keener awareness of the structure of German nationalism; see: *Gesandtschaftsberichte* (1936/1937: v, 86–92).

118   [anon.,] 'Prussia and the Prussian System', *WR* 37 (1842: 141); *Times* (27.3.1843: 4e).

119   There was some discussion of discontent in Bavaria [see: Sulivan to Aberdeen, no. 15, 15.8.1844 and priv., 17.9.1844 (FO/9/87)] but Prussia soon occupied centre stage in British perceptions of *Vormärz* Germany.

120   *Times* (18.6.1832: 2a); *WR* 22 (1835: 135); Cartwright to Palmerston, no. 73, 9.10.1835 (FO/30/57); *Times* (13.9.1841: 4b); [J. Ward,] 'Commercial Tariffs. The German Zollverein', *ER* 79 (1844: 110); Strangways to Aberdeen, no. 13, 17.2.1846 (FO/30/95).

121   Russell to Palmerston, no. 64, 23.12.1840 (FO/64/229), no. 10, 24.2.1841 and no. 15, 31.3.1841 (FO/64/233); Kuper to Aberdeen, no. 3, 27.1.1843 (FO/30/82); Aberdeen to Peel, copy, 15.8.1845 (AP-Add.Mss. 43064).

122   *WR* 37 (1842: 139); [F. Palgrave,] 'Victor Hugo's *Letters on the Rhine*', *QR* 71 (1843: 331); [G. S. Venables,] 'German Political Squibs and Crotchets', *FQR* 35 (1845: 430); [R. Monckton Milnes,] 'Political State of Prussia', *ER* 83 (1846: 224–5).

123   For a summary of Frederick William IV's first steps see: Faber (1979: 182–5); on the constitutional question in *Vormärz* Prussia see: Obenaus (1984: 521–648).

124 *Times* (9.3.1841: 5b; 25.4.1842: 5c); see also: *Times* (7.11.1842: 4a–b; 9.2.1846: 8f; 7.4.1846: 5e; 20.5.1846: 5c; 22.5.1846: 4d); [anon.,] 'The Rhine and Rhenish Affairs', *FM* 27 (1843: 584); [R. Monckton Milnes,] 'Political State of Prussia', *ER* 83 (1846: 228). British liberals praising Prussia's government and administration was nothing new in the 1840s. For Cobden's praise for Prussia's 'bureaucratic liberalism' in the 1830s see: Breuilly (1997).

125 Hamilton to Aberdeen, no. 10, 15.1.1842 (FO/64/238); Aberdeen to Gordon, priv., 4.2.1842 (AP-Add.Mss. 43211 (I)); Wellesley to Aberdeen, no. 3, 13.1.1843 (FO/82/42); Palmerston to Wm Temple, 13.10.1844, quoted in: Bulwer (1874: iii, 159–160).

126 On the 'United Diet' see: Barclay (1995: 122–32); Obenaus (1984: 649–716); Mieck (1992: 222–9); Huber (1968: 491–8).

127 See: Westmorland to Aberdeen, no. 59, 13.3.1846 and no. 64, 18.3.1846 (FO/64/263); Hamilton to Aberdeen, no. 22, 24.6.1846 (FO/64/264); Howard to Palmerston, no. 19, 14.10.1846 (FO/64/266).

128 Palmerston to Westmorland, no. 20, draft, 9.2.1847 (FO/64/270); Palmerston to Westmorland, no. 35, draft, 2.3.1847 (FO/64/270); Palmerston to Malet, no. 7, draft, 6.4.1847 (FO/82/51); Hansard, 3rd ser., vol. 90: 308; *Times* (16.4.1847: 4d); for more favourable articles see: *Times* (19.4.1847: 4a–c and 5.7.1847: 5c).

129 Palmerston to Westmorland, no. 20, draft, 9.2.1847 (FO/64/270); Palmerston to Howard, no. 21, draft, 24.8.1847 (FO/64/271).

130 Ward to Palmerston, genl. no. 9, 7.5.1847 (FO/299/2); Westmorland to Palmerston, no. 161, 25.6.1847 (FO/64/274).

131 Howard to Palmerston, no. 6, 14.7.1847 (FO/64/275); Strangways to Palmerston, no. 22, 16.7.1847 (FO/30/99); Russell: Memorandum, 16.5.1848 (RuP-PRO/30/22/7C); see also Palmerston's praise for Frederick William's policies in: Palmerston to Canning, no. 1, draft, 10.3.1848 (FO/30/117).

132 Barclay (1995: 74, 126); see also: Mieck (1992: 202–10).

Chapter 2

1 Hansard, 3rd ser., vol. 97: 122–3 (1.3.1848).

2 On Britain's European policy in 1848/49 see: Billy (1993); Bourne (1970: 63–8); Clarke (1989: 219–30) and Southgate (1966: 206–57); Palmerston's attitude to Hungary is analysed by Sproxton (1919).

3 The recent 150th anniversary of the revolution has led to a mass of new publications on Germany in 1848/49. See: Dowe (1998); Hardtwig (1998); Pogge (2000) and Siemann (1998). For richness of material, however, Valentin (1930/31) remains unsurpassed.

4 Bligh to Palmerston, priv., 25.2.1848 (BP-GC/BL/84); Palmerston enjoyed his reputation. In his election speech in July 1847 [Palmerston (1847: 23)] he used it as an ironic boast: 'I have been accused all over Europe of being the great instigator of revolution – (laughter) – the friend and champion of popular insurrections, the enemy of all constituted authorities [. . .] I have been charged with disturbing the peace of Europe by giving encouragement to every revolutionary and anarchical set of men – (renewed laughter).' On

Palmerston's undeserved radical reputation see: Chamberlain (1980: 63–4); Chamberlain (1987: 2–3) and Gillessen (1961: 7–9).

5 Kennedy (1980: 12–13); a body of older literature followed this interpretation and emphasized Britain's alleged opposition to German unity; see the summary of these views in: Gillessen (1961: 149–150).

6 [anon.,] 'Political Fly Leaves from Germany', *TEM* 19 o.s. (1848: 595).

7 Palmerston to Westmorland, no. 30, draft, 22.2.1848 (FO/64/282); Milbanke to Palmerston, no. 14, 7.3.1848 (FO/9/100).

8 Malet to Palmerston, no. 9, 2.3.1848 (FO/82/55); Ward to Westmorland, no date [1/2.3.1848] (WeP-M/526/2); *Times* (13.3.1848: 4b; 17.3.1848: 4e).

9 *Times* (25.3.1848: 6d; 18.4.1848: 4c); [J. S. Blackie,] 'The Revolutions in Europe', *BEM* 63 (1848: 649); [W. E. Aytoun,] 'A Glimpse of Germany and its Parliament', *BEM* 64 (1848: 516); *Annual Register* 90 (1848: 356).

10 Cowley to Palmerston, no. 45, 20.8.1848 (FO/30/109); Westmorland to Palmerston, no. 64, 15.3.1848 and no. 75, 23.3.1848 (FO/64/285); similarly: *Times* (29.3.1848: 6e); Ward to Palmerston, genl. no. 15, copy, 30.3.1848 (FO/299/3).

11 Bligh to Palmerston, no. 30, 13.4.1848 (FO/34/53).

12 For instance, in the sources examined the widespread rural unrest in the Black Forest, the Odenwald and parts of Bavaria attracted no more than two superficial references.

13 Canning to Palmerston, no. 11, 24.4.1848 and no. 18, 7.5.1848 (FO/30/117); Canning's mission in the spring of 1848 involved reporting from the German states and preaching the blessings of 'timely concessions'; see: Palmerston to Canning, no. 1, draft, 10.3.1848 (FO/30/117); on Canning's mission see also: Lane-Poole (1888: ii, 167–71); Gillessen (1961: 15–17) and Stürmer (1982).

14 Malet to Palmerston, no. 15, 7.3.1848 (FO/82/55); Orme to Palmerston, no. 17, 7.3.1848 (FO/30/104); Forbes to Palmerston, no. 16, 12.3.1848 (FO/68/68); Canning to Palmerston, no. 10, 3.4.1848 (FO/30/117).

15 Palmerston to Malet, priv., copy, 23.3.1848 (BP-GC/MA/106); Palmerston to Westmorland, copy/extract, 23.3.1848 (BP-GC/WE/191).

16 Canning to Palmerston, no. 3, 23.3.1848 (FO/30/117); Canning to Palmerston, priv., 26.3.1848 (BP-GC/CA/164); Canning to Palmerston, priv., 31.3.1848 (BP-GC/CA/166); Strangways to Palmerston, no. 10, 8.4.1848 (FO/30/106); Canning to Palmerston, no. 11, 24.4.1848 (FO/30/117).

17 Palmerston to Victoria, 18.4.1848, in: (*QVL*: ii, 171); Canning to Palmerston, no. 10, 3.4.1848 (FO/30/117); Palmerston to Milbanke, no. 18, draft, 20.4.1848 (FO/9/99); the same comment that Germany's governments would to well to learn from the way Chartism had been tackled can be found in: Westmorland to Palmerston, no. 147, 20.4.1848 (FO/64/286); for Britain's unflappable attitude in 1848 see: Mitchell (2000).

18 Forbes to Palmerston, no. 39, 19.5.1848 (FO/68/68); on the radicalism and republicanism in Thuringia see also: Forbes to Palmerston, no. 58, 9.8.1848 (FO/68/69); Milbanke to Palmerston, priv., 29.5.1848 (BP-GC/MI/43).

19 Magenis to Palmerston, no. 41, 9.7.1848 (FO/7/354). There are few insightful despatches on German politics from Vienna. This was caused by Italian affairs, which dominated the correspondence with the Austrian capital, and also by the pompous obtuseness of the British ambassador at Vienna,

Ponsonby, whose 'despatches are very dull reading, and add absolutely nothing to our knowledge of the Viennese or Hungarian Revolutions' [Sproxton (1919: 60)]. Two examples of Ponsonby's style will suffice. On 17 March he reported on the revolution in Vienna: 'I have not troubled Your Lordship with details of the occurrences which took place in the streets, nor with reports of the speeches of students and other orators. The commonplaces which figure in such displays, are familiar to all, and my report of them would only be tedious and tiresome' [Ponsonby to Palmerston, no. 54, 17.3.1848 (FO/7/347)]. In June, Ponsonby sent Palmerston some documents from Innsbruck but freely admitted: 'I don't understand enough German to be able to translate what I enclose' [Ponsonby to Palmerston, priv., 14.6.1848 (FO/7/350)].

20 Westmorland to Palmerston, no. 313, 24.8.1848; no. 354, 28.9.1848 (FO/64/289) and no. 402, 9.11.1848 (FO/64/290); Westmorland to Palmerston, no. 389, 1.11.1848 (FO/64/290); Bligh to Palmerston, no. 63, 29.6.1848 (FO/34/53); Malet to Palmerston, no. 63, 5.10.1848 (FO/82/55).

21 [J. S. Blackie,] 'The Revolutions in Europe', *BEM* (1848: 650); Canning to Palmerston, no. 20, 12.5.1848 (FO/30/117); Palmerston to Victoria, 18.11.1850, in: (*QVL*: ii, 275–276).

22 Westmorland to Palmerston, no. 87, 29.3.1848 (FO/64/285) and no. 114, 6.4.1848 (FO/64/286); Westmorland to Aberdeen, priv., copy, 14.4.1848 (FaC-MS Eng d 2577).

23 Forbes to Palmerston, no. 62, 6.9.1848 and no. 64, 26.9.1848 (FO/68/69); Bligh to Palmerston, no. 90, 5.10.1848 (FO/34/54); Milbanke to Palmerston, no. 57, 14.11.1848 (FO/9/101).

24 Westmorland to Palmerston, no. 194, 15.5.1848 (FO/64/287); Forbes to Palmerston, no. 91, 18.12.1848 (FO/68/69); Milbanke to Palmerston, no. 61, 18.12.1848 (FO/9/101) and no. 1, 15.1.1849 (FO/9/103).

25 Forbes to Palmerston, no. 4, 26.1.1849 (FO/68/72).

26 Westmorland to Palmerston, no. 89, 30.3.1848 (FO/64/285); no. 325, 4.9.1848 (FO/64/289) and no. 405, 12.11.1848 (FO/64/290).

27 On the Prussian coup d'état see: Barclay (1995: 153–84 [for the Manteuffel quotation: 168]); Valentin (1930/31: ii, 284–90 [for the Frederick William quotation: 284]); Huber (1968: 746–66); Canis (1972).

28 Westmorland to Palmerston, no. 401, 9.11.1848 (FO/64/290); Westmorland to Palmerston, priv., copy, 20.11.1848 (WeP-M/509/2/ff. 239ff); Westmorland to Palmerston, no. 431, 5.12.1848 (FO/64/290).

29 Cowley to Westmorland, priv., copy, 23.11.1848 (CoP-FO/519/165); for Cowley's approval see also: Cowley to Palmerston, no. 272, 20.11.1848 (FO/30/114).

30 Diplomatic reporting from Austria proved so inadequate as to make a specific discussion of the reimposition of imperial rule in Vienna impossible. However, the few relevant sources found support an interpretation broadly similar to that of the Prussian case. See: Ponsonby to Palmerston, no. 357, 3.10.1848 (FO/7/352); no. 405, 10.11.1848 and no. 421, 20.11.1848 (FO/7/353); Cowley to Ponsonby, priv., copy, 24.11.1848 (CoP-FO/519/165).

31 *Times* (22.11.1848: 4d; 20.12.1848: 4b).

32 Barclay (1995: 182).

33 Westmorland to Palmerston, no. 432, 5.12.1848 (FO/64/290); Cowley to Palmerston, no. 324, 10.12.1848 and no. 334, 14.12.1848 (FO/30/115); Westmorland to Palmerston, no. 439, 14.12.1848 (FO/64/290).

34 Mellish was a remarkably well-informed and prolific official but it is difficult to gauge his influence on the formulation of Britain's German policy; for more biographical information see: Middleton (1977: 295–6).

35 Mellish to Cowley, priv., 13.12.1848 (CoP-FO/519/158); Palmerston to Temple, priv., copy, 9.12.1848 (BP-GC/TE/322); Palmerston to Bunsen, priv., copy, 6.1.1849 (BP-GC/BU/609); Reeve to Mayer, 27.1.1849 (QVP: vol. I.11, doc. 56).

36 Aberdeen to Metternich, priv., copy, 23.2.1849 (AP-Add.Mss. 43128). In all Aberdeen wrote at least nineteen sympathetic letters to Metternich in 1848–9.

37 *Times* (31.1.1849: 4d).

38 Cowley to Palmerston, no. 39, 29.1.1849 (FO/30/122); for the text of the Prussian circular note see: Roth (1850/1852: ii, 253–61); on the note and British reactions to it see: Valentin (1930/31: ii, 360–2), Vogt (1964: 189–90) and Gillessen (1961: 60–2); Russell, Notes on Foreign Affairs, 16.8.1849 (BP-GC/RU/283).

39 *Times* (15.5.1849: 5d).

40 Milbanke to Palmerston, no. 1, 15.1.1849 (FO/9/103); Cowley to Palmerston, priv., 26.2.1849 (BP-GC/CO/162); Milbanke to Palmerston, no. 27, 13.4.1849 (FO/9/103); Malet to Palmerston, no. 15, 22.4.1849 (FO/82/58); Malet to Cowley, priv., 29.4.1849 (CoP-FO/519/160).

41 Cowley to Palmerston, no. 29.4.1849 (FO/30/125); *Times* (4.5.1849, 6a); Milbanke to Cowley, priv., 4.5.1840 (CoP: FO/519/160); [A. Alison,] 'The Year of Reaction', *BEM* 67 (1850: 6–7).

42 Ward to Palmerston, genl. no. 8, copy, 7.5.1849 (FO/299/4); Forbes to Palmerston, no. 26, 9.5.1849 and no. 27, 14.5.1849 (FO/68/72); Cowley to Palmerston, no. 239, 8.5.1848 (FO/30/126).

43 Malet to Palmerston, no. 23, 15.5.1849 (FO/82/58); Milbanke to Palmerston, no. 37, 18.5.1849 (FO/9/103); Cowley to Palmerston, no. 274, 19.5.1849 (FO/30/126); Malet to Palmerston, no. 62, 23.6.1849 (FO/82/59); Malet to Palmerston, no. 62, 23.6.1849 (FO/82/59).

44 Bligh to Palmerston, no. 5, 18.5.1849 (FO/34/56); *Times* (24.5.1849: 4d); Cowley to Palmerston, no. 395, 8.7.1849 (FO/30/128); *Times* (29.6.1849: 5d); Westmorland to Palmerston, no. 255, 2.7.1849 (FO/64/300).

45 Cowley to Malet, priv., copy, 29.6.1849 (CoP-FO/519/165).

46 Malet to Palmerston, no. 19, 16.3.1848 (FO/82/55); John Ward to Westmorland, priv., 1/2.3.1848 (WeP-M/526/2); *Times* (6.3.1848: 5e).

47 Orme to Palmerston, no. 25, 18.3.1848 (FO/30/104); see also: Forbes to Palmerston, no. 11, 4.3.1848 (FO/68/68).

48 Malet to Palmerston, no. 19, 16.3.1848 and no. 24, 22.3.1848 (FO/82/55); Milbanke to Palmerston, no. 17, 18.3.1848 (FO/9/100); Orme to Palmerston, no. 13, 3.3.1848 (FO/30/104).

49 Malet to Palmerston, no. 24, 22.3.1848 (FO/82/55); Orme to Palmerston, no. 28, 23.3.1848 (FO/30/104).

50 Ward to Palmerston, genl. no. 11, copy, 15.3.1848 (FO/299/3).

51 Bligh to Palmerston, no. 76, 10.8.1848 (FO/30/54); see also: Bligh to Palmerston, no. 27, 6.4.1848 (FO/34/53). On the *Vorparlament*, the selection of its members and the governmental attempts to pre-empt and weaken it see: Obermann (1979: 1156–9). The instructions for Friedrich von Wangenheim, the 'Man of Public Confidence' nominated by the Hanoverian government to assist the Diet in its deliberations on possible reforms clearly aim at keeping the reform process 'within strictly constitutional limits' and thus away from the *Vorparlament* [see: Roth (1850/1852: i, 163–5)].

52 Orme to Palmerston, no. 21, 11.3.1848 and no. 25, 18.3.1848 (FO/30/104); see also: Orme to Palmerston, no. 19, 10.3.1848 (FO/30/104), where he suggested action by the Diet to prevent the adoption of the Heidelberg plan; Milbanke to Palmerston, no. 17, 18.3.1848 (FO/9/100).

53 Palmerston to Westmorland, priv., copy, 23.3.1848 (BP-GC/WE/191); for a similar idea see: Palmerston to Malet, priv., copy, 23.3.1848 (BP-GC/MA/106). By 'the subsidiary body' Palmerston was probably referring to the 17 'Men of Public Confidence' who the German governments invited to assist with the reform of the German Diet.

54 Orme to Palmerston, no. 31, 28.3.1848 (FO/30/104); Ward to Palmerston, genl. no. 17, copy, 3.4.1848 (FO/299/3).

55 Strangways to Palmerston, no. 10, 8.4.1848 (FO/30/106); Bligh to Palmerston, no. 30, 13.4.1848 (FO/34/53); *Times* (18.4.1848: 4c); Hansard, 3rd ser., vol. 98: 514; Disraeli to Lady Londonderry, 1.5.1848 and Disraeli to Philip Rose, 12.5.1848, in: Disraeli (1993: 24, 29).

56 Bligh to Palmerston, no. 42, 5.5.1848 (FO/34/53); Milbanke to Palmerston, no. 30, 8.5.1848 (FO/9/100); Malet to Palmerston, no. 41, 21.5.1848 (FO/82/55); Bligh to Palmerston, no. 76, 10.8.1848 (FO/34/54).

57 Milbanke to Palmerston, no. 35, 6.6.1848 (FO/9/101).

58 Given the unsettled nature of the revolutionary institutions, which Britain never formally recognized, Cowley, who replaced Strangways in August 1848, was not accredited until May 1851 [see: Palmerston to Cowley, no. 75, draft, 14.5.1851 (FO/30/146)] and meanwhile occupied a semi-official position of mere observation [see: Palmerston to Cowley, no. 1, draft, 29.7.1848 (FO/30/107)]. Palmerston was so impressed with his performance there that he proposed to promote him to St Petersburg in 1851 [see: Palmerston to Victoria, copy, 14.2.1851 (BP-RC/FF/20)]. In 1852, Cowley was appointed to the even more prestigious post of ambassador to France. On Cowley's position in Frankfurt see: Valentin (1937b: 20–1) and Gillessen (1961: 28).

59 Downie to Couper, 20.5.1848 (QVP: vol. I.4, doc. 77); *Times* (30.5.1848: 7b); *Spectator* (1.7.1848: 636).

60 Palmerston to Ponsonby, priv., copy, 3.7.1848 (BP-GC/PO/814); Palmerston to Russell, 10.7.1848 (RuP-PRO/30/22/7C); Russell to Palmerston, 8.7.1848 (BP-GC/RU/207).

61 *Times* (6.7.1848: 4b–c); the *Times* (20.7.1848, 5a–b) described Johann's arrival as an 'event of most auspicious character.'

62 Palmerston to Cowley, no. 1, draft, 29.7.1848 (FO/30/107).

63 Malet to Palmerston, no. 50, 18.6.1848 (FO/82/55); Milbanke to Palmerston, no. 41, 3.7.1848 (FO/9/101); Cowley to Palmerston, no. 45, 20.8.1848

(FO/30/109); on the lack of appeal of the British parliamentary model for the revolutionaries of 1848 see: Watson (1969: 118); Cowley to Ponsonby, priv., copy, 14.8.1848 (CoP-FO/519/165).

64 Cowley to Westmorland, priv., copy, 8.8.1848 (CoP-FO/519/165); Cowley to Palmerston, priv., 21.8.1848 (BP-GC/CO/146); Cowley to Palmerston, no. 45, 20.8.1848 (FO/30/109).

65 Malet to Palmerston, no. 49, 18.6.1848 (FO/82/55); see also his earlier warning that protectionist demands would be raised in a future German parliament in: Malet to Palmerston, no. 19, 16.3.1848 (FO/82/55); Strangways to Palmerston, no. 88, 28.6.1848 (FO/30/106); Ward to Palmerston, genl. no. 26, copy, 3.7.1848 (FO/299/3); *Times* (20.7.1848: 5b).

66 Palmerston to Cowley, no. 1, draft, 29.7.1848 (FO/30/107); Ward to Palmerston, genl. no. 28, copy, 5.8.1848 (FO/299/3); Palmerston to Cowley, no. 24, draft, 18.8.1848 (FO/30/107); Porter to Addington, 26.10.1848, quoted in: Davis (1997: 56); for a detailed discussion of Britain's reaction to the *Paulskirche*'s commercial policies see: Davis (1997: 48–61).

67 Confines of space forbid a separate and detailed discussion of the British perception of the Schleswig-Holstein question. Although, as Gillessen (1961: 153) points out, contemporaries both in Germany and Britain continually mixed up the questions of German unity and of the Elbe Duchies allowing their reactions to the one to colour their analyses of the other, both questions were really separate issues. While the impact of the Schleswig-Holstein question on British perceptions of the German national movement and the question of German unity will be considered, a treatment of the Schleswig-Holstein question proper was deemed to lie outside its scope. Moreover, there is already a rich literature on the latter question; see: Carr (1963); Gillessen (1961: 30–44, 77–81); Hjeholt (1965); Hjeholt (1966); Hjeholt (1971); Peter (1972); Precht (1925: 25–68, 85–105, 134–57); Sandiford (1975); Scharff (1942: 32–41) and Steefel (1932).

68 Palmerston to Cowley, no. 9, 8.8.1848 (FO/30/107); Cowley to Palmerston, priv., 21.8.1848 (BP-GC/CO/146).

69 Bligh to Palmerston, no. 84, 7.9.1848 (FO/34/54); Mellish to Cowley, priv., 8.9.1848 (CoP-FO/519/157); Palmerston to Cowley, priv., 8.9.1848 (CoP-FO/519/292); *Times* (13.9.1848: 4d).

70 For Cowley's account of the violence in Frankfurt see: Cowley to Palmerston, no. 108, 18.9.1848 (FO/30/110); Cowley to Palmerston, no. 125, 25.9.1848 (FO/30/110).

71 [W. E. Aytoun,] 'A Glimpse of Germany and its Parliament', *BEM* 64 (1848: 530–533); see also the very critical articles in the conservative *Fraser's Magazine*: [anon.,] 'Schleswig and the German Central Power' and [anon.,] 'German Union and Disunion', *FM* 38 (1848: 361 and 379–80).

72 Ponsonby to Cowley, priv., 30.9.1848 (CoP-FO/519/157); Cowley to Palmerston, no. 236, 4.11.1848 (FO/30/113); Mellish to Cowley, priv., 14.11.1848 (CoP-FO/519/158).

73 Bligh to Palmerston, no. 71, 24.7.1848 (FO/34/54); Westmorland to Palmerston, no. 282, 30.7.1848 (FO/64/288); Ward to Palmerston, genl. no. 29, copy, 11.8.1848 (FO/299/3); Cowley to Ponsonby, priv., copy, 22.8.1848 (CoP-FO/519/165); Cowley to Normanby, priv., copy, 8.9.1848 (CoP-FO/519/165).

74 Cowley to Palmerston, no. 146, 2.10.1848 (FO/30/111).
75 Cowley to Westmorland, priv., copy, 29.9.1848 (CoP-FO/519/165); Forbes to Palmerston, no. 67, 8.10.1848 (FO/68/69); Cowley to Palmerston, no. 275, 23.11.1848 (FO/30/114); for an earlier formulation of this argument see: Cowley to Palmerston, no. 236, 4.11.1848 (FO/30/113).
76 Cowley to Palmerston, no. 266, 19.11.1848 (FO/30/114); Blum had gone to Vienna as member of a parliamentary deputation to give moral support to the revolutionaries there. When the imperial troops re-conquered Vienna, Blum fought for the revolutionaries, was captured and executed on 9 November. The Austrian authorities refused to respect Blum's parliamentary immunity. Cowley did not mourn the loss: 'A better deed was never done than shooting that rascal' [Cowley to Ponsonby, priv., copy, 24.11.1848 (CoP-FO/519/165)].
77 Cowley to Palmerston, no. 266, 19.11.1848 (FO/30/114).
78 Cowley to Palmerston, no. 272, 20.11.1848 (FO/30/114); Mellish to Cowley, priv., 5.12.1848 (CoP-FO/519/158); on 14 November, Mellish strongly disagreed: 'I do not see why Prussia if she is strong enough to take the lead in Germany should hold out her hands to the Frankfort marauders [...] But if Prussia is not strong enough then her cordial adherence to the central authority will only be seen as an accession of weakness' [Mellish to Cowley, priv., 14.11.1848 (CoP-FO/519/158)].
79 Ward to Palmerston, genl. no. 29, copy, 11.8.1848 (FO/299/3); Ponsonby to Palmerston, priv., 4.12.1848 (BP-GC/PO/587); Cowley to Palmerston, no. 321, 10.12.1848 (FO/30/115); Milbanke to Palmerston, no. 1, 15.1.1849 (FO/9/103).
80 Cowley to Palmerston, no. 325, 10.12.1848 (FO/30/115); *Times* (20.12.1848: 4b); Cowley to Palmerston, no. 33, 29.1.1849 (FO/30/122).
81 Cowley to Palmerston, no. 84, 25.2.1849 (FO/30/123); Cowley to Palmerston, priv., 28.3.1849 (BP-CG/CO/165); Cowley to Palmerston, no. 183, 14.4.1849 (FO/30/125); Cowley to Palmerston, priv., 28.3.1849 (BP-GC/CO/165).
82 *Times* (4.5.1849: 6a); Cowley to Palmerston, no. 233, 6.5.1849 (FO/30/126); Cowley to Palmerston, no. 245, 12.5.1849 and no. 280, 21.5.1849 (FO/30/126).
83 Malet to Palmerston, no. 38, 2.6.1849 (FO/82/59); Cowley to Palmerston, no. 315, 3.6.1849 (FO/30/127); Malet to Palmerston, no. 53, 15.6.1849 (FO/82/59); Palmerston to Malet, no. 7, draft, 22.6.1849 (FO/82/57).
84 Palmerston to Bloomfield, priv., 18.8.1848 (BlP-FO/356/29).
85 *Times* (6.3.1848: 5e; 16.3.1848: 6a).
86 Lamb to Londonderry, no. 4, 24.7.1822 (FO/30/22); Cowley to Palmerston, no. 45, 20.8.1848 (FO/30/109) and no. 147, 2.10.1848 (FO/30/111).
87 [J. P. Simpson,] 'What would revolutionizing Germany be at?', *BEM* 64 (1848: 374); [W. E. Aytoun,] 'A Glimpse at Germany and its Parliament', *BEM* 64 (1848: 516).
88 Palmerston to Strangways, no. 1, draft, 25.3.1848 (FO/30/105); Russell to Palmerston, 25.3.1848 (BP-GC/RU/191); Palmerston to Albert, 19.6.1849 (QVP: vol. I.15, doc. 50); *Times* (23.3.1848: 4d; see also: 22.5.1849: 6d); [anon.,] 'Political Fly Leaves from Germany', *TEM* 19 o.s. (1848: 599); for Britain's interest in a united Germany stabilizing the European system

see also: Clarke (1989: 224–225); Gillessen (1961: 152); and Mosse (1958: 5–6).

89   Bligh to Palmerston, no. 88, 21.9.1848 (FO/34/54); Mellish to Cowley, priv., 13.12.1848 (CoP-FO/519/158); Malet to Palmerston, no. 11, 8.4.1849 (FO/82/58).

90   Palmerston to Normanby, priv., copy, 28.2.1848 (BP-GC/NO/446); Canning to Palmerston, no. 20, 12.5.1848 (FO/30/117); Strangways to Palmerston, no. 84, 20.6.1848 (FO/30/106).

91   Bligh to Palmerston, no. 65, 6.7.1848 (FO/34/54); [H. A. Woodham,] 'The Germanic Empire', *ER* 88 (1848: 282); [anon.,] 'Europe in 1848', *BQR* 8 (1848: 525); [T. Twiss,] 'Austria and Germany', *QR* 84 (1848: 220); [T. Twiss,] 'The Germanic Confederation and the Austrian Empire', *QR* 84 (1849: 429); Twiss's articles on German politics in 1848 and 1849 were probably based on letters which Metternich wrote to Twiss [see: Gudenus (1988: 41–43)].

92   Palmerston to Albert, 8.5.1849 (QVP: vol. I.14, doc. 25); Malet to Palmerston, no. 59, 28.8.1848 (FO/82/55); [P. B. St. John,] 'General View of the Revolution in Europe', *TEM* 19 o.s. (1848: 455).

93   Cowley to Palmerston, no. 182, 15.10.1848 (FO/30/111); Cowley to Palmerston, priv., 16.10.1848 (BP-GC/CO/157); although Cowley mentioned the difficulty of advocating the mediatization of states like Coburg in view of 'the relations in which the Queen and Prince Albert stand to Germany', Palmerston sent Cowley's private letter on to Albert, who placed a copy in the Royal Archives [see: QVP: vol. I.8, doc. 61]; on the subsequent exchange between Cowley and Albert see: Gillessen (1961: 50–2).

94   Forbes to Palmerston, no. 39, 19.5.1848 (FO/68/68), no. 56, 1.8.1848 and no. 58, 9.8.1848 (FO/68/69).

95   *Times* (13.3.1848: 4c); [H. A. Woodham,] 'The Germanic Empire', *ER* 88 (1848: 282); [anon.,] 'The Archduke-Emperor of Germany', *FM* 38 (1848: 241–242); [anon.,] 'Europe in 1848', *BQR* 8 (1848: 525); Ward to Palmerston, genl. no. 11, copy, 15.3.1848 (FO/299/3); Malet to Palmerston, no. 24, 22.3.1848 (FO/82/55).

96   *Times* (17.3.1848: 4e); Strangways to Palmerston, no. 18, 15.4.1848, no. 45 and no. 46, 10.5.1848 (FO/30/106); Palmerston to Strangways, no. 16, draft, 17.5.1848 (FO/30/105).

97   Hansard, 3rd ser., vol. 98: 515–516, 521; see also Disraeli's interpellation on the Limburg question: Hansard, 3rd ser., vol. 100: 1151–2; for a critical evaluation of Disraeli's bristling but shallow foreign political speeches in 1848 see: Turner (1948: 381); *Times* (20.4.1848: 6e); for Lehmann's authorship see: Hjeholt (1965: i, 89–90); *Times* (8.7.1848: 5e; 11.9.1848: 4b).

98   [H. A. Woodham,] 'The Germanic Empire' and [*idem,*] 'State of Europe', *ER* 88 (1848: 284, 540); [anon.,] 'German Union and Disunion', *FM* 38 (1848: 479); [T. Twiss,] 'Austria and Germany', *QR* 84 (1848: 201, 204–205).

99   Palmerston to Westmorland, priv., 25.5.1849 (WeP-M/509/2/ff. 277ff); Ward to Palmerston, genl. no. 29, copy, 11.8.1848 (FO/299/3); Palmerston to Bunsen, copy, 25.5.1849 (WeP-M/509/2/ff. 281ff).

100 Older works such as Precht (1925: 180), Marcks (1940: 52) and Scharff (1942: 92–3, 95–6) suggested that Britain's rejection of the *Paulskirche* was tantamount to opposing German unity. More recent studies [Mosse (1958:

43, 46–7), Gillessen (1961: 151–2)], on the other hand, intimate that Britain's interest in German unity and her support for constitutional reform amounted to a preparedness to accept a united Germany in a *Paulskirche* mould. The findings of this study support neither interpretation.

101 The central importance of the separate German states to British observers in 1848/9 is also noted by Gruner (2000: 297–8).

102 Palmerston to Strangways, no. 1, 25.3.1848 (FO/30/105); Cowley to Palmerston, no. 325, 10.12.1848 (FO/30/115); Palmerston to Cowley, no. 207, draft, 22.12.1848 (FO/30/108); *Times* (31.1.1849: 4e; 12.4.1849: 4f); Cowley to Malet, priv., copy, 29.6.1849 (CoP-FO/519/165).

Chapter 3

1 The refugees' affair is discussed in Pemberton (1954: 161–5) and Southgate (1966: 257–62).

2 Greville (1888: vi, 356); on the Don Pacifico affair see: Ridley (1972: 486–528) and Southgate (1966: 263–78).

3 For a discussion of Austria's and Prussia's competing concepts against the background of the European system see: Doering-Manteuffel (1989).

4 On the Prussian project see: Barclay (1995: 185–213), Meinecke (1913); Rumpler (1972) and Srbik (1935–42: ii, 17–55).

5 Canning to Palmerston, priv., 1.5.1848 (BP-GC/CA/169); Cowley to Palmerston, no. 161, 8.10.1848 (FO/30/111); Palmerston to Cowley, no. 197, draft, 18.12.1848 (FO/30/108); Cowley to Ponsonby, priv., copy, 25.12.1848 (CoP-FO/519/165); Cowley to Meyer, priv., copy, 31.12.1848 (CoP-FO/519/165); Ward to Westmorland, priv., 1.1.1849 (WeP-M/526/2).

6 Cowley to Palmerston, no. 39, 29.1.1849 (FO/30/122).

7 Cowley to Palmerston, no. 73, 17.2.1849 (FO/30/122); Cowley to Palmerston, priv., copy, 15.3.1849 CoP-FO/519/165); Cowley to Ponsonby, priv., copy 30.3.1849 (CoP-FO/519/165); on Schwarzenberg's reaction to the Prussian circular see: Lippert (1998: 284–6).

8 Palmerston to Russell, 9.4.1849 (RuP-PRO/30/22/7F); Cowley to Palmerston, no. 183, 14.4.1849 (FO/30/125); Cowley to Palmerston, no. 233, 6.5.1849 (FO/30/126); Cowley to Westmorland, priv., copy, 7.5.1849 (CoP-FO/519/165); the Foreign Office knew about Schwarzenberg's opposition to the Prussian proposals; see: Magenis to Palmerston, no. 41, 22.5.1849 (FO/7/367).

9 For Schwarzenberg's rejection of Prussia's proposals in May 1849 see: Lippert (1998: 298–301) and Luchterhandt (1996).

10 The Prussian project consisted of two components: a small-German federal state and an alliance by which it was to be linked to the Austrian monarchy. The constitution of 28 May 1849 called the federal state 'German Empire', but was soon generally known as the 'Erfurt Union' after the city where its constituent parliament was to convene. Confusingly, in its proposal to create a 'narrower and a wider federation' of 9 May 1849, the Prussian government had used the term 'German Union' to describe the alliance between the Austrian monarchy and the proposed German federal state. This proposal, which Schwarzenberg rejected on 16 May 1849,

included provisions for defence, joint diplomatic representations and a four-member directory chaired by Austria to conduct affairs pertaining to the 'German Union'. In the following, the term 'Union' will be used to describe the small-German state. For the 'German Union' proper, the term 'wider federation' will be used. The texts of the 'Erfurt Constitution' and the proposal of 9 May 1849 can be found in: *Dokumente* (1978: 551–9, 538–40).

11 [T. Twiss,] 'The Germanic Confederation and the Austrian Empire', *QR* 84 (1849: 442, 457); [R. Monckton Milnes,] 'Reflections on the Political State of Germany', *ER* 89 (1849: 552); *Times* (22.5.1849: 6d).

12 Cowley to Palmerston, no. 308, 2.6.1849 (FO/30/127); Ward to Palmerston, genl. no. 15, copy, 10.7.1849 (FO/299/4); for more optimism about the 'Union's' commercial policy see: Howard to Palmerston, no. 7, 22.8.1849 (FO/64/302); see also: Doering-Manteuffel (1991: 161–3).

13 Westmorland to Palmerston, no. 205, 24.5.1849 (FO/64/299).

14 Forbes to Palmerston, no. 29, 1.6.1849 (FO/68/72); Cowley to Malet, priv., 13.6.1849 (CoP-FO/519/165); Palmerston to Albert, 19.6.1849 (QVP: vol. I.15, doc. 50); *Times* (4.6.1849: 4c).

15 Cowley to Malet, priv., copy, 2.6.1849 (CoP-FO/519/165); Milbanke to Cowley, priv., 9.7.1849 (CoP-FO/519/161); Malet to Cowley, priv., 5.6.1849 (CoP-FO/519/160).

16 Malet to Cowley, priv., 26.6.1849 (CoP-FO/519/160); Palmerston to Albert, 19.6.1849 (QVP: vol. I.15, doc. 50); Malet informed Cowley of Palmerston's reply in a private letter; see: Malet to Cowley, priv., 8.7.1849 (CoP-FO/519/161).

17 For a printed copy of Palmerston's despatch of 13 July 1849 [Palmerston to Westmorland, no. 183, draft, 13.7.1849 (FO/64/295)] see: *British Documents* (1990: 1–7) or Valentin (1937b: 500–3).

18 Palmerston to Victoria, 18.4.1848 (QVP: vol. I.3, doc. 75); Palmerston informed Cowley about his conversation with Cetto: Palmerston to Cowley, no. 34, draft, 30.1.1849 (FO/30/120); Palmerston to Albert, 19.6.1849 (QVP: vol. I.15, doc. 50); Palmerston to Westmorland, no. 183, draft, 13.7.1849 (FO/64/295).

19 Ibid.; Colloredo to Schwarzenberg, 5.8.1849, quoted in: Precht (1925: 128); according to Cowley, the King of Württemberg also believed that Britain favoured Prussia; see: Cowley to Palmerston, priv., copy, 15.7.1849 (CoP-FO/519/165).

20 Bligh to Palmerston, no. 12, 14.6.1849 (FO/34/56); Malet to Cowley, priv., 26.6.1849 (CoP-FO/519/160); Mellish to Cowley, priv., 29.6.1849 (CoP-FO/519/160); Westmorland to Palmerston, no. 255, 2.7.1849 (FO/64/300); Milbanke to Cowley, priv., 9.7.1849 (CoP-FO/519/161); for Schwarzenberg's manoeuvres to scupper the 'Union' in the summer of 1849 see: Lippert (1998: 303–7).

21 Mellish to Cowley, priv., 31.7.1849 (CoP-FO/519/161); for Palmerston's conflicts with the Court during his time as Foreign Secretary under Russell see: Eyck (1959: 101–60); Gillessen (1961: 99–100); Southgate (1966: 181–297) and Connell (1962). When Palmerston finally resigned in December 1851, Victoria felt 'the greatest pleasure in announcing' the news to King Leopold, knowing that it would give him 'as much satisfaction and relief' as it did her [(QVL: ii, 344)].

22 Bourne (1989: 113); Gillessen (1961: 73); Scharff (1942: 135); Southgate (1966: 254); Valentin (1937b: 47). For Russell's pro-Prussian feelings in the summer of 1849 see: Russell, Notes on Foreign Affairs, 16.8.1849 (BP-GC/RU/283).

23 There were suspicions, though, that the diplomats' hostility towards the 'Union' reflected their own career interests. On 23 March 1850, Prince Albert quoted approvingly from the *Examiner*: 'England keeps a dignified neutrality, with the exception of our *Pumpernickel Diplomats* at the smallest German courts, who fear the extinction of their *twaddlesome nothingness*' [Bolitho (1933: 116)].

24 The importance of the July armistice is emphasized by Mosse (1958: 29).

25 Palmerston to Russell, 9.4.1849 (RuP-PRO/30/22/7F).

26 Palmerston to Normanby, no. 299, draft, 30.6.1849 (FO/27/836).

27 Doering-Manteuffel (1991: 107–19).

28 Palmerston to Westmorland, no. 183, draft, 13.7.1849 (FO/64/295).

29 Palmerston to Westmorland, no. 183, draft, 13.7.1849 (FO/64/295); Bunsen (1868: ii, 226).

30 Throughout the summer of 1849 the war in Hungary prevented Austria from re-asserting herself in Germany. In his despatch of 13 July, Palmerston referred to Austria's 'uncertain and distressed position.' As late as 24 July 1849, Ponsonby assured Palmerston that 'the Austrians [would] do nothing at present as to the proposed arrangement of Germany. [Ponsonby to Palmerston, no. 165, 24.7.1849 (FO/7/368); see also Ponsonby's almost identical no. 171 of 29.7.1849 (FO/7/368)]. It therefore seemed that Prussia had found a window of opportunity to push through her plans without encountering serious opposition.

31 Palmerston to Drouyn de Lhuys, 22.7.1849, quoted in: Guichen (1925: I, 367 [author's trans.]).

32 Palmerston to Normanby, no. 299, draft, 30.6.1849 (FO/27/863); Palmerston to Westmorland, no. 183, draft, 13.7.1849 (FO/64/295).

33 *Times* (7.6.1849: 4e); Cowley to Palmerston, no. 139, 24.3.1849 (FO/30/124); Westmorland to Palmerston, no. 255, 2.7.1849 (FO/64/300); Bligh to Palmerston, no. 20, 12.7.1849 (FO/34/57).

34 Bunsen to the Prussian Foreign Office, 29.7.1849, quoted in: Precht (1925: 128).

35 The apparent success of the 'Union' did not reduce British diplomats' pessimism. By 23 August 1849 25 German states ranging from the kingdom of Saxony to the principality of Schwarzburg-Sondershausen had in some way or another declared their adherence to the 'Union'; see: Aktenstücke (1849: i, XIII).

36 Westmorland to Palmerston, no. 283, 19.7.1849 (FO/64/301); Milbanke to Palmerston, no. 53, 24.7.1849 (FO/9/104); Palmerston to Milbanke, no. 10, draft, 3.8.1849 (FO/9/104).

37 Bligh to Palmerston, no. 31, 9.8.1849 (FO/34/57); Ponsonby to Palmerston, no. 211, 28.8.1849 (FO/7/369); Howard to Palmerston, no. 26, 31.8.1849, no. 31, 6.9.1849 and no. 37, 9.9.1849 (FO/64/302); Ward to Palmerston, genl. no. 20, copy, 3.9.1849 (FO/299/4); Bligh to Palmerston, no. 38, 6.9.1849 (FO/34/57); Forbes to Palmerston, no. 42, 5.9.1849 (FO/68/72).

38 Palmerston to Forbes, no. 10, draft, 18.9.1849 (FO/68/72); Rechberg's

suspicion was reported by Cowley; see: Cowley to Palmerston, no. 495, 1.10.1849 (FO/30/130).

39   For the text of the 'Interim' see: *Dokumente* (1978: 548–50); for Schwarzenberg's motives see: Lippert (1998: 307–14) and Luchterhandt (1996: 149 and n. 56).

40   On Radowitz's interpretation of the 'Interim' see: Meinecke (1913: 331–59).

41   Craven to Palmerston, no. 24, 7.10.1849 (FO/82/60); Milbanke to Palmerston, no. 73, 28.10.1849 (FO/9/104). The negotiations to which Milbanke referred, led to the abortive anti-Prussian 'Four-Kings-Alliance' in February 1850.

42   Howard to Palmerston, no. 187, 22.11.1849 and no. 199, 30.11.1849 (FO/64/304); Howard had already informed Palmerston about Russia's hostile attitude two months earlier: Howard to Palmerston, no. 52, 16.9.1849 (FO/64/302); Bligh to Palmerston, no. 61, 30.11.1849 (FO/34/57); Westmorland to Albert, 8.12.1849 (QVP: vol. I.17, doc. 80).

43   Ward to Bunsen, 16.10.1849 (QVP: vol. I.17, doc. 19); Malet to Palmerston, no. 82, 14.11.1849 and no. 84, 24.11.1849 (FO/82/60); Ponsonby to Russell, priv., 27.11.1849 (RuP-PRO/30/22/8).

44   *Times* (29.10.1849: 6c); Milbanke to Palmerston, no. 73, 28.10.1849 (FO/9/104); *Times* (19.11.1849: 4b); for the Cabinet meeting see: Russell to Victoria, 29.11.1849 (QVP: vol. I.17, doc. 64).

45   Palmerston to Westmorland, no. 234, draft, 26.12.1849 (FO/64/296); this argument corresponded with a line Palmerston had taken earlier; see: Palmerston to Westmorland, no. 50, draft, 14.3.1848 (FO/64/282); on the importance of this distinction for Britain's role in the European system see the far-reaching interpretation in: Doering-Manteuffel (1991: 123–7 and 1996).

46   Russell to Victoria, 29.11.1849 (QVP: vol. I.17, doc. 64); Russell to Albert, 1.12.1849 (QVP: vol. I.17, doc. 70). Russell must have known how loathsome his views were to Albert who, even then, supported the Erfurt plan. Throughout the revolution, Prince Albert pursued his own German policy, which reflected both his liberal nationalism and his dynastic interests. Rather than working through official channels, Albert corresponded with like-minded friends such as Stockmar, Meyer, Bunsen, Leiningen and Duke Ernst of Saxe-Coburg. On this see: Eyck (1959: 66–100) and Fischer-Aue (1953). The Tory opposition found as little to praise about Albert's efforts as the Whig government. Lord Aberdeen, for instance, deplored the Prince's 'violent and incorrigible German unionism' [Greville (1888: vi, 305)]. The Foreign Office was also disgruntled. 'I cannot help wishing we had no Baron Stockmar and Dr Meyer creeping like reptiles about our Court,' Mellish confided to Cowley, 'and that is a feeling in which many here participate' [Mellish to Cowley, priv., 5.5.1849 (CoP-FO/519/160)].

47   Cowley to Meyer, 14.12.1849 (QVP: vol. I.17, doc. 86); Cowley to Palmerston, no. 573, 22.12.1849 (FO/30/131).

48   Ponsonby to Russell, priv., 27.11.1849 (RuP-PRO/30/22/8); Ward to Palmerston, genl. no. 1, 2.1.1850 (FO/299/4); Cowley to Meyer, 14.12.1849 (QVP: vol. I.17, doc. 86); Cowley to Palmerston, no. 573, 22.12.1849 (FO/30/131); for a detailed summary of Cowley's despatch of 22 December 1849 (including Westmorland's hostile marginalia) see: Gillessen (1961: 85–6).

49   Palmerston to Russell, 29.1.1850 (RuP-PRO/30/22/8C); Russell to Ponsonby,

copy, 29.1.1850 (RuP-PRO/30/22/8C); Russell to Albert, 9.4.1850 (QVP: vol. I.19, doc. 80); Russell's worries were fuelled by Cowley who informed Palmerston in March 1850 that 'the democratic spirit in this part of Germany [was] as strong as ever' [Cowley to Palmerston, no. 118, 25.3.1850 (FO/30/137)].

50 Russell to Albert, 9.4.1850 (QVP: vol. I.19, doc. 80).

51 Forbes to Palmerston, no. 8, 7.2.1850 (FO/68/76); Ward to Palmerston, genl. no. 3, 18.2.1850 (FO/299/4); Cowley to Palmerston, no. 118, 25.3.1850 (FO/30/137).

52 For Koch's reprimand see: Eddisbury to Westmorland, draft, 17.4.1850 (FO/64/311); Koch's uninspired reports are filed in FO/64/316.

53 [anon.,] 'Bülow-Cummerow on the German Question, *FM* 41 (1850: 93, 97); [R. Monckton Milnes,] 'Germany and Erfurt', *ER* 91 (1850: 598); *Times* (22.10.1849: 4b; 25.3.1850: 4c; see also: 14.1.1850: 4b–d; 7.3.1850: 4c–d and 19.3.1850: 5b–d); *Annual Register* 91 (1850: 308).

54 Russell to Albert, 24.4.1850 (QVP: vol. I.19, doc. 97); for Palmerston's belief that there was no reason to fear war in the spring of 1850 see: Palmerston to Russell, 31.3.1850 (RuP-PRO/30/22/8D); this conviction was shared by Ponsonby [Ponsonby to Palmerston, no. 51, 9.4.1850 (FO/7/379)]; Cowley to Ponsonby, priv., copy, 27.2.1850 (CoP-FO 519/166); Cowley to Palmerston, no. 154, 30.4.1850 (FO/30/138).

55 Russell to Albert, 9.4.1850 (QVP: vol. I.19, doc. 80).

56 For the Austrian Empire in 1848–49 see: Bridge (1990: 41–8); Evans (2000); Jelavich (1975: 57–79); Lippert (1998: 117–266); Macartney (1968: 322–433) and Okey (2001: 128–56).

57 Report by the Württemberg envoy, 4.2.1849, quoted in: Valentin (1930/31: ii, 361 [author's trans.]); for the texts of the 'Kremsier Declaration' of 27.11.1848 and the letter to the Austrian plenipotentiary of 28.12.1848 see: *Dokumente* (1978: 360, 362–3); see also: Lippert (1998: 267–9, 276–8).

58 The question of what Schwarzenberg was aiming at between 1849 and 1851 has given rise to controversy. Traditionally, his German policy has been interpreted as an aggressive attempt to create an 'Empire of 70 Million' dominated by Austria [for works in this vein see: Austensen (1984: 862 n. 3)]. This interpretation has been challenged by Paul W. Schroeder and Roy A. Austensen, who have argued that Schwarzenberg's policy was not expansive but essentially defensive. [see: Austensen (1977, 1980, 1984 and 1991) and Schroeder (1972: 2–3)]. More recently, however, this revisionism has in turn been challenged by Luchterhandt (1996) and Lippert (1998: 269–76). For a summary of the controversy see: Sondhaus (1991).

59 Cowley to Palmerston, no. 325, 10.12.1848 (FO/30/115); for Schwarzenberg's initial preparedness to contemplate the Gagern plan and his eventual decision to reject it see: Huber (1968: 799–803) and Luchterhandt (1996: 138–42); Palmerston to Cowley, no. 197, draft, 18.12.1848 (FO/30/108).

60 Cowley to Palmerston, priv, 15.3.1849 (CoP-FO/519/165); Cowley to Ponsonby, priv., 30.3.1849 (CoP-FO/519/165); for the text of Schwarzenberg's note of 9.3.1849 see: *Dokumente* (1978: 370–3); see also: Lippert (1998: 269–74).

61 Magenis to Palmerston, no. 41, 22.5.1849 (FO/7/367); Ponsonby to Palmerston, no. 165, 24.7.1849 (FO/7/368).

62 For Palmerston' s and Ponsonby's comments on Austria's weakness in the summer of 1849 see: ch. 3: n. 30. According to Lippert (1998: 303) Schwarzenberg had nothing with which to oppose Prussia in the summer of 1849 but diplomatic notes.

63 Luchterhandt (1996: 149 and n. 56) has suggested that the importance of the 'Interim' for Schwarzenberg lay in its implicit affirmation of the validity of the legal framework established in 1815 which secured Austria's title to be a part of the German Confederation.

64 For Schwarzenberg's November note see: Huber (1968: 892); for Schwarzenberg's lacklustre backing of the 'Four-Kings-Alliance' see: Luchterhandt (1996: 148–50, 159–60).

65 Luchterhandt (1998: 154).

66 On Bruck's life see: Charmatz (1916) and the biographical sketch in Lutz (1994: 361–3).

67 Cf. Luchterhandt (1996: 150–9); on the Bruck plan and Prussia's response see also: Böhme (1966: 19–35); Doering-Manteuffel (1989); Hahn (1984: 140–51); Hoffmann (1959: 84–94) and Srbik (1935–42: ii, 92–101).

68 Ward to Palmerston, genl. no. 28, copy, 30.11.1850 (FO/299/4); Bligh to Palmerston, no. 17, 8.2.1850 (FO/34/60); Palmerston to Bligh, no. 5, draft, 19.2.1850 (FO/34/59).

69 Cowley to Palmerston, priv., 7.1.1850 (CoP-FO/519/166); Cowley to Palmerston, priv., 3.2.1850 (CoP-FO/519/176); Palmerston to Cowley, priv., 11.2.1850 (CoP-FO/519/292); for Britain's reaction to the Bruck plan see also: Davis (1997: 75–9), who argues that British opposition to Bruck's proposal was essentially apolitical, and Doering-Manteuffel (1991: 164–73), who places it firmly in a political context.

70 Ward to Palmerston, genl. no. 25, 26.11.1849 (FO/299/4); Cowley to Palmerston, no. 33, 28.1.1850 (FO/30/136); Cowley to Palmerston, no. 209, 15.7.1850 (FO/30/139).

71 Palmerston to Howard, no. 12, draft, 14.8.1850 (FO/64/312); Hansard, 3rd ser., vol. 112: 1376.

72 On British policy towards the Kassel conference see: Davis (1997: 79–83); Doering-Manteuffel (1991: 170–1) and Ward (1872: 98–9).

73 They were Austria, Bavaria, Württemberg, Saxony, Hanover, Hesse-Kassel, Holstein, Luxemberg-Limburg, Hesse-Homburg and Liechtenstein; by September 1850 they had been joined by Schaumburg-Lippe, Hesse-Darmstadt and Mecklenburg-Strelitz.

74 Ponsonby to Palmerston, no. 60, 30.4.1850 (FO/7/379); Bligh to Palmerston, no. 89, 27.8.1850 (FO/34/61); Forbes to Palmerston, no. 55, 1.9.1850 (FO/68/76).

75 Cowley to Palmerston, no. 156, 21.5.1850 (FO/30/138); Cowley to Palmerston, no. 184, 18.6.1850 (FO/30/138); Milbanke to Cowley, priv., 21.6.1850 (CoP-FO/519/163); Palmerston to Russell, copy, 23.6.1850 (BP-GC/RU/1069); Ward to Palmerston, genl. no. 9, draft, 3.6.1850 (FO/299/4); Cowley to Palmerston, no. 256, 18.8.1850 (FO/30/140).

76 Cowley to Palmerston, priv., 22.7.1850 (BP-GC/CO/181); Cowley to Palmerston, no. 256, 18.8.1850 (FO/30/140).

77 Magenis to Palmerston, no. 52, 30.7.1850 (FO/7/380), no. 65, 20.8.1850, no. 80, 5.9.1850, no. 85, 10.9.1850 and no. 97, 24.9.1850 (FO/7/381).

78 Magenis to Palmerston, no. 55, 6.8.1850 and no. 65, 20.8.1850 (FO/7/381).
79 Magenis to Palmerston, no. 85, 10.9.1850 and no. 97, 24.9.1850 (FO/7/381); Britain's efforts to broker a peace are described in: Hjeholt (1966); for the controversy over ratification and intervention during the summer and early autumn of 1850 see: Gillessen (1961: 101–6) and Hjeholt (1971: 11–122).
80 Cowley to Palmerston, no. 256, 18.8.1850 (FO/30/140).
81 Palmerston to Magenis, no. 80, draft, 30.9.1850 (FO/7/378); see also: Palmerston to Magenis, no. 47, draft, 15.8.1850 and no. 67, draft, 17.9.1850 (FO/7/378).
82 See also: Palmerston to Magenis, no. 89, draft, 15.10.1850 (FO/7/378), where the Foreign Secretary affirmed that he was refusing to accredit a diplomat to the Frankfurt body 'simply out of regard for the treaty of 1815.'
83 Cowley to Palmerston, no. 214, 15.7.1850 (FO/30/139); Howard to Palmerston, no. 58, 29.8.1850 (FO/64/319) and no. 68, 6.9.1850 (FO/64/320).
84 Addendum (31.10.1850), filed with: Magenis to Palmerston, no. 123, 22.10.1850 (FO/7/381). Doering-Manteuffel (1991: 131–2) has interpreted Palmerston's refusal to recognize the Frankfurt assembly in 1850 as indicative of his readiness to accept changes in the 'political and legal organization of the German Confederation.' While this was certainly the case with the 'Union' proposal in the summer of 1849, it does not appear plausible with respect to Schwarzenberg's plans. On the contrary, Palmerston's stand against the complete admission was based on a literal interpretation of the arrangements of 1815.
85 On Bronzell see: Ward (1916: 531–2); on the Autumn Crisis see: Barclay (1995: 206–13), Burian (1974), Lippert (1998: 327–44), Meinecke (1913: 453–522), Schoeps (1972: 19–42) and Srbik (1935–42: ii, 56–91).
86 Hobhouse's diary quoted in: Bourne (1989: 113).
87 For a detailed account of Britain's policy during the run-up to the Olmütz agreement see: Gillessen (1961: 101–28); see also: Doering-Manteuffel (1991: 132–4) and Mosse (1958: 36–40).
88 On the constitutional conflict in Hesse-Kassel see: Huber (1968: 908–14) and Siemann (1990: 85–8).
89 Palmerston to Russell, 1.12.1850 (BP-GC/RU/1076).
90 Magenis to Palmerston, no. 97, 24.9.1850 (FO/7/381); Palmerston to Russell, copy, 17.10.1850 (QVP: vol. I.22, doc. 38); Palmerston to Russell, 29.10.1850 (RuP-PRO/30/22/8F); Russell to Albert, 4.11.1850 (QVP: vol. I.22, doc. 86); Cowley to Palmerston, priv., 2.12.1850 (BP-GC/CO/187); for British views on the Schleswig-Holstein conflict in the autumn 1850 see: Gillessen (1961: 103–5), Hjeholt (1971: 11–122), Precht (1925: 141–57) and Valentin (1937b: 63–5).
91 Cowley to Palmerston, no. 294, 18.9.1850 (FO/30/149); Magenis to Palmerston, no. 102, 1.10.1850 (FO/7/381); Russell to Palmerston, 29.10.1850 (BP-GC/RU/371); Russell to Palmerston, 16.11.1850 [includes Palmerston's affirmative reply] (RuP-PRO/30/22/8F); Palmerston to Magenis, no. 110, draft, 18.11.1850 (FO/7/378).
92 Although Russell privately expressed sympathy with the renitent Hessians [see: Mosse (1958: 39 n. 2) and Precht (1925: 170–1)], there was no official statement in support of their cause.
93 Cowley to Palmerston, no. 89, 4.3.1850 (FO/30/137); Cowley to Palmer-

ston, no. 280, 8.9.1850 and no. 294, 18.9.1850 (FO/30/140); Forbes to Palmerston, no. 73, 30.11.1850 (FO/68/76); Palmerston to Victoria, 18.11.1850 (*QVL*: ii, 275).

94   Russell to [no addressee given], 20.11.1850 (RuP-PRO/30/22/8F).

95   On the illegality of the intervention in Hesse-Kassel see: Huber (1968: 911–12).

96   For Russell's suspicions in connection with Hesse-Kassel see: Russell to Palmerston, 18.11.1850 (RuP-PRO/30/22/8F).

97   Palmerston to Howard, no. 56, draft, 5.11.1850 (FO/64/312); Palmerston to Cowley, priv., 22.11.1850 (CoP-FO/519/92); *Times* (14.11.1850: 4a–b).

98   Palmerston to Russell, 26.11.1850 (RuP-PRO/30/22/8F) and Palmerston to Russell, copy, 27.11.1850 (QVP: vol. I.23, doc. 47).

99   See: Howard to Palmerston, no. 176, 30.10.1850 (FO/64/321). Palmerston marked the passage which predicted that in case of war Russia would side with Austria.

100 Palmerston to Cowley, priv., 22.11.1850 (CoP-FO/519/292); Palmerston to Howard, no. 56, 5.11.1850 (FO/64/312); Cowley to Palmerston, no. 482, 18.11.1850 (FO/30/142); Palmerston to Howard, no. 68, draft, 26.11.1850 (FO/64/312); on Radowitz's mission see: Gillessen (1961: 118–24) and Meinecke (1913: 504–10).

101 Palmerston to Russell, no date [probably November 1850] (RuP-PRO/30/22/9B); for the Court's apprehensions see: Victoria to Palmerston, 18.11.1850 (*QVL*: ii, 274–5); for the disappointment of Prince Albert's Prussophile court party caused by what they felt was British hostility to Prussia and the cause of German unity see: Stockmar to Russell, priv., 8.11.1850 (RuP-PRO/30/22/8F). Russell sent a barbed reply: 'It is not for forty millions of people to complain that they could not obtain good government because England has looked coldly on them' [Russell to Stockmar, copy, 22.11.1850 (QVP: vol. I.23, doc. 23)].

102 Cowley to Palmerston, no. 482, 18.11.1850 (FO/30/142).

103 Palmerston to Magenis, no. 80, 30.9.1850 (FO/7/378); Cowley to Palmerston, priv., copy, 14.10.1850 (CoP-FO/519/166); Palmerston to Magenis, no. 89, 15.10.1850 and no. 110, 18.11.1850 (FO/7/378).

104 Malet to Palmerston, no. 53, 4.11.1850 (FO/82/64); Magenis to Palmerston, no. 137, 12.11.1850 (FO/7/382).

105 For Meyendorff's judgement see: Mosse (1958: 40 n. 1); according to Doeberl (1926: 73), Count Prokesch-Osten, the Austrian envoy at Berlin, also stated that Schwarzenberg was moved to make concessions by declarations from England and Russia; for a discussion of what influenced Schwarzenberg at Olmütz see: Lippert (1998: 339–43).

106 Russell to Albert, 2.12.1850 (QVP: vol. I.23, doc. 62); Palmerston to Russell, 6.12.1850 [Gooch (1925: ii, 41)].

107 For Schwarzenberg's agenda see: *Die Dresdener Konferenz* (1996: XLIX–LI); on the Dresden Conferences see also: Austensen (1977), Lippert (1998: 347–65), Lutz (1994: 390–3); Schoeps (1972: 46–168) and Srbik (1935–42: ii, 102–22). As has been mentioned above (n. 58 (ch. 3)), some scholars have challenged the characterization of Schwarzenberg's policy as aggressive and emphasized its defensive intentions. In the context of this study it may suffice to say that contemporary British observers failed to recognize such a defensive motivation.

108 Palmerston to Russell, copy, 27.11.1850 (QVP: I.23, doc. 47).

109 Cowley to Palmerston, no. 323, 7.10.1850 (FO/30/141); Russell to King Leopold, copy, 5.12.1850 (RuP-PRO/30/22/8F); Palmerston to Bloomfield, no. 456, draft, 16.12.1850 (FO/97/348).

110 Albert to Frederick William IV, 1.12.1850 [Jagow (1938: 170)]; Russell to Albert, 2.12.1850 and Palmerston to Russell, 2.12.1850 (QVP: vol. I.23, docs 59, 60).

111 Mellish to Cowley, priv., 22.1.1851 (CoP-FO/519/164).

112 On the 'Six Points' and the Warsaw meeting see: Friedjung (1912b: 81–7, 551–3), Lippert (1998: 324–5) and Meinecke (1913: 471–81).

113 Russell to Palmerston, 18.11.1850 (RuP-PRO/30/22/8F).

114 Palmerston to Magenis, no. 127 draft, 3.12.1850 (FO/7/378); Hansard, 3rd ser., vol. 114: 3, 115.

115 Palmerston to Magenis, no. 66, 7.3.1851 (FO/7/386); Magenis to Palmerston, no. 48, 15.3.1851 (FO/7/389).

116 Forbes to Palmerston, no. 61, 16.5.1851 (FO/68/81).

117 Russell to Palmerston, 18.11.1850 (RuP-PRO/30/22/8F); Bloomfield to Palmerston, no. 53, copy, 5.3.1851 [enclosed in: Palmerston to Magenis, no. 78, 18.3.1851] (FO/120/253); Palmerston to Magenis, no. 66, draft, 7.3.1851 (FO/7/386); Palmerston to Westmorland, priv., copy, 8.3.1851 (BP-GC/WE/199); Mellish to Cowley, priv., 19.3.1851 (CoP-FO/519/164).

118 Bloomfield to Palmerston, priv., copy, 26.11.1850 (BlP-FO/356/29); Bligh to Palmerston, no. 3, 10.1.1851 (FO/34/63); Bloomfield to Palmerston, no. 65, 2.4.1851 (FO/65/392); Canning to Palmerston, no. 72, copy, 6.3.1851 [in: Palmerston to Magenis, no. 102, 8.4.1851] (FO/120/254); Hansard, 3rd ser., vol. 115: 1354–6.

119 Palmerston to Magenis, no. 127, draft, 3.12.1850 (FO/7/378); Palmerston to Magenis, no. 66, draft, 7.3.1851 (FO/7/386); for the circular see: Palmerston to Bonar, no. 6, draft, 18.3.1851 (FO/9/110); Magenis to Palmerston, no. 48, 15.3.1851 (FO/7/389).

120 Russell to Palmerston, copy, 18.11.1850 (RuP-PRO/30/22/8F); Jermingham to Palmerston, no. 13, copy, 20.2.1851 [in: Palmerston to Magenis, no. 61, 4.3.1851] (FO/120/253); Palmerston to Bloomfield, no. 66, copy, 19.3.1851 [in: Palmerston to Magenis, no. 82, 22.3.1851] (FO/120/253); Westmorland to Palmerston, priv., 6.4.1851 (BP-GC/WE/182); for a description of the Anglo-French initiative and the diplomatic efforts to win over Russia see: Gillessen (1961: 129–48), Doering-Manteuffel (1991: 137–47) and Schoeps (1972: 135–51).

121 Two Foreign Office memoranda of early December 1850 (BP-MM/GE/7–8) tortuously argued that the signatory powers had a right to interfere, but lacked conviction. John Ward [Ward to Westmorland, 8.1.1851 (WeP-M/526/2) and 'Observations', 9.3.1851 (FO/68/80)] declared that Britain was not entitled to object to unanimous decisions by the German states. Initially, even Russell [Russell to Palmerston, 18.12.1850, (BP-GC/RU/387)] wondered if Britain ought not to 'concede a point on which Austria and Prussia seem to be agreed.' Cowley [Cowley to Palmerston, no. 69, 10.3.1851 (FO/30/149)] suggested that the political end might justify legally questionable means and asked 'whether the German element may not be made use of to check Russian influence in the East.'

122 It is difficult to assess how significant a role the strong Austrophobia

amongst the British public (see p. 124) played in influencing reactions to Schwarzenberg's policies. While neither accusations of Austrian atrocities in Italy and Hungary nor anti-Catholic feelings in the context of the 'Papal Aggression' agitation of 1850/51 feature at all prominently in the British diplomatic correspondence, a latent influence of these emotive issues cannot be ruled out.

123 See: Forbes to Palmerston, no. 12, 13.1.1851 (FO/68/80); Bligh to Palmerston, no. 13, 24.1.1851 (FO/34/63) and Ward to Palmerston, genl. no. 2, draft, 29.1.1851 (FO/299/5).

124 Ward to Palmerston, genl. no. 6, draft, 25.4.1851 (FO/299/5); Palmerston to Cowley, no. 75, draft, 14.5.1851 (FO/30/146).

Chapter 4

1 Nipperdey (1987: 674).

2 On the era of 'Reaction' see also: Blackbourn (1997: 225–39); Huber (1970: 129–38, 151–223) and Siemann (1990: 25–88); on police supervision see: Siemann (1983) and Siemann (1985).

3 Gall (1968: 60).

4 Huber (1970: 183–6); Hyde (1994); Okey (2001: 157–90); Okey (2001: 157–76) and Sheehan (1989: 716).

5 *Der deutsche Bund* (1998: XVII–XVIII, LI–LII, LVII–LVIII); see also the report for 1854/55 by Prussia's political police in: Siemann (1983: 128–31); Langewiesche (1974: 270–81).

6 *Der deutsche Bund* (1998: XLVI–LII).

7 Siemann (1998: 1).

8 *Der deutsche Bund* (1998: XV–XVII, XLIV–XLV, LII–LXI); Fuchs (1934: 12–85).

9 Cowley to Palmerston, no. 250, 26.8.1851 and no. 277, 30.9.1851 (FO/30/151); Milbanke to Clarendon, no. 45, 10.7.1856 (FO/9/129).

10 Ward to Russell, genl. no. 3, 8.2.1853 (FO/68/88); Malet to Clarendon, priv., 30.7.1855 (ClP-Clar.Dep. c.36); Clarendon to Loftus, priv., copy, 9.10.1855 (ClP-Clar.Dep. c.133); Milbanke to Clarendon, no. 45, 10.7.1856 (FO/9/129).

11 For an up-to-date account of the Crimean War see: Baumgart (1999b); for Britain's role in the war see: Anderson (1967); Conacher (1968 and 1987) and Wentker (1993).

12 Clarendon to Bloomfield, priv., copy, 15.2.1854 (ClP-Clar.Dep. c. 128).

13 Clarendon to Malet, priv., copy, 22.3.1855 (ClP-Clar.Dep. c.132); Clarendon to Bloomfield, priv., copy, 1.1.1856 (ClP-Clar.Dep. c.135). Britain's relations with Prussia and Austria during the Crimean War are well-covered by Doering-Manteuffel (1991: 191–324) and Schroeder (1972). On the political manoeuvres by the German states between 1853 and 1856 see: Baumgart (1983); Borries (1930); Eckhart (1931) and Unckel (1969).

14 Bavaria, Saxony, Hanover, Württemberg, Hesse-Darmstadt, Electoral Hesse and Hesse-Nassau.

15 On Beust and the Bamberg Conference see: Baumgart (1995); Davis (1998); Doering-Manteuffel (1991: 242–4); Fuchs (1934: 12–53); Meiboom (1931: 64–95) and Schroeder (1972: 176–9).

16 Malet to Clarendon, no. 48, 18.6.1854 (FO/30/167); similarly: Malet to Clarendon, priv., 25.5.1854 (ClP-Clar.Dep. c.13); Ward to Clarendon, genl. no. 22, 31.5.1854 (FO/68/93); Milbanke to Clarendon, no. 51, 29.7.1854 (FO/9/122).

17 Clarendon to Milbanke, priv., copy, 21.6.1854 (ClP Clar.Dep. c.129); Clarendon to Forbes, no. 24, draft, 21.6.1854 (FO/68/91); Clarendon to Bligh, no. 14, draft, 27.6.1854 (FO/34/73).

18 *Times* (26.10.1854: 7f).

19 *Der deutsche Bund* (1998: LI–LII, LVII–LVIII, 312–19, 322–34, 362–4, 426–7); Fuchs (1934: 53–85).

20 Clarendon to Malet, priv., copy, 21.7.1855 (ClP-Clar.Dep. c. 133).

21 Milbanke to Clarendon, no. 49, 23.6.1853 (FO/9/118); Forbes to Clarendon, no. 35, 2.7.1853 (FO/68/87); Ward to Clarendon, genl. no. 7, 28.2.1854 (FO/68/93); Jerningham to Clarendon, no. 10, 27.10.1854 (FO/82/77).

22 Clarendon to Malet, priv., copy, 21.7.1855 (ClP-Clar.Dep. c. 133).

23 Ward to Clarendon, genl. no. 22, 31.7.1855 and no. 24, 9.8.1855 (FO/68/97); l2 to Clarendon, priv., 1.9.1855 (ClP-Clar.Dep. c. 27); see also: Hamilton to Clarendon, no. 15, 29.9.1855 (FO/82/81A) and Loftus to Clarendon, no. 133, 20.10.1855 (FO/64/398).

24 Ward to Clarendon, genl. no. 25, 23.8.1855 (FO/68/97); Clarendon to Ward, no. 12, draft, 8.9.1855 (FO/68/97); Clarendon to Elliot [also to: Milbanke, Malet, Loftus, Bligh and Hamilton], no. 57, draft, 10.9.1855 (FO/7/449).

25 Bligh to Clarendon, no. 114, 15.9.1855 (FO/34/80); Malet to Clarendon, no. 108, 28.9.1855 (FO/30/172); Forbes to Clarendon, no. 40, 14.10.1855 (FO/68/95); Loftus to Clarendon, no. 133, 20.10.1855 (FO/64/398); Milbanke to Clarendon, no. 64, 27.10.1855 (FO/9/126).

26 Ward to Clarendon, genl. no. 29, 8.11.1855 (FO/68/97).

27 I am grateful for Paul Schroeder's shrewd reminder that Britain's unusual anti-Prussian and pro-Austrian posture during the Crimean war was fundamentally in line with her general attitude towards the German question. British support for Austria was highly equivocal – aiming solely at drawing the rest of the German Confederation into the war and at making Austria stand guard against a resurgent Russia. At the same time important makers of British policy continued to believe that Prussia would make a better leader of Germany once Prussia had become less reactionary.

28 For the text of the Regent's speech see: *Dokumente* (1986: 35–7); on the end of the Manteuffel ministry see: Grünthal (1990); on the 'New Era' see: Haupts (1978), Mommsen (1993: 103–20), Nipperdey (1987: 697–704) and Siemann (1990: 190–200).

29 *Times* (1.10.1858: 6b).

30 Paget to Malmesbury, no. 129, 23.10.1858 (FO/64/460); Paget to Malmesbury, no. 149, 6.11.1858 (FO/64/460).

31 Paget to Malmesbury, no. 160, 13.11.1858 (FO/64/462); Paget to Malmesbury, priv., 18.11.1858 (MaP-9M73/11); Bloomfield to Malmesbury, no. 306, 18.12.1858 (FO/64/462).

32 Loftus (1892: I, 288); Malmesbury to Bloomfield, priv., 1.12.1858 (BlP-FO/356/32); 'Memorandum' (QVP: vol. I.21, doc. 37).

33 *Times* (1.10.1858: 6c; 12.11.1858: 6a); see also: *Spectator* (4.12.1858: 1264).

34 Bloomfield to Russell, priv., 30.7.1859 (RuP-PRO/30/22/79); Ward to Russell,

genl. no. 3, 18.1.1860 (FO/68/113); *Times* (16.1.1860: 8e); Hansard, 3rd ser., vol. 157: 1984.

35 Bloomfield to Russell, no. 138, 2.4.1860 (FO/64/491); Russell to Bloomfield, no. 86, 11.4.1860 (FO/64/487); on the re-opening of the Hesse-Kassel question see: Huber (1970: 436–449).

36 Lowther to Russell, no. 4, 2.1.1861 and no. 4, 4.1.1861 (FO/64/506); Russell to Bloomfield, priv., 9.1.1861 (BlP-FO/356/32).

37 QVP: vol. I.21, doc. 37; [W.E. Aytoun,] 'Our Relations with the Continent', *BEM* 85 (1859: 780).

38 Russell to Bloomfield, priv., 1.8.1859 and 5.2.1860 (BlP-FO/356/32); *Daily Telegraph* (26.3.1860), quoted in: Block (1969: 247).

39 Hansard, 3rd ser., vol. 157: 1984; for Russell's reply see: ibid.: 1987–1995; Russell to Malet, no. 27, draft, 23.4.1860 (FO/30/190).

40 Paget to Malmesbury, no. 149, 6.11.1858 (FO/64/460); Bloomfield to Malmesbury, no. 117, 5.3.1859 (FO/64/475) and no. 272, 5.5.1859 (FO/64/477).

41 *Times* (18.7.1859: 10f; 6.11.1860: 8e; 23.1.1861: 8c; for similar articles see: 19.7.1859: 10f; 2.4.1860: 8e–f; 9.1.1861: 8b–c); *Saturday Review* (28.4.1860: 520–1), quoted in: *Block* (1969: 245).

42 Russell to Bloomfield, no. 60, draft, 28.12.1859 (FO/64/472); Ward to Russell, genl. no. 23, draft, 29.9.1859 (FO/299/10); Russell to Loftus, no. 174, draft, 27.6.1860 (FO/7/587); Russell to Milbanke, no. 38, draft, 13.8.1860 (FO/9/143).

43 Gordon to Russell, no. 78, 31.5.1860 (FO/82/94); Milbanke to Russell, no. 55, 27.6.1860 (FO/9/144).

44 On Morier's career in Germany see: Grünthal (1999); Neumann (1919: 5–13); Murray (1997; 1998) and Wemyss (1911).

45 Morier to Bloomfield, draft, 30.6.1860 (MoP-Box 1, 1i); for Morier's great optimism about the 'New Era' see: Murray (1997: 55–78); on the Baden-Baden meeting see: Huber (1970: 403–4).

46 Britain's interest in good Austro-Prussian relations was motivated by a desire to see these two powers united against a possible French attack; see: Palmerston to Russell, priv., 5.9.1859 (RuP-PRO/30/22/20); Russell to Malet, no. 10, draft, 17.2.1860 (FO/30/190); Russell to Loftus, no. 174, draft, 27.6.1860 (FO/7/587); Russell to Howard, no. 30, draft, 25.7.1860 (FO/34/102) and Bloomfield to Russell, no. 282, 31.7.1860 (FO/64/494).

47 Palmerston to Granville, 30.1.1859, quoted in: Hoppen (1998: 227–8).

48 On the war-scare of 1859 see: Dülffer (1997: 47–69), Salevouris (1982) and Zegger (1973); on Britain's attitude towards the Italian war see: Beales (1961); Hearder (1967); Mack Smith (1962) and Weigand (1997: 237–89).

49 On Britain's policy towards Germany in the context of the Italian war see: Adler (1986: 6–29); Metzler (1997: 115–21) and Valentin (1937b: 136–46).

50 Malet to Malmesbury, priv., 29.1.1859 (MaP-9M73/12); Ward to Malmesbury, genl. no. 4, 23.2.1859 (FO/299/10); Loftus to Malmesbury, priv., 24.2.1859 (MaP-9M73/12).

51 Malmesbury to Bloomfield, priv., 2.3.1859 (BlP-FO/356/32); Malmesbury to Milbanke, no. 11, draft, 2.3.1859, (FO/9/139) and Malmesbury to Gordon, no. 9, draft, 2.3.1859 (FO/34/97); see also Malmesbury's reprimand when Gordon appeared lacklustre in pressing this point: Malmesbury to Gordon,

no. 13, draft, 9.3.1859 (FO/34/97); Malmesbury to Loftus, no. 138, draft, 9.3.1859 (FO/7/561); Malmesbury to Malet, no. 20, 1.5.1859 (FO/30/185); Malmesbury to Bloomfield, no. 198, draft, 4.5.1859 (FO/64/471); for Prussia's request see: Bloomfield to Malmesbury, no. 268, 3.5.1859 (FO/64/477); for Russell's commitment to containment see· Russell to Bloomfield, no. 1, draft, 22.6.1859 (FO/64/472).

52 Ward to Malmesbury, genl. no. 15, copy, 9.6.1859 (FO/299/10); Malmesbury to Malet, no. 20, 1.5.1859 (FO/30/185); Bloomfield to Malmesbury, no. 272, 5.5.1859 (FO/64/477).

53 Malmesbury to Bloomfield, no. 210, draft, 11.5.1859 and no. 211, draft, 11.5.1859 (FO/64/471); *Times* (15.10.1859: 8b).

54 Bloomfield to Malmesbury, no. 117, 5.3.1859 (FO/64/475); Malet to Malmesbury, no. 55, 6.5.1859 (FO/30/187); Bloomfield to Malmesbury, no. 319, 28.5.1859 (FO/64/477) and no. 403, 16.7.1859 (FO/64/479); for Prussia's course during the Italian war see: Dülffer (1997: 34–43); Huber (1970: 254–65); Kentmann (1933); Siemann (1990: 180–9) and Weigand (1997: 289–317).

55 Milbanke to Russell, no. 71, 27.7.1859 (FO/9/141); for more reports on Prussia's unpopularity see: Malet to Russell, no. 24, 13.7.1859 and no. 35, 28.7.1859 (FO/187).

56 Russell to Bloomfield, priv., 3.8.1859 (BlP-FO/356/32).

57 Malmesbury to Bloomfield, priv., copy, 1.6.1859 (MaP-9M73/56); Murray to Russell, priv., 21.2.1860 and Howard to Russell, priv., 19.5.1860 (RuP-PRO/30/22/63); *Times* (2.4.1860: 8d–e; 6.4.1860: 6b–d).

58 Milbanke to Russell, no. 14, 27.2.1860 (FO/9/144); Howard to Russell, no. 38, 23.3.1860 (FO/103); Malet to Russell, no. 42, 14.4.1860 (FO/30/191); Murray to Russell, priv., 30.4.1860 (RuP-PRO/30/22/63); Bloomfield to Russell, no. 193, 4.5.1860 (FO/64/492).

59 Milbanke to Russell, no. 14, 27.2.1860 (FO/9/144); Gordon to Russell, no. 2, 2.1.1860 and no. 57, 12.4.1860 (FO/82/94); Malet to Russell, no. 42, 14.4.1860 (FO/30/191); Bloomfield to Russell, no. 176, 21.4.1860 (FO/64/491) and no. 200, 5.5.1860 (FO/64/492); Murray to Russell, priv., 30.4.1860 (RuP-PRO/30/22/63).

60 Russell to Palmerston, 18.7.1859 (BP-GC/RU/508).

61 Russell to Malet, no. 10, 17.2.1860 (FO/30/190); *Times* (2.4.1860: 8d; 13.4.1860: 6c); Russell to Malet, no. 27, 23.4.1860 (FO/30/190).

62 For the revival of the liberal-national movement in 1859 see: Düding (1988: 183–187); Langewiesche (1988: 85–93); Sheehan (1978: 95–107); Schulze (1989: 141–50 and 1991: 82–8). On the *Nationalverein* see: Biefang (1994: 66–206) and Na'am (1987).

63 Ward to Malmesbury, genl. no. 19, draft, 14.10.1858 (FO/299/9); Gordon to Malmesbury, no. 50, 17.11.1858 (FO/34/89).

64 Milbanke to Malmesbury, no. 34, 26.4.1859 (FO/9/140); Ward to Russell, genl. no. 21, draft, 8.9.1859 (FO/299/10); [M. Pattison,] 'Germany – Its Strength and Weakness', *WR* 74 (1860: 166); for further links between the Italian war and the national movement see: Loftus to Malmesbury, no. 409, 12.5.1859 (FO/7/569); Ward to Russell, genl. no. 23, draft, 29.9.1859 (FO/299/10). The Foreign Office valued Ward's expertise on the German national movement. He was instructed to 'report further as to the progress

or decline of this movement' [Hammond to Ward, no. 2, 17.9.1859 (FO/299/10)]. For Ward's good reputation see also Clarendon's statement in: *Parliamentary Papers* (1861a: 1018).

65   Lowther to Russell, no. 39, 22.10.1859 (FO/64/480) and no. 67, 12.11.1859 (FO/64/481); Loftus to Russell, no. 754, 3.11.1859 (FO/7/577); Ward to Russell, genl. no. 27, draft, 17.11.1859 (FO/299/10); on the Schiller celebrations in 1859 see: Mosse (1975: 86–89); Noltenius (1988) and Obermann (1955).

66   Loftus to Russell, priv., 26.7.1861 (RuP-PRO/30/22/79); see also: Loftus to Russell, no. 356, 26.7.1861 (FO/64/512); Murray to Russell, no. 49, 26.7.1861 (FO/68/117); [B. Taylor,] 'The First German Shooting Match', *CM* 4 (1861: 488).

67   Ward to Russell, genl. no. 22, draft, 22.9.1859 (FO/299/10); Malet to Russell, no. 54, 19.9.1859 (FO/30/188); Ward to Russell, genl. no. 31, draft, 13.12.1859 (FO/299/10); Bloomfield to Russell, no. 115, 17.3.1860 (FO/64/490); Ward to Russell, no. 30, 10.9.1860 (FO/33/166); Malet to Russell, no. 36, 1.3.1861 (FO/30/195); Loftus to Clarendon, priv., 17.10.1861 (ClP-Clar.Dep. c.542); Malet to Russell, no. 75, 7.3.1862 (FO/30/200).

68   *Parliamentary Papers* (1861a: 1017).

69   Ward to Russell, genl. no. 24, draft, 13.10.1859 (FO/299/10); Morier's memorandum enclosed in: Bloomfield to Russell, no. 80, 25.2.1860 (FO/64/490); Malet to Russell, no. 36, 1.3.1861 (FO/30/195); Lowther to Russell, no. 22, 1.10.1859 (FO/64/480); on the German Confederation's low standing in European politics in the 1860s and the lack of sorrow at its eventual demise see also: Schroeder (1990).

70   *Times* (18.7.1859: 10f; 19.7.1859: 10f; 18.2.1858: 9b).

71   Loftus to Malmesbury, no. 409, 12.5.1859 (FO/7/569); Lowther to Russell, no. 14, 17.9.1859 (FO/64/480); Crowe to Russell, genl. no. 20, 7.12.1860 (FO/68/113).

72   *Spectator* (27.8.1859: 881; see also: 20.7.1861: 778–9); *Times* (2.9.1859: 8d).

73   Ward to Russell, genl. no. 21, draft, 8.9.1859 (FO/299/10); Bloomfield to Russell, no. 115, 17.3.1860 (FO/64/490); Milbanke to Russell, no. 40, 18.4.1861 (FO/9/149); Loftus to Clarendon, priv., 17.10.1861 (ClP-Clar.Dep. c.542); [B. Taylor,] 'The First German Shooting Match, *CM* 4 (1861: 488).

74   Gordon to Russell, no. 5, 1.7.1859 (FO/34/99); Ward to Russell, genl. no. 22, draft, 22.9.1859 (FO/299/10); Gordon to Russell, no. 12, 29.1.1861 (FO/82/98); Howard to Russell, no. 391, 12.12.1861 (FO/34/122).

75   Malet to Russell, no. 35, 28.7.1859 (FO/30/187); Milbanke to Russell, no. 40, 18.4.1861 (FO/9/149); Malet to Russell, no. 90, 10.6.1862 (FO/30/201) and no. 73, 30.5.1863 (FO/30/206).

76   Milbanke to Malmesbury, no. 34, 26.4.1859 (FO/9/140); Milbanke to Russell, no. 78, 27.8.1859 (FO/9/141); Ward to Russell, genl. no. 22, draft, 22.9.1859 (FO/299/10); Malet to Russell, no. 136, 10.10.1862 (FO/30/202).

77   Loftus to Malmesbury, no. 409, 12.5.1859 (FO/7/569); Loftus to Clarendon, priv., 17.10.1861 (ClP-Clar.Dep. c.542); Crowe to Russell, genl. no. 19, 6.8.1863 (FO/68/128); Russell to Clarendon, 9.9.1861 (ClP-Clar.Dep. c.104).

78   Malet to Malmesbury, no. 134, 28.11.1858 (FO/30/183); Bloomfield to

Malmesbury, no. 272, 5.5.1859 (FO/64/477); Bloomfield to Russell, priv., 30.7.1859 (RuP-PRO/30/22/79); Ward to Russell, genl. no. 29, draft, 24.11.1859 (FO/299/10); Morier to Russell, priv., 26.1.1861 (RuP-PRO/30/22/79).

79 Malet to Russell, no. 14, 1.7.1859 (FO/30/187); Lowther to Russell, no. 87, 26.11.1859 (FO/64/481); Gordon to Russell, no. 2, 2.1.1860 (FO/82/94); Bloomfield to Russell, priv., 11.2.1860 (RuP-PRO/30/22/79); Howard to Russell, no. 64, 11.5.1860 (FO/34/104); Morier to Russell, priv., 26.1.1861 (RuP-PRO/30/22/79); Crowe to Russell, genl. no. 13, 7.5.1861 and genl. no. 15, 22.5.1861 (FO/68/118).

80 *Spectator* (20.7.1861: 779); Russell to Milbanke, no. 20, 22.5.1861 (FO/9/147); Cowley to Russell, no. 771, copy, 22.5.1861 (QVP: vol. I.36, doc. 25); Howard to Russell, no. 177, 25.5.1861 (FO/34/119); Milbanke to Russell, no. 64, 28.5.1861 (FO/9/149); Gordon to Russell, no. 65, 28.5.1861 (FO/82/99); Russell to Gordon, no. 28, draft, 21.6.1861 (FO/82/97); Russell to Milbanke, no. 29, draft, 21.6.1861 (FO/9/147).

81 On the the Würzburg Conferences and the plans for a 'Third Germany' see: Gruner (1973); Srbik (1935–42: iii, 285–99, 318–20) and Wehner (1993: 13–51).

82 Milbanke to Russell, no. 93, 18.11.1859 (FO/9/141); Ward to Russell, genl. no. 29, draft, 24.11.1859 (FO/299/10); Malet to Russell, no. 85, 26.11.1859 (FO/30/188).

83 Malet to Russell, no. 88, 2.12.1859 (FO/30/188); Murray to Russell, no. 13, 9.12.1859 (FO/68/109); Ward to Russell, genl. no. 31, draft, 13.12.1859 (FO/299/10); Bloomfield to Russell, no. 481, 24.12.1859 (FO/64/481); Russell to Bloomfield, no. 60, draft, 28.12.1859 (FO/64/472); Russell to Loftus, priv., copy, 29.2.1860 (RuP-PRO/30/22/98).

84 Russell to Howard, no. 24, draft, 30.5.1860 (FO/34/102); Russell to Milbanke, no. 38, draft, 13.8.1860 (FO/9/143); for Britain's hostility towards the 'Würzburgers' see also: Adler (1986: 52–5, 101–3).

85 Milbanke to Russell, no. 93, 18.11.1859 (FO/9/141); Lowther to Russell, no. 87, 26.11.1859 (FO/64/481).

86 Quoted in: Hoppen (1998: 227–8); for Britain's unfavourable attitude towards Austria between 1859 and 1863 see also: Metzler (1997: 186–95).

87 Malet to Russell, no. 72, 2.11.1859 (FO/30/188); Russell to Bloomfield, no. 60, draft, 28.12.1859 (FO/64/472); Malet to Russell, no. 8, 2.2.1860 (FO/30/191); Howard to Russell, no. 38, 23.3.1860 (FO/34/103); Russell to Palmerston, priv., 30.9.1860 (BP-GC/RU/625); Morier to Russell, 26.1.1861 (RuP-PRO/30/22/79); Crowe to Russell, genl. no. 28, 1.11.1861 (FO/68/118); Palmerston to Russell, priv., 7.11.1861, copy (BP-GC/RU/1140).

88 Palmerston to Russell, 6.9.1859 (RuP-PRO/30/22/20); Russell to Palmerston, 21.1.1861 (BP-GC/RU/1136); Russell to Clarendon, 3.10.1861 (ClP-Clar.Dep. c.104); Russell to Bloomfield, priv., 11.12.1861 (BlP-FO/356/32); *Times* (18.7.1859: 10f; 2.4.1860: 8d; 24.2.1862: 8c).

89 Bloomfield to Russell, no. 177, 15.4.1861 (FO/7/609).

90 On the Prussian constitutional crisis see: Gall (1986: i, 154–228); Helfert (1989; 1994); Huber (1970: 275–369); Pflanze (1990: 164–217); Schulze (1992: 327–33); Siemann (1990: 200–18) and Srbik (1935–42: iii, 26–50).

91 Bloomfield to Russell, no. 470, 17.12.1859 (FO/64/481); Russell to Bloomfield, priv., 5.2.1860 (BlP-FO/356/32); Bloomfield to Russell, priv., 15.2.1860 (RuP-PRO/30/22/79); Bloomfield to Russell, no. 108, 17.3.1860 (FO/64/490); Russell to Albert, 21.3.1860 (QVP: vol. I.31, doc. 88); Russell to Bloomfield, priv., 21.3.1860 and 31.3.1860 (BlP-FO/356/32); in 1862 Russell still supported strengthening Prussia's army [see: Russell to Loftus, priv., copy, 1.1.1862 (RuP-PRO/30/22/112)].

92 Crowe to Russell, genl. no. 20, 7.12.1860 (FO/68/113); Lowther to Russell, no. 26, 14.1.1861 (FO/64/506); Crowe to Russell, genl. no. 1, 17.1.1861 (FO/68/118); Loftus to Russell, priv., 9.2.1861 (RuP-PRO/30/22/79); Loftus to Russell, no. 289, 21.6.1861 (FO/64/511); *Times* (22.6.1861: 10d).

93 Clarendon to Russell, priv., 11.9.1861 (RuP-PRO/30/22/79); Clarendon to Victoria, 19.10.1861 (QVP: vol. I.37, doc. 46); on Clarendon's journey to Prussia see also: Maxwell (1913: ii, 244–9); Loftus to Russell, no. 435, 23.11.1861 and no. 487, 21.12.1861 (FO/64/515).

94 Loftus to Russell, priv., 13.3.1862 (RuP-PRO/30/22/80); Loftus to Russell, no. 183, 22.3.1862 (FO/64/522); Loftus to Russell, no. 216, 5.4.1862 (FO/64/523); Morier's memorandum is enclosed in: Loftus to Russell, no. 246, 12.4.1862 (FO/64/523); for Morier's view on the Prussian constitutional conflict see: Murray (1997: 82–116); Loftus to Russell, no. 291, 10.5.1862 (FO/64/524).

95 Russell to Victoria, 8.6.1862 (QVP: vol. I.39, doc. 43); Russell to Palmerston, 14.9.1862 (BP-GC/RU/726).

96 Loftus to Russell, no. 570, 25.10.1862 (FO/64/529) and no. 581, 1.11.1863 (FO/64/530); *Times* (7.3.1863: 9d); the British press coverage of the Prussian constitutional conflict is summarized in Adler (1986: 132–3); Block (1969: 291–344).

97 For Russell's references to 1830 see: Russell to Loftus, priv., copy, 12.3.1862, 21.3.1862, 14.5.1862, 25.6.1862 (RuP-PRO/30/22/112); Buchanan to Russell, no. 295, 23.5.1863 (FO/64/542); Palmerston to Victoria, 29.5.1863 (QVP: vol. I.40, doc. 56).

98 Granville to Victoria, 24.2.1863, quoted in: Mosse (1958: 113 n. 5); Russell to Buchanan, no. 42, draft, 18.2.1863 (FO/64/536); on Britain's policy with reference to the 1863 rising in Poland see: Adler (1986: 138–47); Mosse (1956 and 1958: 110–28) and Valentin (1937b: 181–188).

99 Russell to Loftus, no. 64, draft, 30.3.1861 (FO/504); *Times* (2.4.1861: 6c); Palmerston to Russell, 27.10.1861 (RuP-PRO/30/22/14B); Palmerston to Russell, 27.6.1863, quoted in: Mosse (1958: 107); for Britain's policy towards the Schleswig-Holstein conflict between 1858 and 1863 see: Adler (1986: 115–17, 126–7); Murray (1997: 180–91); Sandiford (1975: 48–66).

100 Palmerston to Victoria, 29.5.1863 (QVP: vol. I. 40, doc. 56).

101 Bloomfield to Russell, priv., 15.1.1863 (RuP-PRO/30/22/42).

102 On Beust's plan see: Huber (1970: 409–10) and Srbik (1935–42: iii, 366–72).

103 Milbanke to Russell, no. 105, 4.11.1861 (FO/9/159).

104 Malet to Russell, no. 150, 29.11.1861 (FO/30/197); Russell to Murray, no. 21, 27.2.1862 (FO/68/121).

105 For the text of the Bernstorff plan see: *Dokumente* (1986: 121–3); on the plan see: Huber (1970: 410–11) and Srbik (1935–42: iii, 374–6); Loftus to Russell, no. 23, 11.1.1862 (FO/64/520); Howard to Russell, no. 25, 1.2.1862

and no. 33, 12.2.1862 (FO/34/125); Malet to Russell, no. 75, 7.3.1862 (FO/30/200).

106 For the text of the identical notes see: *Dokumente* (1986: 126–7); the anti-Prussian coalition is discussed by Srbik (1935–42: iii, 376–84); Loftus to Russell, no. 79 and no. 84, 8.2.1862 (FO/64/521); Loftus to Russell, no. 102, 15.2.1862 (FO/64/521); Russell to Loftus, priv., copy, 19.2.1862 (RuP-PRO/30/22/112); Bloomfield to Russell, priv., 20.2.1862 (RuP-PRO/30/22/41).

107 On the delegates project see: Huber (1970: 415–20) and Kraehe (1950/1).

108 Loftus to Russell, priv., 16.8.1862 (RuP-PRO/30/22/80); see also Loftus's similar comments in: Loftus to Russell, no. 494, 20.8.1862 (FO/64/527); Russell to Fane, no. 50, draft, 17.9.1862 (FO/7/626).

109 For reports on Bismarck's preparedness to resort to extreme measures see: Buchanan to Russell, no. 25, 20.12.1862 and no. 31, 27.12.1862 (FO/64/531).

110 Howard to Russell, no. 288, 20.12.1862 (FO/34/129); Russell to Bloomfield, priv., 31.12.1862 and 14.1.1863 (BlP-FO/356/32); Russell to Howard, no. 1, draft, 7.1.1863 (FO/34/134).

111 For British efforts to pacify Prussia see: Russell to Buchanan, no. 1, draft, 7.1.1863 (FO/64/536); Buchanan to Russell, no. 14, 9.1.1863 (FO/64/538); Russell to Buchanan, no. 11, draft, 14.1.1863 (FO/64/536); Buchanan to Russell, no. 57, 28.1.1863 (FO/64/538); on this see also: Valentin (1937b: 177–9).

112 Howard to Russell, no. 133, 7.8.1863 (FO/34/137); Bloomfield to Russell, priv., 13.8.1863 (RuP-PRO/30/22/42); Loftus to Russell, no. 78, 14.8.1863 (FO/9/159); Russell to Clarendon, 15.8.1863 (ClP-Clar.Dep. c.104).

113 On the Austrian reform plan and the *Fürstentag* see: Huber (1970: 420–35); Lutz (1994: 440–47); Srbik (1935–42: iv, 1–38) and Wehner (1993: 52–103); on Bismarck's decision to remain aloof see: Gall (1986: i, 230–5); Pflanze (1990: 196–9) and Wehner (1993: 104–15, 307–18).

114 Clarendon to Russell, priv., copy, 20.8.1863 (ClP-Clar.Dep. c.104); Malet to Russell, no. 98, 20.8.1863 (FO/30/207); Morier to Russell, priv., draft, 6.9.1863 (MoP-Box 1, 1i).

115 Howard to Russell, no. 140, 22.8.1863 (FO/34/137); Russell to Palmerston, 26.8.1863 (BP-GC/RU/800); Bonar to Russell, no. 16, 5.9.1863 (FO/9/160); Russell to Clarendon, 13.9.1863 (ClP-Clar.Dep. c.104).

116 On the Franco-Prussian treaty and the subsequent conflict within the *Zollverein* see: Böhme (1966: 91–207); Hahn (1984: 165–80); Henderson (1959: 273–303) and Huber (1970: 615–29).

117 Morier's memorandum enclosed in: Buchanan to Russell, no. 22, 20.12.1862 (FO/64/531); Board of Trade to Foreign Office, 17.8.1863, quoted in: Metzler (1997: 186); on Britain's policy towards the *Zollverein* during the conflict over the French treaty see: Davis (1997: 146–68) and Metzler (1997: 169–86).

118 Layard (Russell) to Lowther, private, copy, 26.8.1863 (FO/64/537); see also: Russell to Buchanan, no. 127, 30.9.1863 (FO/64/537).

119 Howard to Russell, no. 133, 7.8.1863 (FO/34/137); Bloomfield to Russell, priv., 20.8.1863 (RuP-PRO/30/22/42); Clarendon to Russell, priv., copy, 20.8.1863 (ClP-Clar.Dep. c.104); Bonar to Russell, no. 16, 5.9.1863

(FO/9/160); Russell to Clarendon, 4.9.1863 (ClP-Clar.Dep. c.104); Russell to Palmerston, 14.9.1863 (BP-GC/RU/804).

120 Russell to Buchanan, no. 127, draft, 30.9.1863 (FO/64/537); Russell to Bloomfield, 23.10.1863 (FO/356/32).

121 Russell to Palmerston, 4.9.1863 (BP-GC/RU/803).

Conclusion

1 Acton (1862: 148).

2 Bismarck to Gerlach, 11.5.1857, in: Bismarck (1928: 171).

3 It is surprising to note how little importance British diplomats and foreign secretaries appear to have attached to Prussia's Protestantism. Typically, the confessional argument – which was rarely used at all – was added as a lacklustre afterthought. Cowley's attitude was characteristic. 'I have however many unofficial reasons for believing that we are desirous to see Prussia at the head of Germany,' he wrote to Malet on 29 June 1849. 'In the first place it is thought better for our commercial interests. Then people are afraid of the reactionary tendencies of Austria. I presume also that with some persons the religion of Prussia has some weight' (CoP-FO/519/165). Prussophilia in nineteenth-century Britain was further fuelled by memories of the 'glorious' days of Frederick the Great and Blücher; see: Carsten (1982).

4 The findings of this investigation thus strongly support the arguments recently proposed by Hildebrand (1997: 89–90, 111–13, 383–4).

5 The argument that Whig ideology shaped the formulation of mid-Victorian foreign policy is powerfully made by Schroeder (1972: 415–16).

6 See: Chamberlain (1987: 69–70) and Steele (1991: 247); for the Whigs' belief in the importance of proper leadership to make popular demands for reform safe see: Jenkins (1994: 4–6); Mitchell (1980: 63–5); Mitchell (1999: 27, 29) and Southgate (1962: 15).

7 Cartwright to Palmerston, no. 73, 25.6.1832 (FO/30/38).

8 On the non-existence of German Whigs see: Muhs (1988: 228–38).

Manuscript Sources and Bibliography

A) Manuscript sources

Balliol College Library, Oxford:
* *The Morier Papers* (Sir Robert Burnett David Morier).

Bodleian Library, Oxford:
* *The Papers of the Earls of Clarendon/The Clarendon Deposit* (George William Frederick, 4th Earl of Clarendon): Ms Clar. Dep. c.104ff.
* *The Correspondence of John Fane*, 11th Earl of Westmorland: MSS. Eng. d 2577.

British Library/Manuscripts Collection, London:
* *The Aberdeen Papers* (4th Earl of Aberdeen): Add.Mss. 43041ff.
* *The Beauvale Papers* (Frederick James Lamb): Add.Mss. 60455ff.
* *The Palmerston Papers* (3rd Viscount Palmerston): Add.Mss. 48444ff.
* *The Peel Papers* (Sir Robert Peel): Add.Mss. 40453ff.
* *The Westmorland Papers* (11th Earl of Westmorland) [microfilm]: M/509–M/511ff.

Hampshire Record Office, Winchester:
* *The Papers of the Harris Family, Earls of Malmesbury* (3rd Earl of Malmesbury): 9M73/11ff.

Northamptonshire Record Office, Northampton:
* *Cartwright (Aynho) Boxes* (Sir Thomas Cartwright): C (A), Boxes 15ff.

Public Record Office, Kew/Surrey:
* *The Russell Papers (1st Earl Russell)*: PRO 30/22.
* *Foreign Office Papers*:
  FO/7 (Austria/General Correspondence).
  FO/9 (Bavaria/General Correspondence).
  FO/27 (France/General Correspondence).
  FO/30 (Germany [Frankfurt]/General Correspondence).
  FO/33 (Hamburg and Hanse Towns/General Correspondence).
  FO/34 (Hanover/General Correspondence).
  FO/64 (Prussia/General Correspondence).
  FO/65 (Russia/General Correspondence).
  FO/68 (Saxony/General Correspondence).
  FO/82 (Württemberg/General Correspondence).

FO/97 (Supplement to General Correspondence): 326 (Bowring).
FO/120 (Austria/Embassy and Consular Archives/Correspondence).
FO/208 (Germany [Frankfurt]/Embassy and Consular Archives/Correspondence).
FO/244 (Prussia/Embassy and Consular Archives/Correspondence).
FO/299 (Germany [Leipzig]/Embassy and Consular Archive Germany).
FO/356 (The Bloomfield Papers).
FO/519 (The Cowley Papers).

Royal Archives, Windsor Castle:

- *The Papers of Queen Victoria on Foreign Affairs*. Files from the Royal Archives, Windsor Castle. Part 2: Germany and Central Europe, 1841–1900, ed. Kenneth Bourne (Bethesda/Maryland 1993).

Southampton University Library, Southampton:

- *The Political and Semi-Official Correspondence and Papers of Henry John Temple, third Viscount Palmerston 1806–1865* (*MS 62*) (The Broadlands Papers).

B) Printed sources

B.1) Newspapers and Periodicals

The Annual Register
Blackwood's Edinburgh Magazine
The British and Foreign Review
The British Quarterly Review
Cornhill Magazine
The Edinburgh Review
The Foreign Quarterly Review
Fraser's Magazine for Town and Country
The Home and Foreign Review
The Morning Chronicle
The North British Review
The Quarterly Review
The Spectator
Tait's Edinburgh Review
The Times
The Westminster Review

B.2) Other printed primary sources and secondary literature

An Account (1859) *of the Tiverton Election (29th April 1859) with a revised Report of Lord Palmerston's Speech upon that Occasion* (London).

Acton (1862), John E. E. Dahlberg-Acton, Lord: 'Nationality', in Acton, John E. E. Dahlberg-Acton, Lord: *Essays in the Liberal Interpretation of History. Selected Papers*, ed. by William McNeill (Chicago–London), pp. 131–59.

Adler (1986), Matthew: *Great Britain, the 'Bund', and the German Question 1859–1863* (Oxford University, M.Litt. thesis).

Airlie (1922), Mabel Countess of: *Lady Palmerston and Her Times*, 2 vols (London).

Aktenstücke (1849) *betreffend das Bündnis vom 26ten Mai und die Deutsche Verfassungsangelegenheit*, Bd. 1 (Berlin).

Anderson (1967), Olive: *A Liberal State at War. English Politics and Economics during the Crimean War* (London).

Angelow (1996), Jürgen: *Von Wien nach Königgrätz. Die Sicherheitspolitik des Deutschen Bundes im europäischen Gleichgewicht (1815–1866)* (München).

Ashley (1876), E.: *The Life of Henry John Temple, Viscount Palmerston, 1846–1865*, 2 vols (London).

Austensen (1977), Roy A.: 'Felix Schwarzenberg: "Realpolitiker" or Metternichean? The Evidence of the Dresden Conference', *Mitteilungen des österreichischen Staatsarchivs* 30 (1977), pp. 97–118.

Austensen (1980), Roy A.: 'Austria and the "Struggle for Supremacy in Germany," 1848–1864', *JMH* 52 (1990), pp. 195–225.

Austensen (1983), Roy A.: '*Einheit oder Einigkeit?* Another Look at Metternich's View of the German Dilemma', *German Studies Review* 6 (1983), pp. 41–57.

Austensen (1984), Roy A.: 'The Making of Austria's Prussian Policy, 1848–1852', *HJ* 27 (1984), pp. 861–76.

Austensen (1991), Roy A.: 'Metternich, Austria and the German Question, 1848–1851', *IHR* 13 (1991), pp. 21–37.

Barclay (1995), David E.: *Frederick William IV and the Prussian Monarchy, 1840–1861* (Oxford).

Baumgart (1983), Winfried: 'Österreich und Preußen im Krimkrieg, 1853–1856. Neue Forschungsergebnisse aufgrund der österreichischen Akten', in Hauser, Oswald (Hg.): *Vorträge und Studien zur preußisch-deutschen Geschichte* (Köln–Wien), pp. 45–70.

Baumgart (1995), Winfried: 'Die deutschen Mittelstaaten und der Krimkrieg 1853–1856', in Botzauer, Winfried (Hg.): *Landesgeschichte und Reichsgeschichte. Festschrift für Alois Gerlich zum 70. Geburtstag* (Stuttgart), pp. 357–89.

Baumgart (1999a), Winfried: *Europäisches Konzert und Nationale Bewegung. Internationale Beziehungen 1830–1878* (Paderborn).

Baumgart (1999b), Winfried: *The Crimean War 1853–1856* (London).

Beales (1961), Derek: *England and Italy 1859–60* (London).

Bell (1936), Herbert C. F.: *Lord Palmerston*, 2 vols (London).

Biefang (1994), Andreas: *Politisches Bürgertum in Deutschland 1857–1868. Nationale Organisation und Eliten* (Düsseldorf).

Billinger (1976), Robert D., Jr.: 'The War Scare of 1831 and Prussian–South German Plans for the End of Austrian Dominance in Germany', *CEH* 9 (1976), pp. 203–19.

Billinger (1990), Robert D., Jr.: '"They sing the Best Songs Badly": Metternich, Frederick William IV, and the German Confederation during the War Scare of 1840–41', in Rumpler, Helmut (Hg.): *Deutscher Bund und deutsche Frage 1815–1866* (Wien–München), pp. 94–113.

Billinger (1991), Robert D., Jr.: *Metternich and the German Question. States' Rights and Federal Duties, 1820–1834* (Newark–London–Toronto).

Billy (1993), George J.: *Palmerston's Foreign Policy: 1848* (New York).

Binder (1933), Hildegard: *Queen Victoria und Preußen-Deutschland bis zum Ausschluß Österreichs 1866* (Berlin University, D.Phil. thesis).

Bindoff (1935), S. T.: 'The Unreformed Diplomatic Service, 1812–60', *Transactions of the Royal Historical Society*, 4th series 18 (1935), pp. 143–72.

Bismarck (1925), Otto von: *Gesammelte Werke*, Bd. 3 (Berlin).

Bismarck (1928), Otto von: *Gedanken und Erinnerungen*. *Die drei Bände in einem Bande* (Stuttgart–Berlin).

Blackbourn (1997), David: *Fontana History of Germany 1780–1918*. *The Long Nineteenth Century* (London).

Blake (1966), Robert: *Disraeli* (London).

Block (1969), John Martin: *British Opinion of Prussian Policy 1854–1866* (University of Wisconsin, Ph.D. thesis).

Bloomfield (1883), Georgina Baroness: *Reminiscences of Court and Diplomatic Life*, 2 vols (London).

Böhme (1966), Helmut: *Deutschlands Weg zur Großmacht*. *Studien zum Verhältnis von Wirtschaft und Staat während der Reichsgründungszeit 1848–1871* (Köln–Berlin).

Bolitho (1933), Hector: *The Prince Consort and his Brother*. *Two Hundred New Letters* (London).

Borries (1930), Kurt: *Preußen im Krimkrieg* (Stuttgart).

Botzenhart (1977), Manfred: *Deutscher Parlamentarismus in der Revolutionszeit: 1848–1850* (Düsseldorf).

Botzenhart (1996), Manfred: 'Die österreichische Frage in der deutschen Nationalversammlung', in Gehler, M. *et al.* (Hgg.): *Ungleiche Partner? Österreich und Deutschland in ihrer gegenseitigen Wahrnehmung. Historische Analysen und Vergleiche aus dem 19. und 20. Jahrhundert* (Stuttgart), pp. 115–34.

Bourne (1967), Kenneth: *Britain and the Balance of Power in North America 1815–1908* (London).

Bourne (1970), Kenneth: *The Foreign Policy of Victorian England 1830–1902* (Oxford).

Bourne (1982), Kenneth: *Palmerston: The Early Years 1784–1841* (London).

Bourne (1984), Kenneth: 'The Foreign Office under Palmerston', in Roger Bullen, ed., *The Foreign Office 1782–1982* (Frederick/Maryland), pp. 19–45.

Bourne (1989), Kenneth: 'Nationsbildung und britische Politik: Das Kabinett zwischen 1846 und 1852', in Birke, Adolf M./Heydemann, Günther (Hgg.): *Die Herausforderung des europäischen Staatensystems: Nationale Ideologie und staatliches Interesse zwischen Restauration und Imperialismus* (Göttingen–Zürich), pp. 96–118.

Breuilly (1994), John: 'Liberalism in Mid-Nineteenth Century Britain and Germany', in Breuilly, John: *Labour and Liberalism in Nineteenth Century Europe* (Manchester–New York), pp. 228–72.

Breuilly (1997), John: 'Variations in Liberalism: Britain and Europe in the Mid-Nineteenth Century', *Diplomacy and Statecraft* 8/3 (1997), pp. 91–123.

Bridge (1990), F. R.: *The Habsburg Monarchy among the Great Powers, 1815–1918* (New York–Oxford–Munich).

Bright (1907), John: *Selected Speeches on Public Questions* (London–New York).

British Documents (1990) *on Foreign Affairs: Reports and Papers from the Foreign Office Confidential Print*, general editors: Kenneth Bourne & Donald C. Watt, Part 1, Series F, ed. David Stevenson, vol. 18: Germany, 1848–1897.

Brown (1958), Lucy: *The Board of Trade and the Free Trade Movement 1830–42* (Oxford).

Buchner (1955), Rudolf: 'Der Durchbruch des modernen Nationalismus in Deutschland', in *Festgabe dargebracht Harold Steinacker zur Vollendung des 80. Lebensjahres* (München), pp. 305–33.

Bullen (1974), Roger: 'Anglo-French Rivalry and Spanish Politics, 1846–1848,' *English Historical Review* 89 (1974), pp. 25–48.

Bullen (1978), Roger: 'Party Politics and Foreign Policy. Whigs, Tories and Iberian Affairs, 1830–6,' *Bulletin of the Institute of Historical Research* 51 (1978: 37–59).

Bulwer (1870–1874), Hon. Sir Henry Lytton (Lord Dalling): *The Life of Henry John Temple, Viscount Palmerston*, ed. E. Ashley, 3 vols [to 1846] (London).

Bunsen (1868), Frances Baroness: *A Memoir of Baron Bunsen*, vol. 2 (London).

Burian (1974), Peter: 'Die Olmützer Punktuation von 1850 und die deutsche Frage', *GWU* 25 (1974), pp. 668–76.

Canis (1972), Konrad: 'Ideologie und Taktik der junkerlich-militaristischen Reaktion bei der Vorbereitung des Staatsstreiches in Preußen im Herbst 1848', *Jahrbuch für Geschichte* 7 (1972), pp. 459–503.

Cargill (1840), William: *An Examination of the Origin, Progress, and Tendencey of the Commercial and Political Confederation against England and France, Called the 'Prussian League'* (Newcastle).

Carr (1963), William: *Schleswig-Holstein 1815–48. A Study in National Conflict* (Manchester).

Carsten (1982), Francis L.: 'Preußen und England', in Büsch, Otto (Hg.): *Preußen und das Ausland* (Berlin), pp. 26–46.

Chamberlain (1980), Muriel E.: *British Foreign Policy in the Age of Palmerston* (Burnt Mill, Harlow/Essex).

Chamberlain (1983), Muriel E.: *Lord Aberdeen. A Political Biography* (London–New York).

Chamberlain (1987), Muriel E.: *Lord Palmerston* (Cardiff).

Chamberlain (1988), Muriel E.: *'Pax Britannica'? British Foreign Policy 1798–1914* (London–New York).

Charmatz (1916), Rudolf: *Minister Freiherr von Bruck. Der Vorkämpfer Mitteleuropas. Sein Lebensgang und seine Druckschriften* (Leipzig).

Clarke (1989), John: *British Diplomacy and Foreign Policy 1782–1865: the National Interest* (London).

Conacher (1968), J. B.: *The Aberdeen Coalition 1852–1855. A Study in Mid-Nineteenth Century Party Politics* (Cambridge).

Conacher (1987), J. B.: *Britain and the Crimea 1855–56. Problems of War and Peace* (Basingstoke and London).

Connell (1962), Brian: *Regina v. Palmerston. The Correspondence between Queen Victoria and Her Foreign and Prime Minister 1837–1865* (London).

Crowe (1895), Sir Joseph: *Reminiscences of Thirty-Five Years of My Life* (London).

Cunningham (1957), Allen B.: 'Peel, Aberdeen, and the Entente Cordiale,' *Bulletin of the Institute of Historical Research* 30 (1957), pp. 189–206.

Dann (1996), Otto: *Nation und Nationalismus in Deutschland 1770–1990* (München; 3rd edn).

Davis (1997), John Richard: *Britain and the German Zollverein, 1848–1866* (London).

Davis (1998), John R.: 'The Bamberg Conference of 1854: A Re-Evaluation', *European History Quarterly* 28 (1998), 81–107.

Deuchert (1983), Norbert: *Vom Hambacher Fest zur badischen Revolution. Politische Presse und Anfänge deutscher Demokratie 1832–1848/49* (Stuttgart).

Der Deutsche Bund (1998), zwischen Reaktion und Reform 1851–1858, bearb. von Jürgen Müller (München) [= Quellen zur Geschichte des Deutschen Bundes 1850–1866, Bd. 2].

Der deutsche Nationalverein (1995), *1859–1867. Vorstands- und Ausschußprotokolle,* bearbeitet von Andreas Biefang (Düsseldorf).

Disraeli (1993), Benjamin: *Letters,* ed. M. G. Wiebe, vols. V (Toronto).

Doeberl (1926), Michael: *Bayern und das preußische Unionsprojekt* (München).

Doering-Manteuffel (1989), Anselm: Der Ordnungszwang des Staatensystems: Zu den Mitteleuropa-Konzepten in der österreichisch-preußischen Rivalität 1849–1851, in Birke, Adolf M./Heydemann, Günther (Hgg.): *Die Herausforderung des europäischen Staatensystems: Nationale Ideologie und staatliches Interesse zwischen Restauration und Imperialismus* (Göttingen–Zürich), pp. 119–40.

Doering-Manteuffel (1991), Anselm: *Vom Wiener Kongreß zur Pariser Konferenz. England, die deutsche Frage und das Mächtessytem 1815–1856* (Göttingen).

Doering-Manteuffel (1993), Anselm: *Die Deutsche Frage und das europäische Staatensystem 1815–1871* (München).

Dokumente (1978) *zur deutschen Verfassungsgeschichte,* ed. by Huber, Ernst Rudolf, Bd. I: *Deutsche Verfassungsdokumente 1803–1850* (Stuttgart; 3rd edn).

Dokumente (1986) *zur deutschen Verfassungsgeschichte,* ed. by Huber, Ernst Rudolf, Bd. II: *Deutsche Verfassungsdokumente 1851–1900* (Stuttgart; 3rd edn).

Dowe (1998), Dieter *et al.* (eds): *Europa 1848: Revolution und Reform* (Bonn).

Die Dresdener Konferenz (1996) *und die Wiederherstellung des Deutschen Bundes 1850/51,* bearbeitet von Jürgen Müller (München) [= Quellen zur Geschichte des Deutschen Bundes. Abt. III: Quellen zur Geschichte des Deutschen Bundes 1850–1866, Bd. 1].

Düding (1984), Dieter: *Organisierter gesellschaftlicher Nationalismus in Deutschland (1808–1847). Bedeutung und Funktion der Turner- und Sängervereine für die deutsche Nationalbewegung* (München).

Düding (1987), Dieter: 'The Nineteenth-Century German Nationalist Movement as a Movement of Societies', in Schulze, Hagen (ed.): *Nation-Building in Central Europe* (Leamington Spa–New York), pp. 19–49.

Düding (1988), Dieter: 'Nationale Oppositionsfeste der Turner, Sänger und Schützen im 19. Jahrhundert', in Düding, Dieter/Friedemann, Peter/Münch, Paul (Hgg.): *Öffentliche Festkultur: politische Feste in Deutschland von der Aufklärung bis zum 1. Weltkrieg* (Reinbek bei Hamburg), pp. 166–90.

Dülffer (1997), Jost/Kröger, Martin/Wippich, Rolf-Harald: *Vermiedene Kriege. Deeskalation von Konflikten der Großmächte zwischen Krimkrieg und Erstem Weltkrieg (1856–1914)* (München).

Eckhart (1931), Franz: *Die deutsche Frage und der Krimkrieg* (Berlin–Königsberg).

Evans (2000), Robert J. W.: '1848–1849 in the Habsburg Monarchy', in Evans, Robert J. W. and Pogge von Strandmann, Hartmut (eds): *The Revolutions in Europe 1848–1849. From Reform to Reaction* (Oxford), pp. 181–206.

Eyck (1959), Frank: *The Prince Consort. A Political Biography* (London).

Faber (1979), Karl-Georg: *Deutsche Geschichte im 19. Jahrhundert. Restauration und Revolution von 1815–1851* (Wiesbaden).

Fay (1975), Peter Ward: *The Opium War 1840–1842* (Chapel Hill, NC).

Fischer-Aue (1953), H. R.: *Die Deutschlandpolitik des Prinzgemahls Albert von England 1848–1852* (Untersiemau bei Coburg).

Foerster (1982), Cornelia: *Der Preß- und Vaterlandsverein von 1832/33. Sozialstruktur und Organisationsformen der bürgerlichen Bewegung in der Zeit des Hambacher Festes* (Trier).

Foerster (1988), Cornelia: 'Das Hambacher Fest 1832. Volksfest und Nationalfest einer oppositionellen Massenbewegung', in Düding, Dieter/Friedemann, Peter/Münch, Paul (Hgg.): *Öffentliche Festkultur: politische Feste in Deutschland von der Aufklärung bis zum 1. Weltkrieg* (Reinbek bei Hamburg), pp. 113–31.

Freitag (2000), Sabine and Wende, Peter (eds): *British Envoys to Germany 1816–1866. Vol. 1: 1816–1829* (Cambridge).

Friedjung (1912a), Heinrich: *Der Kampf um die Vorherrschaft in Deutschland 1859 bis 1866*, Bd. 1 (Stuttgart–Berlin; 9th edn).

Friedjung (1912b), Heinrich: *Österreich von 1848 bis 1860*, Bd. 2/Abt. 1 (Stuttgart–Berlin; 2nd edn).

Fuchs (1934), Walther Peter: *Die deutschen Mittelstaaten und die Bundesreform 1853–1860* (Berlin).

Fulford (1949), Roger: *The Prince Consort* (London).

Gall (1968), Lothar: *Der Liberalismus als regierende Partei. Das Großherzogtum Baden zwischen Restauration und Reichsgründung* (Wiesbaden).

Gall (1986), Lothar: *Bismarck. The White Revolutionary*, 2 vols (London).

Gesandtschaftsberichte (1936/1937) *aus München 1814–1848, Abteilung 1: Die Berichte des französischen Gesandten*, bearbeitet von Anton Chroust, Bde. 3–6 (München).

Gillessen (1961), Günther: *Lord Palmerston und die Einigung Deutschlands. Die englische Politik von der Paulskirche bis zu den Dresdener Konferenzen (1848–1851)* (Lübeck–Hamburg).

Gollwitzer (1965), Heinz: 'Ideologische Blockildung als Bestandteil internationaler Politik im 19. Jahrhundert', *HZ* 201 (1965), pp. 306–33.

Gooch (1925), G. P. (ed.): *The Later Correspondence of Lord John Russell 1840–1878*, 2 vols (London).

Gordon (1969), Nancy M.: 'Britain and the Zollverein Iron Duties, 1842–5', *The Economic History Review* 22 (1969), pp. 75–87.

Graham (1978), Gerald S.: *The China Station. War and Diplomacy, 1830–1860* (Oxford–New York).

Greville (1888), Charles C. F.: *The Greville Memoirs. A Journal of the Reigns of King George IV., King William IV. and Queen Victoria*, ed. Henry Reeve, 8 vols (London; new edn).

Grünthal (1990), Günther: 'Das Ende der Ära Manteuffel', *Zeitschrift für die Geschichte Mittel- und Ostdeutschlands* 39 (1990), pp. 179–219.

Grünthal (1999), Günther: 'Eine "englische Partei" in Berlin? Sir Robert Morier und die Neue Ära in Preußen', in Ritter, Gerhard A./Wende, Peter (Hgg.): *Rivalität und Partnerschaft: Studien zu den deutsch-britischen Beziehungen im 19. und 20. Jahrhundert. Festschrift für Anthony J. Nicholls* (Paderborn), pp. 29–51.

Gruner (1973), Wolf D.: 'Die Würzburger Konferenzen der Mittelstaaten in den Jahren 1859–1861 und die Bestrebungen zur Reform des Deutschen Bundes', *Zeitschrift für bayerische Landesgeschichte* 36 (1973), pp. 181–253.

Gruner (1977a), Wolf D.: '"British Interests" und Friedenssicherung. Zur Interaktion von britischer Innen- und Außenpolitik im frühen 19. Jahrhundert', *HZ* 224 (1977), pp. 92–104.

Gruner (1977b), Wolf D.: 'Europäischer Friede als nationales Interesse. Die Rolle des Deutschen Bundes in der britischen Politik 1814–1832', *Bohemia. Jahrbuch des Collegium Carolinum* 18 (1977), pp. 96–128.

Gruner (1981a), Wolf D.: 'Der Deutsche Bund als "Centralstaat von Europa" und die Sicherung des Friedens. Aspekte britisch-deutscher Beziehungen in der internationalen Krise von 1819/20', in Kettenacker, Lothar *et al.* (Hgg.): *Studien zur Geschichte Englands und der deutsch-britischen Beziehungen. Festschrift für Paul Kluke* (München), pp. 79–102.

Gruner (1981b), Wolf D.: 'Großbritannien und die Julirevolution von 1830: Zwischen Legitimitätsprinzip und nationalem Interesse', *Francia. Forschungen zur westeuropäischen Geschichte* 9 (1981), pp. 369–411.

Gruner (1983), Wolf D.: 'The Revolution of July and Southern Germany', *The Consortium on Revolutionary Europe 1750–1850. Proceedings* (1983), pp. 509–46.

Gruner (1985), Wolf D.: *Die deutsche Frage. Ein Problem der europäischen Staatengeschichte seit 1800* (München).

Gruner (1986), Wolf D.: 'England, Hannover und der Deutsche Bund 1814–1837', in Birke, Adolf M./Kluxen, Kurt (Hgg.): *England und Hannover* (München), pp. 81–126.

Gruner (1987), Wolf D.: 'The German Confederation and the Rhine Crisis of 1840', *The Consortium on Revolutionary Europe 1750–1850. Proceedings* (1987), pp. 535–60.

Gruner (1990), Wolf D.: 'Der Deutsche Bund, die deutschen Verfassungsstaaten und die Rheinkrise von 1840. Überlegungen zur deutschen Dimension einer europäischen Krise', *Zeitschrift für bayerische Landesgeschichte* 53 (1990), pp. 51–78.

Gruner (2000), Wolf D.: 'Die europäischen Mächte und die deutsche Frage 1848–1850', in Mai, Gunther (Hg.): *Die Erfurter Union und das Erfurter Unionsparlament 1850* (Köln–Weimar–Wien), pp. 271–305.

Gudenus (1988), Georg Philip: 'Metternich as Ghostwriter', in *Manuscripts* 40 (1988), pp. 41–3.

Guichen (1925/1929), Vicomte de: *Les Grandes Questions Europénnes et la Diplomatie des Puissances sous la Seconde République Française*, 2 tomes (Paris).

Hachtmann (1997), Rüdiger: *Berlin 1848. Eine Politik- und Gesellschaftsgeschichte der Revolution* (Bonn).

Hahn (1984), Hans-Werner: *Geschichte des Deutschen Zollvereins* (Göttingen).

Hansard's (1830–1871) *Parliamentary Debates*, 2nd ser., vols 22–5; 3rd ser., vols 1–214.

Hardtwig (1998), Wolfgang (ed.): *Revolution in Deutschland und Europa, 1848–9* (Göttingen).

Haupts (1978), Leo: 'Die liberale Regierung in Preußen in der Zeit der "Neuen Ära": zur Geschichte des preussischen Konstitutionalismus', *HZ* 227 (1978), pp. 45–85.

Hearder (1967), Harry: 'Queen Victoria and Foreign Policy. Royal Intervention in the Italian Question, 1859–1860', in Bourne, K./Watt, D. C. (eds): *Studies in International History. Essays presented to W. Norton Medlicott* (London), pp. 172–88.

Henderson (1959), W. O.: *The Zollverein* (London; 2nd edn).

Heydemann (1987), Günther: 'The "Crazy Year" 1848: The Revolution in Germany and Palmerston's Policy', in Schulze, Hagen (ed.): *Nation-Building in Central Europe* (Leamington Spa–New York), pp. 167–82.

Heydemann (1990), Günther: 'Zwischen Restauration, Reform und Revolution: Britische Deutschlandpolitik 1815–1848', in Birke, Adolf M./Recker, Marie-Luise (Hgg.): *Das gestörte Gleichgewicht. Deutschland als Problem britischer Sicher-*

heit im 19. und 20. Jahrhundert. – Upsetting the Balance. German and British Security Interests in the Nineteenth and Twentieth Century (München), pp. 17–48.

Heydemann (1995), Günther: *Konstitution gegen Revolution. Die britische Deutschland- und Italienpolitik 1815–1848* (Göttingen).

Hildebrand (1980), Klaus: 'Großbritannien und die deutsche Reichsgründung', in Kolb, Eberhard (Hg.); *Europa und die Reichsgründung. Preußen-Deutschland in der Sicht der großen europäischen Mächte 1866–1880* (München), pp. 9–62.

Hildebrand (1997), Klaus: *No Intervention. Die Pax Britannica und Preußen 1865/66–1869/70. Eine Untersuchung zur englischen Weltpolitik im 19. Jahrhundert* (München).

The History of the Times (1939), vol. II (London).

Hjeholt (1965), Holger: 'British Mediation in the Danish-German Conflict 1848–1850, Part 1', *Historisk-filosofiske Meddelelser udgivet af Det kongelige Danske Videnskabernes Selskap*, 41 (1965), pp. 1–236.

Hjeholt (1966), Holger: 'British Mediation in the Danish-German Conflict 1848–1850, Part 2: from the November Cabinet until the Peace with Prussia and the London Protocol (the 2nd of July and the 2nd of August 1850)', *Historisk-filosofiske Meddelelser udgivet af Det kongelige Danske Videnskabernes Selskap* 42 (1966), pp. 1–252.

Hjeholt (1971), Holger: 'Great Britain, the Danish-German Conflict and the Danish Succession 1850–1852. From the London Protocol to the Treaty of London (the 2nd of August 1850 and the 8th May 1852)', *Historisk-filosofiske Meddelelser udgivet af Det kongelige Danske Videnskabernes Selskap*, 45 (1971), pp. 7–323.

Hoffmann (1959), Joachim: *Die Berliner Misson des Grafen Prokesch-Osten 1849–1852* (Free University of Berlin, D.Phil. thesis).

Hoppen (1998), K. Theodore: *The Mid-Victorian Generation 1846–1886* (Oxford).

Huber (1968), Ernst Rudolf: *Deutsche Verfassungsgeschichte seit 1789, Bd. 2: Der Kampf um Einheit und Freiheit 1830–1850* (Stuttgart; 2nd edn).

Huber (1970), Ernst Rudolf: *Deutsche Verfassunggeschichte seit 1798, Bd. 3: Bismarck und das Reich* (Stuttgart; 2nd edn).

Hyde (1994), Simon: *Hans Hugo von Kleist-Retzow and the Administration of the Rhine Province during the Reaction in Prussia, 1851–1858* (Oxford University, D.Phil. thesis).

Imlah (1966), Ann G.: *Britain and Switzerland 1845–60. A Study of Anglo-Swiss Relations during some Critical Years for Swiss Neutrality* (London).

Jagow (1938), Kurt (ed.): *Letters of the Prince Consort 1831–1861*, trans. E. T. S. Dugdale (London).

Jelavich (1975), Barbara: *The Habsburg Empire in European Affairs, 1814–1918* (Chicago).

Jenkins (1994), T. A.: *The Liberal Ascendancy, 1830–1886* (London).

Jones (1981), Raymond A.: 'The Social Structure of the British Diplomatic Service, 1815–1914, *Histoire Sociale – Social History*, 14, no. 27 (1981), pp. 49–66.

Jones (1983), Raymond A.: *The British Diplomatic Service 1815–1914* (Gerrards Cross/Bucks.).

Kennedy (1980), Paul M.: *The Rise of the Anglo-German Antagonism 1860–1914* (London).

Kentmann (1933), H.: 'Preußen und die Bundeshilfe an Österreich im Jahr 1859', in *Mitteilungen des Instituts für Österreichische Geschichtsforschung* 12. Ergänzungsband (1933), pp. 297–415.

Kraehe (1950/51), Enno: 'Austria and the Problem of Reform in the German Constitution, 1851–1863', *AHR* 56 (1950/1), pp. 276–94.

Kriegel (1977), Abraham D. (ed.): *The Holland House Diaries, 1831–1840* (London–Boston).

Laing (1842), Samuel: *Notes of a Traveller on the Social and Political State of France, Prussia, Switzerland, Italy and other Parts of Europe during the Present Century* (London).

Lane-Poole (1888), Stanley: *The Life of the Right Honourable Stratford Canning*, vol. II (London).

Langewiesche (1974), Dieter: *Liberalismus und Demokratie in Württemberg zwischen Revolution und Reichsgründung* (Düsseldorf).

Langewiesche (2000), Dieter: *Liberalism in Germany* (Basingstoke–London).

Lee (1987), Lloyd E.: '1840, the Confederation and German Military Reform', *The Consortium on Revolutionary Europe 1750–1850. Proceedings* (1987), pp. 573–86.

The Letters (1908) *of Queen Victoria. A Selection from Her Majesty's Correspondence between the years 1837 and 1861*, eds Arthur C. Benson and Viscount Esher, 3 vols (London).

Lippert (1998), Stefan: *Felix Fürst zu Schwarzenberg. Eine politische Biographie* (Stuttgart).

Loftus (1892), Lord Augustus: *The Diplomatic Reminiscences of Lord Augustus Loftus, P.C., G.C.B., 1837–1862*, 2 vols. (London–Paris–Melbourne).

Luchterhandt (1996), Manfred: 'Mitteleuropaprojektionen gegen konstitutionelle Bewegung. Schwarzenberg und die preußische Einigungspolitik nach der Revolution 1848–1851', in Gehler, M. *et al.* (Hgg.): *Ungleiche Partner? Österreich und Deutschland in ihrer gegenseitigen Wahrnehmung. Historische Analysen und Vergleiche aus dem 19. und 20. Jahrhundert* (Stuttgart), pp. 135–70.

Lutz (1994), Heinrich: *Zwischen Habsburg und Preußen. Deutschland 1815 bis 1871* (Berlin; new edn).

Macartney (1968), C. A.: *The Habsburg Empire 1790–1918* (London).

Mack Smith (1962), Denis: 'Palmerston and Cavour: Some English Doubts about the Risorgimento, 1859–1860', in Brand, C. P./Foster, K./Limentani, U. (eds): *Italian Studies Presented to E. R. Vincent* (Cambridge), pp. 244–71.

Maxwell (1913), Sir Herbert: *The Life and Letters of George William Frederick Fourth Earl of Clarendon*, 2 vols (London).

Meiboom (1931), Siegmund: *Studien zur deutschen Politik Bayerns in den Jahren 1851–59* (München).

Meinecke (1913), Friedrich: *Radowitz und die deutsche Revolution* (Berlin).

Metzler (1997), Gabriele: *Großbritannien – Weltmacht in Europa. Handelspolitik im Wandel des europäischen Staatensystems 1856 bis 1871* (Berlin).

Meyer (1994), Manfred: *Freiheit und Macht. Studien zum Nationalismus süddeutscher, insbesondere badischer Liberaler, 1830–1848*, (Frankfurt/Main).

Middleton (1977), C. R.: *The Administration of British Foreign Policy* (Durham NC).

Mieck (1992), Ilja: 'Preußen von 1807 bis 1850. Reformen, Restauration und Revolution', in Büsch, Otto (Hg.): *Handbuch der preußischen Geschichte*, Bd. II: *Das 19. Jahrhundert und große Themen der Geschichte Preußens* (Berlin–New York), pp. 3–292.

Mitchell (1980), Leslie G.: *Holland House* (London).

Mitchell (1999), Leslie G.: 'The Whigs, the People, and Reform', *Proceedings of the British Academy* 100 (1999), pp. 25–41.

Mitchell (2000), Leslie G.: 'Britain's Reaction to the Revolutions,' in Evans, Robert J. W. and Pogge von Strandmann, Hartmut (eds): *The Revolutions in Europe 1848–1849. From Reform to Reaction* (Oxford), pp. 83–98.

Mommsen (1988), Wolfgang J.. 'Einführung: Deutscher und britischer Liberalismus. Versuch einer Bilanz', in Langewiesche, Dieter (Hg.): *Liberalismus im 19. Jahrhundert. Deutschland im europäischen Vergleich* (Göttingen), pp. 211–22.

Mommsen (1993), Wolfgang J.: *Das Ringen um den nationalen Staat. Die Gründung und der innere Ausbau des Deutschen Reiches unter Otto von Bismarck 1850 bis 1890* (Berlin).

Mosse (1956), W. E.: 'England and the Polish Insurrection of 1863', *EHR* 71 (1956), pp. 28–55.

Mosse (1958), W. E.: *The European Powers and the German Question 1848–1871 with special reference to England and Russia* (Cambridge).

Mosse (1975), George L.: *The Nationalization of the Masses. Political Symbolism and Mass Movements in Germany from the Napoleonic Wars through the Third Reich* (Ithaca–London).

Muhs (1988), Rudolf: 'Deutscher und britischer Liberalismus im Vergleich. Trägerschichten, Zielvorstellungen und Rahmenbedingungen (ca. 1830–1870)', in Langewiesche, Dieter (Hg.): *Liberalismus im 19. Jahrhundert. Deutschland im europäischen Vergleich* (Göttingen), pp. 223–59.

Murray (1997), Scott W.: '. . . earnest men with ideas and great abilities are sometimes unsafe men': The German Career of Robert Morier, 1853–1876 (University of Calgary, Ph.D. thesis).

Murray (1998), Scott W.: 'In Pursuit of a Mirage: Robert Morier's Views of Liberal Nationalism and German Unification, 1853–1876', *IHR* 20 (1998), pp. 33–67.

Na'man (1987), Shlomo: *Der deutsche Nationalverein. Die politische Konstitutierung des deutschen Bürgertums 1859–1867* (Düsseldorf).

Neumann (1919), Ilse: *Die Geschichte der deutschen Reichsgründung nach den Memoiren von Sir Robert Morier (Darstellung und Kritik)* (Berlin).

Nipperdey (1987), Thomas: *Deutsche Geschichte 1800–1866. Bürgerwelt und starker Staat* (München; 4th edn).

Noltenius (1988), R.: 'Schiller als Führer und Heiland. Das Schillerfest 1859 als nationaler Traum von der Geburt des zweiten deutschen Kaiserreichs', in Düding, Dieter/Friedemann, Peter/Münch, Paul (Hgg.): *Öffentliche Festkultur: politische Feste in Deutschland von der Aufklärung bis zum 1. Weltkrieg* (Reinbek bei Hamburg), pp. 237–258.

Obenaus (1984), Herbert: *Die Anfänge des Parlamentarismus in Preußen bis 1848* (Düsseldorf).

Obermann (1955), Karl: 'Die deutsche Einheitsbewegung und die Schillerfeiern 1859', *Zeitschrift für Geschichtswissenschaft* 3 (1955), pp. 705–34.

Obermann (1979), Karl: 'Die Auseinandersetzungen zwischen Demokraten und Liberalen im deutschen Vorparlament 1848', *Zeitschrift für Geschichtswissenschaft* 27 (1979), pp. 1156–72.

Okey (2001), Robin: *The Habsburg Monarchy c. 1765–1918* (Basingstoke–London).

Orr (1978), Jr., William J.: 'British Diplomacy and the German Problem, 1848–1850', *Albion: Proceedings of the Conference on British Studies* 10 (1978), pp. 209–36.

Owsinska (1974), Anna: *La Politique de la France envers l'Allemagne à l'Epoque de la Monarchie de Juillet 1830–1848* (Wroclaw).

Palmerston (1847), Henry John Temple, 3rd Viscount: *Speech of Lord Viscount Palmerston, Secretary of State for Foreign Affairs to the Electors of Tiverton on the 31st* July 1847 (London; 2nd edn).

Parliamentary Papers (1833), vol. II [Bills, Public, vol. 2: *Act for the more Effectual Suppression of Local Disturbances and Dangerous Associations in Ireland*].

Parliamentary Papers (1840), vol. XXI [Reports from the Commissioners, vol. 6: *John Bowring: Report on the Prussian Commercial Union addressed to the Right Hon. Lord Viscount Palmerston, Her Majesty's Secretary of State for Foreign Affairs*].

Parliamentary Papers (1842), vol. XL [Accounts and Papers, vol. 15 (Supplement): *John MacGregor: Commercial Tariffs and Regulations of the Several States of Europe and America. Part the Fifth: States of the Germanic Union of Customs*].

Parliamentary Papers (1843), vol. LXI [Accounts and Papers, vol. 32: *Copies and Extracts of Despatches from Her Majesty's Ministers Abroad Having Reference to the Recent Modifications in the Tariffs of the German Customs Union*].

Parliamentary Papers (1861a), vol. VI [Reports from the Committees, vol. 2: *Report from the Select Committee appointed to inquire into the Constitution and Efficiency of the Present Diplomatic Service of this Country; together with the Proceedings of the Committee, Minutes of Evidence, Appendix, and Index*].

Parliamentary Papers (1861b), vol. LXV [Accounts and Papers, vol. 32: *Correspondence Respecting the Arrest and Imprisonment of Captain MacDonald at Bonn*].

Parry (1936), Ernest Jones: *The Spanish Marriages, 1841–1846. A Study of the Influence of Dynastic Ambition upon Foreign Policy* (London).

Peel (1977), Peter H.: *British Public Opinion and the Wars of German Unification: 1864–1871* (University of Southern California, Ph.D. thesis).

Pemberton (1954), W. Baring: *Lord Palmerston* (London).

Peter (1972), Michael: *Der Konflikt in Schleswig-Holstein (1846–1852) im Spiegel der englischen Presse. Ein Beitrag zur Geschichte der deutsch-englischen Beziehungen um die Mitte des 19. Jahrhunderts* (Würzburg University, D.Phil. thesis).

Pflanze (1990), Otto: *Bismarck and the Development of Germany. Vol 1: The Period of Unification, 1815–1871* (Princeton).

Pogge von Strandmann (2000), Hartmut: 'The German Revolutions of 1848–1850 and the *Sonderweg* of Mecklenburg,' in Evans, Robert J. W. and Pogge von Strandmann, Hartmut (eds): *The Revolutions in Europe 1848–1849. From Reform to Reaction* (Oxford), pp. 99–133.

Poidevin (1977), Raymond/Bariéty, Jacques: *Les Relations franco-allemandes 1815–1975* (Paris).

Pommerin (1997), Reiner/Fröhlich, Michael (Hgg.): *Quellen zu den deutsch-britischen Beziehungen 1815–1914* (Darmstadt).

Precht (1925), Hans: *Englands Stellung zur deutschen Einheit 1848–1850* (München–Berlin).

Püschner (1977), Manfred: 'Die Rheinkrise von 1840/41 und die antifeudale Oppositionsbewegung', in Bleiber, Helmut (Hg.): *Bourgeoisie und bürgerliche Umwälzung in Deutschland, 1789–1871*, (Berlin/Ost), pp. 101–34.

Rich (1992), Norman: *Great Power Diplomacy 1815–1914* (New York).

Ridley (1970), Jasper: *Lord Palmerston* (London).

Roghé (1971), Dieter: *Die französische Deutschland-Politik während der ersten zehn Jahre der Julimonarchie, 1830–1840* (Würzburg University, D.Phil. thesis).

Roth (1850/1852), Paul/Merck, Heinrich (Hgg.): *Quellensammlung zum deutschen öffentlichen Recht seit 1848*, 2 vols (Erlangen).

Salevouris (1982), Michael J.: *'Riflemen Form': The War Scare of 1859–1860 in England* (New York).

Sandiford (1975), Keith A. P.: *Great Britain and the Schleswig-Holstein Question 1848–64: a study in diplomacy, politics, and public opinion* (Toronto–Buffalo).

Schaarschmidt (1993), Thomas: *Außenpolitik und öffentliche Meinung in Großbritannien während des deutsch-französischen Krieges von 1870/71* (Frankfurt/Main).

Scharff (1942), Alexander: *Die europäischen Großmächte und die deutsche Revolution. Deutsche Einheit und europäische Ordnung 1848–1851* (Leipzig).

Schenk (1939), Karl: *Die Stellung der europäischen Großmächte zur Begründung des Deutschen Zollvereins 1815–1834* (Göttingen University, Dr. phil thesis).

Schieder (1962), Theodor: 'Partikularismus und nationales Bewußtsein im Denken des Vormärz', in Conze, Werner (Hg.): *Staat und Gesellschaft im deutschen Vormärz 1814–1848* (Stuttgart), pp. 9–38.

Schieder (1978), Wolfgang: 'Der Rheinpfälzische Liberalismus von 1832 als politische Protestbewegung', in Berding, Helmut *et al.* (Hgg.): *Vom Staat des Ancien Régime zum modernen Parteienstaat. Festschrift für Theodor Schieder* (München–Wien), pp. 169–95.

Schoeps (1972), Hans Julius: *Von Olmütz nach Dresden 1850/51. Ein Beitrag zur Geschichte der Reformen am Deutschen Bund* (Köln–Berlin).

Schroeder (1972), Paul W.: *Austria, Great Britain and the Crimean War. The Destruction of the European Concert* (Ithaca–London).

Schroeder (1990), Paul W.: 'Europe and the German Confederation in 1860's', in Rumpler, Helmut (Hg.): *Deutscher Bund und deutsche Frage 1815–1866. Europäische Ordnung, deutsche Politik und gesellschaftlicher Wandel im Zeitalter der bürgerlich-nationalen Emanzipation* (Wien–München), pp. 281–91.

Schroeder (1994a), Paul W.: 'Britain, Russia, and the German Question, 1815–1848: Emerging Rivalry or Benign Neglect? in Birke, Adolf M./Wentker, Hermann (Hgg.): *Deutschland und Rußland in der britischen Kontinentalpolitik seit 1815* (München), pp. 15–30.

Schroeder (1994b), Paul W.: *The Transformation of European Politics 1763–1848* (Oxford).

Schulze (1989), Hagen: 'Perspektiven für Deutschland: Nationalverein und Reformverein', in Birke, Adolf M./Heydemann, Günther (Hgg.): *Die Herausforderung des europäischen Staatensystems: Nationale Ideologie und staatliches Interesse zwischen Restauration und Imperialismus* (Göttingen–Zürich), pp. 141–57.

Schulze (1991), Hagen: *The Course of German Nationalism. From Frederick the Great to Bismarck 1763–1867* (Cambridge).

Schulze (1992), Hagen: 'Preußen von 1850 bis 1871. Verfassungsstaat und Reichsgründung', in Büsch, Otto (Hg.): *Handbuch der preußischen Geschichte*, Bd. II: *Das 19. Jahrhundert und große Themen der Geschichte Preußens* (Berlin–New York), pp. 293–372.

Schulze (1996), Hagen: *States, Nations and Nationalism. From the Middle Ages to the Present* (Cambridge, Mass.–Oxford).

Sheehan (1989), James J.: *German History 1770–1866* (Oxford).

Siemann (1983), Wolfram (Hg.): *Der 'Polizeiverein' deutscher Staaten. Eine Dokumentation zur Überwachung der Öffentlichkeit nach der Revolution von 1848/49* (Tübingen).

Siemann (1985), Wolfram: '*Deutschlands Ruhe, Sicherheit und Ordnung*'. *Die Anfänge der politischen Polizei 1806–1866* (Tübingen).

Siemann (1990), Wolfram: *Gesellschaft im Aufbruch. Deutschland 1849–1871* (Frankfurt/Main).

Siemann (1995), Wolfram: *Vom Staatenbund zum Nationalstaat. Deutschland 1806–1871* (München).

Siemann (1998), Wolfram: *The German Revolution of 1848–49* (Basingstoke–London).

Simms (1998), Brendan: *The Struggle for Mastery in Germany, 1779–1850* (Basingstoke–London).

Sondhaus (1991), Lawrence: 'Schwarzenberg, Austria and the German Question, 1848–1851', *IHR* 13 (1991), pp. 1–20.

Southgate (1962), Donald: *The Passing of the Whigs 1832–1886* (London).

Southgate (1966), Donald: '*The Most English Minister . . .*' *The Policies and Politics of Palmerston* (London).

Sproxton (1919), Charles: *Palmerston and the Hungarian Revolution* (Cambridge).

Srbik (1935–1942), Heinrich Ritter von: *Deutsche Einheit. Idee und Wirklichkeit vom Heiligen Reich bis Königgrätz*, 4 Bde (München).

Steefel (1932), Lawrence D.: *The Schleswig-Holstein Question* (Cambridge, Mass.).

Steele (1987), E. D.: 'Palmerston's Foreign Policy and Foreign Secretaries 1855–1865', in Wilson, Keith M. (ed.): *British Foreign Secretaries and Foreign Policy: From Crimean War to First World War* (London), pp. 25–84.

Steele (1991), E. D.: *Palmerston and Liberalism, 1855–1865* (Cambridge).

Stürmer (1982), Michael: 'Die Geburt eines Dilemmas. Nationalstaat und Massendemokratie im Mächtesystem 1848', *Merkur* 36 (1982), pp. 1–12.

Syme (1964), S. A.: 'The Minto mission to Italy, 1847–1848,' *Italian Quarterly* VIII/30 (1964), pp. 35–65.

Taylor (1934), A. J. P.: *The Italian Problem in European Diplomacy 1846–9* (Manchester).

Thomas (1951), R. Hinton: *Liberalism, Nationalism and the German Intellectuals 1822–1847. An Analysis of the Academic and Scientific Conferences of the Period* (Cambridge).

Treitschke (1919), Heinrich von: *History of Germany in the Nineteenth Century*, translated by Eden and Cedar Paul, vol. 5 (London).

Turner (1948), A. C.: *The House of Commons and Foreign Policy between the First and Second Reform Acts* (Oxford University, B.Litt. thesis).

Unckel (1969), Bernhard: *Österreich und der Krimkrieg. Studien zur Politik der Donaumonarchie in den Jahren 1852–1856* (Lübeck–Hamburg).

Valentin (1930/31), Veit: *Geschichte der deutschen Revolution von 1848–1849* (Berlin).

Valentin (1937a), Veit: 'Bismarck and England in the Earlier Period of his Career', *Transactions of the Royal Historical Society*, 4th ser., 20 (1937), pp. 13–30.

Valentin (1937b), Veit: *Bismarcks Reichsgründung im Urteil englischer Diplomaten* (Amsterdam).

Veit-Brause (1963), Irmeline: *Die deutsch-französische Krise von 1840. Studien zur deutschen Einheitsbewegung* (Köln University, D.Phil. thesis) [printed Köln 1967].

Vogt (1963), Martin: *Der deutsche Vormärz im Urteil englischer Zeitschriften, Zeitungen und Bücher* (Göttingen University, D.Phil. thesis).

Vogt (1964), Martin: 'Die deutsche Einheitsbewegung und die Arbeit der Nationalversammlung bis zur Kaiserwahl 1849 in der Darstellung englischer Zeitungen und Zeitschriften', in *Festschrift Percy Ernst Schramm*, Band II (Wiesbaden), pp. 180–92.

Vogt (1965), Martin: 'Das vormärzliche Deutschland im englischen Urteil (1830–1847)', *GWU* 16 (1965), pp. 397–413.

Vorgeschichte (1934) und *Begründung des Deutschen Zollvereins 1815–1834. Akten der Staaten des Deutschen Bundes und der europäischen Mächte*, bearbeitet von W. v. Eisenhart Rothe and A. Ritthaler, 3 Bde (Berlin).

Ward (1872), John: *Experiences of a Diplomatist, being Recollections of Germany, founded on Diaries kept during the Years 1840–1870* (London).

Ward (1916), Sir Adolphus William: *Germany 1815–1890. Vol. I: 1815–1852* (Cambridge).

Watson (1969), D. R.: 'The British Parliamentary System and the Growth of Constitutional Government in Western Europe', in Bartlett, C. J. (ed.): *Britain Pre-Eminent. Studies of British world influence in the nineteenth century* (London), pp. 101–27.

Weber (1963), Frank G.: 'Palmerston and Prussian Liberalism, 1848', *JMH* 35 (1963), pp. 125–36.

Webster (1951), Sir Charles: *The Foreign Policy of Palmerston 1830–1841. Britain, the Liberal Movement and the Eastern Question*, 2 vols (London).

Webster (1961), Sir Charles: *The Art and Practice of Diplomacy* (London).

Wehler (1987), Hans-Ulrich: *Deutsche Gesellschaftsgeschichte. Zweiter Band: Von der Reformära bis zur industriellen und politischen 'Deutschen Doppelrevolution' 1815–1845/9* (München).

Wehner (1993), Norbert: *Die deutschen Mittelstaaten auf dem Frankfurter Fürstentag 1863* (Frankfurt/Main).

Weigand (1997), Katharina: *Österreich, die Westmächte und das europäische Staatensystem nach dem Krimkrieg (1856–1859)* (Husum).

Weisbrod (1967), Kurt: *Lord Palmerston und die Europäische Revolutionen von 1848* (Heidelberg University, D.Phil. thesis).

Wemyss (1911), Mrs. Rosslyn: *Memoirs and Letters of the Right Hon. Sir Robert Morier, G.C.B. from 1826 to 1876*, 2 vols (London).

Wende (1975), Peter: *Radikalismus im Vormärz. Untersuchungen zur politischen Theorie der frühen deutschen Demokratie* (Wiesbaden).

Wentker (1993), Hermann: *Zerstörung der Großmacht Rußland? Die britischen Kriegsziele im Krimkrieg* (Göttingen–Zürich).

Zegger (1973), Robert E.: 'Victorians in Arms: The French Invasion Scare of 1859–60', *History Today* 23 (1973), pp. 705–14.

Index